THE  TIMES
GUIDE TO
EASTERN
EUROPE

The contributors

Keith Sword, the general editor, is Research Fellow at the School of Slavonic and East European Studies (SSEES), University of London, with a special interest in Poland and Polish-Soviet relations.

This book includes contributions from

Dr Jonathan Aves, SSEES, University of London
Dr Marko Bojcun, SSEES, University of London
Professor Richard Crampton, St Edmund Hall, University of Oxford
Mr Denis Deletant, SSEES, University of London
Mr Jim Dingley, SSEES, University of London
Dr Raymond Hutchings, freelance specialist on Albanian affairs
Mr Anton Logoreci, former head of the BBC's Albanian service
Dr Martin McCauley, SSEES, University of London
Mr Stevan Pavlowitch, University of Southampton
Dr Martin Rady, SSEES, University of London
Mr George Schöpflin, SSEES, University of London
Ms Kersti Uibo, Estonian Information Bureau, London

Publisher's note

The publishers would like to express their appreciation to all the contributors for their extraordinary energy, judgement and enthusiasm in this project. Against a constantly shifting background of political change, this book attempts to present a considered assessment of the history and development of the nations of central and eastern Europe from the end of World War II up to July 1991. What has already happened may be recorded as history. What may happen in the immediate future, as many of these nations come to grips with the problems thrown up by their new freedoms and the daunting tasks of adjusting to the free-market, is impossible to predict. But whatever may occur can only be understood in the broader historical and social context which this book seeks to provide.

It should be noted that any opinions expressed in this book are those of the editor and the contributors.

The publishers would also like to thank Professor Norman Davies, of SSEES, Mr George Brock, Foreign Editor of *The Times*, Mr Charles Wilson, former Editor, and Mr Simon Jenkins, Editor of *The Times* for their support, advice and encouragement.

THE TIMES GUIDE TO EASTERN EUROPE

INSIDE THE OTHER EUROPE

EDITED by KEITH SWORD

REVISED EDITION

TIMES BOOKS

First published by Times Books,
77–85 Fulham Palace Road,
London w6 8jb

© Times Books, London 1990
Reprinted with revisions 1991
British Library Cataloguing-in-Publication Data
The Times Guide to Eastern Europe:
   inside the other Europe. – 2nd ed
   I. Sword, Keith
   909.09717

   ISBN 0-7230-0438-2

Typeset by
Rowland Phototypesetting Limited,
Bury St Edmunds, Suffolk

Printed in Great Britain by
Richard Clay Limited, St Ives plc,
Bungay, Suffolk

CONTENTS

INTRODUCTION

1990 marked not only the beginning of a new decade, it heralded a new era for Eastern Europe. The period of post-revolutionary consolidation following the collapse of Communism has led to more open, democratic political systems and to market-oriented economic change. The gradual withdrawal of Soviet troops has been accompanied by the development of independent defence and foreign policies. However, the transition to full sovereignty and democracy is not proving easy.

Widespread frustration and disillusionment have – almost inevitably, some might say – followed the heady optimism of the revolutionary days of 1989. In particular, there has been a growth in unemployment and economic hardship, and the resurgence of strident (at times, violent) nationalism, either or both of which threaten the stability of fragile democracies from the Baltic to the Adriatic.

The magnitude and the unexpectedness of the political earthquake are difficult to capture in words. 1989 has been compared with the two other years in this century when the political face of Europe was radically altered – 1918 and 1945. The similarities are limited, though. These earlier changes came about as the result of world wars, at a time when the exhausted world was looking towards long periods of peace and recovery. They were also the result of conferences of the Great Powers at Versailles (1919) and Yalta and Potsdam (1945).

The events of 1989, by contrast, were not precipitated by major conflict, nor were they imposed by decree. They were the result of an irresistible pressure for reform and change on the part of people who had for too long endured the drabness, stifling restrictions, arbitrariness, untruths and economic shortages of Communist rule. The irony did not escape journalists and commentators that the six-month period of change and upheaval was preceded in July 1989 by the bicentenary celebrations of the French Revolution. Future historians may indeed, as *The Times* leader writer suggested at the end of the year, prefer to compare the events of 1989 with the storming of the Bastille, or perhaps with 'the Springtime of Nations' – the revolutions which swept Europe in 1848.

The upheavals were not restricted to Communist regimes outside Soviet borders. Within the Soviet Union we have also seen the growing momentum of support for democracy, local autonomy and even secession from the Soviet Union. The Baltic States – Estonia, Latvia and Lithuania –

have been the most outspoken, protesting loudly against their forced incorporation into the Union during the Stalinist years. (We should not forget that 1989 also marked the 50th anniversary of the Hitler–Stalin Pact which led soon afterwards to the Soviet takeover of the Baltic states.) Similar voices calling for an end to one-party rule and greater self-determination have been raised in Transcaucasia, Ukraine and Georgia.

The aim of this book is to explain how Communism was imposed and how the structures of Communist rule have been or are being dismantled. It also reviews the changes that have taken place in recent months in post-Communist Eastern Europe.

The geography of Eastern Europe

For the purposes of this book 'Eastern Europe' is taken as being the large area which lies east of a line from Lübeck to Trieste and is bordered by the Ural and Caucasus Mountains. We include, therefore, those central and southern European states which came under Soviet influence at the end of World War II, and also the European republics of the Soviet Union. This may lead to some confusion. We all suffer from the peculiar optical illusion that decades of Cold War have fostered. Accordingly, the expression 'Eastern Europe' has commonly been used to refer to the arc of Soviet satellite states established after World War II between the Baltic and the Black Sea. (Yugoslavia and Albania, which were never subject to Moscow, are sometimes referred to as being in 'Eastern Europe', more often as belonging to the Balkan region or 'southern Europe'.) It refers to what should, in a purely geographical sense, be central Europe. Prague, often during the interwar years taken as being at the heart of Europe, is almost equidistant from Madrid and Moscow. (Though it should not be forgotten that the Urals are almost 900 miles further east than Moscow.) Many people forget that Vienna is further east than Prague or Zagreb, that Athens is further east than Warsaw, Budapest and Belgrade. The terms 'central Europe' and 'east-central Europe' are increasingly used as attention is directed to the political events between the Soviet border and the states of the European Community.

The Ural Mountains are commonly taken by geographers as marking Europe's eastern perimeter, but some readers may feel that this is a somewhat artificial boundary in political terms. After all, even if the USSR is on the point of breaking up into its constituent parts as many observers are predicting, the Russian Federative Republic stretches far beyond the Urals – indeed to Vladivostok. There is some validity in such objections, and this book discusses the Russian Republic as a whole. Yet what are the alternatives? Drawing a line at the present Soviet frontier and excluding all present Soviet territory from 'Europe' does not allow for the prospect that the Baltic states, Ukraine and Byelorussia may eventually find themselves freed from Moscow rule. Conversely, to have included all Soviet territory within the scope of this book would have been too great an undertaking, although we have attempted to locate events in the western republics within the wider context of all-Union structures. As it is, Transcaucasia and the Soviet Muslim Republics are discussed only in passing.

The region we are referring to as Eastern Europe covers an area of 5.5 million square kilometres and contains some 330 million inhabitants. However, there are great differences between the various states and republics. Poland is the most populous state outside the Soviet frontier with a population of 38 million, which contrasts with Albania's 3 million. Within the Soviet frontier differences are even more pronounced; the Ukrainian SSR has 52 million inhabitants, compared with tiny Estonia's 1.5 million. In spatial terms, Poland is ten times the size of Albania, and more than twice the size of Czechoslovakia or Hungary. But the neighbouring Ukrainian Republic, apart from dwarfing the Baltic States in size, is more than twice the area of Poland.

The differences in ethnic and religious terms are also marked. While many of the minority problems that plagued the region in the interwar period have disappeared, most states still have a residue of minorities. Few are as homogeneous in ethnic and religious terms as Poland; but at the other extreme there is Yugoslavia, with its complex ethnic jigsaw of Albanians, Serbs, Croats, Slovenes, Macedonians and others. In religion, too, there is a diversity. The Poles, Lithuanians, Slovaks and Hungarians are predominantly Roman Catholic; Latvia and Estonia are mainly Protestant, although a considerable number are also found in the Czech lands; Bulgaria, Byelorussia, Romania and Ukraine are mainly Orthodox, while Yugoslavia and Albania are mixed.

The dawning of the Communist age

The world's first successful Communist revolution took place in Russia in 1917. The Bolsheviks' 'October Revolution' came as something of a surprise even to most Marxists, since Russia was a relatively backward country economically. Marx had always believed that revolution would occur first in the industrially advanced states. It was the industrial working class – the proletariat – which he thought would be the vanguard of social upheaval and change. During the early days the success of the Bolshevik faction led by Lenin was by no means a foregone conclusion. Indeed, at one time the Bolsheviks believed that only a Communist revolution in the West could guarantee the success of their movement. But similar attempts at this time to create soviet regimes – that of Bela Kun in Hungary or the Soviet Republic declared in Bavaria in 1919 – were shortlived. At home, the 'Reds' faced strong opposition and they had to fight a lengthy and bloody civil war before emerging triumphant.

As they consolidated their revolutionary success the Bolsheviks grew in confidence and came to believe that, far from seeking help from the West, revolution could be exported to the rest of Europe – on the bayonets of the Red Army. Drawn into a war with the resurgent Polish state, Soviet forces were able to reach the approaches to Warsaw in 1920 before being driven back and routed by the Polish army. This defeat persuaded the Bolshevik leadership to concentrate on consolidating their power nearer to home. Although the Bolsheviks were heirs to the vast, multinational empire of the Tsars, it took them several years to reconquer and reabsorb a number of the outlying republics which had tasted independence and had developed along nationalist lines. Soviet Russia became transformed into the USSR (Union of Soviet Socialist Republics) only following acceptance of the 1923 Constitution.

Communist Russia was treated with suspicion by the international community and remained isolated during the early years of its existence (although further Communist states in Central Asia or the Far East, such as the Mongolian People's Republic, were established under Soviet protection). Russia had not been a party to the Versailles treaty, although the 27 signatories included the unlikely names of Honduras and Liberia. The USSR ceased to be an international leper in the late 1920s, when Western states began to give the USSR grudging recognition. In the meantime, however, Soviet Russia had found common cause with Germany – which felt similarly ostracized following its defeat in World War I and believed that it had been unfairly punished at the Versailles Conference. German–Soviet co-operation in the military–industrial sphere was extensive during the 1920s and was suspended only when Hitler came to power.

For a number of years the Nazis' open hostility towards Communism made co-operation impossible. Then, in a remarkable reversal of policy (which dismayed his Italian and Japanese allies), Hitler agreed to a new understanding with the Soviet leader, Stalin. The Nazi–Soviet Non-Aggression Pact of August 1939 resulted from the Soviet leader's belief, on the one hand, that the Western powers (Britain and France) were not serious about opposing Hitler's expansionist aims. They were offering Moscow nothing except the prospect of becoming engaged in a costly war. Stalin considered that rather than oppose Hitler, it would be better to go along with him, especially as Hitler was making extremely attractive offers of territorial gains. The Nazi–Soviet Non-Aggression Pact was, in fact, a misnomer; it was a blueprint for aggression, but against weaker third states. Following Hitler's attack on Poland and the outbreak of war, a new division of Europe into 'spheres of influence' took place. It brought the Soviet Union during 1939–40 half of Poland, the Baltic states, and some parts of eastern Romania.

When in the summer of 1941 Hitler turned his armies east to attack his former ally, the Soviet Union was plunged unexpectedly into a desperate struggle for survival. The earlier alliance with Hitler was expunged from the national memory as all resources were mobilized for the defeat of Nazism. Soviet war casualties were huge (over 20 million dead) and the country suffered enormous material losses during what came to be known as the 'Great Patriotic War'. Immediately Hitler attacked, the Soviet leadership found itself allied with Nazi Germany's existing enemies, notably Britain and, subsequently, the USA. The wartime alliance of the Big Three Powers was born.

The Great Power conferences

The postwar division of Europe can be traced back to the Great Power conferences (particularly those at Teheran in November 1943 and at Yalta, in the Crimea, in February 1945) which took place in the closing stages of the war. The Western Allies in the anti-Nazi coalition were eager to pave the way for a postwar world in which there would be an end to rivalry or squabbling about borders. Western policymakers realized after the Soviet victories of Kursk and Stalingrad that the defeat of Germany was inevitable. They saw, moreover, that the Red Army would liberate most areas of east-central Europe from German occupation. Faced with this inevitability, Churchill and Roosevelt attempted to meet with Stalin at an early stage to agree on the principles of postwar reconstruction.

The crucial role that the Red Army was playing on the eastern front (engaging two thirds of the German Army), and the security concerns of the Soviet regime (attacked from the west for the second time within twenty years) were in the forefront of people's minds. The Americans wanted (at Yalta) to engage the Soviets in the war against Japan. There was also a desire on the part of the USA and Britain to ensure that Stalin, who had been drawn out of his isolation and had made a favourable impression on Churchill and Roosevelt, remain a partner and take a full role in the ordering of the postwar world. Consequently, there was a readiness to make concessions to Stalin and smooth over any points of conflict.

In late October 1944 Churchill had put to Stalin the famous 'percentages agreement' concerning the relative influence of the Great Powers in south-central European countries expected to be liberated by the Red Army's advance. The Soviets were to have a 90% interest in Romania, 75% in Bulgaria and 50% in Hungary and Yugoslavia. In return, the British were ceded a 90% interest in Greece. Significantly, Stalin kept his word on Greece, even though it had a strong Communist movement. (Indeed, once this movement was defeated, thousands of Greek Communists sought refuge, and eventually settled, in the new 'people's democracies' of central Europe.)

At Teheran Churchill made the proposal to Stalin that Poland should be moved bodily westward, forfeiting almost half of its prewar territory and losing major centres of Polish culture such as Wilno (Vilnius) and Lwow. In return, Poland would be compensated at Germany's expense. Stalin accepted this proposal. But he also seized the Baltic states (to the disquiet of the Western allies, who refused to recognize their absorption into the Soviet Union), Bessarabia and northern Bukowina from Romania, and part of Czechoslovakia. In fact, Stalin reclaimed nearly all the territory he had occupied during 1939 and 1940 as a result of his Pact with Hitler. Two results flowed from this. The first was that Poland, having lost almost half its territory in the east, was compensated in the west at the expense of Germany. A large strip of territory from the Baltic coast to Silesia became Polish, including towns such as Stettin (Szczecin) and Breslau (Wrocław). Millions of German inhabitants were expelled to make way for Poles being 'repatriated' from the Soviet-occupied eastern regions of the country. The second was that after 1945 the Soviet Union had a common border with Hungary and Czechoslovakia. This was to have considerable significance in 1956 and 1968.

At Yalta the Declaration on Liberated Europe which was drafted by American officials and signed by the Big Three was couched in fairly elastic language, but it did include the undertaking that the Polish authorities would hold 'free and unfettered elections' once hostilities had ceased and a civilian administration had been restored to the country. (The assumption was that the exiled governments which had taken refuge in London and other centres would be free to return and head temporary administrations.) In retrospect, it may seem surprising that Stalin, whose experience of holding democratic elections was limited and whose track record abysmal, should have been entrusted with such a task. The 'plebiscite' carried out in Soviet-occupied Poland during October 1939 had been a travesty. The 'elections' in the Baltic States during the summer of 1940 were similarly fraudulent. These abuses of power had been brought to the attention of Western politicians and policymakers. Might not, then, provision have been made for international supervision of the elections, as happened in Greece? The answer seems to be that Western politicians did not want to risk Stalin's wrath by suggesting such a course.

It is doubtful, though, whether the Western allies fully understood what Stalin conceived by the term 'influence'. Stalin's comments from his wartime conversations with the Yugoslav Communist Milovan Djilas have often been quoted, but were not known at the time. (Stalin said that this war was not like past wars; in this war whoever occupied a territory imposed his own system.) In the beginning there was little to arouse the fears of Western politicians, although Churchill had been alerted by the Soviets' cynical failure to support the Warsaw Rising. When, in the late summer of 1944, the Red Army were approaching Warsaw an insurrection had been launched by the underground Polish Home Army. The hope of pro-London Poles was that they would be able to liberate their capital and welcome the Soviets as masters in their own house. But the Red Army halted on the eastern bank of the Vistula, and watched as the Germans slowly extinguished the last remnants of resistance. In some sixty days of fighting, a quarter of a million Poles died.

The takeover of east-central Europe

The Communist takeover of east-central Europe between 1944 and 1948 – the imposition of one-party rule – took place by stages. The first was that of military occupation by the Red Army. With the Soviet forces stalled outside Warsaw in the summer of 1944 the offensive moved to the south. Bucharest fell on 31 August 1944. On 5 September Moscow declared war on Bulgaria and the Red Army crossed the Danube. On 19 October Soviet troops were established in Debrecen in eastern Hungary. Only in January 1945 was Warsaw eventually taken, and Soviet troops crossed into Czechoslovakia in March of the same year. The Soviets were sufficiently subtle not to install Communist regimes at the outset. But everywhere (except Yugoslavia, where Tito's partisans took control, and Albania, which was beyond the reach of Soviet units) the Red Army was able to install 'its' people in the local administration and to eliminate (for 'collaboration' or any other charge which could be trumped up) potential opponents.

The second stage of the takeover was marked by the establishment of provisional coalition governments, with the participation of both Communist and non-Communist representatives. The aim of these 'national fronts' or 'popular fronts' was, in all cases, the same: to create administrations which contained members of the prewar parties, including those who had returned from exile, and by so doing to allay Western suspicions. The Communists had, at best, marginal influence in most of these states before the war and were given a role which, in importance, far exceeded their support. They were helped by the outlawing, agreed in the Yalta accords, of parties which were 'fascist' or had 'collaborated' with the Germans. Thus, in Poland the right-wing National Democratic Party, one of the strongest before the war, was not allowed a part in government. Similarly, in Czechoslovakia, the Agrarian Party, which had commanded widespread support before 1938, was excluded because of the collaboration of some of its members.

The third stage involved propaganda and terror. In all cases the Communists took control of key ministries such as Justice, Internal Affairs or Security, and Defence. This put them in an ideal position to use the NKVD-trained security and intelligence forces to break the back of democratic opposition and cloak their actions in legality. Many members of resistance groups which had fought the Germans but were not Communist controlled were arrested (in Poland thousands were deported to the Soviet Union). Skilled use was also made of propaganda. This – especially the use of posters and slogans – had developed as an art form since the earliest days of the Revolution, and had proved very effective, especially among the poorer, less-educated sections of the population. The Communists habitually made lavish promises, whether or not they were able to carry them out. At the same time, they poured abuse on the enemies of 'progress'. As Communist control of the mass media grew, the population became increasingly subject to the Party's line on all matters. Communist ideological censorship was more severe than that imposed during the German occupation.

The fourth stage involved 'salami tactics' to undermine their enemies, by subversion, intrigue and bribery. Communist support varied widely (from 17% in Hungary to 38% in Czechoslovakia), but in all cases they were in a minority in government. They overcame this obstacle by a number of means. In some cases an opposition party could be divided, by turning its leaders against one another. Some were invited to amalgamate or be absorbed. Others faced competition from a bogus rival party which bore a similar name and policies. They watched helpless as their confused supporters were drawn away. In the case of yet others, their leaders and officials were denounced or arrested. By such means the Communists managed to weaken and destroy many of their opponents.

The fifth stage involved the elections themselves. Although the 1946 elections in Czechoslovakia were fairly conducted, those in Poland and Hungary during 1947 were not. In the case of Poland, Stalin was probably convinced that the Poles were such irreconcilable enemies, there was little point in beating about the bush. The final stage involved the further settling of accounts with political opponents once political power had been consolidated.

In asking why the Communists were successful we have to recognize a number of characteristics, in addition to skilful use of propaganda and terror, mentioned above. They were, on the whole, better organized than their democratic opponents. During this period the Party apparatus was highly centralized and extremely disciplined. Many activists had been indoctrinated in the Soviet Union and had a firm grasp of Stalinist methods of seizing power and maintaining control. They planned to take power, and were not merely content to participate in the democratic process. They did not trust improvization or anything so quixotic as a free election. They were ruthless and unscrupulous in the methods they used to achieve their aims. Also, they were prepared to hide or camouflage their real aims from the electorate. All in all, they were playing the political game to a different set of rules from their opponents, who were, in any case, often divided among themselves.

Far from coming out of his shell, as Western policymakers had hoped he would do, Stalin was creating a further barrier – or 'cordon sanitaire' – behind which to hide. Indeed, if, between the wars and as a result of the Versailles settlement, the newly independent stages of central Europe had provided the West with a protective barrier against the contagion of Bolshevism, after World War II, they gave the USSR a security shield behind which it could recover and arm itself.

Hopes that the 'Big Three' alliance would last beyond the war were disappointed. As senior Foreign Office official Sir Frank Roberts observed with some humour, the British and the Americans thought that if only they treated Stalin like a member of the 'club' he might possibly start behaving like one – by joining the United Nations and playing a responsible part in the postwar structure. 'But Stalin did not want to be a member of that club. He much preferred to be the Director General of his own club, which was quite a different club, and which he would not have had us in either.'

The onset of the Cold War

Historians are divided about when the Cold War actually began. Some choose March 1946, when Churchill attempted to draw the world's (and particularly the American public's) attention to what was happening in east-central Europe. Churchill had been awarded an honorary degree by a small American liberal arts college at Fulton, Missouri. His acceptance speech, delivered in the presence of President Truman, echoed around the world. An 'iron curtain', said Churchill, had descended across Europe from Stettin in the Baltic to Trieste in the Adriatic. Behind it the Communist parties which were previously very small had 'been raised to a pre-eminence and power far beyond their numbers' and were seeking everywhere to obtain totalitarian control. They constituted 'a growing challenge and peril to civilization'.

Churchill, who had been in opposition since the July 1945 General Election, went on to say that he did not believe that Soviet Russia wanted war. What it desired were the fruits of war and the indefinite expansion of its power and doctrines. The West could not close its eyes to the danger, he maintained; there was a need for a 'special relationship' between the USA and Britain to counter the threat of Communist expansion. Churchill had used the term 'iron curtain' before. As early as August 1945 he had employed it in a parliamentary speech, when referring to the expulsion of Germans from Poland. But after the Fulton address the term entered into popular usage and became part of the vocabulary of the Cold War.

In fact it was not until 1947 that the pattern of events in east-central Europe became clearer, first with faked elections in Poland and Hungary and then with a campaign of terror against opposition politicians (directed particularly against peasant leaders in Hungary, Bulgaria, Romania and Poland). The year also saw the creation of the Communist Information Bureau, the 'Cominform'. By the end of 1947 the division of Europe was clearer. The Communists were no longer hiding behind coalition governments, but had in most states taken absolute control, had outlawed the opposition and were hounding them.

The West began to respond to Churchill's warnings about Communist expansion during 1947. In March of that year the American President outlined what came to be known in his name as the *Truman Doctrine*. The USA would not abandon those states which sought to avoid coming under Communist domination. Washington would help such countries to retain their freedom and independence. This policy of 'containing' Communist expansion was later superseded under the Eisenhower administration by a more aggressive design to 'roll back' Communism.

The European Recovery Programme, or *Marshall Plan* (named after the

US Secretary of State, George Marshall), was also brought to life during 1947. This was a move to extend economic aid to rebuild Europe's war-shattered economies, a condition being that the Europeans agreed to economic co-operation ($12 billion dollars was sent to Europe between 1947 and 1951). The Soviet government abruptly rejected such help, but the Polish and Czech governments at first welcomed the Plan. Only after Soviet pressure was exerted did they, too, withdraw from it. By the time the first Marshall Plan conference began in Paris on 9 July, with the participation of fourteen nations, Romania, Yugoslavia and Finland had also withdrawn.

The Soviet response was the *Zhdanov Doctrine*. A. A. Zhdanov was an associate of Stalin's who expounded his theory of the 'two camps' to delegates at the founding session of the Cominform in Polish Silesia in September 1947. According to Zhdanov's vision, the world was divided into opposing camps – the 'imperialist', 'anti-democratic' camp (headed by the USA) and the 'socialist', 'anti-imperialist', 'democratic' camp led by the USSR. The speech was couched in extremely aggressive terminology, and was intended to provide a justification for the sovietization of east-central Europe.

If 1947 marked the rupture of the wartime alliance, it is 1948 which is usually taken as marking the onset of the Cold War. This is partly because of the 1948 Berlin blockade and airlift, when the superpowers confronted each other directly, no longer via proxies, and the confrontation threatened to develop into something more than verbal sparring.

Following the defeat of Nazi Germany, Germany had been divided into four occupation zones, to be administered by the victorious Allied powers: the USA, Britain, France and the Soviet Union. (Poles often claim that although they fought from the first day of the war to the last, they were not rewarded with a share in the occupation. But Poland, the Allies could argue, got more than mere supervision of German territory, it 'swallowed' its area of Germany.) The Soviet zone accounted for only one-third of postwar Germany, but it included the prewar capital, Berlin. The Allies had agreed at the Potsdam Conference (July 1945) that they would create a unitary but disarmed German state, and that Berlin would remain under four-power control – itself divided into sectors. When moves to fuse the Western zones were eventually taken in 1947, and currency reform was effected in the West without Soviet agreement or participation, the scene was set for a showdown. The Soviets retaliated in June 1948 by cutting Western road and rail traffic in the 'corridors' which crossed Soviet-occupied territory to the capital. By severing the West's links with its sectors in the German capital the Soviets hoped to starve the inhabitants into submission – or at least force the West into a humiliating climbdown. They were foiled by a massive airlift of supplies along the air corridor into Berlin – which had not been blocked – and it was Stalin who eventually (in May 1949) backed down.

This huge operation demonstrated the West's determination not to be prised out of its foothold in Berlin, but, more importantly, it showed Stalin that he could no longer expect to get his own way quite as easily as he had done during the wartime alliance. Subsequently, the demarcation line with the Eastern, Soviet, zone became virtually a state border. (The German Democratic Republic – East Germany – became *de jure* an independent state from 1949, with its own parliament and decision to frame a constitution. In 1955 it joined the Warsaw Pact.)

In February 1948 Czechoslovakia became the last of the states on the Soviet western border to fall to the Communists. By contrast with Poland, the Communist takeover occurred without any Soviet troops present on Czechoslovak soil (though they returned with a vengeance in 1968). However, Czechoslovakia had what Poland lacked, a strong basis of Communist support. Coincidentally, at the same time that Communist rule was being consolidated in Czechoslovakia, to the south Tito was declaring his independence of Moscow and arousing Stalin's fury. This caused the first split in the Soviet bloc, and reaffirmed Stalin's fears that freedom to follow the national 'deviationist' line would make for untrustworthy, unreliable partners. Hostility grew between the two Communist parties. Consideration was given by Moscow to military intervention, but in the end the USSR reluctantly allowed Tito to go his own way.

The consolidation of Communist rule

The twin blows to Stalin's ambitions that occurred during 1948 (defeat in the Berlin confrontation and Tito's defection) were added to by the signing of the Atlantic Pact in Washington during July. These events served only to increase Stalin's paranoia, and moves began to consolidate Communist rule in the satellite states and to weld them into a political bloc. In the economic sphere, industrialization was pushed forward and central planning bodies set up. Tighter censorship was imposed, and a greater cultural and artistic conformity demanded. Increasing pressure was exerted on the Church. In December 1948 the Hungarian Roman Catholic primate, Cardinal Mindszenty, was arrested and later imprisoned. The Polish primate, Cardinal Wyszyński, met the same fate in 1950. Church property was confiscated and church charitable organizations wound up or taken over by the state. Actions of this nature prompted the Pope to issue a declaration that members of the Communist Party and its sympathizers would be excommunicated.

The use of secret police to eliminate political opponents was soon directed inwards towards the ranks of the Party itself. In June 1949 the Hungarian Interior and Foreign Affairs minister, Laszlo Rajk, was arrested, together with seventeen other people. He was accused to having had contact with American intelligence before the war, of being a Gestapo agent during the war, and of having spied for Yugoslavia since the war – a colourful and damning inventory of misdemeanours. He was sentenced to death along with two of his 'co-conspirators'. The Rajk affair set the tone for a series of Party purges over the next few years. (The next took place in Bulgaria during December 1949 and ended with the hanging of former deputy premier, Trajcho Kostov.) The lesson ostensibly being taught was one of constant vigilance against the enemies of socialism. But the real message was one of absolute conformity; that deviation from Moscow's line would not be tolerated.

Czechoslovakia managed to avoid such extreme measures for rather longer than its neighbours, but eventually had to submit to Moscow's prompting. This country was an important piece in the jigsaw, one of the most highly industrial regions in the Eastern bloc, and had to be secured for socialism. When the purges did come they were ruthless and extensive. Almost 10,000 people were in prison for political offences in the Czech lands alone at the end of 1950, and more than 16,000 arrested over the next two years by the state security forces. In the four years to the end of 1952 almost 200 people were executed. The best-known victim of these purges was Rudolf Slánský, Party general secretary, who was arrested and put on trial along with thirteen other people for 'Trotskyist, Titoist, Zionist, bourgeois-nationalist treason'. (The anti-semitic character of these trials has been seen by some historians as a legacy of Moscow's failure to transform the infant state of Israel into a left-wing, pro-Moscow outpost in the Mediterranean.) At the end of 1952 Slánský and ten other people received the death sentence.

In January 1949 the Communist world's trade organization, the *Commission for Mutual Economic Aid* – known as Comecon or CMEA – was called into being in Moscow. Six nations (the USSR, Poland, Czechoslovakia, Romania, Hungary and Bulgaria) took part in its early meetings, although Albania joined later in the same year. The forming of Comecon was regarded by most observers as the Soviet answer to the Marshall Plan. While violently hostile to the Americans' initiative, the Soviets had not hitherto been able to respond with any positive moves of their own. Although Soviet-bloc spokesmen denied that this was the case, the communiqué which announced Comecon explicitly stated that 'broader economic co-operation between the peoples of the people's democracies and the Soviet Union' was being planned, because 'these countries do not consider it possible to subordinate themselves to the dictates of the Marshall Plan, as this plan infringes on the sovereignty of countries and the interests of their national economies'.

The aims of Comecon, as outlined in the communiqué, were to 'exchange economic experience', to extend technical aid and encourage trade between the member states. Its stated political aims were to 'strengthen the unity and solidarity of members' and encourage co-operation 'in the interest of the building of socialism and communism'. The initial setting up of Comecon seems to have been more for propaganda purposes than for anything else. The Organization remained virtually inactive until 1954, when its Secretariat was created, and only in December 1959 – more than ten years after the announcement of its formation – was the Charter of the Organization signed in Sofia. Gradually, more began to be achieved in co-ordinating five-year national economic plans, in encouraging special-ization and co-operation of production (particularly in chemicals and engineering). But much of this co-ordination was done on a bilateral basis. Although Comecon was created as an organization of equals, one was more equal than others; the Organization was dominated by the Soviet Union. Soviet personnel took most of the top positions, and the secretariats were eventually concentrated in Moscow. In the early days, at least, the Organ-ization served Soviet economic, as well as political, interests.

The fusing of the Soviet bloc nations in a military alliance did not take place until 1955, when the *Warsaw Treaty Organization* (better known as the *Warsaw Pact*) was created. As with Comecon, its creation was largely a response to events in the West; the creation of West European Union in the previous year and the inclusion of the newly created German Federal Republic in the North Atlantic Alliance, which the Treaty saw as 'increas-ing the danger of a new war and creating a threat to the security of peace-loving states . . .'. The Treaty provided for consultation on military and defence matters and for assistance to be offered to a member state in the event of an armed attack. It specified 'armed attack in Europe', and therefore, by implication, did not oblige any intervention by Eastern bloc countries should the Soviet Union become embroiled in a conflict in Central Asia or the Far East. (Perhaps ignorant of this or else sceptical that it would be observed, many citizens of the Warsaw Pact states were nervous during the Afghanistan conflict about the possibility of 'allied contingents' being sent to fight the mujahaddin.)

Western analysts have suggested that the formation of the Warsaw Pact was an early Soviet gambit to bring about the dismantling of NATO and the withdrawal of American troops from Europe – on a *quid pro quo* basis. Indeed, the proposal to liquidate both organizations – NATO and the Warsaw Pact – which has been revived recently by Gorbachev was first made at the 1955 Geneva summit meeting.

The Pact had a useful effect, from the Soviet viewpoint, of 'locking in' the member states to Moscow. The prospect of a rearmed Germany so soon after the war, and before memories of the ravages of Nazi occupation had subsided, was frightening to Germany's neighbours in east-central Europe, who had suffered so terribly at its hands in the past. It was put to excellent propaganda use by Moscow, which was then able to represent itself as defending the true interests and freedom of these peoples. This was effective with the Poles, especially, who, despite a traditional sus-picion of the Russians, feared that growing German economic strength and military power would be accompanied by attempts to reclaim their eastern territories acquired by Poland in 1945. True, East Germany had signed a treaty with Poland in 1950 confirming the inviolability of the new border. However, sections of West German opinion had remained hostile and felt that the Berlin Communists did not have the right to sign in the name of the German nation.

In addition to the USSR, seven countries signed the Warsaw Treaty – Poland, Czechoslovakia, East Germany, Hungary, Romania, Bulgaria and Albania. Yugoslavia never became a member following the split with Moscow in 1948; indeed, it signed the Balkan Pact with Greece and Turkey during 1954. But some of those that did join showed a great deal of unease with the Pact. During the course of the 1956 Hungarian uprising the government of Imre Nagy stated its intention to leave the Organization. Naturally, with the suppression of the Rising, such moves were foiled. Romania too was early in adopting a cautious attitude to the Treaty, although it avoided a complete break. From 1962 onwards it allowed no Warsaw Pact troops on its soil for 'joint manoeuvres'. Albania withdrew from the Organization in 1968, shortly after the invasion of Czechoslovakia. Since it is completely surrounded on the land side by Yugoslav and Greek territory, the Albanian regime presumably felt safe from the intervention of Warsaw Pact tanks!

Soviet justifications for the creation of the Eastern bloc pacts – that they were reacting to developments in the West – ignore the reasons why the Cold War began; the aggressive methods undertaken by Moscow, especially during the Stalinist period, to enforce Communist rule on its Western neighbours.

The nature of Communist rule

The regimes which came into power in east-central Europe after 1945 called themselves 'people's republics' or 'socialist democracies'. In fact they were neither socialist in the accepted Western sense of the word nor were they democracies, since they did not allow for free choice in competitive elections. Nor were the regimes in any way the choice of the people. Misuse of such terms and misinformation about the true nature of conditions obtaining under Communist rule have been characteristic of Communist regimes.

The emerging Communist states did have a number of things in common. The first is that they were all buttressed by an official ideology – Marxism or Marxism–Leninism. This had three important elements which adherents found attractive: it provided a 'scientific' interpretation of history in class terms; it explained that the victory of the proletariat and the triumph of Communist rule was logical and inevitable; finally, it presented a vision of a more egalitarian society, with the elimination of poverty and exploitation. The concept of 'building socialism', the society of tomorrow, was portrayed as a thoroughly worthy and progressive exercise. Social engineering on a wide scale was used to further the interests of the workers (for example, preferential selection for university education for their children).

Marxism provided the moral and theoretical justification for Communist Party rule in the name of the working classes. Once this foundation stone of Party rule had been set in place any challenge to the arrangement – even from within the working class itself – could be branded 'reactionary' or 'counter-revolutionary'. The Communists' claims to be bringing social justice and an end to extremes of wealth and poverty were powerful moral arguments, and beguiled sections of the electorate in many of the states concerned, not to mention more credulous groups in the West. Increasingly, as corruption, abuses of power and stark inequalities under Communist rule became evident the ideological underpinning became frayed and then completely discredited.

The second characteristic was the introduction of single-party rule. Although other parties were tolerated throughout the period, these were 'fellow-travelling' parties which were completely subservient to the Communists. Party control was extended outwards and downwards by means of the *nomenklatura*, Party nominees selected for key posts in all areas of public life – from the economy and local government to the media and the diplomatic service. It was also an invaluable source of political patronage. Over a period of time the Communist Party tended to develop into an elite caste. Indeed, the Polish former dissident, Adam Michnik, compared the division between Party and people to the apartheid system in South Africa. The Party, he suggested, was the white community. Privileges such as special shops, better housing and jobs, and easier foreign travel existed for members. This, however, had a deleterious long-term effect on Party morale and discipline. It attracted careerists, those who were not ideologically motivated but merely wished to share the benefits of Party membership.

The economic systems introduced into east-central Europe were modelled on the Soviet type; that is, the market relationship between consumer and producer was largely removed. As large areas of the economy were drawn into public ownership a large bureaucracy came into being to cope with economic management. Consumer wants or demands became largely an irrelevance, as the state increasingly determined what should be produced, allocated the necessary resources and set targets. Typically, this meant large investment in the extractive industries, in engineering and heavy industry at the cost of living standards. Heavy and wasteful use of labour, raw materials and energy produced early results, but by the 1970s (if not earlier), the Communist economies were looking decidedly unwieldy. Central planning meant lack of initiative and innovation. The incentives which in the West led to the development of new ideas and entrepreneurship were missing, since not only was the profit motive distrusted but the road to advancement was blocked by Party appointees.

The result all too frequently was empty shops and queues for basic necessities. Stalin's successor, Nikita Khrushchev, once boasted during a visit to the USA that the Soviet economy would be turned to service the needs of its consumers and would outstrip the West, but no significant improvement in the supply of consumer items took place.

The Polish attempt to reverse the downward trend under Edward Gierek's regime in the 1970s involved the large-scale import of Western technology and investment. The rush for growth failed because the structures which would have enabled it to work were not in place. The whole system needed reform, as was belatedly realized.

Communist economic systems almost everywhere failed in terms of the efficiency and the standards of living achieved under the successful market economies. It is true that in their early stages they took steps towards a more egalitarian system by attempting to eliminate most traces of absolute poverty; true also that massive state subsidies kept prices artificially low. But the end result was negative, and could be seen at its worst in Poland and the Soviet Union. Currencies which were not convertible and had little purchasing value led to a black market in dollars. The empty shops, queues and absence of much-sought Western consumer items resulted in black market trade, speculation and hoarding. The government 'bought off' elite groups of workers by allocating them a greater flow of resources together with higher pay, special shops and other privileges.

The fourth characteristic that the postwar Communist regimes shared was elimination of civil society. 'Civil society' is a term used by historians and political scientists to describe the change that took place when societies emerged from the feudal era. Using the term in this context draws an interesting parallel between the tendency of both feudal and Communist systems to exert control over all aspects of an individual's life. In a totalitarian society, as Václav Havel has argued, the state aims not only to control all areas of political and economic life, it is suspicious of all forms of social organization which do not come under its aegis – be they angling clubs or scouting groups. It reduces and atomizes society, and at the extreme treats its subject people as prisoners or slaves, denying them the right to independent thought, action, association.

Fifthly, Communists everywhere worked to achieve a monopoly on the supply of news and information to the public. At the outset, this helped them to gain and consolidate power. In later years, it aided in concealing the shortcomings of their policies. The Party-controlled censorship became an important part of the power structure, creating a further bureacracy with well-paid posts for the *nomenklatura*. The censors' painstaking attention to detail can be illustrated by reference to the Black Book of the Polish Censor, an instruction manual smuggled out to Sweden in 1977 and since published in the West. The importance the regimes attached to preserving this news monopoly can be deduced by the persistence with which they jammed Western radio stations such as the BBC, Voice of America, and Radio Free Europe. The London assassination of journalist, Georgi Markov (widely attributed to the Bulgarian secret police), and the death sentence passed by the Polish Government *in absentia* on RFE head, Zdzisław Najder (in May 1983), are further evidence of the damage done to the domestic propaganda efforts of the Communists.

Further characteristics which the regimes shared were their lack of legitimacy and accountability. The power they wielded had been achieved illegally and retained by force, or the threat of force. They did not rule with the authority and legitimation that comes with political consensus. The absence of democratic procedures meant that mistakes could be concealed or, at the very worst, a member of the *nomenklatura* could be replaced by another Party nominee. True, at the top, where the buck stopped, some degree of accountability was evident, as indeed it had to be. Once other scapegoats had been exhausted, government or Party leaders (in Communist systems there is little difference between them; the same people often fill posts in both the government and the Party's Politburo) could be replaced when popular discontent reached the level of demonstrations and strikes. But the Party monolith remained in place. 'Change' meant a shuffling of the leadership pack and the ritual, token sacrifice of a disgraced member.

How the web began to unravel

What were the factors which led to the break-up of Soviet hegemony over east-central Europe? Much has been written about the 'changing of the guard' in the Kremlin, of the passing away of the gerontocracy which had maintained a hold on power for so long. Certainly the new Party leader, Mikhail Gorbachev, who came to power in 1985, represented a new generation – one for whom the days of the Red Army's triumphs during World War II were scarcely more than a childhood memory. But from his early policy statements there was little to suggest that we would see the far-reaching transformation which has occurred, both in East–West relations and in those between Moscow and its Eastern European satellites.

It seems clear that the radical change in policy leading to the Soviet disengagement from central Europe was not just a spontaneous process. Influences of an almost irresistible nature on the Kremlin leadership forced a reassessment of traditional policies and relationships. These influences or pressures came from three areas; pressure for change from within Eastern Europe itself, pressures due to developments in Moscow's relationship with the West, and domestic Soviet policy considerations.

The nations of east-central Europe did not submit happily to Communist rule and became increasingly turbulent over the four postwar decades. Protests and unrest were apparent from an early stage. The first major upheaval of any consequence occurred in East Germany in June 1953 – shortly following the death of Stalin. Strikes and demonstrations broke out throughout the country and were put down savagely by police, who shot at demonstrators in Berlin. In 1956 came the Polish October – this following Khrushchev's denunciation of Stalin at the Soviet Party's Twentieth

Congress. Mass strikes and demonstrations occurred in Poznań, following which workers stormed the headquarters of the Party and the security police. Over fifty people were killed in putting the unrest down, but it had the effect of returning Władysław Gomułka to power. The Polish events were followed by the Rising in Hungary, during which Nagy declared not only Hungary's withdrawal from the Warsaw Pact but also the introduction of a multi-party system. This revolt against the twin principles of Communist one-party rule and alliance with Moscow was put down by Soviet tanks.

Strikes and demonstrations were not the only means by which subject peoples, deprived of recourse to the ballot box, could make their dissatisfaction known. Many took the chance to vote with their feet, despite the bureaucratic and financial restrictions on travel abroad. Large numbers of East Germans were able to abandon Communism in this way, by travelling to Berlin and passing over to the Western sectors of the city. By the end of the 1950s this route had become so popular it was becoming an embarrassment to the Communist authorities – an estimated 20,000 people a month were flooding across. On the night of 12/13 August 1961, barbed wire was put up along the boundary between Soviet and Western sectors, to be replaced within days by a more substantial structure – the Berlin Wall.

The Wall became a symbol of the postwar division of Europe – and of Communist repression. It illustrated in stark form the lost freedoms of the people who lived behind it. Many Germans were henceforth cut off from their families and friends across the border, and only in the 1970s did the restrictions on cross-border contacts ease. The flood of refugees was reduced to a trickle – those brave, hardy, and sometimes ingenious souls, who were prepared to risk death in challenging the Wall's defences. The erection of the Wall and the storm of international protest which resulted detracted significantly from the propaganda value of Yuri Gagarin's first manned space flight, which took place during the same year.

A mere seven years later, the Czechoslovak Communist Party made a courageous attempt to reform the system from within. Without going quite as far as Nagy had gone in Hungary – there were no plans to abolish one-party rule – the Prague leadership under Dubček hoped to make state socialism more tolerable, to give it a 'human face'. The intervention by Warsaw Pact troops and tanks was a further disastrous move in political terms for the Kremlin. It harmed East–West relations, increased Warsaw Pact members' suspicion of the Organization, and undermined Moscow's standing with previously sympathetic leftist groups in the West.

No sooner had the Prague Spring been nipped in the bud, than unrest broke out again, this time along Poland's Baltic coast. Strikes and demonstrations resulted in repressive police action and the shooting of dozens of workers. Popular discontent led to a change of leadership – Gomułka was replaced by Edward Gierek. The 'recurrent crises' which afflicted the Communist regime in Poland struck more tellingly ten years later, though, when Gierek himself fell from power. The rise of the Solidarity trade union under Lech Wałęsa's leadership proved the most serious threat to Soviet control of the region, and the most difficult to put down, precisely because it clearly had such huge public support (10 million members).

The introduction of martial law in December 1981 removed the need for Soviet tanks to intervene directly, but it presented the world with the unlikely spectacle of 'proletarian rule' being maintained following a military coup – a coup directed, moreover, against the very industrial working class whose interests the Party was supposed to be representing! The vision of Poland, the largest of Moscow's central European satellites, being ruled during the 1980s by a South American-style military junta forced the Soviet leadership to rethink its policy in the region. The line of states that had been acquired by Stalin in the 1940s to provide a 'cordon sanitaire' and a zone of stability had itself become unstable – and therefore a liability. Furthermore, the trade costs of maintaining the defensive cordon had become prohibitive. Moscow was selling its partners valuable supplies of oil at below world prices in return for poor-quality manufactured goods.

Developments in East–West relations were also important in influencing Soviet policy towards Central Europe. One of the early moves to defuse tension was the reorientation of West German foreign policy towards rapprochement with Eastern Europe. This 'Ostpolitik' was set in motion as early as 1966 under Chancellor Kurt Kiesinger, but flourished under his successor, Willy Brandt, with whom it is now chiefly associated. It resulted in the signing in Warsaw (in 1970) of a treaty by which the Federal Republic recognized Poland's western borders, removing fears of German revanchism. (Similar treaties were later signed with Czechoslovakia, Bulgaria, Hungary and East Germany.) Earlier, a visit by Brandt to Moscow had resulted in the signing of a Treaty on the mutual renunciation of force in relations between states. This led to closer ties with Moscow and helped convince the Soviet leadership that Germany was no longer a threat in military terms.

Brandt's Ostpolitik led to the process of East–West détente in the 1970s. It paved the way for a thaw in relations between East Germany and the Federal Republic, but, more significantly, led to the Helsinki Conference on Security and Co-operation in Europe (CSCE). An important aspect of the Helsinki talks was that for the first time all the European states (with the exception of Albania) and the North Americans participated as equals. There had been no general peace treaty at the end of World War II – only the Great Power conferences which had 'imposed' the postwar settlement. Some influential Western voices were critical of the subjection of Eastern Europe to Moscow rule and even called for the Yalta accords to be revised. So the main aim of the Soviet side, which was the instigator of the Helsinki talks, was to secure general recognition of Europe's postwar frontiers. Indeed, it was a desperate attempt to guarantee the stability of the existing structures, given the growing threat to security, not so much from the West's military or economic power but from within Eastern Europe itself, from the inherent instability of the Soviet satellites.

The Helsinki talks were divided into three 'baskets': confidence-building measures of a mainly military kind, economic co-operation, and the third 'basket' on security and human rights. The Soviets were persuaded to recognize that international security was not just something that could be determined by governments sitting around a table. They were shown that the causes of insecurity were inherent in the Soviet system. The security of states was inextricably linked with the security of individuals. In order to encourage security and stability it was necessary to foster internal order – an order which could only be guaranteed by reference to human rights. Soviet policymakers were forced to recognize that the stifling of the aspirations of its citizens was a greater threat to stability than NATO tanks.

By signing the Helsinki Final Act, Moscow acknowledged the linkage between co-operation in other spheres and the observance of certain standards in the treatment of its citizens. It had effectively forfeited (though was slow in realizing it) the excuse that human rights violations were 'an internal matter', and was henceforth denied recourse to the argument that principles of non-intervention in the domestic affairs of a sovereign state should apply. The determination of the West to monitor human rights abuses gave the impetus to indigenous dissident groups to carry out their own monitoring process. Groups came into existence both in Eastern Europe (KOR in Poland, Charter 77 in Czechoslovakia) and in the USSR. The Helsinki talks revealed the need for continuing East–West dialogue, and so the Helsinki process was born. A series of meetings took place such as those on disarmament at Madrid (1983), Stockholm (1984–6), and Vienna (1986–9).

In the USA, however, right-wing critics of détente saw it as a form of appeasement and, unwilling to treat the Soviets as an equal, rejected the concept of military balance or parity with the USSR. The Soviet invasion of Afghanistan led to the collapse of détente and the return to a Cold War atmosphere in the last years of the Brezhnev period. This, in turn, resulted in a renewal of the arms race. In President Ronald Reagan the Kremlin found a leader who was firm and prepared to confront the Soviet leadership. He was ready to increase US military spending, and forcefully backed the 'Star Wars' programme (to develop a satellite-borne umbrella of laser weapons to counter Soviet ballistic missiles). Soviet attempts to drive a wedge between the Americans and their European allies (for example, the campaign to prevent dispersal in Europe of Cruise missiles) failed.

If increased military spending was creating imbalance for the US budget, it was making the economic pips squeak in Moscow, which was banned from receiving advanced technology and found it almost impossible to increase the burden of military spending. (Western experts estimate that the USSR was spending twice as much proportionately to maintain its position in the arms race as the USA.) The war in Afghanistan constituted a further drain on the resources and the international standing of the Soviet Union. Further east, the Chinese Communists had introduced limited economic reforms and were achieving impressive 9% annual growth rates throughout the decade. Not only was Japan now an economic super-power, but the nations of the Pacific Rim, with their market economies, were making commendable efforts to emulate it. It was against this background that the Soviet leadership looked to the West, saw the impressive moves towards economic and political union made by the West European states and their prosperity, and realized that greater hope for stability lay in courting, rather than confronting, their West European neighbours.

From this the principles that have characterized Soviet policy in the closing years of the decade developed; liberalization at home, abandonment of the arms race and rapprochement with the West, enunciation of the concept of the 'Common European home', and, in regard to the central European satellites, rejection of the Brezhnev Doctrine in favour of the so-called 'Sinatra Doctrine' ('let them do it their way').

How and why change came

In both Hungary and Poland change began earlier and was altogether more gradual and less dramatic than elsewhere. In Hungary the ousting of Kádár as early as May 1988 signalled the beginning of a more open political discussion between Party and opposition elements. The elevation of reform-minded Imre Pozsgay to the Politburo forced the pace of reform from within the Party. In the early months of 1989 the Party made repeated concessions to an opposition movement headed by the Democratic Forum, until the way was eventually cleared for a multi-party democracy. The Hungarian Party reshaped itself in preparation for elections in the spring of 1990. In Poland, too, the first concrete moves took place in the autumn of 1988, with attempts by the Jaruzelski regime to reach an accommodation with the Solidarity opposition. Solidarity representatives were invited to round-table talks, which took place in the spring of 1989. These led to the 'partly free' elections in June and to the appointment of the first non-Communist premier of a Warsaw Pact state.

During this period the eyes of analysts were repeatedly turned to Moscow. How far would the Soviet leadership permit the liberalization in their vassal states to go? Could it be taken as far as real democracy and possible divorce from Moscow? In the Eastern European capitals the message had been received early that the Soviets were prepared for a liberalization and a loosening of ties. Gorbachev made his views clear during two key speeches in July 1989 – one to the Council of Europe in Strasbourg and the other at the Warsaw Pact summit in Bucharest. In Bucharest, the Soviet leader stressed to his allies his rejection of the

Brezhnev Doctrine; there was no set model for the building of socialism. Each Communist party had the right to pursue its own strategy in line with national conditions. Henceforth, he hoped there would be 'unity in diversity' – a looser, more pluralistic alliance of equals.

At Strasbourg, Gorbachev signalled his desire to 'consign to the archives the postulates of the Cold War, when Europe was regarded as an arena of confrontation'. In a final break with the doctrine of interventionism, he stated,

> The affiliation of the states of Europe to different social systems is a reality, and the recognition of that historical state of affairs, respect for the sovereign right of every people to choose a social system as it sees fit, is a vital prerequisite for the normal European process. The social and political orders of one country or another changed in the past and may change in the future as well. However, that is exclusively the affair of the peoples themselves, a matter for their choice. Any interference in internal affairs, any attempts to limit the sovereignty of states, both of friends and allies, no matter whose it is, is impermissible.

While Gorbachev gave the green light to change it is unlikely that even he realized how rapidly change would come.

In August and September of 1989 (28 years after the erection of the Berlin Wall) waves of East Germans began once more to exercise their choice of political order. East German 'tourists' flooded to the West via Hungary, Czechoslovakia and the West German embassy in Poland. This outflow – heading, of course, for the Federal Republic – was an acute embarrassment for the state, which had perhaps the most successful economy in the socialist bloc. Not least embarrassing was the fact that its neighbours and allies (no doubt with an eye on relations with the Federal Republic) were not prepared to lift a finger to stop the migrants. The refugee exodus was followed by mass demonstrations in East German cities against the leadership, which led in October to the resignation of Party leader, Erich Honecker, in favour of a younger colleague, Egon Krenz. The reforms which Krenz introduced brought no relief for the leadership. The demonstrations continued, the ultimate goal now, it was clear, being the complete removal of the Communists from power. On 7 November the government resigned, to be followed a day later by the whole Politburo. On 9 November the Berlin Wall was breached by the authorities, by which time some 200,000 East Germans (1% of the population) had left the country. Krenz himself was eventually forced to resign in early December, after only 49 days in office.

On the day after the Berlin Wall was breached, Bulgarian leader Todor Zhivkov was toppled by Party colleagues. The 78-year-old leader had been the longest serving in central Europe (he had come to power a year after

Stalin's death and seven years before the Berlin Wall was erected in 1961). Zhivkov precipitated his own downfall when his despotic policies to 'Bulgarianize' the country's Muslim community resulted in a mass exodus across the Turkish border. This, in turn, had led to severe problems for the Bulgarian economy, and to Zhivkov's replacement by Petur Mladenov.

Within days, the Czechoslovak regime capitulated. Hitherto defiant and resolute in its determination to retain socialist policies, the Prague leadership overreacted to student demonstrations in the capital on 17 November. The police violence (now widely believed to have been instigated by a faction inside the secret police apparat, and not the leadership) caused outrage and led to further demonstrations, which grew in support and spread to other towns. The Party's hold on power was loosened by the end of the month and was finally shaken off completely in early December.

Finally, the dramatic and bloody events in Romania erupted in the days before Christmas 1989. The rule of the Romanian leader Nicolae Ceauşescu – labelled the 'Balkan Caligula' in a *Times* leader – had been harsh, even by Communist standards. He had treated the country as his personal fiefdom and ruled with his family like a true despot. The arrest of a Hungarian pastor in Timişoara provoked demonstrations which were put down by the security forces with great bloodshed. The protests moved to the nation's capital and gathered strength when the army refused to shoot at demonstrators. Ceauşescu's attempt to flee failed, and he was executed with his wife after a summary trial.

What came as the greatest surprise to onlookers was the speed with which the old structures of power collapsed. Their frailty surprised even those opposition elements responsible for their downfall. The movement for change and reform seemed to gather its own irresistible momentum. Once it began, and not without justification, observers began to refer to the 'domino theory' working in reverse. (The 'domino theory' was formulated during the 1960s to account for the predicted collapse of neighbouring states in South-east Asia to Communist rule.)

Why did the regimes collapse so quickly in central Europe? It is difficult to generalize. But we can say first, that the states that fell to Communism after World War II, while having far from lengthy traditions of democracy, lacked the almost unbroken tradition of absolutism that the Russians had inherited from Tsarist rule. In their philosophical, religious, cultural and political traditions they identified more closely with the West. We can also refer to the collapse of belief in Marxist ideology (and therefore in the future it promised), the economic failures, the removal of the threat of force (both domestic and external). The Soviet policy of greater openness – *glasnost* – also had an effect. It encouraged re-examination of the past and a questioning of Party legitimacy. Finally, there was the 'behaviourist' policy adopted by the West. The system of financial rewards or incentives offered as aid but linked to progress in liberalization.

In the aftermath of revolutions

Whereas the second half of 1989 saw the toppling of Communist regimes in much of central Europe, in the first half of 1990 there was a consolidation of the reforms that had been set in motion. The most significant events to take place during this period were the elections in East Germany, Hungary, Romania, Czechoslovakia and Bulgaria – the first democratic, multi-party elections to be held in the region for more than four decades. In Yugoslavia elections were also held in the northern republics of Croatia and Slovenia. (Poland, a notable absentee from the list, now seems likely to have a general election before its new Constitution is ready in the spring of 1991.) The elections did not pass without surprises. In East Germany they brought the unexpected victory of the conservative alliance led by the CDU over the Social Democrats. In Romania and Bulgaria, they provided controversial, but convincing victories for former Communists. The pattern was subsequently – in March 1991 – repeated in Albania. Indeed, even in Czechoslovakia, where Civic Forum won resoundingly, the Communists fared better than expected with 13% of the vote.

In the second half of 1990 a good deal of the euphoria and optimism generated by the collapse of Communist regimes evaporated, as the states of east-central Europe discovered that there is more to democracy than merely holding elections. As one East European academic put it, they woke up with a post-revolutionary hangover. Their lack of a rooted political culture, and of established, experienced political elites, have been sorely felt and the problems have not been made easier by the economic problems faced. The necessary strains of running a democracy led to the break-up of the Solidarity consensus in Poland and that of Civic Forum in Czechoslovakia. Local elections in Poland, Czechoslovakia and Hungary showed reduced public support for the administrations which guided the countries' first faltering steps towards democratic rule. There was unrest in Bulgaria and Romania. Indeed, the belief in the latter country that nothing has changed led to pressure on the Iliescu regime and calls for 'a second revolution'. Yugoslavia has faced perhaps the most intractable problems; its two northern republics, Slovenia and Croatia, voted in right-wing governments, while the dominant Serbs chose to remain under Communist leadership. Given the strength of underlying nationalist feelings, the centrifugal forces in Yugoslavia seem irresistible.

German reunification occupied the thoughts of policymakers of both East and West during 1990. Concern in Western Europe that this new 80 million-strong superstate will dominate the European Community economically were matched in the east by concern about the military and strategic ramifications of the merger. A series of 'two plus four' talks (the victorious wartime allies – the US, the USSR, Britain and France – with representatives from both Germanies) set in motion in May aimed to solve the problems arising from unification. Although German economic and monetary union took place on 1 July, it was not until 12 September – after seven months of negotiations – that the 'two plus four' treaty was signed in Moscow. While Moscow conceded that the new Germany could remain in NATO, there was agreed limitation on German troop numbers, and that Soviet troops should remain in eastern Germany until 1994. The Germans also agreed to sign a treaty with Warsaw settling, once and for all, the Polish–German border issue. This paved the way for Germany to regain full sovereignty on 3 October, and formal unification took place on 2 December.

One of the most disappointing features of this first year and a half of post-Communist rule in central Europe has been the resurgence of nationalism, often in its most bigoted and intolerant form. There have also been positive features, though. One has been the gradual emergence of tiny Albania from its self-imposed isolation, and the holding of democratic elections there. Many achievements have been made in the political and economic fields, as well as in those of diplomacy and regional security.

On the economic front moves have been made to end central planning and introduce market mechanisms, to cut spending on the defence, armaments and security forces. Steps are being taken to remove state subsidies, to privatize state-owned concerns and to encourage foreign investment. Many states are making efforts to balance budgets and strengthen currencies in anticipation of full convertibility. (Some already have internal convertibility.) During the period of upheaval, and later, as democratic rule was being consolidated, promises of aid arrived thick and fast from governments in the West (as well as the Japanese) and international organizations. In the USA an initial offering of $145 million in aid to Poland and Hungary in July 1989 rapidly expanded into a Senate Bill promising aid of $2.75 billion to seven central European states by the end of 1992. In early June 1990, following pressure from exporters and from Western governments, COCOM restrictions on the export of advanced technology goods to the Soviet Union and central Europe were relaxed. The European Bank of Reconstruction and Development (EBRD), headed by Frenchman Jacques Attali, was opened in London in April 1991. As its name suggests, its aim is to promote economic development in Eastern Europe, and to this end it has received financial backing from 41 governments and institutions, of which the largest shareholder is the USA. At the same time, however, the Bank's brief is to keep a discreet eye on the democratic and human-rights records of potential beneficiaries.

Many Western firms have been quick to see the possibilities of these emerging economies – and of the sizeable potential market they represent. The result, as controls have been lifted, has been the establishment of numerous 'joint ventures' between Western firms and partners in central Europe. By the end of 1990 2000 such undertakings had been established in Hungary alone. It is by no means certain, though, that east-central Europe will prove to be the dynamic, thrusting economic force that Japan was in the 1960s and 1970s and the countries of the Pacific Rim proved to be in the

1980s. Economic forecasts for the region vary widely. The reality is likely to be considerably more complex, with possibly significant divergences in economic performance between individual states.

The former German Democratic Republic, having been absorbed into the Federal Republic in the course of 1990, is widely tipped to prosper, despite the large costs that reunification entails and the inevitable difficulties of up-grading its largely moribund industries. Hungary has, too, attracted considerable interest from investors. If there is a question mark over Poland, it is because of uncertainty as to whether the drastic reform programme which the Solidarity-led government introduced at the beginning of 1990 will take effect in revitalizing the economy. There are further doubts about the average Pole's readiness to tolerate indefinitely the austerity these measures have brought.

Political stability of course, is a major factor in determining where foreign investment will be directed, and in the south of the region Yugoslavia, in particular, has been showing worrying signs of instability. There is the further problem in all the new democracies of changing attitudes to work and developing the skills necessary to run a market economy. Its not proving easy to develop an entrepreneurial culture rapidly in societies where private trade has been condemned for decades as 'speculation'.

The collapse of Communist rule in east-central Europe also led to a crumbling of the Communist bloc alliances. Poland, Czechoslovakia and Hungary showed particular eagerness to wind up the trading bloc, Comecon. Agreement was reached that from 1 January 1991 bilateral trade between the member states would be conducted in hard currencies, rather than the dubious 'convertible rouble'. At the beginning of 1991 the dissolution of Comecon was announced, together with the information that work would begin on creating a new trading organization (the International Organization for Economic Co-operation) based on free-market principles. It is difficult to see what attraction such a successor would have for the countries of Eastern Europe, particularly if it is headed by the ailing Soviet giant – currently something of a liability in trade terms. The Poles and the Hungarians in particular have made creditable efforts to redirect their exports from Comecon to Western markets and they, like several other post-Communist states, are looking forward to early entry to the European Community.

The Warsaw Pact was dissolved as a military organization in March 1991. One rationale for its existence disappeared in July 1990, when NATO members declared at their London summit that they no longer looked upon the Warsaw Pact states as adversaries. The organization soon lost one member – East Germany – following German reunification. However, Soviet troops, due to leave both Czechoslovakia and Hungary by the summer of 1991, will remain on German soil until 1994.

Throughout the region steps have been taken to reduce the burden of defence spending which Pact membership involved, to convert their armed services into truly national forces, and to develop independent defence policies. A move by Moscow to negotiate bilateral treaties of friendship with its former satellites has been received with caution. The draft treaties would enjoin both parties not to participate in alliances directed against either of the parties – a clear warning against seeking NATO membership. Many states feel that this would immediately impose limits on their newly won freedom. But Romania has already agreed to sign.

One way of filling the vacuum caused by the collapse of the old bloc structures is to form regional sub-groupings. The Pentagonale is such a grouping and is also perceived in some quarters as providing a 'fast track' for entry into the European Community. At the end of 1989 four central and southern European states (Hungary, Austria, Italy and Yugoslavia) came together to discuss co-operation on such issues as trade, tourism and environmental matters. In the course of 1990 this loose association of states was strengthened by the addition of a fifth member, Czechoslovakia, and began to organize itself along more formal lines. A summit of the five was held in Venice during August 1990. Poland has shown an eagerness to join and will probably become a member before the end of 1991, thus trans-forming the group into a Hexagon.

During October 1990 a conference of foreign ministers from countries on the southern tier (Albania, Bulgaria, Greece, Romania, Turkey and Yugoslavia) met in the Albanian capital, Tirana, to discuss regional co-operation. It is possible that a Balkan regional grouping similar to the Pentagonale is in the making here. Ironically, the one member state common to both groups – Yugoslavia – is also the most unstable in the region. It is not beyond the realm of possibility, though, following the outbreak of fighting between Slovenia and Croatia on the one side and Serbia on the other at the end of June 1991, after the former had announced their independence, to envisage Slovenia and Croatia gravitating to their northern neighbours (especially Austria and Hungary) in the Pentagonale, while the Serbian-dominated remainder retained links with the Balkan group.

Between 19 and 21 November 1990 a CSCE summit took place in Paris. Thirty-four nations took part – all the signatories of the Helsinki Final Act with the exception of East Germany. Even little Albania was present as an observer, although attempts by representatives of the Baltic States to be accorded similar status were rebuffed at Soviet insistence. The Paris summit was hailed as the peace conference to end the 50-year division of Europe. At the Elysée Palace NATO and Warsaw Pact members signed an agreement to cut arms in Europe. The conference gave its blessing to German reunification. The 'Helsinki process' was also given institutional form – in the shape of a secretariat to be based in Prague and a Conflict Prevention Centre in Vienna. There is, as yet, to be no European Security

Council and no peace-keeping force. (The Americans in particular were worried that this might diminish the role of NATO.) But these are early days. Further CSCE summits are planned, the next being when the conference returns 'home' to Helsinki in 1992. If the growing fires of ethnic and national unrest show no signs of abating, there may be greater readiness to consider a Continental peacekeeping force.

Part 1
Eastern Europe

1 ALBANIA

Following the dramatic collapse in 1989 of Communist rule in central and eastern Europe, Albania still remained as a Stalinist bastion. However, changes in economic policy, including a number of fundamental significance, have since been announced; by mid-1991, Albania had as its avowed aim a market economy. Furthermore, in May 1991 the country officially became the 'Republic of Albania', dropping the words 'Socialist People's' from its name. Nonetheless, to understand why Albania was the last Eastern European country to turn away from Communism, one has to look at its history.

Recent history

Albania gained its independence in 1912, the last colony of the Ottoman Empire to do so. But true independence proved short-lived. Its territory – the mainly mountainous Balkan hinterland of the Strait of Otranto – was overrun by several foreign armies during World War I. The Albanian state only came into being in 1920.

The 1920–39 period, fraught with great political, economic and international difficulties, was dominated by Ahmet Zogu, who served as cabinet minister, prime minister and president of the republic. In 1928 he finally proclaimed himself King Zog. Under his authoritarian rule the country became entangled, politically and economically, with Mussolini's fascist regime. This policy led eventually to the Italian invasion of 1939 and the end of independence as well as Zog's reign.

Albania became the base for Italy's invasion of Greece in 1940, which was repulsed by Greek troops who pushed forward into Albania. However, after Nazi forces had overwhelmed both Greece and Yugoslavia, Albania was enlarged through the addition of adjacent areas of Yugoslavia where ethnic Albanians lived. The emergence of any resistance movement within Albania was very gradual. When, at the end of 1941, the Communist Party of Albania was founded it set up its own resistance group. Right-wing resistance also appeared on the scene: the National Front (*Balli Kombetar*) and a royalist organization. Resistance became really active when German occupiers replaced Italian ones in 1943. It soon aroused tension between right-wing and left-wing groups. Broadly speaking, the Communists were the more willing to fight whenever there was an opportunity, regardless of the reprisals which might be taken against civilians.

ALBANIA

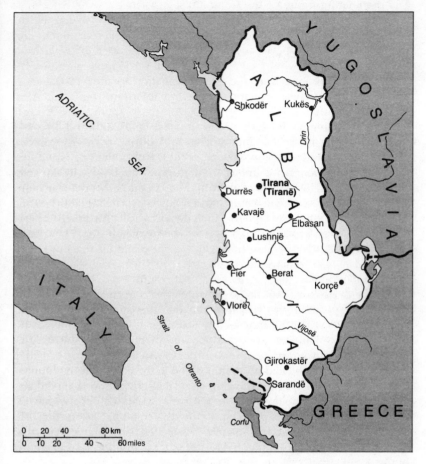

Official name	Republic of Albania
Area	28,748 sq. km (11,100 sq. miles)
Population	3,182,400 (1989, annual growth rate 2%)
Capital	Tirana (Tiranë)
Language	Albanian (Gheg, Tosk)
Religion	Outlawed in 1967, relegalized 1991: Muslim, Roman Catholic and Greek Orthodox minorities
Currency	lek

The rise of Enver Hoxha

The dominating figure of the Communist resistance movement almost from the beginning was the party leader Enver Hoxha (1908–85). Hoxha rose from a crucible, which included among several explosive ingredients: the daily travail of poorly armed and badly organized guerrilla units fighting against well-equipped and highly trained occupying armies; the exigencies of the civil war; and a determination to prevent the more powerful Yugoslav resistance movement from interfering unduly in Albanian domestic affairs.

After pursuing the retreating Nazi armies from Albania and defeating their right-wing rivals the Communists set up their own government, under Hoxha's leadership, in November 1944. Unlike the Yugoslav Communists, their Albanian counterparts had no direct links with Moscow during the war. This state of affairs continued in the early post-war years, when the Albanian regime was in effect a Yugoslav satellite. But Tito and his colleagues soon discovered that their desire to make Albania part of the Yugoslav federation was strongly opposed by Hoxha himself. They consequently tried hard to replace him with a more pliant leader. But Hoxha employed all his Machiavellian deviousness to thwart Yugoslav efforts to topple him, and succeeded in averting that result.

Hoxha came to display the same ruthlessness in creating a one-party state. All opposition was crushed with the utmost brutality. The only group towards whom he showed any wariness or consideration was the peasants, who made up the great majority of the population. He first introduced a mild agrarian reform in order to win their support. But later, when he had consolidated his own position in the party and the country, he embarked upon a fierce campaign of full collectivization of agriculture.

The Yugoslav ambition to annex Albania created a split within the Albanian party between a pro-Yugoslav and an anti-Yugoslav faction. The situation was exacerbated by the fact that the leader of the pro-Yugoslav faction, Koci Xoxe, was appointed Minister of the Interior, thus in control of the secret police (*Sigurimi*) and all other security forces.

The 1948 schism between Stalin and Tito suddenly gave Hoxha an opportunity to achieve three main political ambitions: to escape once and for all from Yugoslavia's clutches; to eliminate pro-Tito opponents; and to establish his first direct links with Moscow. From 1948 onwards he embraced Stalinism with unparalleled fervour. Hoxha visited Stalin in Moscow on several occasions, when he discovered, to his delight, that there was great affinity between them. Both believed in absolute personal power, which was justified (and disguised) by a very flexible ideology. Like Stalin, Hoxha was determined to destroy all opponents and to remove every obstacle his orders and policies encountered. Hence under his rule every trace of natural justice and of freedom of expression was wiped out in his country, just as it had been in the Soviet Union.

After the break with Yugoslavia, the Albanian leader set in motion a series of party purges which, in one form or another, went on for most of his career. Koci Xoxe, the Interior Minister, and several other politicians and officials were tried and executed as pro-Yugoslav traitors in 1949. During the next few years a large number of people were expelled from the Party. Most of them were accused of being 'enemies of the people'. Some were executed after secret trials. The purges affected institutions including the Party's central committee, the government, and the People's Assembly. As late as 1981 the resistance military commander and long-term prime minister, Mehmet Shehu, was alleged to have committed suicide and (later) to have been a multiple traitor.

The rift with Belgrade left the Albanian economy in a very poor state. In order to stave off disaster and the possible collapse of the isolated regime the Soviet Union and its allies rushed food and other essential supplies to the country. This urgent aid operation marked the beginning of a long-term programme of economic and industrial aid which continued until 1961, and in which the Soviet Union and other Communist countries, particularly Czechoslovakia and East Germany, took part. Experts in various fields were sent to Albania, and many Albanians received their training in the Soviet Union and other parts of Eastern Europe. The Albanian *Sigurimi* also established close links with the KGB in Moscow, as did the Albanian armed forces with their counterparts in the Soviet bloc.

The death of Stalin

Stalin's death in 1953 and the emergence of Nikita Khrushchev as party leader in Moscow were a severe blow to Hoxha. Not only did he lose a powerful friend and like-minded teacher, he suddenly passed under the control of a volatile political leader who held dangerous reformist ideas. Hoxha's first shock came in 1955, when Khrushchev decided to bring about a reconciliation between Moscow and Yugoslavia, whose relations had remained frozen since 1948. The Albanian leader was asked to bring to an end his regime's long hostility towards Yugoslavia and establish normal relations with it. Although he made a few superficially friendly gestures towards his neighbour, Hoxha was at heart opposed to any genuine reconciliation, and he remained so mainly because he feared Tito's reformist ideas. Yugoslav attempts to overthrow him a few years earlier also played a part in his decision not to give in to Khrushchev's demands.

Another and greater shock was Khrushchev's denunciation of Stalin in his 'secret speech' of 1956. Hoxha saw this as an attack not only against the policies of his regime but also against his own personal position in the Party and government. The Soviet leader's efforts to persuade Hoxha to reform his rule and give up some of his Stalinist policies also proved ineffective. As a result, tension between Moscow and Albania steadily grew from 1955 to 1961, when the final break occurred. So did Hoxha's anti-Soviet, anti-Yugoslav and anti-Western paranoia. The first signs of trouble in the

Soviet–Albanian alliance appeared in 1960, when Hoxha sided with China in the early stages of the Soviet–Chinese ideological dispute. Matters came to a head at the international conference of 81 Communist parties held in Moscow in November 1960, where the Albanian leader openly defied Moscow by supporting China's cause. A year later Moscow broke off diplomatic relations with Albania and stopped all economic, industrial and military aid.

The Chinese quickly came to the rescue of their small ally in Europe with a package of economic help. They undertook to build 25 industrial plants in Albania with the assistance of Chinese technicians. But relations between the two countries faced great difficulties from the beginning because of their immense difference in size and the cultural chasm that divided them. Nevertheless, Mao's 'Cultural Revolution' did have one profound impact on Hoxha: it led him to make all religious practices illegal in 1967. However, serious strains between the two countries arose when the Chinese government opened up to the USA and Yugoslavia in the early 1970s. Hoxha rejected China's advice that his government should do the same. The alliance finally came to an end in 1978, when Peking stopped all economic and military aid and withdrew its experts. As a result, not only was Albania deprived of foreign aid, it was militarily isolated. Reacting to this, the regime launched a large-scale programme of building pillbox fortifications.

Economic and industrial stagnation

The end of the alliance with China marked the beginning of a period of steady economic and industrial stagnation. Industrial plants built in the 1950s with Soviet bloc aid became outdated. Shortage of equipment led to the widespread use of manual labour in collective farms. The situation was aggravated by a highly centralized bureaucratic system and inefficient management. At the same time there were incessant exhortations to increase output, relying on people's own efforts and on national resources. The most critical requirement was to increase food production to feed a population growing at more than 2% annually. Since 1963, and especially between 1971 and 1978, a very extensive work of terracing of hills was undertaken with the aim of enlarging the cultivated area; but this activity has almost certainly gone beyond what is useful.

1985 was an important watershed for all Communist countries of Europe but especially for Albania. In March, Mikhail Gorbachev became Soviet Communist leader. In April, Enver Hoxha died at the age of 76. He was succeeded by Ramiz Alia, a member of the Politburo who had served for several years as Hoxha's principal deputy.

Alia made it plain that Hoxha's policies would still be pursued, and indeed propaganda glorifying Hoxha continued and has included the erection of numerous and substantial statues. However, the new administration did admit more shortcomings. Serious failures were reported in agriculture (particularly dairy farming) and in the system of distribution. Another significant admission was that young people were bored and alienated by the mediocre level of newspapers, books and entertainment.

Gorbachev's coming to power frightened the Albanian leadership. A campaign was soon mounted against his *glasnost* and *perestroika* policies. It was stressed that Albania would avoid similar policies, and would introduce only such reforms as were appropriate to its needs and conditions. Radical reforms were clearly – and indeed rightly – seen as a dangerous threat to the Communist Party's monopoly of power.

Reforms: overdue, cautious, but accelerating

Nevertheless, a number of factors have pushed the new leadership towards reforms. This is partly in response to pressure from within the Party, intellectuals and the public. In large part it amounts to a response to worsening economic prospects in the face of increasing needs.

Even before Hoxha's death there had been a number of signs that the regime wanted to take some steps to break out of international isolation and to expand its diplomatic and trade links with Western countries. Hoxha himself made a literary contribution to the movement to improve relations with Greece, with whom Albania still remained formally at war. In January 1985 the border with Greece was opened and in August 1987 formal peace was concluded with that country. Diplomatic relations were established with Spain in 1986, West Germany in 1987 and Canada in 1988. The West German accord was particularly important: besides agreeing to exchange specialists and scholars the Bonn government, which had shown interest in Albania's chrome mining, made Albania a gift of DM26 million. The more general economic purpose of these approaches became clear when on 31 July 1990 one of the most striking changes was approved: foreigners would henceforth be permitted to invest in Albania. Directly contrary to both the philosophy and the practice hitherto of the Communist regime, this change of course shows how far economic considerations have gained precedence.

Economic structural reforms were also initiated. A 'New Economic Mechanism' called for decentralization of decision making, but since this was limited to 94 industrial and 100 agricultural enterprises it can be called a halfway house. One reform which did begin to have an immediate effect was the legalization of peasants' rights to sell their produce. (One market was set up near to Scanderbeg Square, near the centre of Tirana.) Unfortunately, in recent years summer droughts in Albania have become normal and have caused acute shortages of supplies.

Replacing the *nomenklatura* system, the only criteria governing many appointments would henceforth be 'loyalty to socialism' and professional qualifications. The right of legal defence and of appeal would be introduced in court cases. The Ministry of Justice, dismantled some years earlier, would be reinstated. Other changes concerning human rights were introduced in May 1990, just before the UN Secretary-General, Pérez de Cuéllar, visited the country. The number of capital offences was reduced from 34 to 11, though this punishment would still apply to stealing state property, economic sabotage, spying and murder. For the first time since World War II Albanian citizens could apply for passports. This last measure quickly resulted in a massive influx of citizens into certain foreign embassies with the aim of escaping from the country, in obvious imitation of the successful experience of the East Germans; a result which the Alia government even permitted.

Political change gathers momentum

This government soon found itself compelled to make political concessions of a more orthodox type. In January 1990 Alia was urging Party members to forge the closest possible links with the people though making the utmost use of existing Communist organizations. However, a subsequent law required a minimum of two candidates for each constituency, although it imposed conditions upon the policies which candidates might espouse in their campaigns which, if enforced, must have emasculated any effective opposition. In August 1990 Alia had still been denouncing pluralism, but in December 1990 he reported that the Politburo had approved the removal of Stalinist symbols, though he still attacked those who wished to 'denigrate' Enver Hoxha. Above all, following the defection to France of Albania's best-known writer, Ismail Kadare, and a meeting of Alia with student leaders it was announced that other political parties might be formed. The Democratic Party (DP), headed by Sali Berisha (a cardiologist), was set up at once.

Disturbances, which the government labelled 'hooliganism', broke out in several towns, but those claimed to be responsible were quickly tried and sentenced to long terms of imprisonment. On the other hand, the first legal religious services for 23 years (Roman Catholic in Shkodër, Muslim in Tirana) were held. A student demand that the Enver Hoxha University of Tirana should have its name changed was at first refused, then accepted. The widow of Hoxha was deposed from the Chairmanship of the Democratic Front and other top leadership changes were announced. A new constitution was published. But such changes were now no longer enough. On 20 February the large bronze statue of Enver Hoxha in Tirana's city centre was toppled, as were statues of him in Durrës and Korçë, while copies of his works were set on fire. On the other hand, other monuments in Tirana, including the Enver Hoxha museum, were protected by paramilitary forces with armoured personnel carriers. In Korçë the toppled statue was replaced by a bust, which thereafter was under continuous guard. Hardliners in various parts of the country began to mobilize and the army was employed to transport Albanian Workers' Party (AWP) supporters to rallies. Under the impact of so much disorder, with few people working and unrest and revenge in the air, the economy was growing weaker.

An exodus of Albanians from the country began. On certain days, up to 2,000 people of Greek origin were crossing the Greek border on their way to refugee camps, though some were sent back by both Greece and Yugoslavia as being economic rather than political migrants. More than 20,000 Albanians crammed into ships and reached southern Italy, especially Brindisi, where they stayed in appalling squalor. The defectors included the crew of a naval tanker. Some Albanians returned to Albania, but in early May some 23,000 were still distributed in camps in various parts of Italy. Albania's entire Jewish population, over 300 people, was evacuated to Israel. The official Albanian responses to these extraordinary events were, on the whole, consistent. In December 1990 Alia had referred positively to employment possibilities outside the country. It was now announced that no measures would be taken against returnees, though in Durrës a crowd suspected of trying to board a ship was forcibly dispersed. On the other hand, Albania has asked 13 countries for work permits to enable Albanians to work abroad.

Political prisoners have been released: 563 between mid-1990 and January 1991. The Minister of Justice said that all would be freed eventually, but it remained doubtful whether those detained following the December disturbances would be among them.

A multi-party election was set for 10 February 1991, but at the Opposition's request was postponed until 31 March. President Alia gave an assurance that if the AWP was defeated it would relinquish power. In the event, however, the AWP won the election, gaining 168 out of 250 seats (67.2%) while its only serious rival, the Democratic Party, gained 75 (30%): 98.9% of the electorate voted in the first stage and 96.6% in a run-off. Although Ramiz Alia was defeated in his own Tirana constituency by a previously unknown engineer, he was re-elected President, though for the first time a non-Communist prime minister, Fatos Nano, was appointed.

The election made very clear that political opinion in Albania is polarized along several distinct fault-lines. There is a conflict between generations, older people tending to be more inclined to the Communists, as well as one between town and countryside, the latter mainly siding with the Communists, the former generally opposed to them. For example, in Korçë, the country's sixth-largest city, all five DP candidates were elected. A belief that the Democratic Party intended to privatize and redistribute land seems to have carried weight among people in rural areas, who also would be more fearful of change. Finally, the north, with its tradition of fierce independence, tends to be opposed to the Communists whereas the south (except for its Greek minority) favours them. Where these fault-lines coincide the gulf is naturally widest, the northern city of Shkodër having even suggested secession from Tirana.

Change becomes irrevocable

However, as the economy continued to deteriorate – during five months little work was done, as workers struck for higher wages, or supplies could not get through due to transport strikes – economic imperatives dictated further political change. A coalition government was formed and on 1 May Albania abandoned the title 'Socialist People's Republic' to become simply 'Republic'; words like 'Parliament' or 'majority' appeared for the first time in living memory. Ramiz Alia was elected President. Ylli Bufi became prime minister while Fatos Nano, a reformer, now heads the Socialist Party of Albania – as the Albanian Party of Labour is now renamed. At the Party's Tenth Congress, which effected this change, the accent was on distancing the Party from its 'mistaken theoretical and practical baggage'. First Xhelil Gjoni and then Alia blamed Enver Hoxha for various mistakes, including excessive centralism, human rights violations and excessive national self-reliance. Ramiz Alia – himself criticized by Gjoni for senti-mentalism and not being sufficiently energetic, though praised for his policy of avoiding confrontation – admitted to certain faults.

By now, public order had in part broken down while the state of the economy was catastrophic. The prime minister told Parliament on 12 June 1991 that the country was on the brink of disaster. Rail transport, import-ant sectors of road transport, the ports, light industry, construction, many mines, agriculture and exports were paralyzed. The budget situation, already bad, had grown much worse. The countryside, having suffered a deep economic and social shock, was at a standstill. Production was therefore almost paralyzed, and the prospect of famine loomed. The country had only days' reserves of main foodstuffs, with many essential supplies blocked in the ports; foreign firms, understandably concerned that they would not be paid, had delayed sending other supplies. There was the same situation in industrial goods. The black market raged unchecked. Public property had been attacked and the security forces had been fired on. Hooliganism was on a massive scale and there was a continual illegal outflow of people across the state frontiers.

The government's objectives in confronting looming disaster seemed unexceptional, but what it can do is unclear. Help from abroad is urgently sought, and has started to be promised, notably by Italy which has offered £28 million. Albania remains independent, but shorn of its ideological extremism and unviable self-reliance it is revealed as far from monolithic and as facing economic disaster. Though the more distant future possibly holds some element of promise the real question is whether the country can survive the next months.

2 BULGARIA

The modern Bulgarian state was created by the Treaty of Berlin in July 1878. Its internal affairs were soon the preserve of corrupt politicians dominated by Prince Ferdinand. In external politics its chief desire was to secure control of Macedonia, whose Slav inhabitants the Bulgarians regarded as their co-nationals, but before 1914 their only gain was the small area of Pirin Macedonia.

It was the desire to possess Macedonia which determined Bulgaria's alignment with Germany in World War I. Defeat in that war meant the discrediting of the established political parties, and a struggle therefore took place between the nation's two major radical forces: the Communists and the Bulgarian Agrarian National Union (BANU). The former's origin could be traced back to the early 1890s while the latter were essentially a product of the agrarian crisis which affected the country at the turn of the century. The Agrarians proved victorious, but their radicalism and their willingness to compromise with the Yugoslavs, who controlled Macedonia, created many enemies. In 1923 the Agrarians were deposed and their leader, Alexander Stamboliiski, murdered.

There followed over a decade of instability, which ended on 19 May 1934 with a *coup d'état* staged by army officers and discontented elements from the intelligentsia. They did not last long. After they had succeeded in containing disruptive Macedonian elements they were elbowed aside by King Boris and his advisors. The King's major preoccupation was with foreign affairs. By the end of 1938 Bulgaria was the only European power defeated in 1918 not to have recovered some of its lost territory, a condition which was a strong impulse towards alignment with the revisionist powers, primarily Germany. By 1941 the pressures to join Germany were irresistible, but although Bulgaria joined the Axis it would not commit itself to war against the Soviet Union, nor would Boris agree to the deportation of Bulgarian Jews.

Boris died in somewhat mysterious circumstances in August 1943, by which time Bulgaria was anxious to escape from the conflict. In this it failed. The Soviet attack which so many Bulgarians had feared materialized in September 1944 and was aided by the small partisan units of the Fatherland Front, an opposition group consisting of Communists, Agrarians, supporters of the 1934 coup, and a number of left-wing 'bourgeois' parties.

On 9 September 1944 the Fatherland Front formed a government.

BULGARIA

Official name	Republic of Bulgaria
Area	110,910 sq. km (42,810 sq. miles)
Population	8,973,600 (1988) (annual growth rate 0.2%)
Capital	Sofia (Sofiya)
Languages	Bulgarian, up to 10% Turkish
Religion	Eastern (Bulgarian) Orthodox, 10% Muslim
Currency	lev

During the following three years the Communists systematically under-mined their coalition partners, the major confrontation coming in 1947 when the Agrarian leader, Nikola Petkov, was arrested and executed after a grotesque show trial. Within a year all real opposition to Communist domination had been broken; what was left of the Agrarians capitulated to the Communists and became junior partners in the nominal Communist–Agrarian coalition which was to rule the country for over 40 years.

The first years of Communist rule saw industrialization, collectiviz-ation, and the general sovietization of Bulgaria. After Stalin's death changes took place which brought to prominence Todor Zhivkov, who was to lead the Bulgarian Communist Party (BCP) from 1954 to 1989.

Pressure for change

Zhivkov's position began to weaken in the early 1980s. Unsavoury inci-dents such as alleged Bulgarian involvement in the attempted murder of the Pope in 1981 tarnished Zhivkov's image while at home the regime failed to fulfil all its promises with regard to increasing living standards. To improve economic performance a series of reforms were initiated. These did little more than tinker with the administration of the economy, thus causing further dislocation. To retrieve credibility, Zhivkov hauled out the chauvinist drum. He decided to go down in history as the man who united all Bulgarians into one, homogeneous, socialist nation. More crudely put, he decreed that the Turks, who formed around 10% of the population, must be assimilated. To this end, Turks were required to adopt Slav names, broadcasts and publications in Turkish ceased, and it was made illegal to speak Turkish in the streets.

Many Bulgarians were revolted by such policies. To mitigate oppo-sition, Zhivkov extended his 'reforms' from the economic to the political sector. The doctrines of 'self-management' and pluralism were widely debated and even incorporated into seemingly advanced legislation such as the Labour Code of 1986. In the summer of 1987 Zhivkov delighted the reform-minded with the so-called 'July concept', which promised liberaliz-ation, pluralization and many of the other attractions which were now on offer in other East European states. At the end of 1987 the Bulgarian reformists made full use of these new-found freedoms.

The city of Rousé had for some years been suffering from periodic poisoning by emissions from a metallurgical plant across the Danube in Romania. An exhibition staged in Rousé at the end of 1987 showed that the incidence of lung disease in the city had risen from 969 per 100,000 in 1975 to 17,386 per 100,000 in 1985. There was a huge national outcry. An unnerved Zhivkov began to backtrack. The Party newspaper, *Rabot-nichesko Delo*, dilated upon the distinction between positive and negative *glasnost*, and in the summer Zhivkov sacked one of the Party's leading reformists, Choudomir Alexandrov.

In previous years Zhivkov's opponents would have been cowed by such menaces but now, with the Soviet Union a bastion of reform rather than reaction, they were not to be intimidated. By the beginning of 1989 a number of opposition groups had been formed, including The Discussion Club for the Support of Perestroika and Glasnost (later changed to Democracy), the Independent Association for the Defence of Human Rights, the independent trade union, *Podkrepa* (Support), the environmental organization Ecoglasnost, and the Committee for the Defence of Religious Rights. Government attempts to bludgeon these groups into quietude were totally ineffective, and by the spring of 1989 it was clear that a major political confrontation between government and opposition in Bulgaria was imminent.

The first serious clash came over the Turkish issue. A number of the new political groups sympathized with the Turks and their determination to resist assimilation. In late May 1989, immediately before the opening of the Paris Conference on Security and Co-operation in Europe, a handful of leading Turkish protesters began staging hunger strikes. These led to clashes with the police and to the expulsion of a number of Turkish activists who immediately appeared as honoured guests at the CSCE conference. Zhivkov now made worse of a bad job. He challenged the Turkish government to open their borders and allow Bulgaria's Muslims a free choice between their socialist homeland and Turkey. The Turks called his bluff, and by late August over 300,000 Bulgarian Turks had fled to Turkey, which was forced once more to close its frontiers.

The uneasy calm produced by the closing of the borders lasted until October, when Sofia was the venue for a meeting of the EcoForum, another Helsinki follow-up conference. The growing Bulgarian ecological movement, headed by Ecoglasnost, staged a number of demonstrations, one of which, on 26 October, was disrupted by the police in full view of the international press. Public frustration increased, as did the anger of many leading BCP officials. By early November an anti-Zhivkov cabal had formed and, once the support of the military had been assured, the plotters moved, deposing the dictator and his closest supporters during a Central Committee plenum on 10 November. Zhivkov was arrested soon after on charges of corruption.

End of an era

The removal of Zhivkov inevitably marked the end of an era. The collapse of the old regime in Bulgaria, however, was the result of a palace coup, not a popular revolution. 'People power' had not been totally absent but it was as much, if not more, the result than the cause of the end of the *ancien régime*, with the largest demonstrations taking place in December and January rather than October and November. For that reason, the non-Communist opposition forces are much less confident of the permanence of their gains than the equivalent groups in other East European states.

Zhivkov was replaced as Party leader and head of state by his foreign minister, Petur Mladenov. Mladenov moved rapidly to consolidate his position, and by early December had replaced all the remaining Zhivkovites in the Politburo and had reduced their strength in the Central Committee. The new leadership pledged itself to end the abuse of personal liberties, to allow free, multi-party elections at the earliest feasible opportunity, and to inaugurate a massive economic restructuring which would abolish the 'administrative-command' system and allow much greater play to market forces. Political relaxation was immediately apparent. Within days of Zhivkov's fall, old parties were being reborn and new ones founded. Most prominent among the former were the Social Democrats, and the Nikola Petkov Agrarians, a revived version of those Agrarians who had refused to compromise with the BCP in the 1940s. The new groups included a Green Party. On 14 November the more prominent of the opposition groups achieved a loose form of unity in the Union of Democratic Forces (UDF), which by March 1990 had fifteen constituent elements.

The Turkish issue

Before further progress towards structural political change could be made, the new leadership and the opposition alike were faced with the possible threat of counter-revolution. The issue on which the reactionary forces chose to make their stand was that of the Turkish minority.

Mladenov, as foreign secretary, had been all too aware of how much damage Zhivkov's assimilationist policies had done to Bulgaria's international reputation. Given the crushing need for foreign aid, such policies had to be disavowed. This was done by a government decree of 29 December 1989. It produced a furious reaction. In Kurdjali, Haskovo and other areas with mixed populations the Bulgarians were loud in their protests. Demonstrations were organized, strikes were staged and on Sunday 7 January 1990 coachloads of protesters descended on Sofia to besiege the *Subranie* (National Assembly) with complaints that so important a change could not be enacted without a referendum. The Turkish issue had indubitably roused many passions, but there can be little doubt that the protests were exploited, if not instigated, by BCP officials, particularly those middle-ranking full-time Party employees who stood to lose position, power and privilege as a result of the reforms.

The demonstrations of 7 January may well prove to be the turning point of the Bulgarian revolution. Those demonstrations were raucous and threatening, yet the new leaders were undaunted, not least because in the following week Mladenov was to travel to Kuwait to hold discussions with the Turkish foreign minister. Concessions to the chauvinists would have wrecked these talks and, with them, realistic hopes of loans from the Arab world. The week after the nationalist protests there were even larger demonstrations, this time sponsored by the UDF but condoned by the

BCP, and now demanding that full liberty be granted to all Bulgarian citizens irrespective of ethnic identity or religion. The authorities responded by setting up a Social Council on which 65 organizations covering a wide variety of interests were represented. The Council was to investigate the ethnic question and to recommend appropriate legislation to the *Subranie*. On 17 January, acting on the Council's recommendations, the Assembly adopted a bill allowing all Bulgarians to choose freely the names which they wished to bear, and removing any discrimination based upon religion or race. As a *douceur* to the nationalists, the bill also stated that only the Bulgarian flag could be raised in the country, that Bulgarian was the only official language, and that no political parties based purely on religious affiliation would be allowed. The latter was a great disappointment to many Muslims.

From BCP to BSP

It was significant that the session of the *Subranie* which endorsed this bill also modified Article One of the 1971 constitution, the article which enshrined the leading role of the Communist Party. The resolution of the Turkish problem played some part in this. If the confrontation of early January seemed to have drawn the teeth of the nationalist dragon, it had also shown that the government and the major opposition groups did have some common objectives. This was a reassuring discovery, because contact between the two sides had, until then, been fitful and hardly fruitful. There was clear need for dialogue, but the opposition was wary of being trapped, and would do nothing without reassurance that the BCP was prepared to abandon its leading role. The BCP leadership had given many such assurances, not least in a self-flagellating Central Committee plenum on 11–13 December 1989, when a total restructuring of Party and state was promised. There had also been some moves to dismantle the Party's primary organizations in educational institutions, the armed forces and the media. But there had been no legislation, and this problem had been partially responsible for slowing down moves towards the round-table talks which both sides had wanted. The deadlock was not resolved until early January, and full talks did not begin until 18 January, the day after the *Subranie* had legislated to end the BCP's leading role.

The UDF was not entirely satisfied with the bill of 17 January. It repealed only clauses two and three of Article One, those which designated the BCP as the leading force in society and the state, and which allotted to it and its BANU allies the task of constructing an advanced socialist society. Clause one remained intact. It stated that Bulgaria was 'a socialist state of the working people of the town and the countryside, led by the working class', a wording which left many non-socialists feeling distinctly uneasy.

The BCP had, however, sacrificed some of its privileges, and it now set about preparing itself for the electoral contest that was to come in the early summer. Soon after the fall of Zhivkov it had been agreed that the next party congress should convene earlier than its scheduled date of late 1991. In fact the 14th Extraordinary Congress met from 31 January to 2 February 1990. It was the most turbulent and radical congress in living memory. First, Mladenov announced that he would no longer serve as head of party and head of state, relinquishing the former post to Alexandur Lilov. The party congress also agreed that prime minister Georgi Atanasov should be replaced by Mladenov's close confidant, Andrei Loukanov. Much more surprising, however, was the decision to abolish the Central Committee and the Politburo which were replaced by a Supreme Party Council and a Praesidium. The new structure was intended to be more democratic and to encourage greater participation by the mass of party members. It was also intended, no doubt with the forthcoming elections in mind, to mark a determined shift away from old practices and old personalities, and in the latter regard at least it must be accounted a success, for no more than 10% of those elected to the Supreme Council had been members of the previous Central Committee. Furthermore, the Supreme Council included representatives of the various factional groups which had by now become visible in the BCP, including the Democratic Forum, the Movement for Democratic Socialism, the Road to Europe Platform, and the Alternative Socialist Organization. On 3 April the BCP renamed itself the Bulgarian Socialist Party (BSP). Its newspaper, *Rabotnichesko Delo*, was henceforth to appear as *Duma*.

The January–February restructuring of the BCP was followed by the formation of a new government. Ironically, shortly after the BCP had renounced its leading role, Bulgaria was to have its first purely Communist administration. The reason for this lay in the dynamics of opposition politics. The emergence of the Nikola Petkov Agrarians had alarmed the official BANU leaders, whose previous co-operation with the BCP was denounced as collaboration by the Petkovists. The 'official Agrarians', leaping at the chance to disassociate themselves from the Communists and to initiate talks with the Petkovists for union, refused to re-enter the government. The BCP leadership, meanwhile, was clearly hoping that the UDF and other opposition parties might join in a government of national unity to guide the country through to the general elections which were soon, because of opposition pressure, put back from May to June. The opposition, however, were not prepared to co-operate. They insisted that they would not be part of any government which had to rely for its support on a *Subranie* elected under the old conditions. Nor were they happy to join with the Communists while so little had been done to dismantle the *nomenklatura* and to limit the powers of the secret police. Furthermore, the opposition, learning from the experience of the 'official Agrarians', feared that cohabitation with the Communists now would appear as collaborationism in the electoral battle which lay ahead.

The elections of June 1990

The round-table talks had determined that elections for a Constituent or Grand National Assembly (GNA) should be held on 10 and 17 June. Half the 400 delegates would be elected by a simple majority and half by the proportional system. The round tables had also drafted legislation for the regulation of political parties. A myriad of new parties appeared but the major contenders for power were the BSP, the UDF, BANU, and the Movement for Rights and Freedoms (MRF). The latter was and is primarily a Turkish organization campaigning for minority rights.

The elections were, in the words of the then UDF leader, Zheliu Zhelev, 'free but not fair', a judgement with which most foreign observers would probably agree. The BSP's electoral success was based upon the vested power of the Communists, particularly in the countryside, where the old traditions of political clientism were strong. Furthermore, the BSP insisted that now it was shed of the incubus of the Zhivkov clique the party was the only body capable of bringing about the regeneration of which the country was so much in need. The opposition, on the other hand, were inexperienced, lacking in basic equipment such as fax machines, telephones, and offices, and they could not find an obvious and dominating leader; there was, as yet, no Bulgarian Wałęsa or Havel. Nor was the main opposition force, the UDF, entirely united in its policies, with important differences on how far privatization, particularly of land, should proceed.

The failure of the socialist government

The elections produced a socialist government but not political stability. Students took to the streets to demand full publication of the details concerning electoral irregularities and to these demands were soon added many others. Shortly before the Assembly was to convene, the protesters declared they had a videotape which showed Mladenov urging the use of tanks against demonstrators in December 1989. Mladenov denied the accusation but technical examination of the tape proved the students' claim and on 6 July he resigned, the UDF leader Zhelev being made President in his place. When the Assembly convened on 10 July it did so to a background of considerable tension in the mixed Bulgarian-Turkish areas, the chauvinists complaining at the presence in the Assembly of the MRF which they regarded as illegal because the law on political parties had proscribed organizations based on ethnic or religious affiliations.

These tensions did not prevent the Assembly from beginning its work but it soon became plain that there would be little constructive legislation. There were long procedural wrangles which prevented much real progress towards defining a new constitution, and, more urgently, the opposition refused to vote for the programme of economic reforms presented by Prime Minister Loukanov. He, in turn, insisted that the cures for Bulgaria's economic ills were so drastic that they must be supported by all elements in the Assembly. The opposition refused. They did not want to carry the blame for having to rectify the mistakes made by the BCP of which Loukanov and many of his colleagues had been prominent members.

The past conduct of the BCP and the present attitudes of its successor were rapidly becoming central political issues. By the end of August little progress towards dismantling the Communist apparatus of power seemed to have been made and two protesters declared they would burn themselves to death if the red star, the symbol of that power, were not removed from the roof of the Party headquarters in Sofia. Reassuring promises were given but in a highly charged atmosphere a crowd broke into the building on the night of 26–27 August, ransacking and burning some of the lower floors. There were rumours that the incident was a *provokatsiya*, not least because the crowd had unhindered access to what was usually one of the best-guarded buildings in the country. The fire did concentrate political minds somewhat, and in the following two months the Assembly outlawed membership of a political party for those in the judiciary, the army, the police and the diplomatic corps. The Assembly also passed legislation to allow local elections. The mandate of existing local authorities had expired on 28 August but the opposition insisted that reform of the system and the removal of Communist Party power must precede any further elections. In the interim local government was to be in the hands of coalitions reflecting the votes cast in the June poll. These concessions, however, did not satisfy the opposition, partly because they seemed to have been made with bad grace, but also because the BSP was refusing to hand over to state care the archives of the BCP. This was an emotional issue because by October many of the opposition were demanding legal action against those responsible for the 'national catastrophe'. The archives, it was believed, would provide the evidence the courts would need.

By this time the decline in the economy had indeed reached 'catastrophic' proportions. The 1989 harvest had been affected by the exodus of Turks and the revelation in December of that year that the foreign debt was $10 billion rather than $4 billion meant an end to food imports at previous levels. Furthermore, the prospect of price deregulation was encouraging hoarding by producers and distributors. Food shortages intensified and prices soared. At the same time, industrial production plummeted, the figures for the first ten months of 1990 being 10.4% below the already poor 1989 level. There were also problems with fuel supplies. Bulgaria has little in the way of native fossil fuel reserves and was already affected by the prospect of higher, hard-currency prices being charged by its chief supplier, the USSR. Then came the Gulf crisis in August 1990. Sofia loyally observed UN sanctions but at a terrible immediate cost. Iraq was Bulgaria's largest foreign-currency debtor and in May it had been agreed that this debt should be repaid in oil, 640,000 tons of which was to be delivered in 1990 alone.

Bulgarians were facing their worst winter since the war. Economic hardship and political frustration deprived Loukanov of much of his support. He came under increasing pressure to resign, finally agreeing to do so on 28 November. The immediate causes of his downfall were student sit-ins, street demonstrations, signs of serious fissures in the BSP, and the probability of widespread strike action. However, one of the main long-term reasons was the intensifying fear that the BSP had not broken away from its former BCP habits and policies, nor did it intend to.

On 20 December a new government was formed under the non-party Dimitur Popov, who had gained widespread respect as secretary to the electoral commission in June. The critical post of Minister of the Interior was also placed in non-party hands. The street confrontations of November had sobered political opinions, and the new government of Popov would have been impossible without the multi-faction agreement of December to guarantee a peaceful transition to democracy. This political agreement was followed in January by a social contract between government, trade unions and managers which promised social peace for 200 days while the government introduced economic reforms and devised a new constitution.

Neither of these two massive tasks proved as easy as had been anticipated. No-one contested the need for economic reform – indeed it had been made a condition of essential loans from the IMF – but it was delayed by wrangles over the legitimacy of one MP's election, over police files on deputies, on demands that Turkish be taught for four hours per week in state schools in Turkish areas, among many other issues. However, a law on the decollectivization of land was passed in February 1991, and in May came new regulations concerning foreign investment in Bulgaria and measures to encourage the sale of state enterprises. The reform which most affected Bulgarians was the lifting of most price regulations with effect from 1 February 1991. Many goods had been hoarded pending price liberation and when they first appeared on the market they were greatly over-priced, a condition that led to considerable unrest and even threatened the social agreement of the previous month. In subsequent weeks prices drifted downwards somewhat but they remain astronomic compared with the days of regulation and subsidy.

If economic reform progressed, albeit in hesitant fashion, advance towards a new constitution was much slower. By May a sizeable group of UDF deputies had decided that the Assembly, with its BSP majority, was incapable of producing a purely democratic constitution, and these deputies walked out of the Assembly demanding immediate elections. The old fear of BSP intentions had surfaced again, it being argued that a socialist-dominated Assembly could not be trusted because it would tailor the constitution to the needs of the old *nomenklatura*. The dispute threatened to split the UDF and made it even more difficult to secure progress towards fundamental constitutional change. In May President Zhelev promised that elections would be held in September 1991 and that before then the Assembly would have decided upon the new constitution. It did so in July, but again fears of the BSP's intentions produced alarm among non-socialist deputies.

3 CZECHOSLOVAKIA

The modern Czechoslovak state emerged in 1918 out of the ruins of the Austro-Hungarian empire. The new republic was composed of two contrasting regions. In the west were the Czech lands – Bohemia and Moravia – with their large areas of flat plain, which had seen considerable industrial development under Habsburg rule. The Czech people, after almost 300 years of Austrian rule, were more advanced in economic, political and cultural terms than their Slovak neighbours to the east. Slovakia, a region of largely mountainous, forested terrain, had been dominated for centuries by Hungary. It had little industry and its mainly peasant population depended upon agriculture for their livelihood. While the growth of industrialization in the western regions had led to the rise of a Czech urban middle class, in Slovakia the towns were mainly peopled by Germans and Jews.

Czechoslovakia under Masaryk

Tomáš Garrigue Masaryk, a prime mover in the drive for Czechoslovak statehood, became the country's first president and remained its leader for most of the interwar period. A Slovak from Moravia, Masaryk was of humble origins, but had risen to become Professor of Philosophy at Prague University. He was a firm believer in unity between the Czech and Slovak people, since only by the creation of an alliance or federation of the two peoples, he felt, could a state be formed which would be strong enough to survive. He also believed in unity on cultural grounds (although the Czech and Slovak languages have differences, they are closely related and mutually comprehensible offshoots of the west Slavonic group of languages).

Until its loss of sovereignty in 1938–9, Czechoslovakia was unique in east-central Europe in retaining the democratic system of government with which it had been endowed in 1918. Its success in this respect and the relative political stability it enjoyed compared with its neighbours can be attributed to several factors. First, it was prosperous and most sections of society benefited from this prosperity. Land reforms did much to satisfy the peasants' craving for land, while financial reforms helped to avoid the kind of uncontrolled inflation which undermined political stability elsewhere in the region. Second, for most of the interwar period the country was governed by a coalition of five parties, the Pětka, members of which had developed the habit of working together while representing

CZECHOSLOVAKIA

Official name	The Czech and Slovak Federative Republic
Area	127,870 sq. km (49,360 sq. miles)
Population	15,620,000 (1988) (annual growth rate 0.3%)
Capital	Prague (Praha)
Languages	Czech, Slovak
Religion	65% Roman Catholic, 4.5% Protestant (Czechoslovak Church)
Currency	koruna (Kcs)

Czech affairs in the Austrian parliament. Third, the Czechoslovak constitution, based on the French model, provided for a strong executive, and in the person of Masaryk, a president was elected who was widely respected and who contributed personally to the political stability of the federation.

This is not to say that the country did not have problems. The sense of grievance felt by the Slovak minority mounted, as earlier promises of political autonomy continued to be ignored. More of a problem in the western border regions (the Sudety uplands) was the 3 million German population, which became increasingly restive with the growth of Nazism across the border. The effects of the Depression were severe in Czechoslovakia, and as they set back the country's prosperity, so there was a corresponding growth of radicalism and militancy among both Slovaks and Sudeten Germans.

Munich and after

The year 1935 marked a watershed in Czechoslovak politics. In November the 'President Liberator' Tomáš Masaryk stood down as president and was replaced by a disciple and colleague, Eduard Beneš. Earlier, in May, the pro-Nazi National Front Party had captured 62% of German votes in the election. This rejection of a future with their Slav neighbours in favour of a resurgent German imperialism was an ominous sign for Prague politicians. They made efforts to strengthen diplomatic links with France and the Soviet Union, but proved impotent to stem the tide of National Socialism. In March 1938 Hitler staged his *Anschluss* – the annexation of Austria – and in September of the same year came the tragi-farce of Chamberlain's meeting with Hitler at Munich. The attempt to buy peace was made at Czechoslovakia's expense. The Prague government was persuaded not to resist Germany but to cede the Sudety region with its German population to the Reich. Independence and democracy were sacrificed without a shot being fired. As George Kennan, then a young diplomat, wrote: 'A remarkable little people . . . found themselves standing out in lonely bitterness against what they felt to be an unjust and unsympathetic Europe.' As a direct result of Munich, Czechoslovakia was dismembered. The Sudety region was immediately incorporated into the Reich. But in the following year Hitler annexed the remainder of the country. An independent Slovak state was declared and a German 'Protectorate' of Bohemia and Moravia created. In the east an area of the Carpathian foothills and its mainly Ruthenian population was ceded to Hungary, while Poland took a small piece of disputed territory around Těšin (Cieszyń).

German rule in Czechoslovakia was by no means as harsh or destructive as in neighbouring Poland. The most dramatic event was the assassination of Reinhard Heydrich by members of the Czech resistance movement, an operation which resulted in reprisal executions and the massacre of the male population of the village of Lidice. In the summer of

1944 a rising took place in Slovakia which took the Germans several weeks to put down. Throughout the war an exile government in London, under the presidency of Beneš, maintained the continuity of the Czechoslovak state.

The greater part of Czechoslovakia was liberated by the Red Army. Although American forces entered the country, and Patton's troops were at one point closer to Prague than the Soviets (they liberated Pilsen), they were ordered to withdraw. While some historians have seen this withdrawal as a further abandonment of Czechoslovakia by its Western allies, in fact Soviet troops also withdrew within six months. There were no foreign troops in the country by the time of the first postwar election. In the wake of the Red Army came both Czechoslovak Communists who had found refuge in Moscow during the war years and members of the 'London' camp – headed by Beneš – who had reached an understanding with the Communists in Moscow. Beneš had become convinced that Czechoslovakia could not rely on the support of the Western democracies; the country needed friendly relations with the Soviet Union. He was hopeful that Czechoslovakia, situated in the centre of Europe and with its traditions of humanism and democracy, could act as a 'bridge' between East and West. As the Polish historian M. K. Dziewanowski has written, though, Stalin was not seeking 'bridges' in central Europe but rather 'bridgeheads'.

On crossing the border and reaching Košice, Beneš appointed a provisional government which included six Communist ministers as well as a number of 'fellow-travellers'. The programme outlined by the new government reflected the Moscow Agreement. It provided for free elections, nationalization and land reform, the outlawing of fascist organizations, and for preventing the renewal of political parties which 'had transgressed so gravely against the interests of the nation and the Republic' during the war. This included the Agrarian Party, the largest in Czechoslovakia before the war, and the Slovak Populist Party, both of which were banned. A further measure was the immediate expulsion of the German population from the Sudety region. Here, as in Poland, the Communists ensured that they controlled the redistribution of land vacated by the Germans. This valuable form of political patronage helped them to build support and party membership. Border changes were small but significant. The Soviet Union, having seized Polish and Romanian territory, proceeded to take the small area of Carpathian Ruthenia, following a 'plebiscite'. By contrast with its prewar situation, Czechoslovakia now had a common border with the Soviet Union.

The postwar elections

The elections foreseen under the Moscow Agreement took place on 16 May 1946, and their results provide us with one of the surprises of postwar Eastern Europe. Just as, before the war, Czechoslovakia was the one country in the region which retained democracy until the end, so in the immediate postwar years it was the only one in which the Communists gained a measure of support at the polls. In the only free elections in postwar Czechoslovakia, at least until 1990, the Communists took 38% of the vote (40% in the Czech lands).

Why was this? It is true that there had been a strong Communist movement in the country between the wars, particularly in the Czech lands, where there was a sizeable industrial working class. The Communists had also gained prestige by their hostility to the Munich capitulation, by their acts of resistance to wartime German rule, and by the fact that it was the Red Army which had liberated most of the country. But perhaps most important was that in 1945–6 their programme seemed attractive. The Communists were not calling for revolution, for violent overthrow, but masked their real aims behind calls for reasonable reforms and national unity. Many of the proposals which had been discussed in Moscow during the talks with Beneš seemed very sensible to voters. Although the Czechoslovak Communist Party (CPC) had only some 50,000 members at the war's end – less than half its prewar membership – it worked hard to attract support, and by March 1946 could boast over 1 million members in the Czech lands alone.

Although the elections left them without an overall majority, the Communists were the largest single party. Their political opponents were divided among themselves, and in any case were bound by the coalition agreement which brought the National Front government into power. Few opposition politicians realized that their days were numbered, that they had come up against determined opponents who had clear objectives and were prepared to abandon principles in pursuit of them. The lack of a unified and coherent opposition enabled the Communists to strengthen their hold on power. Klement Gottwald, leader of the 'Moscow' group of Communists, became prime minister and out of the 26-member Cabinet, nine ministers were Communists.

Despite this evidence of their growing political muscle, the Communists were hesitant about carrying out a coup. They were worried that a violent seizure of power, going against the country's strong democratic traditions, might bring an outraged and hostile reaction from the community. Although they had increasing control of the mass media, the police and the security apparatus, made use of violence, blackmail and intimidation against political opponents, and encouraged marches and street demonstrations to exaggerate the strength of their support, the Communists were aware that, as things stood, they would not be able to capture power at the next election. Yet during 1947, as the political and ideological battlelines were drawn ever more clearly across Europe, the pressure from Moscow for a consolidation of Communist power became irresistible.

In the end the crisis which brought the Communists total control was engineered by ministers of the 'opposition' non-Communist parties them-selves. A threat of group resignation, which they hoped would curb the excesses of the Communists and force them from office, backfired. Gott-wald, by a mixture of cajoling and threats, managed to persuade the ageing, sickly president, Beneš, to accept the resignations. The Commu-nists were able to take power 'legally' through what was, in effect, a bloodless revolution, and Gottwald was able to announce the victory to an excited crowd in Prague's Old Town Square.

Consolidation of Communist rule

In the aftermath of the February coup, the Communists – as if to make up for lost time – began to tighten their hold on the country by all the means at their disposal. There was, as Hans Renner has written in a recently published history of modern Czechoslovakia, a 'rapid metamorphosis of Czechoslovakia into a totalitarian society of the Stalinist type'. In economic life the first five-year plan (1949–53) covered the nationalization and reconstruction of industry. Czechoslovakia was to become the foundry-workshop of Comecon, concentrating on producing heavy machinery for its socialist partners. The imposition of Stalinist orthodoxy also brought with it a cultural purge. Hundreds of thousands of ideologically harmful books were removed from shops and libraries, to be replaced with trans-lations of Soviet literature and textbooks – not always of the highest quality, but always in enormous quantities.

As in the rest of east-central Europe at this time, 'counter-revolutionary elements' were arrested, evicted or thrown out of work. Some 130,000 people were despatched to prisons, labour camps and mines. The remain-ing vestiges of political tolerance vanished and many opposition poli-ticians were forced into exile. Jan Masaryk, son of the country's first president and the only surviving non-Communist in the government, died in suspicious circumstances – widely presumed murdered by agents of the Soviet or Czechoslovak security forces. The Church was also persecuted, with members of religious orders and Catholic intellectuals among those who were sent to labour camps.

But the terror did not only engulf the Party's opponents. In the early 1950s a bloody purge of the Party's own ranks was carried out, ordered by Moscow and supervised by its advisers. Indeed, the purging of the 'inner enemy' took a form which closely resembled the Stalinist show trials of the 1930s and 1940s. The purge claimed, among others, Rudolf Slánský (the Party secretary-general) and Vlado Clementis (Minister for Foreign Affairs). Both were hanged in 1952. It seems that anti-semitism lay at the root of the affair. Not only were most of the victims Jewish; when their names were listed in *Rudé Právo* they were followed by the words 'of Jewish origin'.

Gottwald, the architect of Stalinist rule in postwar Czechoslovakia, died in March 1953, a matter of days after his political mentor, Josef Stalin.

In his place, Antonín Novotný became first secretary of the Party and, in 1957, took the post of president as well. But the death of Stalin and Khrushchev's leadership had little effect upon Czechoslovakia. In 1956 there was no 'thaw' as in Poland, no challenge to Communist rule, as in Hungary. Indeed, measures to consolidate the Communist system, such as liquidation of private trade, carried on apace, and in 1960 the country's new Constitution renamed the country the Czechoslovak Socialist Republic. Article 4 of the Constitution confirmed the Communist Party's 'leading role' in society and Marxism–Leninism was declared a cornerstone of cultural life.

The 1960s proved to be a decade of impatience with the chafing restrictions of Communist rule. Criticism emerged from within the party itself, particularly from the younger generation of intellectuals – those who had been in their teens and twenties at the end of the war. Economic failures led to calls for changes in policy, and, in turn, to pressure for liberalization in other areas. An internal power struggle developed in late 1967, with criticism directed at Novotný's leadership. When Leonid Brezhnev, visiting Prague in December of that year, pointedly refused to intervene, Novotný found himself isolated. His resignation as Party leader in January 1968 was followed by the election of the Slovak Party leader, Alexander Dubček, as first secretary of the CPC. The Party split into two camps – reformers and conservatives – and a bitter internecine struggle began for its soul.

'Socialism with a human face'
In April 1968 the reformers' manifesto – their Action Programme – was published. This blueprint for change envisaged greater democracy within the Party, a new constitution, rehabilitation of the victims of the 1950s purges, freedom of speech and of assembly, and devolution of powers to federal (Czech and Slovak) governments. Democratization of economic life was also foreseen, devolving power to workers' councils and restoring to trades unions the power to defend their members' interests. What came to be known as the 'Prague Spring' was accompanied by an unprecedented loosening of controls on the mass media, which began to report and debate political issues quite openly. Significantly, though, there were no moves to threaten the Party's position by ending its 'leading role'. Demands for the re-establishment of an opposition party, the Social Democrats, were stalled and subsequently overtaken by events.

There is no doubt that a majority of citizens supported the reforms – and supported Dubček, who attained a stature and popularity that no other Communist leader in postwar Czechoslovakia has even approached. But Dubček's moves to introduce 'socialism with a human face' were viewed with increasing concern, both in Moscow and by Czechoslovakia's Warsaw Pact neighbours. Moscow applied strong pressure on the Czechoslovak leadership during the summer of 1968, using such tried and tested methods as 'troop manoeuvres', but the reformists refused to alter course. On the night of 20–21 August, Czechoslovakia was invaded by troops from five of its Warsaw Pact allies – the USSR, Poland, Hungary, Bulgaria and the GDR; in all, 27 divisions.

The end of the Prague Spring

The world watched in astonishment and horror as Soviet tanks rolled into Prague. Older citizens could draw the parallels with the German takeover in 1938/9. The operation was not without casualties, and dozens died on both sides, but there was no mass resistance. The lasting impression is of a concerted, but peaceful, effort by the populace to convince the soldiers of the injustice they were doing. Attempts were made to confuse the operation by removing or altering road signs. Many of the troops were very shaken when they realized how they had been lied to, and units were rapidly recalled and replaced. The operation was accompanied by a campaign of misinformation in the Soviet bloc media. Meanwhile, Soviet theoreticians had worked hard to devise a rationale for the move. They came up with an answer. The brave experiment in seeking a Czechoslovak road to socialism had been suppressed in the greater interests of the 'socialist commonwealth' (the Brezhnev Doctrine).

Dubček and his supporters on the Politburo were treated disgracefully. They were arrested and taken to the Ukraine. Only when the ageing president, General Svoboda, who had decided to go to Moscow of his own accord, refused to begin negotiations without them, did the Soviets produce the Dubček group. During October the Soviet leadership bullied the reformers into reversing the reforms and signing a 15-point protocol, ensuring that Moscow's demands were met. The treaty also provided for Soviet troops to be stationed 'temporarily' on Czechoslovak soil (although as a small and rather hollow concession, there was agreement that they would not intervene directly in the country's internal affairs!).

To the ageing Kremlin leadership, the 'Prague Spring' represented a threat to the stability of the entire socialist bloc. But the return to orthodoxy, the process of 'normalization' which Moscow had indicated that it wanted set in motion, did not begin immediately. Slow to recover from the shock of the violent intervention, the reformists still believed that there was room for compromise and some of the gains could be retained. The desperation of reformist-minded Czechs and Slovaks not to return to the 'ice age' of Stalinist-style repression was tragically highlighted by the public self-immolation of a student, Jan Palach, in January 1969. The one lasting gain was the confirmation of a federal structure, ensuring complete equality between the Czech and Slovak nations. Both were to have parallel institutional structures – a Czech National Council (200 members) and a Slovak National Council (150 members) – and were to receive a just allocation of seats in the Federal Assembly.

'Normalization' under Husák

Dubček was quickly relegated to obscurity. An initial posting to Turkey as Czechoslovak ambassador was followed by his expulsion from the Party's Central Committee. In June 1970 he was expelled from the Party and removed from the public spotlight to a lowly job with the state forestry administration in Bratislava. Dubček's fall was spectacular, but it was not isolated. In the months that followed, thousands of Party members were expelled and lost their jobs in a mass clear-out of the reformist elements. Some one and a half million members were interrogated by screening commissions. There were heavy casualties in the media and in cultural life, and large numbers of the persecuted (over 100,000 by the end of 1970) chose to leave the country.

Ironically, the man who took over as Party leader from Dubček and began to 'normalize' Communist rule was not only, like Dubček himself, a Slovak. Gustáv Husák had been arrested in 1951 – one of the victims of the Party's earlier purges of its own ranks. (He had been amnestied in 1960.) Husák had even at one time been a Slovak nationalist. He took over in April 1969, following prolonged 'armtwisting' of the Party hierarchy by the Soviet leadership.

The process of 'normalization' which took place under Husák meant inflexible, unresponsive leadership and public apathy. The stand-off which ensued can be compared to the situation after the 1981 suppression of Solidarity in Poland. People felt cheated of the freedoms they had tasted all too briefly. They resented the 'depoliticization' which followed. Many had begun for the first time to engage in true democratic debate and to interest themselves in the political process, as something they could influence, and which could bring change for the better into their lives. The Husák regime anxiously attempted to deflect unrest by engineering a rise in living standards. Private consumption rose considerably in the course of the 1970s and car-ownership alone increased threefold between 1969 and 1981. But this induced boom did not signify underlying economic health.

By 1980–81 there was a growing crisis in the economy and growth of national income had slowed to zero. The structure of the Czechoslovak economy had not been altered appreciably from its earlier Stalinist model. It was still functioning as the workshop of Comecon, producing steel and heavy machinery. Furthermore, much of the Czechoslovak industry was outdated and many of its products of low technical standard. The central planning restrictions and curbing of private enterprise stifled innovation and the growth of new industries – particularly the new technologies developing in the West and Japan. In the course of the 1970s Czechoslovakia lost one third of its share of Western markets. This meant an important loss of Western currency with which to finance imports.

Meanwhile the country was still having to import large quantities of raw materials and energy, and these were becoming increasingly expensive on world markets. Czechoslovakia's huge and inefficient consumption of energy led it to exploit large quantities of brown coal (lignite) to fire thermal power plants – but at enormous environmental cost.

Charter 77

The Husák period was marked by the growth of an intellectual and cultural opposition – dissident writers, academics, artists – who began to bypass the offical media by publishing their works in the unofficial (*samizdat*) press. The dissidents included both disaffected former Communists and those who had remained outside the Party, yet they had a common purpose, and their chief spokesman became playwright Václav Havel. In the spring of 1975 Havel wrote an 'open letter' to Husák in which he pointed out that far from returning to normality or order, Czechoslovakia was passing through a crisis – and the crisis was getting deeper. A continuation of present policies would only lead to disaster, and history would judge Husák and his colleagues most severely for driving Czechoslovakia into this impasse. This letter, like other products of the dissident press, was broadcast back to the country by Western radio stations. It remains an important testament to the courage of the man who was himself later to become the country's president.

In December 1976 Havel was one of the founders of a dissident group which became known as Charter 77 (the movement's declaration, written in large part by Havel, was dated 1 January 1977). Other founder members included Jiří Němec, Pavel Kohout and Zdeněk Mlynář. The movement was formed, like similar groups in neighbouring countries, to protest against abuses of human rights by reference to the Helsinki agreements and to draw infringements to the attention of the world media. A catalyst leading to the fusion of many dissident groups in just one movement was the regime's arrest, in March 1976, of a group of young rock musicians and fans. The youngsters, borrowing ideas from their Western counterparts of the 1960s, had decided to turn their backs on the sterile, official culture and develop an alternative one. They were, though, not a political opposition group, and the fact that the authorities should seek to extinguish all independent organizations, even an inoffensive group of musicians, struck many people as being both an appalling and a ridiculous misuse of power. The mobilization of opposition resources brought an awareness of how many groups there were and the realization that greater co-ordination was needed.

The founding of Charter 77 was the most significant political event in the period between the Prague Spring and the 'velvet revolution' of 1989. Charter 77 was not a political party, nor a trade union like Solidarity. It was not even an organization, but merely a loose association of like-minded citizens concerned that political and social life should be ordered along ethical lines, and that infringements of human rights should not be passed over in silence. It hoped, its manifesto stated, to engage in a constructive dialogue with the authorities over such abuses. This was too optimistic. In ensuing years the Charter signatories were threatened, harassed and hounded by the authorities. Some, like Jiří Lederer, were imprisoned early on (for 'undermining the republic'). Václav Havel received a prison sentence of four and a half years, Jiří Dienstbier (now foreign minister) one of three years. But those at liberty faced dismissal from their jobs, telephone threats against themselves or their families, or physical assault on the streets. A large number of Charter signatories were hounded out of the country. Despite such pressures, in the twelve years of its existence the 'Chartists' produced scores of letters, reports, pamphlets, analyses and declarations about a wide range of subjects – from history to nuclear power. Charter 77 did not become a mass movement – it had few working-class members – but gave hope to many and inspired others to form opposition groups.

The 'velvet revolution' of 1989

The 1980s in Czechoslovakia marked a change in the relationship between the Party and the people. There was a new spirit abroad of optimism and defiance which strengthened as the decade progressed. Three factors influenced the public mood. The first was the success – despite its suppression – of the Solidarity trade union in Poland in confronting the Communist authorities and attracting mass support. The second was Gorbachev's assumption of power in the Kremlin in 1985, and the introduction of a more liberal Soviet regime. The third was a resurgence of religious belief and activity – particularly among the Roman Catholic population.

The Soviet liberalization was perhaps the most important for the Prague authorities. The Czechoslovak censorship could hardly stem the flood of new articles appearing in Soviet party journals. Yet the unprecedented questioning and self-criticism ran directly counter to the stern, uncompromising approach of the Husák regime. The position of the Prague regime became increasingly awkward as Czechs and Slovaks realized that the changes taking place in the Soviet Union were more radical even than the modest reforms they had called for during the Prague Spring. In April 1967 when Gorbachev visited Prague he was generally complimentary towards the leadership but pointedly refused to endorse the Soviet intervention of 1968. His silence had a similar sequel to that of Brezhnev's visit in 1968. In December 1987 Husák resigned as Party secretary general (though he remained president). His successor was another hardliner, Miloš Jakeš. Jakeš had been right-hand man to Vasil Bilak, when the latter was charged with purging Party reformers in 1970.

In the course of 1988 and early 1989 Czechoslovakia seemed on the surface to remain almost unaffected by the historic moves towards dismantling of Communist rule that were taking place in her neighbours Poland and Hungary. True, the country saw the largest protest demonstration for twenty years in August 1988, on the anniversary of the Soviet-

led invasion. Perhaps because of this, the government displayed nervous-
ness the following January when a series of peaceful demonstrations in
Prague to commemorate the death of Jan Palach were broken up by police.
Václav Havel and thirteen other dissidents were arrested when they tried
to lay flowers at the spot where Palach had set fire to himself. The 52-year-
old playwright was originally charged with 'hooliganism', although he
was later sentenced for breach of the peace and obstructing the authorities.

Yet Havel's arrest proved an embarrassment, particularly as the news
broke that he had been nominated for the Nobel Peace Prize. Amid the
international chorus of protest, over a thousand prominent figures from
the Czechoslovak world of art and culture signed an appeal for Havel's
release. Since they were all state employees, and faced loss of employment
for their heresy, this was a move which demanded courage. On 20
February 1989 the premier Adamec returned from Moscow, evidently
affected by the new mood of liberalization there. He told a Czech reporter,
'We want to hold a dialogue with all those who honestly desire to help
socialism in a creative way . . .'

By the summer the Prague leadership was looking forward with
apprehension to the twenty-first anniversary of the Soviet invasion. Three
of the five Warsaw Pact countries which had taken part in the invasion had
already condemned the act. The Czech leadership's response had been
that such statements 'helped the cause of anti-socialist forces'. They could
scarcely say otherwise. A repudiation of the 1968 invasion and attempts to
rehabilitate Dubček called the legitimacy of the post-1968 regimes directly
into question. (In fact, later in the year demonstrators were to taunt Jakeš
with the chant that he was 'installed by tanks . . .'.) In the event the Prague
demonstrations of 21 August 1989 were small. Only a few thousand people
took part, probably due to the fact that opposition leaders, fearing a
repetition of police violence (and no doubt mindful of the savage violence
of China's Tiananmen Square), had advised people to stay away.

The Prague authorities began to take steps to soften discontent and to
show that, along with the moves towards liberalization in its neighbouring
states, Czechoslovakia too could show a human face to its citizens. On 1
August the Czech branch of International PEN Club held its first meeting
since being disbanded in 1971. There followed in September a liberalization of the travel laws for those who wanted to visit the West. A greater
openness was also evident on economic matters, belated recognition by
the Party that economic failure lay at the root of much of the popular
discontent. A government spokesman with responsibility for nationalized
industry admitted that 30% of Czechoslovak industry was hopelessly
uneconomic. The Party daily *Rudé Právo* reported on 30 August that there
were 38 state enterprises for which bankruptcy proceedings had been
started and 147 agricultural enterprises which had to balance their books
within five years or be dissolved.

A turning point in the Czechoslovak situation came in October 1989 with the toppling of two hardline Soviet bloc regimes – in East Germany and Bulgaria. These developments brought to the opposition – and the hitherto uncommitted – the realization of how shaky were the foundations of Communist rule. At the same time, and in due proportion, the Party leadership began to lose confidence, finding itself to be an anachronism – an island of orthodoxy in a sea of reform and change.

Ironically, the event which led to the collapse of the Communist regime in Czechoslovakia had been approved by the authorities themselves. It was a student march in the centre of Prague on 17 November to commemorate the death at the hands of the Gestapo of a student, Jan Opletal. When the rally turned into an anti-government demonstration, the tens of thousands of people who had gathered in Prague's Wenceslas Square were attacked by riot police. Over 140 people were reported injured. Indignation at the news of the violence was increased when the rumour (later denied) spread that a student had been killed at the hands of the police. Instead of deterring opposition, the government's action provoked further marches, which grew in size on successive days. The Prague regime found itself confronting a new generation of dissidents – young people who had grown up since the 1968 events and had not the same fear of repression as their elders. In the early stages, though, the students had little support from working people.

On 19 November more than a dozen opposition groups met in Prague to form an opposition coalition, Civic Forum. (In Slovakia a parallel movement called Public Against Violence came into being.) They were joined by representatives of the Socialist Party and the People's Party, for 40 years the docile partners of the ruling Communists. Their joint resolution called for dialogue with the government and for the resignation of several Party leaders. Support came in the form of strikes and occupations of schools and universities throughout the country. Students prepared posters and made dozens of video copies of the film of the police violence, which were circulated to small towns and villages as a counter to the official, censored version. Actors, musicians and theatre staff also went on strike and theatres quickly became the scenes of public debates.

By Monday 20 November extraordinary scenes were taking place in Wenceslas Square as flowers were placed and candles lit at the foot of St Wenceslas's statue, the national flag waved and the national anthem sung. Keys were jangled, reminiscent of the closing-time ritual in Czech inns, to remind the leadership that their time, too, had come. Premier Adamec, clearly prompted by the paralysis that affected his older Party colleagues and wishing to dissociate himself from the earlier violence, met with opposition leaders and offered 'a different concept of the leading role of the Party', including the idea of non-Communists joining the government.

On 24 November both Havel and Alexander Dubček had addressed crowds in Prague. Dubček, speaking publicly for the first time in the current crisis, called for the resignation of the leadership. As he appeared on the balcony he was greeted by a huge roar of welcome. A two-hour national strike was called for Monday, 27 November. It met with the support of 60% of the workforce, and persuaded the Party leaders that the mood of defiance now extended to their traditional supporters.

Jakeš handed in his resignation and that of the entire Party secretariat. He was replaced as Party leader by a 48-year-old former railwayman, Karel Urbánek, who was relatively unknown and, because of his age, was untainted by association with the events of 1968. The opposition forces had developed a confidence and a momentum, however, and were not to be fobbed off by yet one more attempt to 'shuffle the pack'. Crowds continued to gather in the centre of Prague, to chants of 'Free elections'. Havel made clear to the crowds that dialogue with the Party must include abolition of the Party's leading role.

Although this was conceded by the Party – as was the demand for free elections – a government reshuffle on 3 December which still left 16 of the twenty Cabinet posts in Communist hands created an administration which lasted a mere seven days. Marián Čalfa was called upon to supervise the Party's retreat by forming a coalition with opposition leaders. Miloš Jakeš and Miroslav Stěpán, the former Party boss for Prague, were both expelled from the Party, after the public had been treated to the unedifying spectacle of the two men denying responsibility for the police violence on 17 November, while apologizing for it.

The new government dominated by non-Communists was sworn in on 10 December. Immediately afterwards the president, Gustav Husák, resigned. Premier Čalfa, a 43-year-old Slovak, soon left the Communist Party – as did two deputy premiers and a number of ministers of this Government of National Unity. It had become evident to many that in the rapidly changing political climate Party membership had become a liability and a hindrance to career prospects. Thousands of Party members at the lower levels returned their Party cards. (Between 600,000 and 800,000 – or 40% of the membership – are thought to have left the Party by the end of February 1990.) For the more active members, though – the editors, directors, heads of departments, ambassadors – there was nowhere to hide. Positions occupied by the *nomenklatura* during the Husák–Jakeš era were vacated – from government down to district and workplace level. They were quickly replaced by members of Civic Forum. Jan Czarnogursky, released from prison on one day, found himself deputy premier the next. Jiří Dienstbier, spokesman for the opposition movement, became Minister for Foreign Affairs. Havel's translator, Rita Klímová (before 1968 a professor of economics), became ambassador in the USA, while the son of Rudolf Slánský, victim of the Stalinist purges, became ambassador in Moscow.

President Havel

On 29 December Havel, a man who had been imprisoned four times and frequently detained by the régime, was elected President. He became the most popular and respected holder of that office since the country's founder, Tomáš Masaryk. The election result was important, since presidential office confers considerable powers – a legacy of the Communist period. Havel promised to use his new powers as a stabilizing force during the period of transformation to come and as a guarantee that full democracy would be restored to Czechoslovakia.

Immediately after his election, Havel visited Germany, where he stressed his support for German unification and in a wise but controversial move requested forgiveness for the brutality with which Germans had been expelled from Czechoslovakia at the end of World War II. Visits to Poland, Hungary, the USA, the Soviet Union, Britain and France were also to come within three months of Havel taking office. His Soviet visit at the end of February 1990 was of particular importance, since he went with the mission of persuading Soviet leader Gorbachev to remove one of the last vestiges of the 1968 invasion – the 'temporarily' stationed 75,000 Red Army troops – from Czechoslovak soil. Agreement was reached that all would be removed by the summer of 1991.

The new democracy

The June 1990 elections determined the composition of the bicameral Federal Parliament and the two (Czech and Slovak) national councils. The run-up to the election proved eventful. First came an unseemly quarrel over the new name the Republic should bear in the post-Communist era. Then the caretaker government came under fire for being 'soft' on the Communists and Interior Minister, Richard Sacher, was accused of failure to root out all influence of the state security police, the *Statni Bezpecnost* (*StB*). Rumours circulated that former security agents aimed to destabilize the new democracy. These were given substance by a bomb incident in central Prague during the election campaign.

As if to contribute to the uncertainty and further undermine the government's standing, it was revealed that the origins of the 'velvet revolution' of the previous November had not been as straightforward as popularly imagined. The police violence which triggered off popular protest had apparently been orchestrated by the KGB in an operation to unseat Husák and the hardliners in the Party.

All this might have damaged Civic Forum's chances. Yet the election result was a vote of confidence in the Civic Forum/PAV camp, which secured more than half of the seats in the Federal Parliament. The greatest surprise was the poor showing of the Christian Democrats, who trailed in third place behind the Communists. Yet it was to the Christian Democrats that the prime minister designate turned to form a coalition. Marian Čalfa's new government was reduced in number from 23 ministers to 17.

The new government did not please everyone, however. There was criticism of Havel within the Civic Forum camp for retaining a number of figures, including former Communist Čalfa as premier. One figure who did go was Interior Minister, Sacher, replaced by Slovak former dissident, Jan Langos. On 5 July, Václav Havel was re-elected President. Despite the formation of a strong team of presidential advisers at Prague Castle, headed by the returned exile, Count Karl von Schwarzenberg, his position was not as strong as it had been. A growing influence and a potential threat to Havel had emerged in Václav Klaus, the right-wing finance minister. Although not overpopular with colleagues, Klaus largely won the battle over the need for far-ranging economic reforms. He also became Chairman of Civic Forum in October, beating Havel's nominee, Martin Palous, by a margin of more than two to one.

Economic reforms

Under Communism Czechoslovakia had a more successful economy than most of its Comecon partners and, following the 'velvet revolution', could afford to face the transition to a market economy with some confidence. It possessed an educated and skilled workforce. Its level of inflation was low (between 2.5% and 3.5%) and its $8 billion foreign debt was considered manageable by Western bankers. It also enjoyed relatively high standards of living: food shops, for example, were kept well-stocked and prices low thanks to government subsidies.

Nevertheless, problems existed. First there was the need to rein in government spending. The state budget account for a massive 70% of national income. Some 8% of this (50 billion crowns) went on defence and security, with further large sums being spent on the government bureaucracy and state subsidies. Second there was the need to break up some of the large industrial conglomerates and encourage the development of skill-intensive, high-tech industries. Third, there was the requirement to lessen the country's dependency upon its Comecon partners for export markets. Demand from the Soviet Union, which took over 40% of Czechoslovakia's exports, was expected to drop markedly. There was also a need, for both economic and environmental reasons, to look closely at the efficiency of energy usage.

At the beginning of 1990 opinion was divided about how far-reaching a reform programme should be and how quickly it should be implemented. While some (led by Finance Minister, Václav Klaus) called enthusiastically for a tough budget and an early privatization programme, others were more cautious, fearing the effects such policies might have on unemployment levels and thus on their electoral chances. In the end the painful decisions were put off until a government with a proper mandate was returned.

Moves towards market reform gathered pace in the second half of 1990, following the June elections. A series of laws was passed, intended to encourage foreign investment. These allowed for the privatization of small enterprises, the creation of joint stock companies and the liberalization of foreign trade. At the end of October the Czechoslovak crown was devalued by over a third, a measure adopted to prepare for its internal convertibility from 1 January 1991. This was one of a number of reform measures introduced by the government, which included the freeing of prices, proceeding with plans to support privatization and private-sector activity, an anti-inflationary macro-economic policy and welfare provision (including unemployment benefits).

As in Poland a year earlier, the measures came as a shock to the system. In January prices rose by 26% (31% for food prices) compared with the previous month. By the end of February industrial production had dropped by 6% compared with the first two months of 1990. Unemployment had risen to 15,000 (some 2% of the workforce), although government 'worst-case' estimates were that it might reach as high as 12–15%. Some 7% of the state budget (10 billion crowns) had been set aside for unemployment benefits and re-training costs.

There is no doubt that 1991 and 1992 will be a crucial period for the Czechoslovak economy. The collapse in Comecon trade has affected the country more seriously than its neighbours. The need to pay for oil and gas imports in dollars was also a major setback. Its high degree of centralized planning and scant experience of attempts at reform under the Communists also weigh against it.

Civic Forum splits

In the latter half of 1990 the Civic Forum movement began to show signs of disintegrating. Like Solidarity in neighbouring Poland, it was an umbrella organization, containing a wide range of political opinions. It was inevitable as the time came to take difficult decisions – particularly crucial ones concerning economic policy – that cracks in the movement's consensus would begin to appear. A grouping of right-wing members of federal and republican parliaments came into being around Finance Minister, Klaus, who insisted that the Forum's organizational structure was too loose and its political programme too vague. Following Klaus's assumption of the Forum chairmanship, his followers made efforts to shift the Forum further to the right. Naming themselves the Democratic Right, their immediate target was left-of-centre groups such as Obroda, which was composed mainly of former Communists.

At the very end of 1990, a more centre-left grouping known as the Liberal Club emerged, supported by many prominent politicians, including foreign minister Jiří Dienstbier. At the Forum's conference in mid-January the Liberal Club resisted attempts to transform the Forum into a political party. However, at a further congress in late February the Forum officially split into two parties, both of which will carry the 'Civic' title; the Liberal Club became the Civic Movement and Klaus's rightist grouping the

Civil Democratic Party. Both groups will remain under the Civic Forum umbrella until the next parliamentary elections, when the Forum will be dissolved.

Nationalism

Pressures of a rather different kind have led to a split in Civic Forum's Slovak partner, Public Against Violence. Indeed, apart from economic reform, some of the most heated political debates have centred on resurgent Slovak nationalism. Although Public Against Violence gained agreement from the federal authorities during 1990 that control over most industries should devolve to the republic, this was not enough for the Slovak Nationalist Party, which argued that Slovakia should have its own budget and control its own economic policy. Slovak demands caused deep concern, particularly when opinion polls in the autumn of 1990 gave them 35% support. President Havel, who in late October made a whistle-stop tour of Slovakia to calm local feelings, warned a few weeks later that extreme devolutionary demands might provoke a constitutional crisis – the break-up of the country's federal structure might lead to economic collapse. Pressure on the federal government seemed to have eased, however, when voting figures from the local elections showed that SNP support (at 3.2%) was nowhere near as high as the polls had indicated.

Despite this temporary relief, Slovak demands (which, at their most extreme, include calls for secession) have made the country increasingly harder to govern. Growing popular support for nationalist demands has forced other Slovak parties to adopt a more extreme line. In February 1991 the Slovak National Council stalled moves to extend the powers of the President (he would have received emergency powers in time of crisis), arguing that it would have left too much power in the hands of the Federal Government. In the same month the Slovak Christian Democratic Movement (a member of the government coalition) demanded that before new federal and republican constitutions be prepared a state treaty be signed by the Czech and Slovak republics. (Havel was against the idea of confederation, but agreed that both republics should have the right to secede.) At more or less the same time the comparatively moderate Public Against Violence lost its premier, Vladimir Meciar. Meciar had argued that PAV should give more prominence to Slovak issues, and in particular had argued that the federal government's reform programme should be modified to take account of the specific problems facing less-industrialized Slovakia.

At the beginning of 1991 the chorus of regional (if not nationalist) demands shifted from the east to the north of the country, as Moravian and Silesian groups began to campaign more stridently for a 'fairer share' of the republic's budget. Calls for Moravia and Silesia to be reconstituted as a third republic (along with Bohemia and Slovakia) received a sympathetic hearing in the Czech republican council. However, such a move would downgrade the position of the Slovak republic – since regional criteria would be introduced alongside those of nationality – and would arouse Slovak opposition. A more likely outcome seems to be some kind of regional autonomy for Moravia and Silesia.

4 EASTERN GERMANY – THE FORMER GDR

The German Democratic Republic – the GDR – was born on 7 October 1949. It was laid to rest on 3 October 1990. Its death was not solemnly observed but was greeted with a euphoria that knew few bounds.

Today, as part of the Federal Republic of Germany, eastern Germany, much like its western half, is finding that the true cost of unity is infinitely higher than anyone had imagined. Teething problems were expected, but nothing on the scale of those actually encountered. While western Germans complain that they are being expected to shoulder the huge financial burden of righting 40 years of Communist mismanagement, eastern Germans face the prospect of widescale unemployment and seeing what remains of their economy taken over wholesale by the west. They complain that they are being made to feel that they have little or nothing to contribute to the new state. The culture shock is causing deep wounds which will take, perhaps, a generation to heal.

The German Democratic Republic (GDR) was a latter-day Holy Roman Empire, which was disparagingly referred to as neither holy, nor Roman, nor an empire. It foundered because it was neither German nor democratic. The ruling Socialist Unity Party (SED) tried to sustain the myth that Germans in East and West Germany belonged to different nations. The GDR occupied a unique place in contemporary European history as the only state which has voluntarily voted itself out of existence. The GDR declared proudly that it was the first socialist state on German soil. It may turn out to have been the first and last socialist state on German soil.

Historical background
The Republic was a war baby, and its father was Josef Stalin. It was born officially on 7 October 1949 but it had existed ever since the unconditional surrender of Nazi Germany on 8 May 1945 under the name of the Soviet Occupied Zone of Germany. The Allies had agreed that after defeat, Germany was to be occupied, and therefore three occupation zones (American, British and Soviet) were agreed. Berlin was to be divided into three sectors. Later, a French occupation zone and a French sector in Berlin were added, but Stalin insisted that they be taken from the American and British occupied territories.

Since the Red Army had conquered Berlin, the Soviets had a free hand in the city until the Western Allies arrived on 1 July. A Soviet Military

EASTERN GERMANY

Official name	Federal Republic of Germany
Area	108,333 sq. km (41,828 sq. miles)
Population	16,666,000 (1988) (annual growth rate 0%)
Capital	Berlin
Languages	German, Sorb
Religion	30% Evangelical Protestant, 6% Roman Catholic
Currency	D-mark

Administration (SMAD) was established to run the city and the Soviet zone. Its aim was to have a functioning city government in place by the time Berlin was again declared the capital of Germany. However, the Potsdam Conference could not agree on the future of Germany and the Allied Control Commission (ACC) fared no better. The Soviet Zone was stripped of many of its assets, which were declared by Moscow to be reparations. All important enterprises were nationalized in 1946 and a land reform eliminated large landowners. The onset of the Cold War in 1947 speeded up the Stalinist revolution and in March 1948 the Soviets left the ACC.

This ended the masquerade of a common German policy by the four occupying powers. All they had ever agreed on was their right as victors to determine the future of Germany, and that Germany should never again be a threat to European peace. Lying at the heart of Europe, the country was too important to be allowed to slip into the other camp. The Soviets wanted a socialist Germany, the Americans a capitalist one and the British and French were so concerned about resurgent German political and economic power that they preferred the country to remain divided.

The introduction of the deutschmark in the Western zones and Berlin in June 1948 divided Germany. The Soviet response was the Berlin blockade and the Western answer, the Berlin air lift. The longer the blockade dragged on, the more certain it was that a separate West German state, anchored in the Western alliance, would come into being. There was a real fear of the Soviets using their military power to expand westwards, and this gave birth to NATO, which obliged the USA to maintain troops in Western Europe.

Politically, the Soviets attempted to seize the initiative in Germany in 1945, and legalized parties in their zone in June without consulting the other occupying powers. The parties which came into being were conceived of as all-German ones; the Communists (KPD); the Social Democrats (SPD); the Christian Democrats (CDU) and the Liberal Democrats (LDP). Later, a National Democratic Party and a Peasants' Party were founded. Only in 1989 were more parties added to the list. The parties formed the National Front with the Communists playing the leading role.

Under the skilful leadership of Walter Ulbricht the Communists made headway but the SPD became more popular. It had always been the avowed intent of the KPD and SPD to merge, but when the fusion did come, in April 1946, it was a forced marriage. The relatively free elections later in 1946 did not provide the Communists with the mandate they desired, and thereafter only lists of candidates could be voted for.

When the GDR came into being on 7 October 1949 it was effectively a one-party state. The Communist Party then began the process of transforming the country into a socialist one. However, a Stalinist political and economic model was not to the liking of the great majority of the population. This led to a massive exodus of skilled personnel, but on 17 June

1953 those who remained revolted against increased work norms. Without Soviet help, Ulbricht and the SED would have been swept from power.

By the late 1950s Ulbricht had ousted all his rivals and defeated efforts to retain aspects of the market economy. The border with West Germany had been closed but Berlin was still an open city. In order to complete the building of socialism by imposing collectivization of agriculture Ulbricht needed to close off the Berlin outlet. Khrushchev finally agreed, and on 13 August 1961 the building of the Berlin Wall began. The SED believed that only if the GDR were isolated from capitalist West Germany could socialism be built at home.

Thereby began an isolation which was to last to 1989. In a world of increasing economic interdependence the SED attempted to do the impossible – build a modern, industrial state in isolation. In the 1950s and 1960s certain sectors of the GDR economy were on a European, even world, level but, over time, these achievements were lost. Autarchy became an obsession with Erich Honecker after he succeeded Ulbricht as party leader in June 1971.

The drive for autarchy led to endless efforts to raise the legitimacy of the SED regime. The GDR proclaimed itself a separate nation, and attempts were made to engender a specific GDR state consciousness. The GDR evolved a specific economic model which was claimed as the most developed anywhere. The leadership began a cult of past German heroes, including Frederick the Great, Luther and Goethe, but all in vain. Had the GDR become a vibrant, economically successful society it might have survived. However, economic malaise afflicted it from the early 1980s and the SED's inability to halt this condemned the GDR to accelerated decline. As the economic and social situation deteriorated, the regime descended to half truths and then lies. The educated segment of the population found the lack of dialogue with the regime extremely frustrating, and eventually assembled to debate the deteriorating position. With hindsight, the key variable in the collapse of the GDR was the Gorbachev phenomenon. His bold initiatives in the Soviet Union, at a time of leadership paralysis in the GDR, inspired many, and revealed that there could be an alternative to existing socialism.

Seven key factors led to the demise of the GDR:

1 The political, economic and social decline of the country during the 1980s and the startling revelations about the abuse of power and unbridled corruption of the GDR elite;

2 The advent of Gorbachev in the Soviet Union. His policies of *perestroika*, *glasnost* and democratization undermined the legitimacy of a GDR socialist model;

3 The swelling stream of GDR refugees during 1989. This led to the crucial decision by the Hungarian government on 11 September 1989 to permit GDR citizens to cross unhindered into Austria;

4 The events surrounding the 40th anniversary celebrations of the GDR
state in October 1989. Gorbachev, as the main foreign guest, came not
to honour Honecker and the SED regime but to contribute to their
overthrow;
5 The power of the crowd;
6 The opening of the Berlin Wall;
7 The resurrection of politics and the march to German unity.

Political, economic and social decline

GDR published statistics were systematically falsified during the 1980s and
presumably long before that. The SED's legitimacy rested on its ability to
fashion an economically successful state as a viable alternative to West
Germany. The GDR had significant achievements to its credit, especially in
the realm of social policy, but these were all before 1980. Competitiveness
vis-à-vis West Germany declined. The technological gulf between East and
West increased as East German industry failed to invest in new equipment
and keep pace with world technology. Labour productivity was a critical
factor. In an economy in which there were no labour reserves, economic
output could only grow through productivity gains. Annually the gap
widened between labour productivity in East and West Germany. There
were islands of excellence, such as Carl Zeiss Jena, but the overall picture
was one of gloom. This led to a rising curve of mendacious statistics. While
these fooled many foreign observers, they increased the frustration felt by
most GDR citizens. They knew their living standards were declining but
the state insisted that things were rather rosy. The lack of investment led to
critical shortages of housing, medical and other social services. Many
citizens were shocked to hear, on 13 November 1989, that the state had run
up debts of 130 billion ostmarks. Most industrial enterprises were also in
debt, as were most local authorities. Hard currency debts, on 3 January
1990, were put at US$20.6 billion.

The person rightly blamed for this monumental mismanagement of the
national economy was Günter Mittag, SED secretary for the economy since
1976. Deeply unpopular, arrogant and dictatorial, Mittag ran the GDR like
a family firm – *his* family firm. Like several other members of the GDR elite,
he became addicted to hunting and delighted at shooting at anything that
moved. (Finding a factory on his game reserve he ordered its removal! This
makes clear his economic priorities in the 1980s.) Other members of the
elite enjoyed unheard-of privileges, and could be likened to feudal robber
barons. They had special residences built for themselves at Wandlitz, just
outside Berlin, the whole area being out of bounds to ordinary GDR
citizens, and every luxury imaginable was available to them. The state's
hard currency reserves were plundered to pander to the whims of the elite.
One device for adding to the stock of imported goods was the annual
Christmas barter deal. Freedom for political prisoners in GDR jails could be
bought by West Germany at princely sums. Some of the negotiators began

to confuse state and personal profit during the 1980s. Alexander Schalck-Golodkowski was said to have been involved in illegal arms and currency deals. Other leading politicians were less expensive. Harry Tisch, head of the trade union movement, was so obsessed about cleanliness that he had a shower installed in his garage! Needless to say, Honecker had most. He even had his own island in the Baltic.

During the 1980s Honecker and his elite gradually lost contact with reality. They all lived under Communism, where money was no longer necessary. Wealth and luxury sapped the moral fibre of even the most resilient Communist. Only those who deliberately avoided becoming members of the elite, such as Hans Modrow, evaded its deadly embrace. Top officials could not complain of being kept in the dark. Honecker dismissed the criticisms of one First Party Secretary by advising him to concern himself with matters in his own district.

The SED claimed that it was building real socialism in the GDR, but the party permitted no debate about priorities or policies within its ranks. Frustration built up, and churches became an alternative venue for discussions. As disillusionment grew with the Honecker regime so, too, did police brutality. Honecker appears to have believed that he was facing a counter-revolution which, by definition, had to be controlled from abroad. He was quite incapable of appreciating that it was not an exogenous force which was threatening socialism in the GDR but the SED's own incompetence and corruption, undermining it from within.

Enter Gorbachev

The advent of Gorbachev in the Soviet Union was an embarrassment to the SED leadership. It had become accustomed to setting its own priorities under the ailing Brezhnev and his successors. Gorbachev began to undermine the legitimacy of the SED by offering a fresh vision of socialism. Honecker found the principles of *perestroika*, *glasnost* and democratization deeply distasteful and alarming in their implications for the SED regime. *Neues Deutschland*, the party organ, censored Gorbachev's utterances, especially those which attacked party and governmental corruption. This did not prevent East Germans from discovering what the Soviet leader had said, since West German radio and television carried full coverage. Honecker's message to his members was that party discussion was to be restricted to the excerpts printed in *Neues Deutschland*. When *perestroika* was on the agenda many party and trade union officials insisted that it only applied to the USSR.

Honecker argued that the SED did not need the changes being introduced by Gorbachev since its economy had not declined. However, the increasing shortages and poverty of political life transformed Gorbachev into a symbol of hope for many GDR citizens. He was greeted with genuine warmth during his visits to the republic.

Events in Poland and Hungary began to isolate the SED. The GDR congratulated the Chinese leadership on slaughtering students in Tiananmen Square in June 1989. Gorbachev made no secret of the fact that he believed that the present kind of socialism had no future. Although all socialist regimes were sovereign, he expected them to follow in his footsteps and introduce a more democratic system.

Given the opportunity, Honecker lectured the Soviet leader and party on the virtues of East German socialism, and was quite incapable of grasping that his analysis of GDR reality was ludicrously wrong. Other members of the SED elite found original ways of justifying the do-nothing policy. Kurt Hager, Central Committee Secretary for Ideology, asked rhetorically if one's neighbour papered his house, was one supposed to do the same? He was forever dogged by this unfortunate remark.

Emigration

A tangible measure of the dissatisfaction felt by East Germans was the increasing numbers trying to emigrate to West Germany. A rising flood began to seek refuge in West German embassies in Eastern Europe and in the West German mission in East Berlin. On 3 August 1989 the Hungarian Foreign Ministry stated that it was considering granting GDR citizens political asylum. Hungary began to turn a blind eye to East Germans crossing the Austrian frontier, and by 10 August about 1,600 had reached Austria. Bonn was forced to close its mission in East Berlin and its embassy in Budapest to stem the flow of those seeking to move to the West.

Animated diplomatic discussions between Bonn, East Berlin and other capitals failed to staunch the flow of refugees. Remarkably, the GDR authorities did not cancel visa-free travel to Czechoslovakia. Most refugees then moved on to Hungary. The Hungarian government regarded the refugees as a German problem and eventually presented the GDR with an ultimatum. Either solve the problem or Hungary would open its frontiers to Austria.

At about midnight on 11 September Hungary did this, and over 25,000 East Germans crossed into Austria *en route* to West Germany. This unilateral decision infringed a 1969 agreement, but the Hungarians had come to the conclusion that the SED regime could not survive very long. The decision to open the frontier was of enormous political and psychological significance, since it was the breaking of the first link in the chain which had isolated the GDR since 1961. This decision had a catastrophic impact on SED morale, and led to a flood of refugees making for Hungary. The GDR responded by dragging passengers off trains and raiding flats to seize identity papers. East Germans, in turn, made for West German embassies in Warsaw and Prague. East Berlin capitulated, and on 30 September special trains, accompanied by West German officials, carried 800 refugees from Warsaw to Helmsted and 5,500 from Prague to Hof in Bavaria. The following day, over 6,000 more travelled by special trains from Warsaw and Prague to West Germany. There was no respite for the embassies, since new refugees immediately replaced those who had left. On 4 October over 7,600 refugees travelled to West Germany in special locked trains. Their departure had been delayed while all the stations they were to pass through in the GDR were cleared of would-be émigrés. On 4 November the Czechoslovak authorities secured an agreement from the GDR government that permitted GDR refugees to cross into West Germany. Over 40,000 people made use of this between 4 and 9 November. By 31 December 343,854 GDR citizens had moved to the West.

Alarmingly for the GDR, the refugees were predominantly between 25 and 45 years old. They and their families had chosen to turn their backs on their homeland and abandon their flats, cars and most worldly possessions. The refugees included many doctors, teachers, engineers, railway workers and others desperately needed in the GDR. This produced a knock-on effect throughout the economy. Medical services, for instance, were badly hit as doctors and nurses left.

Gorbachev's visit

The chief guest at the celebrations marking the 40th anniversary of the GDR was Mikhail Gorbachev, but he came not to praise but to stab Erich Honecker in the back. At a gala in the Palast der Republik on 6 October the SED General Secretary spoke of the '40 years of successful struggle for progress in the GDR'. He devoted no attention to the gathering crisis and clearly had no intimation of how serious the situation was. He also failed to grasp that he could not hold back the tide of *perestroika* flowing from the Soviet Union. Gorbachev spoke of his hope that the SED would come up with 'political answers to all the questions which were on the agenda and which were troubling the population'. The following day, 7 October, the occasion of the anniversary, was crucial. In talks at Schloss Niederschönhausen Honecker again painted a rosy picture and failed to address the pressing problems of the hour. Gorbachev, however, devoted considerable attention to the changes in Eastern Europe and in an interview on Soviet television after his return made it clear that he had pressed for reforms in the GDR. After the military parade, accompanied by stirring Prussian music, Gorbachev went on a walkabout. His message to onlookers was clear and unambiguous: 'Those who arrive late will be punished by history.' He went even further: 'If you really want democracy take it and it will be given to you.' This was an extraordinary appeal to make in the land of 'real, existing socialism' and was tantamount to saying that SED democracy was false. Gorbachev's words spread like wildfire among the opposition grapevine. If the Soviet leader was in favour of change how could Honecker resist it? A new impetus was given to the struggle for reform.

At the dinner in the evening in the Palast der Republik Gorbachev demonstrated to all that the Honecker era was over. On arrival, the Soviet President merely shook hands with the GDR leader. Honecker waited for

Gorbachev to embrace him and kiss him on both cheeks, the traditional greeting between the Soviet and GDR leaders. Mikhail Gorbachev merely smiled and then walked up to Willi Stoph, the GDR Prime Minister, and ostentatiously shook hands, embraced and kissed him on both cheeks. Gorbachev had already agreed that Egon Krenz was to be the next leader. The latter had a short meeting with Valentin Falin, a Gorbachev adviser on German affairs, during the pre-prandial reception. The message was that things would change.

Official parades and demonstrations marked the anniversary but counter-demonstrations, involving tens of thousands of people in favour of reform and freedom of opinion, took place in East Berlin, Leipzig, Dresden, Plauen, Jena, Potsdam and many other cities, and were broken up by police, often with great brutality. Many of the demonstrators were injured and over a thousand arrested. Foreign journalists were also caught up in the violence; they were beaten and their equipment smashed. Renewed demonstrations took place on 8 October and again the security forces dispersed them by force. Many were arrested.

The power of the crowd

Those who wished to practise free speech in the GDR had to go to church. In a party-run state, churches were the only buildings not directly licensed by the SED. Over the years, a dialogue had developed between the churches and the regime and a certain amount of free speech was tolerated. Many clerics were embarrassed by their role but gradually, over time, the churches evolved a social theology which was based on dialogue, opposition to violence and reconciliation between conflicting groups. Various pastors emerged who enjoyed great authority and represented an alternative way of life to the increasingly moribund Marxist–Leninist dogma of the SED. During the 1970s there was considerable contact between the churches and Honecker, but this stopped in the 1980s. The Roman Catholic Church was more conservative than Evangelical churches in the 1970s but gradually became more radical. However, it never produced clerics who were as prominent as Rainer Eppelmann, for instance. The fact that Catholics made up about one in six believers in the GDR also played a role.

It is a custom for believers to pray for peace, but this began to assume greater significance as political tension rose. Leipzig became a focal point and St Nicholas's Church the source of a new movement. Regularly on Mondays after prayers, believers and others assembled outside and demonstrated peacefully. This was copied in many other cities and the security services became alarmed and dispersed the crowds. On 29 September 1989 church authorities in Leipzig stated that eleven demonstrators had been sentenced to up to six months' imprisonment and that about two dozen had been fined up to 5,000 ostmarks. Instead of this intimidating protesters, a remarkable phenomenon developed. Each successive Monday evening saw an increase in the number of demonstrators in Leipzig. On 2 October over 20,000 demonstrated and were attacked by the security services, with many injuries and arrests. Large demonstrations took place throughout the GDR on 6, 7 and 8 October with security forces dispersing the crowds. Again, many were injured and arrested. On 4 October over 3,000 demonstrators and police clashed violently in front of Dresden's main railway station, and the following day the same happened. Demonstrators in Magdeburg were also attacked by the security forces.

The violent conduct of the security forces became a focus of protest. On 9 October the crowd in Leipzig had swollen to 70,000, but this time the police did not intervene. This was due to the fact that three Leipzig SED secretaries, Kurt Masur, conductor of the Leipzig Gewandhausorchester, Pastor Peter Zimmermann and the artist Bernd Lutz Lange, had signed an appeal which had been read out in churches and broadcast. The appeal stated that a 'free exchange of views about the further development of socialism in our country was needed. Therefore the signatories promise all citizens that this dialogue will not be restricted to Bezirk Leipzig but will also be conducted with our government'. The same day, Wolfgang Berghofer, Mayor of Dresden, received a delegation of 20 who were acting as spokespersons for the thousands of demonstrators who had been on the streets the day before. A nine-point programme was presented which demanded an explanation for the violent behaviour of the police on the previous day; the right to freedom of opinion, demonstration, travel and free elections; and the legalization of the political grouping 'Neues Forum'. Berghofer offered to examine the demands and to pass them on to higher authorities. On 10 October 500 of those arrested in Dresden were released. In the Gethsemane Church in East Berlin, Gottfried Forck, Bishop of Berlin, read an appeal signed by leading members of the Evangelical Church in Berlin-Brandenburg. It requested the GDR leadership to come up with credible suggestions which could serve as a basis for 'broad general agreement about a democratic, socialist future'. On the same day, Honecker received Yao Yilin, Chinese deputy Prime Minister, and drew parallels between the 'counter-revolutionary uprising in Beijing' and the 'present hate campaign against the GDR'.

On 15 October thousands demonstrated in Halle and Plauen for democratic reforms and Walter Leich, Bishop of Thuringia and chairman of the GDR Evangelical Church Union, in a circular, warned the GDR leadership against classifying demonstrators as 'enemies of the state' and to refrain from the use of force.

By 16 October the Leipzig crowd, demonstrating for reforms and democratic renewal, had grown to 120,000. Again, the police did not intervene. In Dresden about 10,000 people assembled in front of the Rathaus (town hall) to hear about the second round of talks between the mayor and city representatives and Church leaders. The results were to be read out the following evening in five Dresden churches. *Neues Deutschland* carried an interview with Berghofer on 18 October. The party newspaper also reported worker dissatisfaction with the information policy of the regime. However, it did not report the meeting of the leadership of the Writers' Union on 11 October. It called for 'revolutionary reform' in the GDR and demanded that an 'open democratic dialogue' at all levels of society should begin.

On 17 October over 20,000 packed five Dresden churches to hear reports on discussions with Wolfgang Berghofer which had taken place the day before. In Leipzig Mayor Bernd Seidel and other councillors met Church representatives for discussions. *Neues Deutschland* reported that talks between the SED, the government and trade unions had been taking place. It underlined that everything should be openly spoken about but socialism was not to be undermined. One of the National Front parties, the Liberal Democrats, proposed more freedom of travel and the ability to renounce GDR citizenship as well as greater legal protection for citizens.

The resignation of Erich Honecker on 18 October and his replacement by Egon Krenz accelerated demands for reform. On 20 October about 50,000 demonstrated in Dresden and over 5,000 in Karl-Marx-Stadt. In East Berlin the deputy police chief met the press and answered allegations about police brutality on 7–8 October. He stated he had many complaints against police officers and every complaint would be investigated. In Dresden, Bishop Johannes Hempel, addressing the Evangelical Synod, cast doubt on the right of the SED to rule.

On 21 October tens of thousands demonstrated in East Berlin, Plauen and other cities. In the capital Erhard Krack, Mayor of East Berlin, and Günter Schabowski, SED First Secretary, engaged in debate for over an hour with demonstrators. Schabowski promised that a new travel law had 'top priority'. He also lamented the fact that everything the SED did in the short term would be perceived by the population as a 'trap'.

Bishop Johannes Hempel called on the GDR leadership to apologize for brutal police behaviour against demonstrators. The Dresden Church authorities had prepared a document which included statements by eye witnesses. The report called for an independent enquiry, and this was supported by other groups, such as Demokratischer Aufbruch (Democratic Awakening). The report had been held back until after Honecker's resignation because of the appalling story it had to tell. The feeling was that had it been published beforehand it would have inflamed passions and led to possibly more bloodshed.

On 22 October 1989, in the Gewandhaus in Leipzig, over 500 people debated the situation in the GDR with Kurt Masur, Klaus Höpcke, deputy GDR Minister of Culture, and SED officials. It was agreed that similar meetings would take place on future Sundays.

On 23 October, on the eve of Egon Krenz's election as the GDR's head of state, about 300,000 demonstrated in Leipzig for free elections and against a 'new concentration of power'. Thousands also protested in

Dresden, Magdeburg, Zwickau and East Berlin. Demonstrations against Krenz's election were called for the following day.

On 25 October in a live television interview on West German television Günter Schabowski stated that discussions with opposition groups had been under way for some time. He had also asked Church authorities to use their influence to ensure that demonstrations remained peaceful. In Neubrandenburg, after prayers for peace, 20,000 took part in a 'march of hope'. Mayor Heinz Hahn proposed discussions during the weekend and on following Saturdays.

On 26 October about 100,000 people attended a meeting in Dresden at which the mayor reported on a special session of the city council. Specialist groups, including citizens among their members, had been set up. On 28 October tens of thousands demonstrated in Plauen, Greiz, Rostock, Senftenberg and elsewhere for 'meaningful reforms in all areas of social life'. On 30 October over 200,000 in Leipzig cross-examined Mayor Seidel and other officials about the 'desolate housing situation' and the slow 'processing of complaints'.

On 4 November in East Berlin over 500,000 attended a demonstration for reform in the GDR, the largest ever demonstration in the GDR not organized by the SED. At the five-hour event, called by the artists' associations, 26 speakers, including the writers Stefan Heym and Christa Wolf, accused Erich Honecker of 'mistakes, omissions and crimes'. Similar demonstrations, stressing the urgency for political, economic and cultural change, took place throughout the country. On 7 November in Wismar 50,000 and in Meiningen 20,000 demonstrated for 'free elections and against the power monopoly of the SED'.

On 18 November over 150,000 demonstrated in East Berlin, Leipzig and Dresden against the power monopoly of the SED and for free elections. Over 50,000 attended the first legal meeting of 'Neues Forum'. Forum speaker Jochen Lässig called Egon Krenz an 'election falsifier and a friend of Chinese terror'.

On 11 December over 100,000 Leipzigers participated in the tenth Monday demonstration since 7 October; 90,000 came together in Dresden, 40,000 in Karl-Marx-Stadt, and there were large crowds in many other cities. At all demonstrations there were calls for and against German reunification. On 18 December 150,000 took part in Leipzig in the traditional Monday evening demonstration. On the initiative of Kurt Masur, it was dedicated to the 'victims of violence and spiritual oppression under Stalinist rule'. In East Berlin several hundred people commemorated the 'victims of Stalinism' in a silent march.

The traditional Monday demonstrations continued to take place in Leipzig and other cities, but the focus of attention changed. They orientated themselves more towards policy and the future. Issues such as German reunification became very important and, with elections brought forward to 18 March, West German politicians began to take part. This became very widespread in February and presented Federal politicians with a ready-made opportunity to address electors.

The power of the crowd played a major role in destroying the power of the SED. The party's refusal to enter debate about priorities was circumvented by large crowds, week after week, demanding reform and dialogue. The cradle of this revolution was Leipzig, and contributed to the weakness of the SED there. SED tactics were to disperse the crowds, but this could only be done if they remained relatively small. Once a crowd exceeded 100,000 in a city centre it became extremely difficult to control it. This was one of the reasons the security forces became so brutal and violent. A crowd of 200,000 or 300,000 could not be dispersed by them, and then the question of the use of the military had to be faced. Krenz has maintained that he was given an order by Honecker to use the military to break up the demonstrations in Leipzig but he refused to carry it out. Worker militias placed a statement in the *Leipziger Volkszeitung* to the effect that they would use force if ordered to do so. The fact that so little blood was spilt in Leipzig is due to the role of the Church and others, especially Masur, who became one of the heroes of the revolution. After Honecker had warned the population to remember what had happened in China Masur turned the Gewandhaus into a place for debate, and he and many other musicians tore up their SED party cards. The crowds throughout the GDR forced SED politicians to debate with them, and under these circumstances it is not surprising that they enjoyed little credibility and authority.

The inability of the SED to formulate cogent responses to popular demands handed the initiative over to other groups whose aims differed radically from those of SED socialism. The continued flow of refugees testified to the lack of hope about the future and the revelations about the corruption of the SED elite led to a precipitate decline in SED fortunes. Seldom has a political party lost power so rapidly.

Breaching the Wall

The opening of the Hungarian–Austrian border to GDR refugees on 11 September was the first link to break in the chain which isolated the country from the West. Breaching the Berlin Wall on 9 November tore the rest of that chain asunder. It also broke the spell of SED power. Before the opening of the Wall almost all East Germans had regarded the collapse of SED power as inconceivable. Now the impossible might happen, and with it the end of the fearfully efficient security police, the Stasi. Moreover, the holes in the Wall revealed that there was only one German nation. Honecker had previously defended the existence of the GDR by pointing to the achievements of existing socialism. He conceded that without such socialism the state had no reason to exist. He never expected socialism to fail, but his words proved very prophetic in November. Its collapse meant that it would have to give way to an economically more dynamic system – capitalism. The SED paid a high price for failure – extinction.

The resurrection of politics

The longer Honecker stayed in power, the more likely it was that all he stood for would go with him. His destructive role can be likened to that played by János Kádár in Hungary. Both men hung on too long, and in so doing failed to address all the key questions on the political agenda. They belonged to the Brezhnev generation, and their parties could only have survived if they had ruthlessly removed both men from power in the mid-1980s.

Honecker was in hospital several times during 1989 and when he left the Berlin Charité hospital after an operation for a malignant kidney tumour on 29 January 1990 he was judged too ill to be arrested. The lack of decisive action by the leadership to staunch the flow of refugees during the summer (such as ending visa-free travel to Czechoslovakia) was remarkable. This may have been due to Honecker's state of health, which paralysed decision-making, or to an inability to decide whether making concessions or using force was more likely to resolve the crisis. Using force was only an option while the size of the crowds did not exceed 100,000. But only a certain number of medium-sized crowds could be controlled by the security forces. The opposition realized that the authorities could not cope with demonstrations in many GDR cities simultaneously. Hence Monday evenings became a focal point for protest.

Since there could be no dialogue with the SED, initiative groups, such as New Forum, began forming. They were composed of artists, intellectuals, clergy and others who expressly avoided using the word 'party' to describe their group. The first opposition group to apply for recognition as an association was the New Forum. Their application was rejected by the Ministry of the Interior on 21 September 1989 on the grounds that they were 'hostile to the state'. New Forum actively recruited new members, and those involved were often fined. By 14 October, when 100 New Forum representatives met in East Berlin to co-ordinate their efforts, there were about 25,000 members.

After Gorbachev's visit it was only a matter of time before Honecker was forced to resign. However, he was determined to cling on to power as long as possible, and this split the SED Politburo. Some of his supporters remained loyal to the bitter end, and thereby ended their own political careers. Honecker commented publicly on the flight of refugees for the first time on 13 October. His lame comment was that no one could be 'indifferent' to the loss of citizens. All he could offer the beleaguered party and state was the promotion of the 'strategic concept of continuity and renewal'. No tangible reforms were in sight.

The coup against Honecker

Key roles in the conspiracy against Honecker were played by Günter Schabowski, SED leader in East Berlin, General Markus Wolf, head of GDR counter-intelligence until he was dismissed by Honecker in late 1986 for being Moscow's man rather than the General Secretary's man, and General Erich Mielke, Minister of State Security. Honecker explicitly trusted Mielke but, in the end, confused personal friendship with loyalty to the Party leader. It appears that Mielke had discovered that Honecker had not been a model anti-fascist inmate during his imprisonment under the Nazis. It was probably Markus Wolf who had procured the relevant documents for the Stasi chief. Schabowski liaised closely with the Soviet ambassador in East Berlin, Vyacheslav Kochemasov.

Seven of the 23 members of the SED Politburo were privy to the plot. At a Politburo meeting on 18 October Stoph rose to propose that Honecker be relieved of all his functions. The startled General Secretary soon recovered his balance and stoutly defended himself. His self-confidence evaporated when Mielke hinted that he would publish the incriminating prison material if the General Secretary did not go.

At the 9th Plenum of the SED Central Committee on 18 October Honecker asked to be relieved of all his functions: as SED General Secretary; Member of the Politburo, Chairman of the GDR Council of State and Chairman of the National Defence Council. Joachim Herrmann and Günter Mittag, who had stood shoulder to shoulder with the General Secretary, were also dismissed from their functions as Politburo members and Central Committee Secretaries. Egon Krenz, long regarded as the *Kronprinz* (crown prince), became the new SED leader, Krenz's career pattern was almost identical to that of Honecker's. He was a previous leader of the FDJ, the Communist youth movement, and afterwards Central Committee Secretary for Security. He had been cultivated by the Soviets, and although Gorbachev would have preferred Hans Modrow, he had to make do with Krenz who, however, remained a prisoner of his own background and proved quite incapable of imaginative leadership.

Krenz had several crosses to bear from the beginning. Due to a previous illness, he had dark shadows under his eyes, and this gave him the appearance of being always the worse for drink. He was linked to the blatant falsification of the results of the May 1989 elections, which purported to show that the SED was as popular as ever. Then there was his ill-advised trip to China. But worst of all, he was the overlord of the Stasi. On the following day, Krenz met Bishop Werner Leich, chairman of the GDR Evangelical Church Union, and resolved to 'engender trust and to dare to build up trust'. The official communiqué was silent about demands for an open and very frank dialogue with the population and the involvement of reform groups such as New Forum.

On 22 October the first Soviet criticism of the Honecker leadership appeared in the trade union newspaper *Trud*. This was scathing in its condemnation of the old regime, and in a nice turn of phrase claimed it had 'erected a wall without windows and doors' to keep out GDR reality. The result of this short-sighted policy was that tens of thousands had quit the country.

On 24 October the Volkskammer (Parliament) elected Krenz as Chairman of the Council of State (President) with 26 voting against and 26 abstaining. The votes all came from the non-socialist parties. Only eight voted against and 17 abstained when he was elected Chairman of the National Defence Council. Krenz spoke of a possible change in the electoral law, but the same evening 12,000 demonstrated in East Berlin against his election to the two high state offices.

On 1 November, on his first visit to Moscow as Party leader, Krenz referred to *perestroika* and the new political thinking as a 'constant stimulus to social progress'. Gorbachev was confident that the SED was capable of 'boldly pursuing the course of renewal'.

The Central Committee plenum on 8 November 1989 opened with a sensation. The whole Politburo resigned and a new, slimmer, Politburo replaced it. There were up to 66 votes against some of the candidates. The new Politburo had eleven (formerly 21) full members and six (five) candidate members. The new full members were Hans Modrow, First Secretary in Bezirk Dresden and soon to succeed Willi Stoph as Prime Minister; Wolfgang Herger, chairman of the Volkskammer youth committee; Wolfgang Rauchfuss, deputy Prime Minister; and Gerhard Schürer, chairman of the State Planning Commission. All the others were from the old Politburo. Among those dropped were Kurt Hager (responsible for ideology); Erich Mielke (Stasi chief); Willi Stoph (Prime Minister) and Harry Tisch (trade unions). This did not satisfy Party members, and thousands demonstrated in front of the Central Committee building in East Berlin for a 'party leadership that listens to the people'.

This was the plenum which took the decision to open the Berlin Wall. Hundreds of thousands crossed into West Berlin, most of them without any checking of documents. By 30 November another 50 crossing points had been opened.

The Central Committee plenum ended on 10 November with an 'action programme' which included free elections, a new criminal code and freedom of association. It was also announced that four Politburo members, elected two days before, had been forced by pressure from below to resign. They included three district first secretaries who were obliged to resign these positions as well. Also, as a result of pressure from below, the Party Conference called for mid-December was transformed into an extraordinary Party Congress.

On 17 November Hans Modrow presented his new government to the Volkskammer. There were 28 (previously 44) ministers, of whom 16 were from the SED. Four were Liberal Democrats, three Christian Democrats, two National Democrats and two from the Peasants' Party. Nine ministers, including Oskar Fischer, Foreign Affairs, survived from the old government. The Ministry of State Security (Stasi) was dissolved and replaced by the Office of National Security under Wolfgang Schwanitz (SED). The Volkskammer also set up a commission to examine 'abuses of power, corruption and personal enrichment' of members of the Honecker regime.

Modrow built up a solid reputation as prime minister mainly because he emphasized that he spoke for all GDR citizens. Nevertheless, the government had limited authority, since it still excluded the new political groupings. Pressure told, however, and the first meeting of a Round Table was called by the SED for 7 December 1989.

Turmoil within the ranks of the SED resulted in the whole Politburo and Central Committee resigning on 3 December. This astonishing move was necessary in order to protect the party from 'extinction'. A working committee was set up to guide the party until the extraordinary Party Congress. It was also decided to expel Honecker and eleven other members of the old party and state leadership from the SED. Gregor Gysi, later to become Party leader, headed a commission to examine illegal activities by previous and present officials. Gysi reported on 5 December that his commission already had 'thousands of examples' of malfeasance.

On 6 December Krenz resigned as Chairman of the Council of State and Chairman of the National Defence Council. On the same day, the SED Congress was brought forward a week and was due to open on 8 December. It began its deliberations during the evening and stayed in session for 17 hours. Gysi was elected Party Chairman with over 95% of delegates in favour. The Party Congress concluded its deliberations on 16–17 December. It still claimed 1.7 million members, and in an attempt to change its fortunes it changed its name. The new party was called the SED-Party of Democratic Socialism (SED-PDS). This mouthful would last until party members agreed on a new name.

A new leadership (Parteivorstand) was elected with a ten-member Presidium. The SED-PDS was only nominally one party. Several groups established themselves with their own platforms. Krenz's party career ended on 21 January 1990, when he and 13 former full and candidate members of the Politburo were expelled from the party. Forty-seven members, expelled under Ulbricht, were rehabilitated. On the same day, Wolfgang Berghofer, Mayor of Dresden and deputy chairman of the SED-PDS Parteivorstand, and 39 other Dresden party members, resigned from the party and called for its dissolution. It did not dissolve, but on 4 February 1990 changed its name to the Party of Democratic Socialism (PDS). Gysi reported on 15 February that the PDS had about 700,000 members – a long way short of the 2.3 million the SED had had in mid-1989.

Gysi, a bespectacled Berlin Jewish lawyer, totally lacked charisma but was accepted as a comrade with clean hands. He failed to revive the fortunes of a party racked by deep antagonisms between the base and the leadership. One of the reasons for this was the daily revelations of corruption of the SED elite. The announcement of criminal charges against Honecker and others did not help matters. Probably the only SED official who could have salvaged something from the wreck of a once-omnipotent party was Hans Modrow, but he was politically too astute to try.

If Gysi's task was well-nigh impossible that of Modrow, the Prime Minister, was almost as difficult. Head of a government which was composed of the old political forces, he had to contend with the rising authority of the new political parties and groups. The front-runner had been the New Forum. It made a breakthrough on 26 October when Schabowski, Berlin First Party Secretary, met two of its leaders, Jens Reich and Sebastian Pflugbeil. Its first officially sanctioned meeting, which attracted 50,000 people, was in Leipzig on 18 November 1989. New Forum was a coalition of opponents of SED rule but did not develop into a political party. There were in reality two CDU parties until the elections of 18 March 1990. One consisted of those members elected to the Volkskammer under Honecker, many of whom continued to support the SED-PDS. The other CDU was modelled on its Western sister party and developed, against all expectations, into the strongest party in the GDR. On 10 November 1989 Lothar de Maizière, later to become GDR Prime Minister, was elected chairman. On 20 January 1990 twenty conservative Christian, liberal groups came together in Leipzig to form the German Social Union (DSU), and Pastor Hans-Wilhelm Ebeling was elected its first chairman. Democratic Awakening (DA), another conservative group, led by Wolfgang Schnur and Pastor Rainer Eppelmann, also had its base in Leipzig. These three formed a coalition on 1 February to fight the elections of 18 March. On 5 February in West Berlin it was given the name of Alliance for Germany, and thereby declared its main aim to be the rapid unification of Germany.

The Social Democrats chose 7 October 1989, the 40th anniversary of the founding of the GDR, to re-emerge from their long-enforced cohabitation with the SED. A Social Democratic Party in the GDR (SPD) was founded in Schwante, near Potsdam. The historian, Ibrahim Böhme, was elected leader. It developed close relations with the West German SPD and on 27 October, in Bonn, Steffen Reiche, one of its leaders, stated that the West German party would support its application for membership of the Socialist International and 'preferred' it as future discussion partners in the East.

A major problem for the Social Democrats was their attitude to the reunification of Germany. They proposed at their programme congress on 18 December in Berlin that a community treaty be negotiated between the two German states. This would then lead to a confederation. At the founding congress of the GDR SPD in Leipzig on 25 February Böhme was elected chairman and Willy Brandt, honorary chairman. An SPD aim was to ensure that the tender plant of democracy in the GDR would be allowed to flourish before the two Germanies embraced one another tightly. Despite the eloquence of Brandt and other leading Social Democrats, this message fell on deaf ears. The economic plight of the country swayed many workers to vote for the Conservatives, who promised economic union and the introduction of the deutschmark.

GDR liberals could count on the support of Hans-Dietrich Genscher's party in the Federal Republic, the FDP. An Alliance of Free Democrats, consisting of the German Forum Party (DFP), the Liberal Democratic Party (LDP) and the Free Democratic Party (FDP), came together to fight the election. The original front-runner, New Forum, moved to the left and linked up with Democracy Now and Peace and Human Rights Initiative to form Alliance 90 for the election.

On 7 December 1989 an 'alternative' government came into being, one which represented the new constellation of political forces. Called a Round Table, it met on the initiative of the Evangelical Churches in the GDR and twelve parties and groups were represented. The CDU, Peasants, LDP, National Democrats and New Forum had three representatives. The SED, Democracy Now, Democratic Awakening, the Greens, Peace and Civil Rights Initiative, SDP and United Left each had two. After protests by trade unionists, two FDGB members joined as did two from the Independent Women's League. Three other organizations were granted observer status. The Round Table proposed Volkskammer elections for 6 May 1990 and the preparation of a new constitution to be confirmed by referendum. It also demanded that the Office for National Security be dissolved under civilian control, that the true ecological, economic and financial plight of the country be revealed, that the government informed the Round Table of key pending decisions and that members participated in the decision-making process. The election date was subsequently brought forward.

The Round Table met 16 times under the able chairmanship of the theologian Wolfgang Ullmann. A founder-member of Democracy Now and a minister in Modrow's government, Ullmann deftly brought the often acrimonious debates back to basic essentials. When an embarrassed Krenz apologized awkwardly for falsifying the May 1989 election results Ullmann, in the silence which greeted these words, replied: 'I accept, as a citizen and as a Christian, your apology.'

The worsening economic situation made Modrow's position almost untenable, and on 29 January 1990 he announced the formation of a 'government of national responsibility', which would run the country until the 18 March elections.

The change of mood towards German reunification emerged from opinion polls. A *Neues Deutschland* poll of East Berliners, published on 24 November 1989, found that 83% were in favour of the continued existence of a sovereign, socialist GDR but only 19% would be willing to vote SED. A poll of young people in Leipzig between 20 and 27 November found 16% strongly in favour of a united Germany and 29% strongly against; 31% would vote SED, 17% for the New Forum and 10% for CDU. Also in late November a poll in Neubrandenburg revealed 39% in favour of a united Germany. On 29 December a poll in East Berlin resulted in 34% saying they would vote for the SED-PDS and 7.9% for the CDU. A Leipzig poll, published on 6 February 1990 about the forthcoming elections, found 59%

preferring the SPD, 12% the PDS, 11% the CDU but only 4% the New Forum. By then, the SPD and PDS were in favour of a united Germany, but the crucial question was how quickly this would come about.

The election results of 18 March 1990 stunned the SPD and delighted the Alliance for Germany and the PDS. It overturned all the opinion polls, since it had been expected that the Social Democrats would gain most from the discomfiture of the Communists. The Alliance lost a few votes due to the revelation that Wolfgang Schnur, chairman of Democratic Awakening, had been a Stasi informer for over a quarter of a century. The campaign was a personal triumph for the West German Chancellor Helmut Kohl. During the week before the elections he addressed over a million people in six cities, ending with a huge rally in Leipzig attended by up to 300,000 on 15 March.

The first and last democratically elected GDR government was agreed on 9 April. A grand coalition of the Conservatives, Social Democrats and Liberals, it was headed by Lothar de Maizière. Social Democrats obtained the key posts of Foreign Affairs, Health and Employment.

The contentious issue of the exchange rate between the ostmark and the deutschmark was resolved on 23 April 1990. Monetary union was set for 1 July with salaries, wages, pensions, and cash and savings up to 4000 ostmarks being exchanged at parity.

The grand coalition lasted until mid-August, when the Prime Minister, Lothar de Maizière, dismissed Walter Romberg (SPD), the Finance Minister, and Peter Pollak (non-party but nominated by the SPD), the Minister of Agriculture. Two other ministers, one CDU and the other non-party, also resigned. Romberg and Pollak were dismissed for 'incompetence' but refused to go. This led to the SPD withdrawing its other five ministers and the collapse of the grand coalition. The Prime Minister did not call for new elections but nominated state secretaries to carry out the functions of the former ministers. Social democrats were very critical of de Maizière's action, seeing it as the beginning of the election campaign. These were to take place in East Germany on 14 October when the region was again to be divided into five Länder. The SED had abolished the Länder in 1952, replacing them with Bezirks. Each Land was to elect its own parliament and government – as in West Germany. A provisional agreement to unite the two German states also on 14 October foundered when the SPD refused to agree. Instead, 3 October 1990 was nominated as unification day. Pan-German elections were set for 2 December 1990.

The main political parties, the Christian Democrats (CDU), Social Democrats (SPD) and Liberals (FDP) fused to become all-German parties. The West German electoral law – according to which the pan-German elections were to be held on 2 December – requires a party to obtain at least 5% of the total vote in order to enter parliament. The SPD was keen to retain this clause since it wished to keep the Communists (PDS) out of the new Bundestag. The PDS and other small parties appealed against this and the Constitutional Court upheld the appeal. In order for the PDS and other minnows to enter the new parliament they only had to poll at least 5% of the East German vote.

The East German economy declined alarmingly and unemployment soared to over a million by the time of unification. Part of the problem was the inexperience of the East German government and officials. The lack of impact of the Treuhandanstalt, responsible for keeping the 9000 enterprises afloat, was painfully obvious. West German businessmen were unwilling to invest heavily for four main reasons: the complicated and confused legal system, which made it impossible to decide quickly who owned what; the heavily indebted East German enterprises; the pollution problem; and rapidly rising unemployment. Who was to pay for the cleansing of the environment and the redundancy pay (if any) of the dismissed workers and employees? Confidence about the viability of some sectors of the East German economy quickly evaporated. Chemicals, open-cast mining, steel, textiles and even agriculture soon proved to be liabilities. Some West German concerns were holding back until the East German elections of 14 October, but most were waiting for the results of the pan-German elections on 2 December. A CDU–CSU victory was needed to boost investment confidence.

Critical foreign policy decisions had to be taken before the new Germany could become a sovereign state. The key player was the Soviet Union. President Mikhail Gorbachev's triumphal tour of West Germany in June 1989 was a watershed in relations between the two countries. By February 1990 Gorbachev was giving the green light to German unification. It was up to the Germans themselves to decide on the terms, conditions, speed and timing. However, a major problem was the future Germany's membership of NATO. Chancellor Kohl insisted on it but Gorbachev, mindful of the increasing influence of the Soviet military on Soviet decision making, refused to concede this point. Gorbachev and his Foreign Minister Eduard Shevardnadze began to promote the idea of Germany belonging to both NATO and the Warsaw Pact. The Soviets pushed this idea at the 'two plus four' talks (the two German states; and the USA, the USSR, Britain and France) which got under way in Bonn on 5 May 1990. However, the proposal was turned down by President Bush at the Washington summit with Gorbachev in May-June 1990. The Soviet Union's economic weakness turned the tide in favour of the West Germans. At a very relaxed meeting on Gorbachev's home ground in Stavropol the Soviet leader conceded that Germany could be a member of NATO. Soviet troops were to be out of East Germany by 31 December 1994, Bonn was to pay much of the cost of garrisoning Soviet troops and rehousing them in the Soviet Union (DM12 billion plus a DM3 billion loan), no nuclear, biological or chemical weapons were to be stored on East German soil by the Bundeswehr and its numbers were to be cut to 370,000 troops. It was a personal triumph for Chancellor Helmut Kohl and his Foreign Minister, Hans-Dietrich Genscher. In face-to-face diplomacy with the Soviet superpower they had achieved the unification of Germany and the restoration of full sovereignty. Germany and the Soviet Union also signed a treaty of friendship and co-operation which envisages that Germany will become the USSR's main trading partner. In late September East Germany withdrew from the Warsaw Pact and ceased to be a member of Comecon. However, East German obligations entered into before unification will be honoured by Germany. Four-Power responsibility for Germany ended on 12 September 1990 with the Moscow treaty.

The treaty unifying the two German states was signed on 31 August 1990 in East Berlin by Wolfgang Schäuble, the West German Minister of the Interior, and Günther Krause, state secretary to the GDR Prime Minister. The document, over 200 pages in length, had been initialled in Bonn the previous night. Unification day was 3 October and Berlin was to become the German capital. It was stated that the seat of parliament and the government would be decided after unification (in the event, and despite much procrastination and intense lobbying by those with vested interests in keeping Bonn the home of the parliament of the new Germany, in June 1991 it was decided that Berlin would once more be made the seat of parliament and government). President von Weizsäcker, who became President of Germany, will, however, reside in Berlin.

Unification was celebrated at midnight on 2 October, when the federal flag was hoisted in front of the Reichstag in Berlin and a bell rang out. Over a million people passed under the Brandenburg Gate to mark the occasion. Their joy was not shared by two groups, Communists and Anarchists. The latter took to the streets on 3 October, a national holiday, and riot police had to intervene. Mindful of international concern about the political and economic power of the new Germany, Chancellor Kohl and President von Weizsäcker appealed to Germans, in the euphoria of the present, never to forget the guilt of the past.

The elections of 14 October saw the CDU, with 43.6% of the vote, strengthen its position as the leading party in the East. The SPD moved up to 25.2% and the FDP also gained, up to 7.8%. The losers were the Left/ PDS, which dropped to 11.6% from 16.4% in March 1990. All five Land governments were coalitions but the CDU provided the Prime Minister in four Länder and only Brandenburg has a Social Democrat as head of government.

The pan-German elections of 2 December 1990 were a triumph for Chancellor Kohl. The CDU became the strongest German party, securing 36.7% of the national vote (43.4% in East Germany) and replacing the SPD, which dropped to 33.5% (23.6% in the East). The coalition of CDU–CSU and FDP (11% of the national vote) has an overall majority of 108 seats in the Bundestag, the largest ever in postwar German politics. The PDS polled 9.9% of the East German vote (down from 15.2% in March 1990) but only 0.3% of the West German vote. Nevertheless, it entered the Bundestag with 17 deputies. The Alliance '90/Green coalition obtained 5.9% of the East German vote and therefore joined the PDS in parliament. The other East German parties failed to reach the 5% threshold and were therefore excluded.

End of an era

Many people will be sorry to bid farewell to the GDR. It represented a Germany which had developed distinct characteristics. Life for the opposition was never easy, but it engendered a camaraderie which may now be lost. The GDR had a distinct smell about it. Most of the odours were (and are) life-endangering – such as in Halle and Bitterfeld – but there is often an old-world charm which reminds one of pre-war Germany. In many towns the cobbled streets and shops have hardly changed over the last half century, and the country must have the largest collection of antique railway stations in the world.

Not all party members will mourn the passing of the SED. Under the leadership of Erich Honecker it managed to lead the country to ruin. Possessed of immense power and a population which knew the limits of dissent, it nevertheless ended in oblivion. In postwar Eastern Europe the Polish Communists were held to be the least gifted, to put it politely, but there must now be some doubt about this. The SED must be in the running for the prize for incompetence, corruption and stupidity. During his many appearances before the commission of enquiry into party behaviour, Honecker never conceded that he had been wrong. He appears to have led a life apart, and to have become detached from reality. After he left hospital in January he was judged too frail to be imprisoned. A pastor and his family offered to welcome Honecker and his wife Margot (the long-serving Minister of Education) into their family circle. Eventually the Honeckers had to leave since there were too many people who wanted to send them to the next world. Moscow intervened in April 1991 to spare Honecker the indignity of standing trial for the murder of GDR citizens trying to leave the country. He was moved from a Soviet military hospital near Berlin to Moscow to undergo special medical treatment. It was conveniently overlooked that medical facilities in Berlin were superior to those in Moscow. It is not known whether Erich and Margot requested Moscow's permission to die in the Soviet Union or whether the Soviet authorities decided that the former SED General Secretary was privy to too many secrets to be allowed to stand trial in a German court.

The Honeckers and the GDR elite lived under Communism – they had everything they wanted and did not need money – but they forgot that the population had to live under socialism. Only one or two of the elite were capable of showing remorse about the past. The others blithely defended themselves before the commission, arguing that they performed their functions and the leader led. Krenz claimed that the Soviet ambassador in East Berlin made them believe that Moscow would rescue them. This is one reason why the SED failed. At some point of time during the 1980s it passed the point of redemption. The GDR was the SED's child. It was most healthy in its thirties (in the 1970s) but at forty it was senile, and expired soon afterwards.

A hard road to prosperity

The German Democratic Republic was swallowed up by the Federal Republic at unification, as if the GDR had never existed. In the ecstasy of unity it was expected that the five East German Länder would sit easily – after a few teething problems – with the existing eleven West German Länder. Nothing could have been further from the truth. The East German mood has turned quickly to one of disillusionment over the bitter fruits of unity.

Bonn got the economics of East Germany all wrong. At monetary union the exchange rate was much too generous. The first 4000 marks of savings were exchanged at parity, then the rest, savings and debts, were exchanged at one to two, against a former black market rate of one to ten. The exchange rate chosen by Bonn made most people instantly better off while ruining the competitiveness of East Germany's industry by straddling it with large deutschmark debts. East Germans are now asked to work for wages which are a mere fraction of their new deutschmark savings. They are used to regarding equal wages and employment opportunities as civil rights.

The Treuhandanstalt, responsible for the privatization of about 9000 enterprises, has been fiercely criticized. On 1 April 1991 its head, Detlev Rohwedder, was assassinated. By then, its record on paper did not appear so dreadful: only 1.5% of enterprises closed down (including Interflug, the former state airline), 12.5% sold off and another 25% under negotiation. However, many of those sold had large workforces, and West German companies were only willing to make the investment at the cost of large-scale redundancies. For example, Robotron, an electronics firm, reduced its staff from 68,000 to 15,000. Many fear that by the end of 1991 the ever-rising rate of unemployment in eastern Germany will embrace 50% of the workforce. Chancellor Helmut Kohl was forced to break his electoral promise not to raise taxes to pay for East German development. An aid package of DM80 billion has been agreed, but this is a drop in the ocean of what eventually will be needed. Cleaning up eastern Germany's rivers, lakes and water supply would run to DM60 billion alone, according to one estimate.

The political and social consequences of the collapse of the East German economy are still unknown but East Germans believe as Germans they should live as well as West Germans. Most wages, at present, are 40–60% of West German rates and are to achieve parity by 1994. However, it will be extremely difficult to get East German productivity rates up to the level of West Germany by 1994.

A gradual approach towards transformation has been adopted by other

East European states. Eastern Germany is unique in attempting to adjust to a full-blooded market economy overnight. Not surprisingly, the results have been disastrous. However, what matters is the long-term. Few doubt that eastern Germany has a future – or that the road to prosperity will be long and hard.

5 HUNGARY

The reason Communism fell apart in Hungary, according to the Budapest version, is that it rotted away. This contains an element of truth and begs a number of questions as well. Above all, it demands, almost insistently, why? What made conditions in Hungary so different from the other Communist countries that the Soviet-type system disintegrated quietly? Why did the ruling Communists not put up much of a fight? What determined the composition of the forces that replaced them?

The answers are partly to be found in the remote past, in the origins of the Kádár régime and in the way in which the system was put together after the revolution of 1956, and partly in the particular circumstances of the mid-1980s, when the system needed a new infusion of energies, which was impossible because of the way in which it had been put together. Crucially Kádár's own role as a conservative innovator who could not move with the times requires particular scrutiny.

The modern Hungarian state emerged from the ruins of the Austro-Hungarian Empire in 1918. It was much reduced in size, however, losing some two-thirds of its territory (to Romania, Serbia and Czechoslovakia) at the Treaty of Trianon in 1920. A four-month Communist regime, headed by Béla Kun, ended in August 1919 when the Romanian army marched into Budapest. Hungary subsequently came under the conservative rule of Miklós Horthy, a former admiral in the Austro-Hungarian Navy who was appointed head of state in 1920.

In the course of the 1930s Hungary came under German influence. When war came it profited from German goodwill by regaining some of the territories lost in 1920. Although it also sent a contingent to fight alongside the Germans on the eastern front Hungary was never more than a lukewarm ally of the Nazis. After Horthy had signed a treaty with the Soviets in October 1944, he was arrested by the Germans and replaced by a fascist stooge, Ferenc Szálasi. By April 1945 Hungary had been liberated by the Red Army.

Hungary emerged then from the war under Soviet occupation and was reduced to its pre-war territory. Its people were exhausted and eager for reform of the social and political order. The Communist Party had been declared illegal for most of the interwar period. At the end of the war some of its members (Mátyás Rákosi, Ernö Gerö, Imre Nagy) returned from abroad, while others (László Rajk, János Kádár, Gyula Kállai) came out of hiding. Although its base of support was weak – it had only 3,000 members in November 1944 – within twelve months this figure had grown to almost

HUNGARY

Official name	The Republic of Hungary
Area	93,030 sq. km (35,910 sq. miles)
Population	10,569,000 (annual growth rate 0.2%)
Capital	Budapest
Language	Hungarian
Religion	54% Roman Catholic, 22% Hungarian Reformed Church, Lutheran and Orthodox minorities
Currency	forint

half a million. It was not sufficient to gain them political hegemony. In the first, largely free, postwar elections in November 1945, the Communists received support from only 17% of the electorate. The outcome was a victory for the Smallholders Party (KGP) but Soviet pressure led to the inclusion of Communists in the government.

By the next elections, in August 1947, although Communist support had increased only to 22%, the Communists formed the largest single party. At the beginning of the following year they exercised effective control of the Hungarian state and government having used their notorious 'salami tactics' to eliminate the rival parties one by one as serious opponents. In the May 1949 election, the Hungarian 'People's Front for Independence' was able to put forward a single list of candidates before the electorate. Following their predictable success the Communists introduced a new constitution modelled on Soviet lines. Hungary became a republic of 'workers and peasants'.

Under Stalinist rule, Hungary followed a predictable pattern; it became a police state, with all opposition crushed and dissent stifled. In the economic sphere there was emphasis upon the development of heavy industry, agriculture was collectivized, and there was a rapid shift from private to state ownership. Following Stalin's death in 1953 a struggle developed between Imre Nagy and Mátyás Rákosi, Party first secretary, for political supremacy. In 1955 Rákosi regained political dominance, and Nagy was expelled from the Party. By the time the Soviets realized their mistake and removed him in mid-1956, Rákosi's hardline regime had stirred up so much hostility and opposition that the Party and its security apparatus were unable to control it. What began as a student demonstration in Budapest at the end of October turned into a full-scale uprising and a battle for the capital.

Although Imre Nagy was restored as premier and victory seemed assured (the secret police was disbanded and Soviet tanks withdrew), impressions were deceptive. While the country prepared to take a new political course, which included a multi-party system and neutrality (Nagy issued a declaration on 1 November that Hungary was leaving the Warsaw Pact), the Soviet leadership was planning how to crush the revolution. The second and decisive stage of the campaign began on 4 November when the Red Army returned in force, inflicting heavy damage on the capital and thousands of casualties. Dozens of the insurgent leaders were arrested and tried. Imre Nagy and a handful of close collaborators were executed for their 'treason' – martyred in the eyes of the overwhelming majority of the nation.

In the wake of the revolution the Soviets chose János Kádár to be the new premier and Party leader. After 1956, Kádár had a complex task and little time in which to do it. He had to re-establish his power, reorganize the Communist Party that had fallen apart in the revolution, break down the resistance of the population, end the general strike and liquidate the institutions that the revolution had created. He could not be too discriminating about the means and he did not have much of a choice either. He had to use harsh methods and to rely on discredited Stalinist elements, who wanted revenge for the shock they had suffered in the revolution. Kádár's tactics were to use every possible lie in negotiating with the Workers' Councils, the strongest representatives of the people, and to arrest and imprison opponents.

He had to convince the population that resisting the might of the Soviet Union was useless and that the Communist system was there to stay. For five years, he operated or presided over a reign of terror, in which thousands were executed, imprisoned and interned. Imre Nagy and four other leaders of the uprising were shot. By the early 1960s, Hungarian society was thoroughly cowed.

Kádár, however, was not Stalinist himself and he did not want to rule over a country run solely on the basis of terror, always assuming that this was possible. He had, after all, been a victim of Stalinism personally and his vision, presumably, was of an orderly, economically prosperous, disciplined system, in which everyone accepted his version of 'socialism' and worked towards it. Pivotally, he drew the lesson from the 1956 revolution that the people were not to be trusted with power. If they were given a choice, they would not exercise it in the way that he wanted. On the contrary all sorts of undesirable political aims would be pursued, such as a multi-party system, workers' self-management and spontaneity. In Kádár's view political choice was to be the preserve of the few and of individuals like himself, honest socialists.

Depoliticizing society

From that time, Kádár's tactics could be described as having evolved towards a strategy – depoliticize society and keep the population happy through economic concessions. To this end, the system needed both economic and administrative adjustments, many of which had political implications. The Communist Party would continue to insist on its monopoly of power, but this would no longer be defined in Stalinist terms as an absolute monopoly. The individual could now have some choice, as long as this did not impinge on the power of the Party, and when such trespasses took place was something defined solely by the Party. In other words, political monopoly was retained under a new and considerably more sophisticated redefinition. This dispensation was arrived at in its final form more by good luck than by good management, but it proved to be a most successful one from the Party's standpoint.

It offered a considerable flexibility in dealing with society, in the management of power and in the routinization of administration. Essentially, it gave the power elite wide-ranging discretion in the exercise of power – there were no fixed criteria for anything. This meant that every concession remained a concession and could not be transformed into a right. It provided opportunity for pragmatism – much admired by those in the West who entirely failed to understand the true nature of the system – and created just enough social space for different groups to find satisfaction. The satisfaction of social aspirations was, of course, made much easier by their previous forcible suppression after 1956 – people expected much less.

The trouble with this degree of discretion was that it gradually undermined the system of power itself. A power elite is not a small club of people who know each other personally, but a complex organism and, as such, it requires basic ground rules, some relatively clear and understandable criteria for the exercise of power. In Hungary, as in other Communist countries in the 1970s, the official ideology lost this cementing quality and it was not replaced by anything other than the ideology of power itself, coupled with the external threat of Soviet intervention. In the mid-1980s, the latter vanished and the former proved too weak to sustain the edifice of power for long. But in the 1960s, it still held.

In effect, the foundations of Kádárism were laid by the early 1960s. The peasantry, once it had reluctantly accepted that collectivization was there to stay, was left alone and given an incentive to produce. The output of the private plot could be sold on urban markets and the urban population's consumption of foodstuffs was secured thereby, unlike Poland where the rulers failed completely to achieve this. Collective units are notoriously inefficient in producing fruit, vegetables, poultry and eggs, but private enterprise, by relying on cash incentives for work done, could do so. At the same time, sections of the peasantry also prospered.

The industrial working class was offered the prospect of high levels of collective consumption through a variety of welfare provisions, coupled with lenient labour discipline, low productivity and a steady improvement in the standard of living. Egalitarianism, the crude levelling down of the 1950s, on the other hand, was off the agenda.

Intellectuals and intelligentsia

The deal extended to intellectuals and the intelligentsia (the former create values, the latter administer them as teachers, lawyers, managers, engineers, etc.) was the most complex, and went to the heart of the Kádár system. Under Stalinism, the creative independence of intellectuals and the administrative autonomy of the intelligentsia were brusquely ended because the system had no need of them. They were expected to sing the praises of socialism and that was all, because the Party, through its control of the past and the future, had the answers to everything.

Kádárism sought instead to incorporate these social-professional groups in order to use their talents. So the word went out that anyone honestly ready to use his or her talents would be deemed to be engaged in 'the construction of socialism'. This dealt adequately with the intelligentsia, which did not have serious aspirations to gain autonomy as well.

The creative intellectuals were more problematical, but here the system found a brilliant device. Instead of being forced to proclaim, as in the 1950s, that 'socialism was the most marvellous system in the world', they could say, in effect, 'the system that we have here in Hungary is full of defects, it does not work very well, it is open to criticism on a whole variety of grounds; but it is the best that we can hope to have'. This formula completely immobilized critical intellectuals and built self-censorship into their public utterances.

To secure its position, the Party let it be understood that there were two rules that had to be strictly observed – neither the basics of the system nor the relationship with the Soviet Union could be questioned. Not, the Party would hasten to add, because this was something that the Hungarians liked, but because the Soviet comrades preferred it that way. This subtly mendacious system of blackmail and self-deception was augmented by giving intellectuals and the intelligentsia access to material privileges, to information, to the outer fringes of power and *de facto* control over entry to higher education, which meant that those who had succeeded could live secure in the knowledge that their children would inherit their privileges and status.

The character of the system was, therefore, deeply opportunistic. There were no fixed standards. Everything was subject to the needs of the day, decided on by a political leadership that had largely lost its vision. It knew it wanted to hold on to power, but it could no longer justify it in any terms other than those of power. As the 1970s progressed, the official ideology was increasingly emptied of content. The ideals of equality, modernity and rationality – central to the Marxian idea of the future – were gradually lost as power-holders and intellectuals recognized that the system could not be adapted any further to meet these goals.

The forcible suppression of the 1968 'Prague spring' sent out the unmistakable signal that no East European country – Hungary included – had the freedom to go farther and faster than Moscow. Ideology was dead except as rhetoric. The Party then tried to legitimate its rule by insisting that it was the repository of rationality and efficiency, a claim that was increasingly difficult to make good in practice and, as far as the population was concerned, disproved by everyday life.

To make the mixture more palatable, the Party added a judicious amount of nationalism: that the Communist Party's rule was the most successful expression of Hungary's national destiny. This, too, was disproved by practice. Apart from the inherent implausibility of a self-proclaimed Marxist party pretending to be the best representative of the nation and of nationhood, the fate of the Hungarian minorities in the neighbouring states increasingly exercised Hungarian opinion, and the country's rulers were seen as incapable of doing anything to help the ethnic Hungarians in Czechoslovakia and Romania.

This left the Party with the threadbare proposition that it was the agent of a 'revolution', which no-one took very seriously, though it did make it impossible for Kádárism to come to terms with the (genuine) revolution of 1956. For Kádár, the events of that year were forever a 'counter-revolution', because it had defined its own myth in having seized power as a Marxist–Leninist party against the anti-Communists. That was the limit to the Kádárist integration strategy.

Declining legitimacy

As far as justification by power was concerned ('we rule because we rule'), this was vulnerable to any direct challenge to that power or threat of a challenge. Essentially, legitimation by power alone was a dangerously thin support, because any loss of power would weaken the core of the Party's rule, as eventually happened. Buying peace through economic expansion proved to be exposed to economic failure. Hence the successful management of the economic system was crucial for keeping it together.

The Kádár system earned many plaudits from Western observers for its apparent ability to run a reformed economy and to have discarded Marxist dogmas about central planning. The 1968 New Economic Mechanism (NEM) appeared to many to be a well-intended and intelligent attempt to combine central planning with market instruments, to mix the best of capitalism with socialism. It gave up physical allocation, instructing enterprises what and how much they should produce, and no longer treated the country's economy as a vast, single firm, the functioning of which could be known precisely by the country's central planning office. It appeared to accept that complexity and unforeseen transactions, conflicts of interests and individual choice were normal parts of a modern economy.

The authorities sought to reach their stated goals by indirect means. That was the theory. In practice, neither enterprise managers nor the central bureaucracy was ready to give up power and live with the risk of market failure, constant adaptation, technological change and high information flows required by the market model. But unlike Czechoslovakia, where the post-1968 restoration actually reversed similar reforms overtly, in Hungary the backward move took place behind a façade of reform-oriented language. This was a deception, but it had the advantage that the language of reform was never excluded from public discourse, so that the limits of debate were significantly wider than in Czechoslovakia. Nor did the Party attach issues of ideology and prestige to non-reversal of Marxist–Leninist orthodoxy, as happened in Prague, where the very word 'reform' was excluded from public utterance for the best part of two decades.

The reality was also different in Hungary, though not that different. The central plan was replaced by the 'plan bargain', by which every enterprise did a deal with the relevant branch ministry to regulate conditions for its operations – supplies, subventions and market shares. In this system, no-one ever had an incentive to make improvements. On the contrary, it favoured conservatism and bureaucratic politics rather than economic efficiency, though it maintained the external appearance of market operation.

It also left the economy firmly fenced in by political constraints. What enterprises could do were, beyond a certain point, determined by political power. When an enterprise was plainly uneconomic, its fate was decided not by financial criteria but by the economic power of the manager and his patrons in the Party and the branch ministry. If they had enough power, the enterprise would not be closed down but would be rescued and 'reorganized', and then helped to stay afloat through ever-higher central subventions. Clearly, there was no economic incentive to operate more efficiently, by, say, cutting costs or improving productivity.

The consequence was that the level of central support for much of industry was dangerously high – dangerously, because it could only be sustained by continuous and increasing foreign borrowing. It was evident by the late 1970s that the country's heavy industry was a severe burden, that it cost the country more than it produced and that restructuring, including closure, was the best way of saving the economy the large subsidies that it was paying to keep these firms alive. Politics, as ever, intervened. The heavy industry lobby was well entrenched politically. It was the source of power and patronage for Party secretaries and managers, so that the last thing they wanted was bankruptcy. Political power predictably won the day over economic rationality. Despite the sophisticated public relations job performed by Hungarian spokesmen in the 1970s and 1980s, the economy was declining, and only a steady infusion of Western credits kept it afloat. The legacy of this was a foreign debt of $21 billion by 1990 and the highest per capita indebtedness in Eastern Europe.

The New Economic Mechanism

The principal milestones of the rise and fall of the NEM are simply chronicled. The reform project came on stream on 1 January 1968 and looked dangerously bold on 21 August that year, the day when Czechoslovakia was invaded by the Warsaw Pact, including Hungarian troops. In November 1972, the Central Committee of the Hungarian party introduced a variety of restrictions on the reform, largely depriving it of its marketizing qualities while pretending that these were little more than course-corrections.

Two years later, the main architects of the reform were dropped from the Politburo and the new strategy was to give subventions to enterprises whose weaknesses had been exposed by the NEM and by the growing openness of the Hungarian economy to the world market. The size of central support increased quickly, until by 1979 even Kádár was convinced that a move back towards economic rationality – supply and demand – was advisable. The outcome was a cautious, conservative course that eliminated the worst excesses but left the main problem – the political obstacles to market rationality – untouched. Kádár's conservatism, as ever, got the better of him.

At this point it is worth noting again how significant it was that reform language (and hence the potential for re-opening the debate on reform) remained within the ambit of politics. Criticism of the situation began to grow and sections of the elite were influenced by this, so much so that the pressure to introduce more radical measures resulted in Kádár declaring in 1983 that there would be 'no reform of the reform'. Unlike Czechoslovakia, the intellectuals were not tied down by a narrowly circumscribed political system but had some leeway for thought and debate. The habits of criticism had not been marginalized by political power.

This had two consequences. The political leadership needed the intellectuals up to a point, more than they had thought, in order to legitimate their own ideas and strategies and were, as a result, vulnerable in this respect. Second, the intellectuals themselves were aware that they could make an impact on the political system. This was the sense in which the decay of the Kádár system took place from within, with only minimal popular participation.

From that point on, it was evident (though few accepted this in public) that as long as Kádár remained at the helm the system could only disintegrate from within. The external proprieties were maintained, but by the mid-1980s the stagnation was unmistakable. When, instead of adopting a market-oriented course, Kádár launched yet another 'acceleration' in 1986 (an investment drive with funds that he did not have but had to borrow from abroad), he was really saying that, despite his reputation for flexibility, he was no longer capable of changing with the times. From having been a conservative reformer he had become an opponent of all change, a true reactionary. That was the moment when Kádárism lost the backing – political, intellectual, psychological – of those supporting intellectuals who had played such a vital role in sustaining him from the early 1960s onwards.

Because the process in Hungary was a gradual one, there was no clear, visible, dramatic moment from when it is possible to date the beginning of the end. Nevertheless, the last months of 1986 saw increasing signs of the growing alienation from the regime of the previously supportive intellectuals. At the end of November, the country's writers, who traditionally enjoyed the role of being a surrogate opposition, met at the Writers' Union Congress and rebelled against the wishes of the Party, which essentially told them not to meddle with politics, as this was not their concern. On the contrary, the writers insisted, the alarming state of deterioration in Hungary was something that concerned all responsible intellectuals.

The economists, who formed an influential group and on whose ideas the Party and the economic bureaucracy leaned heavily (even if much of their advice was ignored), likewise withdrew its support from the Kádár system. In a wide-ranging document entitled *Turning-point and Reform* the economists strongly argued that, without radical changes in the direction of marketization, Hungary would head towards inevitable decline and collapse. 'Collapse' was, of course, a metaphor, but the physical reality of collapse was represented by next-door Romania, which had been dragged into an appalling state of poverty by Nicolae Ceauşescu's misconceived development strategy. What was particularly striking and influential in the document was the argument that the Communist model of development, when viewed in a perspective of four decades, had been much less effective than the market-based strategies employed in the Pacific Rim countries – Taiwan, South Korea, Singapore – which had already over-taken the Communist world economically.

Finally, the Kádár system also lost the support of the country's journalists at this time. Their role was an important one in reporting the general state of affairs, and their growing consternation at the state of the economy and society, coupled with the apparent complacency of the political leadership, represented a major loss to the regime. The journalists could not, of course, simply write what they saw, but whereas until then they had been prepared to live with the Kádárist constraints and respected the rules, they now insisted on writing more freely. This resulted in a constant battle with editors, who acted on Party instructions as censors, and over the months the editors' resistance was worn down. The result of this was that, by 1987, the Hungarian media were reporting more of the real situation. This major gap in the Party's control of the information available to the public made it possible for alternative, competing ideas to circulate and gradually, but irreversibly, undermined the Party's hold on public opinion. By the beginning of 1988 it was widely accepted that a change was essential, but the way in which this was to happen remained contested.

The central issue was, of course, that economic reform on its own was not enough. In order for the economy to respond effectively to supply and demand, the political impediments to this would have to be removed, and that obviously meant that the Party's control over the political system and power would have to be loosened. The recognition of this was the key element in the changing consciousness of the intellectuals. There were two broad strands – the work of the Party reformers and of the democratic opposition.

The Party reformers

The group known as the Party reformers were historians, jurists, sociologists and political scientists, with official posts, who had for some time been calling for a transformation of the Party's political monopoly into something more responsive to public opinion. The democratic opposition, on the other hand, had consciously taken a stand outside officialdom and chose marginalization. It had launched itself tentatively in 1977 and, in its earliest phases, relied on Polish and Czechoslovak models. After 1982 it embarked on a more directly political form of activity, mostly through *samizdat*, in calling for a transformation in Hungary on the basis of human rights and democracy. Their influence was hard to assess or quantify, but in the 1985 elections to parliament they were pleasantly surprised to discover that many of their ideas had been espoused by independent candidates who otherwise had no links with the democratic opposition at all. The implication was that the *samizdat* writings of the democratic opposition had much wider currency than they had imagined.

At more or less the same time, both the democratic opposition and the Party reformers launched a concept that has come to be known as 'constitutional Communism'. The idea behind this was that of one-party pluralism. The Communist Party would retain power, but this would no longer be absolute or a monopoly. Rather, it would be circumscribed by legal and political constraints, thereby enabling the market to function in the economy and the political leadership to gain greater legitimacy. The key document from the democratic opposition was entitled 'Social Contract', and it came from the group around the *samizdat* journal *Beszélő*. Its most striking feature was a call for Kádár to go. Without Kádár's removal from the leadership, the document recognized, no change was possible. The Party reformers were more circumspect in this respect, but they too demanded a political system with constraints on the power of the Party. Both groups proved to be influential, especially on sections of the Party itself, which was not, of course, immune to the growing ferment in the country.

By the early months of 1988 the atmosphere in Hungary had changed beyond recognition. The tight control of the Party over intellectual opinion was a thing of the past. There were dozens, if not hundreds, of discussion groups, many of them formally constituted, with explicitly political objectives. The most significant of these at the time was the Hungarian Democratic Forum.

The Forum, which subsequently went on to become the largest single political party in the 1990 general elections, was initially a loose discussion circle set up by the populists. The populists (in many respects a uniquely Hungarian phenomenon) were drawn from writers rather than social scientists, and they addressed their message to the country as a whole rather than to the intellectuals. They were a part of the opposition, but were in many ways more ready to deal with the Party than the democratic opposition proper, something which resulted in constant tension between the two. Both were committed to democracy, but the language of the populists was more nationalistic and more concerned with returning to true Hungarian traditions than the democratic opposition liked.

The social background of the two groups also set them apart. The democratic opposition was drawn primarily (though not exclusively) from the urban, Budapest, Jewish middle class and intelligentsia. Many of them were the children of established Communist figures and had had a Communist background themselves. They had abandoned this by the time they moved into opposition, of course, and were committed to human rights and democracy. The populists, on the other hand, were generally from the country, of a more humble background, mostly non-Jewish and had had no part in Marxism at all. This social difference also contributed to the tension between them.

Opposition rivalries

Over the years, some co-operation between the opposition currents did take place, though it was never easy. In 1987, in part as a direct response to the 'Social Contract' document (in the drafting of which they had played no role), the populists held a meeting at Lakitelek, a small town outside Budapest, from which the democratic opposition was largely excluded. This had long-term and highly negative consequences, and explained much of the rivalry between the two groups. The reason for the exclusion was that the Forum had succeeded in persuading the Party reformers to go to Lakitelek and, crucially, the leader of the Party reformers, Imre Pozsgay, had agreed to take part. Pozsgay had asked that the most radical members of the democratic opposition not be invited, calculating that thereby he could legitimate at least a section of the opposition without excessively offending the Party hardliners.

In this Pozsgay was successful, and the Forum thereafter had a recognized existence, neither legal nor illegal, but the price of this was a final and fatal breach with the democratic opposition. From September 1987, when the Lakitelek meeting took place, until November 1988, when the democratic opposition constituted itself as the Alliance of Free Democrats, the Forum held the initiative. It organized more or less monthly meetings (open forums) at which the democratic opposition was free to speak, but which were dominated by the populists. Various topics were debated – the state of the country, the national minorities in the successor states and the media. In this way, the Forum made a major contribution to the political radicalization of the intelligentsia.

By the spring of 1988, the situation in Hungary was widely described as 'fluid' and 'decaying'. The Party leadership (above all, Kádár himself) had no response to the increasing ferment except to make threatening noises. When four well-known intellectuals, who were also Party members, attended meetings of the Forum, all the Party could do was to expel them from its membership. This, if anything, made things worse. In effect, the leadership was not leading, and the ferment in intellectual life was beginning to affect the Party membership, which was far from immune to the country's problems and the changing mood.

The personality of Kádár became an important factor in this complex situation. Born in 1912, he was 75 years old at this time and was manifestly losing control. His speeches had become hesitant, repetitive and unconvincing. There were rumours circulating about his mental and physical health. Whether these were true or not was irrelevant. The fact that they were circulating was a symptom of his declining authority. When two senior Party figures came to him to suggest that perhaps he might like to retire, he is said to have retorted, 'You know what will happen then. They'll rehabilitate Imre Nagy'. It was like Banquo's ghost at the feast. This obstinate refusal either to change or to go evidently persuaded his opponents in the party to prepare a coup for his removal.

In one respect, Kádár made it easier by a speech that he made in March 1988, which destroyed all lingering respect for him. He insisted, in the face of all the evidence, that there was no crisis in Hungary. As far as the Soviet Union was concerned, the Kremlin had already signalled that there were no objections to getting rid of Kádár. At the 1987 celebrations of the anniversary of the October Revolution, Kádár was given a very low protocol position, a significant pointer to the declining esteem in which he was held.

The fall of Kádár

The Kádárist leadership was forced to make the concession of permitting the convening of a Party Conference (an event where all the Party bodies are represented, but without the weight of a Party congress) and this was scheduled for May 1988. Kádár's opponents used this to remove him, and relied on classic tactics. They established unity among themselves, agreed on a candidate of their own to succeed Kádár (Károly Grósz, the prime minister) and indicated that the post-Kádár leadership would be open to major changes. It went as expected, with only one surprise – the Conference was more radical than anyone had thought and sacked not only Kádár but all the senior Kádárists as well, so that eight out of 11 Politburo members were voted out.

The new leadership, however, turned out to be much weaker and more divided than expected. It seemed afterwards as if removing Kádár was the only point on which they were agreed. Grósz essentially looked towards some kind of an authoritarian model of economic efficiency and high levels of coercion. Pozsgay and the party reformers, on the other hand, were increasingly attracted by an open, democratic system. For all practical purposes, the outcome was a stalemate.

Grósz did nothing during the summer months, while Pozsgay accepted that the media could widen their already extensive freedom to comment. The situation deteriorated very rapidly and by August the questioning of Grósz's leadership had begun. Then Grósz made a mistake, which destroyed virtually all his authority. Hungarian opinion was increasingly worried over the fate of the ethnic Hungarian minority in Romania in connection with the 'systematization' policy of forced resettlement pursued by Ceauşescu. Grósz agreed to a one-day meeting in Arad with the Romanian leader and returned empty-handed, and was also rather offhand about it. This was enough to make him unacceptable to public opinion, and the signs of a widening political vacuum were unmistakable. Within a few days of the Arad meeting, the Hungarian Democratic Forum announced its existence as a political movement.

The months between the beginning of September and the end of November represented the watershed. In September, with a more determined leadership, the Communists might just have been able to seize the agenda and push through a reform programme of their own. By the end of November, it was too late. During those weeks, Hungarian society became aware of the weakness of Communist rule and of its own mounting political weight. Thus at a Central Committee meeting in early November the hardliners in the Party launched a major attack on the media, in the expectation of halting the trend towards greater openness. This was simply ignored. In addition, the Soviet Union, the conservatives' last redoubt, had also kept silent. In the past, the hardliners had always been able to eliminate criticism by referring to Soviet disapproval. This pretext for doing nothing had gone, as Gorbachev's reform programme progressed. To underline this, as it were, Hungary was visited at this time by the Soviet Politburo reformer, Alexander Yakovlev. From fragmentary evidence, it seems likely that Yakovlev told his hosts that the Kremlin had no objections to the Communist Party abandoning its monopoly, if that was the only way of revitalizing the country.

From the end of November, overtly political organizations began to emerge. Hungary had begun to assume the appearance of a multi-party system. The democratic opposition established itself as the Alliance of Free Democrats at this time and the so-called 'nostalgic parties', the Smallholders and the Social Democrats, which had taken part in the post-1945 coalition and briefly revived in 1956, once more returned to the political stage.

It was still far from clear, though, that the Party reformers had won the battle. Pozsgay had some supporters, but the Party as a whole was hesitant about accepting pluralism. In January 1989 Pozsgay made a major move, when he announced that a Party commission, working on the history of the previous 40 years, had concluded that Imre Nagy had been correct in 1953–5, when he sought to introduce liberalizing reforms, and that the events of 1956 were not a 'counter-revolution', as the Kádárists had insisted, but a popular uprising. There was a major row in consequence, the outcome of which was a fudged compromise coupled with the simultaneous announcement that the Party accepted a multi-party system. The Party recognized that its strength was draining, and its strategy at this time was to try to guarantee itself a reserved position in the political structure, while allowing other parties to exist.

The Party loses control

The contest turned on a number of interlocking factors. The reformers argued that change was urgent and would only work if pluralism was accepted. Otherwise Hungarian society would not accept the authority of the political leadership and hence its energies could not be mobilized. The conservatives disliked this, but were stripped of all counter-arguments by their fear of popular upheaval as in 1956 and the fact that they did not have an intellectually viable alternative strategy. The break-up of political monopoly was merely a question of time.

Nevertheless, it was not all over by the spring of 1989. The conservatives' retreat was a step-by-step affair. While the celebration of 15 March as Hungary's national day (in commemoration of the 1848 revolution and, as such, a potent symbol of freedom) was fairly easily accepted, the ceremonial re-interment of Imre Nagy was much more contested. By acceding to this, the conservatives tacitly acknowledged that everything that had happened after 1956 was, in some senses, illegitimate. On 16 June, the thirty-first anniversary of the execution, Imre Nagy and the others who died with him were formally reburied, thereby symbolizing the acceptance of democracy.

In the summer, the Party finally sat down with the opposition parties at a round table (in reality, the two sides sat opposite each other) to try to work out the method of handing over power and to construct a new political system. Work on drafting a new constitution had been going on for some time in the Ministry of Justice, but the political sanction came from the round-table agreement in September. This approved a political structure with a weak presidency and an over-strong but democratically elected government. The thinking underlying this was the expectation that the Communists would retain much of the strength even after the forthcoming elections, so that the position of the government *vis-à-vis* parliament would be a weak one.

No-one actually expected what happened in October – the complete collapse of the party-state, the Communist system in its entirety. The Communist Party held a congress at the beginning of October and was deeply split between reformers and conservatives. A compromise was patched up, by the terms of which the Party reconstituted itself as the Hungarian Socialist Party. This appeared to break the spell, and the control exercised through the *nomenklatura* system vanished. Party discipline over parliament and government went too, so much so, that in the middle of October, parliament passed a series of laws depriving the Communists of their power, abolishing the Workers' Guard (the Party's private army), banning the Communists from organizing cells in places of work and insisting that the Communists disclose all their assets. Finally, on 23 October, the anniversary of the outbreak of the 1956 revolution, Hungary was formally declared to be a 'Republic' and no longer a People's Republic. Communist rule was over.

The 1990 election

The main rivals in the election campaign which followed did not include the successor to the Communists, the Hungarian Socialist Party, but were instead the Forum and the Free Democrats. The Free Democrats offered the voters a radical, anti-Communist programme, based on rapid marketization. They stressed individual rights and freedoms, including support for minorities and deprived groups. The Free Democrats drew their membership from the intellectual and professional classes, and were particularly strong in Budapest. The close allies of the Free Democrats, the democratic youth organization FIDESZ (Alliance of Young Democrats), won substantial backing from young people and disillusioned pensioners.

The Forum represented provincial, small-town Hungarian society, and the interests of tradesmen. Although it advocated a dismantling of the state economic sector, the Forum's policies were more cautious than those of the Free Democrats. During the course of the campaign, the Forum increasingly espoused a conservative position. Much stress was laid in its propaganda on 'Hungarian national values' (these the Forum never defined, since they were considered too obvious to Hungarians to merit description). The more extreme, populist elements, whose message was sometimes infused with anti-semitism, were cold-shouldered by the Forum's leadership. Henceforward, they largely confined their obscurantist venom to the Forum's journal, *Hitel*.

The election was held in two rounds on 25 March and 8 April 1990. Of the 386 seats in the new parliament, 176 were elected by constituency and 152 by 20 regional lists. The remaining 58 seats were allocated to parties in such a way as to compensate for the inequities of the 'first past the post' system used in the constituencies.

The Forum took 164 seats in the new parliament and the Free Democrats 92. The strength of the Forum's vote allowed it to form a ruling coalition with the Independent Smallholders Party and the Christian Democrat Peoples Party. Both broadly shared the conservative and Christian-nationalist philosophy of the Forum's leadership. With their support, the Forum had a working majority of 35 in the new parliament.

The Forum government

The new Forum-led coalition government was sworn in on 23 May 1990. The Prime Minister was József Antall, a historian who had previously been imprisoned for his activities in the 1956 Uprising. The Foreign Minister, Géza Jeszenszky, and Minister of Defence, Lajos Für, were similarly historians by training. Of the fifteen other cabinet seats, four posts were given to Independent Smallholders, one to the Christian Democrats and three to non-party specialists.

According to legislation passed in 1989, a two-thirds majority was needed in parliament to pass the budget and amend legislation. The Forum controlled less than 60% of the parliamentary seats, which meant that its programme could have been obstructed by the opposition. Accordingly, Antall struck a deal with the Free Democrats. In return for having the Free Democrat, Árpád Göncz, elected by parliament as President of the

Republic, the Free Democrats agreed to limit the two-thirds majority rule to only the most important parliamentary bills. Co-operation of this sort between government and opposition soon gave way, however, to re-crimination and to stormy parliamentary sessions.

The centrepiece of the government's programme, as outlined in May by József Antall, was the creation of a 'social market economy', the gradual privatization of state industry and the elimination both of inflation and of the foreign debt. Although expecting difficulties in the short term, Antall held out the prospect of a 3–4% growth rate.

Although Hungary exported more to the West than had been antici-pated, the economy proved to be as resistant to change as under the Communists. In the first year of the Antall government, inflation reached 40%; interest rates were set at 35%; the registered workless grew to 80,000; and industrial output fell by 10%. The budget presented in December 1990 additionally envisaged a record deficit. By this time, it was reckoned that over 2 million Hungarians were living below the poverty line and earning less than 6000 forints (£50) per month.

The continuing economic crisis and the new austerity policies intro-duced by the government made it increasingly unpopular among ordinary Hungarians. In October 1990 taxi- and lorry-drivers blockaded the centre of Budapest in protest at an increase in petrol prices. For a short time it seemed that the government might collapse under pressure from the streets. Two months later, 10,000 teachers demonstrated for higher pay and in February 1991 there were lively protests in front of parliament over the government's agricultural policy. Discontent also extended to the army, and in April 1991 part of the garrison of the town of Törökbálint mutinied.

Disillusionment with the Forum registered itself in the municipal elections in October 1990. The Free Democrats took Budapest and the larger cities; independents, among whom were a number of ex-Communists, were successful in the localities. Opinion polls taken in 1991 suggested that the Free Democrats and FIDESZ would win 45% of the vote if an election were to be held; and that the Forum would take only 14%. By-elections held in March/April 1991 confirmed the electorate's deep dissatisfaction with the Forum.

The Forum's record in foreign policy also proved lacklustre. Although Jeszenszky took Hungary into the Council of Europe in November 1990, the Forum failed to assuage the sensitivities of its neighbours with regard to the issue of the Hungarian minorities living abroad. Antall's declaration in the autumn of 1990 that he felt himself to be a Prime Minister for all Hungarians, regardless of citizenship, alarmed the Romanian govern-ment. The despatch of 10,000 assault rifles, allegedly by bureaucratic oversight, to the government of Croatia caused equal consternation in Belgrade. The dismissal in April of the Hungarian ambassador to Washington, Péter Zwack, on account of his severe criticism of the government's handling of foreign policy, greatly embarrassed his political masters.

Despite its blundering and failure to deliver on its promises, the government seemed reasonably secure in 1991. Its coalition partners, despite occasional sabre-rattling, appeared unlikely to desert the alliance. Given this circumstance, it is likely that the Forum government will remain in power until the next elections in 1994. Nevertheless, a schism between the 'left' and 'right' wings of the Forum cannot be ruled out; nor should the revitalized and increasingly popular Hungarian Socialist Party be omitted from the political equation. The passage to the elections of 1994 is bound to be a troubled one for the present government.

6 POLAND

The political transformation which occurred in Poland during 1989 has been called a 'step-by-step revolution'. Although Poland produced the first non-Communist prime minister in the Soviet bloc, and the first government not controlled by Communists, the changes which occurred were not so much an overthrow of Communist power as a negotiated withdrawal by the Party. In order to understand the historic compromise which occurred in Poland, we must know what went before.

Prewar Poland

Modern Poland is the descendant of a powerful and prosperous kingdom which once stretched from the Baltic to the Black Sea. Its decline in the seventeenth and eighteenth centuries ended in partition at the hands of three powerful, imperial neighbours – Russia, Austria and Prussia. Released after over a century of captivity, when the three empires collapsed during World War I, Poland was reborn in 1918.

Poland's short-lived period of independence between the wars was plagued by political, economic and social problems. Rapid attempts were made to unite the three partition zones – their economies, administration and transport systems. The early years, however, were marked by political instability, and in 1926 a *coup d'état* was carried out by Marshal Józef Piłsudski. Subsequently government, although more stable, became increasingly less democratic and tolerant. Poland's economic plight grew worse in the wake of the Depression, and the position of her large minority populations also deteriorated.

In 1939 Poland became the first nation to resist Hitler's territorial demands. The Nazi–Soviet Pact paved the way for the invasion of Poland and the outbreak of World War II followed. Partitioned again by two powerful neighbours, Poland succumbed to a long and bloody occupation. Some six million of Poland's inhabitants died, including virtually the whole of its Jewish population. Material damage and cultural losses were also severe. Polish resistance was stout and heroic – but was treated with savagery. The Warsaw Rising in August 1944 resulted in a quarter of a million people killed and the capital being razed to the ground by the Germans. The Polish government took up residence first in Paris and later in London. Throughout the war its soldiers, sailors and airmen fought alongside the Allies, under British operational command.

At the end of the war Poland faced once again the consequences of its

POLAND

Official name	The Republic of Poland
Area	312,685 sq. km (120,695 sq. miles)
Population	38,210,000 (annual growth rate 0.9%)
Capital	Warsaw (Warszawa)
Language	Polish
Religion	95% Roman Catholic
Currency	złoty

geographical position. Strategically located on the Soviets' route to Berlin, the country found itself under Red Army occupation. At the 'Big Three' wartime conferences of Teheran and Yalta it had been agreed that Poland would come under Soviet influence. The Polish government, although a wartime ally, was not consulted. In a sense one could say that Poland was the price the West paid Stalin for the Red Army's successes, and sacrifices, on the eastern front.

Postwar

The postwar Polish state was a very different structure from that of 1939. First, it was moved bodily to the west, losing half of its territory to the Soviet Union and being compensated at the expense of Germany with territory in the north and west. The transfer of territory was accompanied by massive exchanges of population – 3½ million Germans were expelled from the 'recovered' territories in the west, while almost 4½ million Poles 'returning' from Soviet-acquired territory took their place. Second, Poland was now a remarkably homogeneous state, with relatively small numbers of non-Poles and overwhelmingly Roman Catholic.

The Western leaders hoped that Stalin would be content with this settlement (he gained virtually the same area of Poland that he had been allotted under the 1939 Nazi–Soviet Pact), would consider that Soviet security interests had been satisfied and would not feel it necessary to communize Poland. Their hopes were misplaced. Stalin was unsure of whether Communist rule could be imposed on Poland or whether it would be wise to try (he once likened it to 'putting a saddle on a cow'). There was a long legacy of hostility in Polish–Russian and Polish–Soviet relations, which had not been assuaged by Stalin's cynical and brutal policies from 1939 onwards. Indeed, if it is true that Poland suffered more than any other nation during World War II, then much of that suffering was due to Soviet actions; the mass deportations to the USSR, the murder of Polish officers at Katyn and failure to help the Warsaw insurgents during the 1944 Rising.

In addition, there were few native Communists Stalin could count on, since he had liquidated the leadership of the Polish Communist Party in 1938. The few Party members who had survived the purge were those who had been in Polish jails or else who had refused the summons to Moscow and gone to ground. The pro-Soviet Poles who had gathered in Poland towards the end of the war and formed the Lublin Committee (a pro-visional government under Soviet auspices) were a poor bunch of non-entities, who had little following. Indeed, they were regarded as traitors by many of their own people. Their great virtue from Moscow's viewpoint, though, was that they would do Stalin's bidding. The word 'Communist' was intentionally dropped.

The Communist Party was recreated in 1942 as the Polish Workers Party – later (in 1948) to become transformed into the Polish United Workers Party (PUWP). It did not start from any significant base of support, although from an estimated 8000 members at the beginning of 1943 the Party had built up its membership to some 20,000 in mid-1944 and 30,000 by January of the following year. As people saw which way the wind was blowing, more and more decided to join the Party as the road to political or vocational advancement. In the summer of 1947, some six months after the elections, there were one million members (out of a population of some 24 million).

In July 1945 the USA and Britain recognized a 'Provisional Government of National Unity', in which both 'Moscow' Poles and members of the Polish exile government in London took part. Stanisław Mikołajczyk, leader of the Peasant Party, was the most prominent of the 'London' group, and his return to Poland was something of a test of Soviet intentions and good faith. The distribution of Cabinet posts was significant; some two-thirds of the portfolios, including the key posts of Internal Security and Defence, went to Moscow nominees.

The Yalta formula provided for 'free and unfettered elections' in Poland, but not for any mechanism for international monitoring of these elections (as in Greece). It was to be a year and a half before elections took place (in January 1947). They were preceded by a campaign of terror and intimidation against opposition parties, including the murder of many supporters of Mikołajczyk and the splitting of his party. Even so, the election results when they appeared were grossly falsified, the Communists and their allies receiving 80% in official figures. Western protests that the conditions set out in the Yalta agreement had not been met were rejected by Moscow. A few months after the elections, Mikołajczyk fled to the West, fearing for his life.

Poland's period of Stalinism lasted until 1956 and was relatively bloodless, by comparison with neighbouring Czechoslovakia. In 1948 a campaign was mounted on Moscow's orders against Władysław Gomułka for advocating a 'Polish road to socialism'. Gomułka had objected in particular to the demand that agriculture be collectivized. In the flurry which followed Tito's heresy in rejecting the Stalinist line, Gomułka became a victim of Moscow's clampdown on all forms of national deviationism. He was denounced publicly and in the following year removed from his position as deputy premier and from his seat on the Party's Central Committee.

In 1956 the first Polish protests against deteriorating economic conditions took place. Following Khrushchev's intervention, Gomułka was rehabilitated and assumed the mantle of Party leader, but despite his popularity the reforms he introduced were ineffective. The economy became increasingly inefficient and declining living standards resulted in further outbreaks of popular unrest, notably in 1970, when Gomułka himself was removed from office and replaced by Edward Gierek.

Gierek's period of office was notable for three factors, all of which were setbacks to Communist rule and were to stimulate the Polish drive for freedom and democracy. First, Gierek's policy of a massive, investment-led drive for growth – funded by Western banks and governments – failed miserably due to the structural inadequacies of the Polish economy. Debts accumulated and the huge interest repayments required to service this debt handicapped later attempts to improve investment and trade performance. Gierek stated at the XVI Party Plenum in October 1979 that the 1980s would be 'the decade of the greatest progress (economic and social) in the history of People's Poland. We have created a fine basis on which to build the future of our country.' The future was anything but sure or rosy, and within a year Gierek himself was forced out of office, the victim, once again, of popular protest.

The second major event was the formation in September 1976 of KOR, the Workers' Defence Committee, following the arrest of striking workers at Radom. It was the first organized body to oppose the Communist authorities and to defy them in the name of the workers. Although its members were harassed by the authorities (one of them, a young student named Stanisław Pyjas, was killed in Kraków in May 1977), the movement, nevertheless, gathering confidence from the Helsinki accords, extended its activities to include defence against all infringements of human rights. It provided a training ground for many of the dissidents (such as Adam Michnik and Jacek Kuroń) who were later to advise the Solidarity trade union.

The third event was an act of God – the election in October 1978 of Kraków's Cardinal Wojtyła as Pope. Not only was Wojtyła (or John Paul II as he chose to become) the first Pole to ascend the Throne of St Peter, he was a living contradiction – the head of a universal church numbering hundreds of millions of adherents who came from a formally atheist, Communist-bloc state. It is difficult to overstate the emotional effect that Wojtyła's election had on the people of Poland. It was a matter of national pride that a son of Poland had been elected to such an illustrious position, but it was also a reaffirmation of Poland's place in Christian and Western civilization – to which Poles had always felt they belonged. What is more, henceforth ordinary Poles were to feel the confidence that they had a stout and powerful defender on their side. The Pope's first return visit to his homeland in June 1979 inspired scenes of mass enthusiasm, and seasoned observers of the Polish scene were not slow to contrast them with the dour demeanour of marchers on the Party-orchestrated May Day parades.

The rise of Solidarity

In the summer of 1980, instigated by sudden food price rises, a wave of strikes swept across Poland, from Lublin in the south-east, to Silesia and the Baltic Coast. The mood of protest reached the Lenin Shipyard in Gdańsk, where a Strike Committee was set up on 16 August under the leadership of a shipyard electrician named Lech Wałęsa. The Committee drew up a list of 21 demands which included the 'acceptance of free trade unions independent of the Party and the employers'. Following much-publicized negotiations with the government, agreement was reached, although at a political cost. Prime Minister Babiuch was removed and at the beginning of September, Gierek himself stood down as Party First Secretary. The official reason given for his departure was 'health grounds'. A caretaker leader, Stanisław Kania, was brought in.

Moves towards the creation of independent unions did not go smoothly. The authorities dragged their feet over registration and were clearly unhappy about licensing unions to act on a national, as opposed to a local, basis. Nevertheless, the success of the union in forcing the government to talk and then to recognize it officially was considerable, and a landmark in the history of postwar east-central Europe. At last the Party, self-professed champion of proletarian interests, was forced to admit that it did not command the loyalty or support of the working masses. The momentum which had been created by the historical agreement in Gdańsk did not slacken. The 'Solidarity' union increased its following across the country until it had an estimated 10 million members.

As Solidarity attracted the hopes and the loyalty of millions of Polish citizens, so the morale of the Party membership, ashamed and disenchanted by the incompetence of their own leaders, plummeted. Many Party members flocked to join the ranks of Solidarity. A movement within the Party for reform and renewal scarcely got off the ground. In the course of 1981 it became clear that events in Poland had moved too fast for the Soviet leadership. A power vacuum had formed in Poland, as those holding the reins of power proved impotent to control events and those who enjoyed popular confidence and support were blocked from the positions of true authority.

A state of martial law was declared on 13 December 1981 and was accompanied by the arrest and internment of several hundred Solidarity activists. The move came as a complete surprise, although it had clearly been planned well in advance. The operation was put into effect by General Wojcich Jaruzelski, Kania's replacement as Party leader. It was essentially a move by the military wing of the Party to bolster the sagging morale of the civilian Party's leadership and to restore order and discipline, on both the political and the economic fronts.

It now seems clear that Jaruzelski and his colleagues acted to forestall possible Soviet intervention, along the lines of Budapest in 1956. At the time, however, the repressive measures which came into force were greeted with a chorus of protest both inside and outside the country. The protest demonstrations and strikes which broke out were put down harshly and a number of deaths resulted. In the international arena, the Jaruzelski leadership became a diplomatic leper – shunned by all except its extremely relieved socialist bloc allies. Most damagingly, the USA imposed economic sanctions on Poland, thereby considerably hindering the task of economic recovery.

Indeed, although martial law ended a period of extreme uncertainty, it is arguable whether its introduction facilitated the task of governing Poland. The formation of a Military Council of National Salvation (Polish acronym, WRON) was designed to override the established structures and political – and Party – rule. Jaruzelski added the chairmanship of WRON to his Party first secretaryship and several other posts, concentrating power in his own hands. He faced though a sullen and unco-operative people whose history had taught them that, if it was unwise to engage in any dramatic and fruitless gestures of resistance against such overwhelming military force, they could not be compelled to do any more than the bare minimum by way of co-operation. The spirit of wartime occupation was revived among a younger generation as a flourishing underground press sought to evade the censor's blockade.

Indeed, the Communist regime, having proceeded to outlaw the Solidarity opposition, found that it had no-one to talk to. Wałęsa, as the Polish media and Party spokesmen insisted, was merely a private citizen. (For a while, he had been detained by the authorities, but never subjected to long-term imprisonment or internment, like other Solidarity figures.) The desire of the Communists to relegate him to obscurity proved unsuccessful. He had already achieved too great a status, having become famous far beyond Polish borders. When eventually foreign leaders began to make their way to Warsaw they made a point of visiting Wałęsa during their stay. This meeting with the unofficial opposition leader was always made during the private section of their visit. (In 1983 he was awarded the Nobel Peace Prize.)

Although Solidarity was outlawed in October 1982, martial law itself was lifted some nine months later. The Communist leadership made strenuous efforts to achieve 'respectability' and to convince world opinion that the situation in Poland had returned to normal. Unfortunately, the leadership's hopes that a mood of reconciliation and unity would result from the Pope's second visit to Poland during June 1983 were disappointed. In October 1984 news of the brutal seizure and killing of the pro-Solidarity priest, Father Jerzy Popiełuszko, shocked the world. The fact that the murder was carried out by agents of the Interior Ministry drew attention to the murky role of the Polish security forces in establishing 'order' in the country. In the course of the decade scores of deaths were to occur in mysterious circumstances.

Economic reform

Gradually, following successive amnesties of interned Solidarity activists, there was a slight thawing of the diplomatic atmosphere which resulted in the lifting of US trade sanctions in 1983. The sanctions certainly damaged the Polish economy, and helped exacerbate the most serious underlying economic problem – foreign debt repayment, the legacy of Gierek's profligacy. Although the economy had picked up from its low point of

1981–2, shortages and queues remained. Attempts undertaken during 1983–5 to decentralize economic decision making had no noticeable effect and the poor foreign trade performance indicated that more radical measures were called for. At the beginning of 1988 the Polish authorities launched a new initiative – the 'second stage' of economic reform – having first appealed to the population in a referendum. This was received by a weary community with scepticism. Party organs also began to voice the opinion that there was no way out of the morasse if the traditional forms of one-party rule were not relaxed.

Throughout the 1980s thousands of Poles left the country, seeing no future for themselves. They went abroad as tourists and remained as refugees. Special camps were created in Austria, a favourite destination, to house them. From there they sought to move on to Canada, South Africa and Australia. They included large numbers of trained and qualified personnel – engineers, for example – which Poland could ill afford to lose.

In mid-January 1988 the Party weekly *Polityka* published an open letter to both Jaruzelski and Wałęsa from the Warsaw historian, Professor Jerzy Holzer. Holzer's message was apocalyptic. He pointed out that the crisis which had engulfed Poland was rapidly reducing it from membership of the mid-developed group of countries to that of a backward state in terms of civilization. A feeling of helplessness and apathy hung over the country. The authorities had not managed to enlist the support of the majority of the population since the introduction of martial law. Their struggle with Solidarity had undermined the authority of both sides and left a gulf. It was important, continued Holzer, that those who were able to influence the future of Poland should meet and – if only temporarily – overcome their animosities. Otherwise, he warned, Poland stood before a threat equal to that which faced the country in the eighteenth century (i.e. extinction). History would not forgive those who had a chance to save Poland and failed to act.

Other analysts pointed to the cyclical nature of Polish upheavals, and the pattern that these confrontations demonstrated. While there was no doubt that each crisis had left some permanent change to the system of government, Poles could perhaps hope for a more evolutionary, less painful and damaging means of bringing about change. Even political commentators from the Party ranks admitted that the era of ideological confrontation was in the past. The vocabulary of socialism was bankrupt; no-one now wanted to talk about 'improving socialism' or 'introducing real socialism'. The need for greater co-operation with the opposition had dampened polemics.

The 'second stage' of economic reform, the attempt to rally support for one more 'push' on the economic front, was undermined by ill-conceived price rises in the early part of 1988. A further wave of strikes in the spring and summer of 1988 forced Jaruzelski and his advisors to the conclusion that Poland could no longer be governed by force. Some kind of compromise had to be found with the opposition.

The consultations begin

The breakthrough came in August 1988 on the eve of the Party's VIII Plenum, when Interior Minister General Czesław Kiszczak offered to convene a series of meetings with 'representatives of various social and workers' organizations' to take the form of round-table talks. This face-saving formula – stressing 'various' groups, including 'workers' groups, but omitting the name of Solidarity – was intended as an olive branch to the opposition, which, nevertheless would not unduly alarm hardline Party elements (or Moscow). The Plenum agreed to base the system of government in Poland on a wider national understanding.

Kiszczak's offer of talks was quickly taken up. The Interior Minister had a series of meetings with Wałęsa and opposition leaders (including Church representatives) during the late summer. At the same time, Wałęsa invited groups of expert advisers to consult with him in Gdańsk about the way in which negotiations with the authorities should be conducted. Meetings had begun in 1987, and the fifth such conference took place on 18 December (of 135 people invited, 119 attended). These advisers represented more than purely political and economic expertise; they included Church representatives, and figures from the world of culture. In Western terms, the consultations amounted to the drawing up of a political manifesto by a party's policy-making committee. This loose assembly of experts was eventually transformed into a 'Citizens' Committee' linked to the Solidarity leadership. It developed fifteen sub-commissions dealing with specific topics such as political reform, trade union pluralism and the national minorities.

When, on 19 September 1988 the Sejm passed a vote of no confidence in the government of Zbigniew Messner, Poland's eighth prime minister in the postwar period, he was replaced by Mieczysław Rakowski. Rakowski, formerly editor of the Party weekly *Polityka*, took the unusual step of consulting with Cardinal Glemp before appointing his Cabinet. In another departure from orthodoxy, he appointed a millionaire private business-man, Mieczysław Wilczek, his Minister for Industry.

The year 1988 proved a crucial one for the ending of one-party rule in Poland. (The decision to enter into round-table talks was, as one political commentator wrote, like 'giving the opposition the ball and inviting them to play . . .') Communists themselves voiced their perplexity at times that there should be a crisis of confidence in the government at precisely the moment when it had attempted to introduce new policies of openness and consultation, when radical economic reforms were being attempted, and when people could say and write almost what they wanted. This was naive, though, and if genuine, indicated how little they understood the strength of the distrust and resentment that lay beneath the surface. The desire to get the Communists out after years of mismanagement, of official lies and of subservience to Moscow was overpowering.

Although formal round-table talks had been planned for November 1988 they did not take place until February of the following year. The talks lasted for nine weeks and the legislative proposals which resulted were far-reaching. They involved significant changes to the Constitution and to political structures. First, they recommended the creation of a second, upper chamber (Senate), which meant a return to the bicameral system of government abandoned by the Communists in 1946. Second, they foresaw the restoration of the presidency, the candidate to be elected by a National Assembly (i.e. a joint session of the Sejm and Senate). Most importantly, they recommended multi-party, competitive elections – the first in Poland since 1947, and a departure from the 'plebiscites' by which the Communists had formerly called on the populace to support a closed list of Party nominees. There were also far-reaching economic proposals. The Sejm approved the measures in April 1989.

The elections

The elections were held in two stages in June 1989. All seats to the Senate were fought competitively, but in the Sejm only 35% of seats were 'open'; the other 65% remained reserved for the Communists (PUWP) and their allies (ZLP and SD). While this meant that the Communists were guaranteed a continued presence in government, it was conceived as an interim measure – a period of coalition or 'guided democracy', leading to completely free and competitive elections planned for 1993. All parties were to be free to conduct their own election campaigns. In May 1989 a new independent daily newspaper, *Gazeta Wyborcza* (*Election Gazette*), came into being with official approval. Its chief editor was Adam Michnik, historian and long-term dissident who had been imprisoned under martial law. The *Gazeta Wyborcza* was founded to report the election campaign and especially the point of view of the opposition candidates.

The course of the two-stage June elections and the subsequent manoeuvring to form a government was unprecedented for a state in the Soviet bloc. As expected, Solidarity candidates virtually whitewashed the Communists, securing 99 out of 100 seats in the Senate and all the 35 seats which they were able to run for in the Sejm. However, this still left them in a minority in the lower chamber, and most onlookers expected that Solidarity would be content to continue its opposition role, except this time in a more formal setting. Statements from Wałęsa and other Solidarity leaders confirmed that they would bide their time, and not participate in any Communist-led administrations.

In the aftermath of the elections the office of presidency had to be filled. General Jaruzelski, the architect of martial law, made an early announcement of his decision not to stand, fearing that his record would count against him and would result in a humiliating defeat. When it became clear, though, that Wałęsa was not standing for office, the general reversed his decision. On 19 July he was elected president after an eight-hour televised debate, having received 270 votes against 233 votes opposed to his candidature (34 deputies abstained). The majority of Solidarity deputies voted against him.

Jaruzelski's subsequent decision to ask former Interior Minister, Kiszczak, to form a government was greeted with hostility. It was a blow to Solidarity, since Kiszczak was the person responsible for interning so many people during martial law. With the prospect that they would capture both the presidency and the premiership, many felt that the Communists were merely taking over where they had left off. Wałęsa issued a statement opposing the choice, which deepened the crisis. Faced with such firm opposition, Kiszczak found it impossible to form a government. Solidarity persuaded the Communists' formerly loyal allies, the Democrats (SD) and the Peasant Party (ZSL), to turn against them. Kiszczak was forced to admit defeat.

The way now became clear for adoption of the formula proposed by Adam Michnik in the columns of *Gazeta Wyborcza* – 'Your President, Our Premier'. On 24 August 1989 Tadeusz Mazowiecki, a Catholic journalist and one of Wałęsa's advisors since the early days of confrontation in the Gdańsk shipyard, was appointed prime minister. He immediately set about constructing a Cabinet. By 12 September he was able to submit 23 names to the Sejm. While eleven of the Cabinet posts were allocated to Solidarity deputies, and only four to the PUWP (Communists), the latter were granted key ministries of the Interior and Defence. (Since control of the military and security forces had been the springboard from which the Communists had taken power in the period 1945–7, this raised some eyebrows, but it was a necessary part of the compromise.) Other Cabinet posts were allocated to the Democrats (3) and to the Peasants' Party (4), with one portfolio going to an independent.

The assumption by Mazowiecki of the premiership, the first non-Communist prime minister in the Soviet bloc, was received with justified acclamation and even incredulity in the West. Within the Communist world reactions varied, from the guardedly welcoming to the openly hostile. It was the Romanian leader Ceauşescu whose hostility went furthest. While Ceauşescu had not supported the Warsaw Pact invasion of Czechoslovakia in 1968 and had broken with Moscow over it, he now tried to persuade Soviet leader Gorbachev that intervention in Poland by friendly socialist states was necessary. Such entreaties were futile, of course. The Soviet leader had been hinting for some time that he was not in sympathy with the Brezhnev Doctrine and had made his rejection public in a number of speeches during the summer. The Poles immediately made soothing noises, by stressing their intention to honour existing agreements, and specifically to remain members of Comecon and the Warsaw Pact.

'The first comprehensive market-oriented reforms in Eastern Europe'

The new government rapidly set about rolling back the frontiers of Communism. This process began with changes to the Constitution, including the deletion of Article 3, concerning the leading role of the Communist Party. A team was charged with drafting a new Constitution, which, it was hoped, would be ready by May 1991 – the 200th anniversary of Poland's, and Europe's first. Poland's official name reverted to the prewar 'Rzeczpospolita Polska' (that is, Polish Republic, rather than People's Republic). The country's symbol, the white eagle, had its royal crown – a legacy of the Polish monarchy – restored. Across the country, the symbols of Communist rule were stripped or torn down. Busts and statues of Lenin were toppled, and there was great satisfaction when the statue of Feliks Dzierzyński, the Pole who created Lenin's secret police, was taken down in the Warsaw square that had borne his name.

The most difficult task facing the incoming administration was that of tackling the economy. In addition to the crippling burden of overseas debt which aproached $40 billion by the end of 1989, inflation had accelerated dramatically and was estimated at 1000%. Part of the boost to prices had been caused by the Rakowski government's attempts during August to 'marketize the food economy'. While the measures had given producers free rein to raise their prices, they had not been able to ensure an adequate supply of goods to satisfy market demand.

The young Finance Minister and Deputy Premier, Leszek Balcerowicz, had to consider with his colleagues how to control the rampant inflation, and at the same time put the Polish economy on the road to recovery. Negotiations began with the International Monetary Fund (many loans from Western governments were dependent upon IMF approval of the restructuring arrangements). The package eventually agreed was the most radical break with socialist policies ever attempted, and in the words of *The Economist*, 'the first comprehensive market-oriented reforms in Eastern Europe'. There was to be an end to price controls and remaining subsidies. Prices would be determined by the market, but wages would be held down to avoid a wage–price spiral that would accelerate inflation. The private sector would be freed from government restrictions, while the state sector would be slimmed down by privatizations, and subjected to the discipline of the marketplace. The government undertook to adopt responsible monetary and fiscal policies (e.g. balanced budgets), and stressed its eventual aim to bring about convertibility of the złoty.

The measures were introduced on 1 January 1990. The first twelve months of the Balcerowicz programme produced notable achievements and a number of surprises. Inflation was forced down from the stratospheric levels of late 1989 and in August 1990 – the best month – prices rose by only 2%. The złoty also held firm against the dollar, following its 30% devaluation at the beginning of the year. Queues and empty shelves in the shops – so much a feature of life under Communist rule – largely disappeared. There was evidence of greater work discipline; strikes were fewer and the number of days lost through sickness or absenteeism dropped appreciably.

These achievements, though, were gained at a high cost. The drop in output was far greater than the 5% the government had expected. Furthermore, many sections of the population began to experience great hardship. Unemployment, as expected, rose steadily through the year. It reached 443,000 by May 1990 and in October passed the million mark – 7% of the working population outside of the agricultural sector. Unhappily, the unemployment level is set to go higher – possibly to double – during 1991.

Added to this misery is the fact that public-sector pay levels have been prevented from rising with inflation. As a result, disposable incomes have dropped by between 30% and 40% since the beginning of 1990 – this from a figure which was already low at the end of 1989. An average monthly wage in the summer of 1990, of just under a million złoties, sounds a lot, but at a rate of 18,000 zł to the pound this amounted to only £55. By April the Poles were spending 60% of their incomes on food.

A major surprise was the improvement in the balance of trade. As declining incomes led to a dampening of demand, import levels fell while domestic producers had to seek overseas markets more vigorously. Therefore although the government had expected the trade balance to deteriorate, in fact 1990 produced a series of monthly trade surpluses. But the surplus on overseas trade, even if it could be sustained, would not be enough to solve Poland's debt problem. In February 1990 the 17-member 'Paris Club' of international debtors agreed to defer interest payments on the massive Polish debt for twelve months to allow the Polish reforms time to take effect. The interest was not being written off; it was being added to the debt already outstanding and this had reached $46 billion by the end of 1990. During a visit to Washington in May 1990, Finance Minister Balcerowicz made an early attempt to have the country's official debt reduced to manageable proportions – say, by 80%. His efforts brought success. In March 1991 the USA had agreed to write off some 70% of the (admittedly relatively small) debt owed them, and encouraged their Western allies to follow suit. The 'Paris Club' members agreed to a 50% reduction in the existing value of the official debt. (Poland has been more fortunate than the South American debtor countries in that a large proportion of its overseas debt was owed to governments, rather than to commercial banks.)

The Polish privatization programme was slower in getting off the ground than expected. Indeed, the government's original aim to privatize half of state enterprises in the course of the first five years began to look extremely ambitious. The privatization bill was passed by the Sejm in July 1990 and a fully fledged Ministry of Ownership Transformation created under the leadership of economist, Waldemar Kuczyński. The first group of firms were sold off to the public during November.

The Polish government's bold measures have excited admiration and interest, not least among Soviet economic advisors. But what are the chances of success for the Balcerowicz programme? The 'turn-around' in the Polish economy (initially forecast for 1991) now looks even further off. There is concern over whether the reform programme has been effective in changing underlying structural weaknesses in the economy. Is it in fact the most efficient of the industrial enterprises that have been going out of business? Furthermore, like other states in the region, Poland had been hit heavily by the collapse in Comecon trade and the effects of the Gulf crisis. Finally, it remains to be seen whether social pressures force the government to 'soften' or slow down the reform programme.

Politics

The political landscape altered radically during the course of 1990. So much so that Poland ended the year with a new President, a new Prime Minister and the Solidarity movement in tatters.

In January the Polish United Workers' Party disbanded and became the Social Democratic Party of the Polish Republic. A breakaway faction named itself the Social Democratic Union. The efforts of these successor parties to inherit the massive estate of the defunct PUWP were largely foiled. A government commission discovered that the Communists and their allies had occupied some 5000 buildings, only 86 of which, however, were legally in their possession; the remainder had been appropriated from the state. In early April, the great majority of these were returned to the people.

As in the other post-Communist states of the region, a multitude of political parties came into being. In the June elections to some 2383 local councils many of the smaller parties were still campaigning under the Solidarity banner. The election itself, an important further step in the gradual removal of the Party *nomenklatura* and the first completely free election in Poland for more than half a century, resulted in a disappointing turnout (42%). Solidarity-backed candidates, as expected, did well in the traditional centres of opposition support (e.g. Gdańsk, Kraków), but the much-reduced support for the movement shown elsewhere was an indication of disenchantment with the government's performance and with squabbles in the Solidarity leadership.

In the spring of 1990 Lech Wałęsa began to demand that General Jaruzelski should step down as president, making it clear that he saw himself as the natural successor. But he also attacked the performance of the Mazowiecki government – composed for the most part of former Solidarity colleagues and advisers he himself had nominated for office.

What caused this change of tack? Certainly, Wałęsa sensed the frustration felt by many Poles that they had been left behind in the region's transition to democratic rule. Apart from the presidency, two-thirds of the seats in the lower house were still occupied by former Communists and their allies. This legacy of the 1989 'round table' agreement had become an anachronism. But Wałęsa was also aware that public anger was growing at the hardship caused by the government's economic policies. Resentment was fuelled by a belief that the Mazowiecki government had not done enough to root out the old Communist *nomenklatura* and to prevent the former Party apparatchiks from setting themselves up comfortably in consultancies and enterprises created with funds appropriated from the state.

Wałęsa later played on latent anti-semitism and paranoia in the community to suggest that the transition to full democracy had been hijacked. He demanded that the reform programme be accelerated (especially the privatization programme), that the *nomenklatura* be removed and be held accountable for past excesses, and that more urgent moves be made to remove Soviet troops from Polish soil. A rift with former colleagues rapidly developed as criticism of government policies turned into personal attacks. Wałęsa chided the government intellectuals for their remoteness from the people. In calling for a 'permanent political war' and talking of 'spontaneous democracy and mass social activity' he framed an unashamedly populist appeal. But opponents were alarmed by the authoritarian tones in Wałęsa's statements (e.g. that when elected President, he would rule by decree if necessary).

On 22 September 1990 the Sejm voted its approval for a presidential election to take place on 25 November. By the beginning of September two political groupings had already been formed. One, the Centre Alliance (*Porozumienie Centrum*), was to support Wałęsa's candidacy for the presidency; the other, Citizens' Movement – Democratic Action (known by its Polish acronym ROAD), was formed to oppose Wałęsa's bid for power. While Wałęsa declared his candidacy early, and stated publicly his confidence that he would receive 60% of the votes, Mazowiecki's late decision betrayed perhaps some reluctance to stand, and even a lack of confidence.

The hesitation was, perhaps, justified. For Mazowiecki the election was a disaster and a humiliation. He received just 18% of the first-round vote and was relegated to third place. But Wałęsa too suffered from the electorate's disillusionment. His 40% of the votes was enough to gain him first place, but insufficient to avoid a second round of voting. His opponent in the second round would be an unknown émigré businessman, Stanisław Tymiński, who claimed to have made millions from business interests in Peru and Canada. The 42 year-old Tymiński, who won almost a quarter of the votes cast (23.1%), profited from the electorate's disillusionment with the squabbles in the Solidarity camp.

The second round of voting on 9 December was preceded by a strong campaign against Tymiński. His mental health was questioned, and accusations made that his campaign was directed by former Communists (there were former security service personnel in his team of advisers). This did not, however, seem to greatly harm the 'Peruvian Pole', and in the second round – although soundly beaten by Wałęsa – he still received one in four of the votes cast. Wałęsa was sworn in as President on 22 December. The ceremony was marked by the return to Poland, after 50 years in London, of the historic insignia of office, handed over by the President-in-Exile, Ryszard Kaczorowski.

Mazowiecki, following his first-round defeat, had immediately offered his resignation and that of the government, while remaining in a caretaker capacity until a successor could be found. He also requested his electoral support team to continue its work, signalling his intention to serve in opposition to Wałęsa and the new government. Wałęsa's initial attempts to nominate a new Prime Minister ran into difficulties. However, some three weeks after Wałęsa's election a little-known 39-year-old economist, Jan Krzysztof Bielecki, was able to form a government. Key figures from the Mazowiecki Cabinet, such as Finance Minister Balcerowicz and Foreign Minister Skubiszewski, have been retained, thus ensuring continuity of policy in two key areas.

Bielecki was expected to be a stop-gap figure, since new elections were expected in the spring. However, in April the Sejm voted to postpone a general election until the autumn, thus prolonging the life of the Bielecki government. The vote defied a presidential proposal for early elections, and disappointed members of Wałęsa's entourage suggested that former Communists (and others with no political mandate) were desperately clinging to power. (The existing Sejm is still that formed from the 'controlled' elections held under the 1989 'round-table' agreement.) In fact, the reality was more complex: opposition to an early election also came from former Solidarity members now ranged in opposition to Wałęsa. It remains true, however, as presidential supporters pointed out, that Poland will not gain membership of the Council of Europe until free elections are held.

The 1990 presidential campaign signalled an end to the Solidarity consensus and paved the way for the development of a true party political system. Apart from the pro-Wałęsa Centre Agreement and the opposition ROAD (Citizens' Movement) group, a number of other parties will be in contention when elections arrive. These include the Democratic Union formed by former premier Mazowiecki, various PSL (Peasant Party) groupings, the Social Democrats (successor to the Communists), the right-wing Catholic National Christian Union (ZChN), and Party X. The last is the creation of the defeated presidential candidate, Tymiński, and, after his exploitation of the 'disaffected vote' during the presidential campaign, it would be unwise to dismiss his chances completely.

7 ROMANIA

Romania as we know it today is, territorially speaking, largely the product of the Paris Peace Settlement which followed World War I. Much of the country was under foreign imperial rule until 1918. Transylvania and Bukovina had been part of the Habsburg Empire, and Bessarabia, having been lost to Russia in 1812, was regained in the turmoil produced by the Bolshevik Revolution. Even the Black Sea coast province of Dobrogea had only been severed from the Ottoman Empire and awarded to the infant Romania by the European Powers in 1878.

The legacy of a different historical experience of the Romanians in these constituent lands, coupled with the diverse ethnic mix of the large Hungarian, German and Jewish minority populations which they contained, posed major problems of harmonization and consolidation in the enlarged Romanian state, problems which, in the brief interlude of the interwar period, Romania's leaders had little time, capacity and will to address. The failure to solve them (and the Western democracies provided little help to this end) was to blight the country's progress towards modernization and the exercise of genuine democratic rule.

Although a radical land reform was introduced after World War I, the economic and social reforms sought by the peasantry (80% of the population of 18 millions lived in villages) were not introduced by governments, which remained subservient to the sectional interests of the banks and prominent industrialists. The economic recession of the 1930s doomed such hopes and fostered a decade of instability in which the xenophobia of the impoverished peasantry was exploited by right-wing movements, principally by the Iron Guard, and directed against the Jews. The growth in support for the Guard, which stemmed in part from a widespread disillusion with the experience of parliamentary government, led King Carol II to institute a personal dictatorship in 1938. At the same time, Romania's geographical position, and its economic predicament, forced it into Hitler's arms.

Involvement with Germany

After the Munich agreement of 1938 Romania found itself increasingly drawn into the web of German military and economic policies. With Britain unwilling to buy Romania's wheat in large quantities, and with Germany in control of the Czech Skoda works with which Carol had placed orders for arms, Romania was now dependent on Hitler for the means to save its

ROMANIA

Official name	Romania
Area	237,500 sq. km (96,699 sq. miles)
Population	23,050,000 (1988) (annual growth rate 0.4%)
Capital	Bucharest (Bucureşti)
Languages	Romanian, Magyar
Religion	70% Romanian Orthodox Church, 10% Romanian Uniate Church, 5% Roman Catholic, 5% Lutheran
Currency	leu

economy and territorial integrity in the face of threats from the Soviet Union and Hungary.

In June 1940, on German advice given in accordance with the Nazi–Soviet pact of August 1939, Carol agreed to the Soviet demand for Bessarabia and Northern Bukovina, and two months later he accepted Hitler's own imposition of the Vienna Award, by which Romania was forced to cede Northern Transylvania to Hungary. The loss of these provinces cost Romania almost one third of its territory and population of whom half, some 3 million, were ethnically Romanian. Unable to resist popular demands for his abdication following these supine concessions, Carol renounced the throne in favour of his teenage son Michael, after having appointed General Ion Antonescu as Prime Minister. In January 1941 the Iron Guard, which had shared power with Antonescu, rose against him and Hitler, anxious to have a stable Romania as a springboard for his attack upon the Soviet Union, allowed the general to crush the rebellion. Antonescu now assumed supreme powers and willingly joined the German invasion of the Soviet Union on 22 June 1941 in order to gain the lost eastern provinces.

As the military situation steadily deteriorated after the battle of Stalingrad, in which Romanian losses were put at 155,000 dead, wounded and missing, Antonescu tolerated the emission of peace feelers, both from within his own government and from the opposition leader, Maniu. These efforts foundered on the Anglo-American insistence upon 'unconditional surrender', which could not be reconciled with Antonescu's desire to guarantee Romania's postwar independence from the Soviet Union. Antonescu's reluctance as a soldier to abandon his German ally who was now on the defensive forced the opposition parties to plot his overthrow, and with Soviet troops rapidly advancing on Romanian territory the young King Michael boldly arrested the general on 23 August 1944. This *volte-face*, the most decisive of World War II, exposed the German Army's southern flank and opened the whole of south-eastern Europe to the Red Army.

The Russians arrive

When Soviet troops entered Bucharest on 31 August they found an interim Romanian government ready to negotiate an armistice and to hold free elections. To regain the initiative, Stalin fashioned from the Soviet–Romanian armistice a legal framework for securing a dominant political and economic interest in Romania, one conceded to him by Churchill at their meeting barely a month later in Moscow under the so-called 'Percentage Agreement'. The British and American co-signatories, and their representatives on the aptly titled Allied (Soviet) Control Commission in Romania, were reduced to the role of spectators in the application of the armistice according to Soviet dictates.

In order to impose Stalin's will on the Romanian people the Soviet authorities employed blatant political engineering. On the grounds that they needed stability in a country that was behind their lines in their continuing war effort against Germany, they installed a puppet government under Petru Groza on 6 March 1945. This government oversaw the first steps to communize the country, which involved abolishing the freedom of the press and of political assembly, and the arrest and imprisonment of virtually all political opponents. Most of the Romanian army was demobilized and the policing of the country placed in the hands of the Soviet Army of occupation. At the insistence of Britain and the USA, elections were finally held in November 1946. The results were not announced for three days, and the government was suspected of having falsified the returns in presenting a total defeat as a major victory. The subjugation of Romania to the Soviet Union was completed at the end of the following month, when King Michael, on being presented with an ultimatum by Groza to abdicate or face the prospect of civil war, renounced his throne. On the same day, 30 December 1947, the Romanian People's Republic was proclaimed.

The postwar period

The principal political figure of the early postwar period in Romania was Gheorghe Gheorghiu-Dej, General Secretary of the Romanian Communist Party (from 1947 the Romanian Workers' Party) between 1945 and 1954, and First Secretary from 1955 to his death in 1965. Under his leadership, Romania emerged from subservience to the Soviet Union to challenge the latter's supranational pretensions by resisting pressure to become the granary of Comecon and by rapidly developing its own industry. Underlying the emphasis given to rapid industrialization was also a political goal: that of enabling Romania to break its dependency upon the Soviet Union. The achievement of the greater economic self-reliance needed to underpin the political autonomy from the Soviet Union sought by Dej and his party in the late 1950s and early 1960s was based not only upon the further development of agriculture but also upon an extension of the industrialization drive to the countryside. The policy had important sociological, occupational and economic consequences, generating a movement of labour from the land to the factory and increasing the urbanization of the population. The proportion of the urban population rose from 22% in 1948 to 30% in 1965 and 49% in 1983, and was projected to rise to 75% in the year 2000.

The autonomous policies inaugurated by Dej were continued by his successor, Nicolae Ceauşescu, who was elected First (later General) Secretary of the Party in March 1965. Romania developed relations with China, who became its principal partner in the international Communist movement, was the first country in the Eastern bloc to establish diplomatic relations with West Germany in 1967, and did not break diplomatic ties with Israel after the Six-Day War. The most forceful affirmation of independence from Soviet dictates was Ceauşescu's refusal to participate in, and condemnation of, the Warsaw Pact intervention in Czechoslovakia in 1968. Growing recognition of Romania's political usefulness as a thorn in the flesh of the Soviet Union opened a period of increasing Western courtship of Ceauşescu, exemplified by President Richard Nixon's visit in August 1969. Ceauşescu returned the visit in December 1970. There followed a succession of economic favours. In 1971 Romania was admitted to GATT (General Agreement on Trade and Tariffs) and in 1972 it was accepted into the International Monetary Fund and the World Bank. Romania's trading position was further enhanced when the country acquired preferential trading status with the Common Market in 1973. In March 1975 President Gerald Ford granted Romania Most Favored Nation status and Ceauşescu visited the USA again in April 1978. Three months later he was given an honour unprecedented to the head of a Warsaw Pact country – a state visit to the United Kingdom.

Economic decline and 'systematization'

At the same time, disturbing trends began to emerge in the country's economic performance. Soviet opposition to Romania's rapid industrialization was translated into a refusal to provide financial aid for the programme and therefore Ceauşescu turned to the West for loans. Romania's creditworthiness was assessed on over-optimistic estimates of its ability to repay through exports which were generally of poor quality. Not only did exports fail to generate the income anticipated, but the energy-intensive heavy industry plants became increasingly voracious due to inefficient running. In the mid-1970s Ceauşescu expanded Romania's oil-refining capacity in excess of the country's own domestic output, and in 1976 was forced to begin importing crude oil. When the price of oil soared on the international market in 1978 Romania was caught unprepared, and soon faced a major trade deficit. The problem was exacerbated by the revolution in Iran, a chief supplier to Romania of oil, which interrupted deliveries. With the Soviet Union refusing to make good the oil deficit unless Ceauşescu showed greater conformity in foreign policy, a third of Romania's oil-refining capacity became idle in 1981.

Nature was also against the regime. A severe earthquake in 1977 and floods in 1980 and 1981 disrupted industrial production and reduced the exports of foodstuffs which Ceauşescu now looked to in order to reduce the foreign debt incurred through industrialization. In late 1981 Romania's foreign debt rose to $10.2 billion and Ceauşescu decided to request its rescheduling. On the recommendation of the IMF, imports were reduced and exports, especially of machinery, equipment and petroleum products, increased. The implications of this reduction of imports has not been fully appreciated, since in 1981 Romania was a net importer of food from the industrialized West (Romanian food imports from the West in 1981 totalled $644 million and exports $158 million; in the same year Soviet statistics show that Romania exported 106,000 tons of frozen meat to the USSR).

Therefore in order to reduce Romania's hard currency debt Ceauşescu reduced food imports from the West from a peak of almost $1 billion in 1981 to $300 million in 1982 and $27 million in 1984. Cutting back on food imports, while at the same time continuing to export meat to the Soviet Union, forced Ceauşescu to introduce meat rationing.

More importantly, the very act of having to accept conditions from the Western banks was a great blow to Ceauşescu's inflated pride. He declared defiantly in December 1982 that he would pay off the foreign debt by 1990, and to achieve this introduced a series of austerity measures unparalleled even in the bleak history of East European Communist regimes. Rationing of bread, flour, sugar and milk was introduced in some provincial towns in early 1982, and in 1983 it was extended to most of the country, with the exception of the capital. The monthly personal rations were progressively reduced to the point where on the eve of the revolution they were, in some regions of the country, two pounds of sugar, two pounds of flour, a half-pound pack of margarine, and five eggs. At the same time, heavy industry was also called upon to contribute to the export drive, but because its energy needs outstripped the country's generating capacity drastic energy-saving measures were introduced, which included a petrol ration of 30 litres per month for private car owners. Other strictures stipulated a maximum temperature of 14°C in offices (in winter outside temperatures usually drop to well below zero) and periods of provision of hot water (normally one day a week in state-owned flats). In the winter of 1983 these restrictions were extended, causing the interruption of the electricity supply in major cities and reduction of gas pressure during the day so that meals could only be cooked at night. During the severe winter of 1984–5 it was calculated from medical sources in the capital's hospitals that over 30 children had died as a result of unannounced power cuts affecting incubators.

Ceauşescu's relevance on the world stage was undermined by the accession to power of Mikhail Gorbachev in March 1985. A number of the very positions which Ceauşescu had been adopting in his foreign policy, and which had gilded his 'liberal' image in the West, now became features of Soviet policy; withdrawal from Afghanistan, removal of short-range nuclear weapons from Europe, and reductions in nuclear arsenals. Ceauşescu's usefulness as a bridge between East and West rapidly evaporated. Furthermore, the reforms to the Communist system advocated by Gorbachev were rejected by Ceauşescu, who continued to apply his Stalinist policies in an even more draconian manner by introducing in November 1987 a seven-day working week and reduced domestic heating quotas. On the very day when the Party newspaper reported the proceedings of a Central Committee plenum at which Ceauşescu dismissed the idea of Gorbachev-style reform, the first major challenge to Ceauşescu was launched by several thousand workers in Braşov, the country's second largest city, when they sacked the local Party headquarters on 15 November in protest at his new measures. The leaders of the protest were rounded up, beaten and jailed as Ceauşescu defiantly refused to make any concessions.

Ceauşescu's fanatical commitment to modernizing the country was exemplified by his announcement of the 'systematization' policy, and in this respect he scored a spectacular own goal. With it disappeared the popular image of him in the West as a benign figure, as 'one of Europe's good Communists' as Vice-President George Bush described him after a visit to Romania in September 1983. In March 1988 Ceauşescu announced plans to complete by the year 2000 the urbanization or 'systematization' of the country which would involve a reduction by half in the number of Romania's 13,000 villages. How the number of villages was to be reduced soon became clear from the demolition, in one case at only 48 hours' notice, of a handful of villages around Bucharest.

As the pace of reform grew within the rest of Eastern Europe the president became more and more defiant. The extremism of his thinking found expression in his attempt at the July 1989 Warsaw Pact meeting in Bucharest to obtain support for armed intervention against the Solidarity government in Poland when his most sympathetic listener was Erich Honecker. He found another partner in the resistance to reform in Deng Xiao-ping, to whom he offered free holidays in Romania for Chinese soldiers and policemen who had suppressed the demonstrating students in Tiananmen Square. Deng was one of the few Communist leaders to send a high-ranking representative to the Fourteenth Romanian Party Congress in November 1989, where Ceauşescu received 67 standing ovations during his opening address, which once again made no concession to *perestroika* and *glasnost*. The popular despair and frustration at Ceauşescu's re-election as General Secretary manifested itself a month later.

The pastor in Timişoara

The spark which ignited the revolution against Ceauşescu was a local protest in the western Transylvanian town of Timişoara against the harassment of a Hungarian pastor, Laszlo Tokes. Members of his flock maintained a vigil on the night of 15 December outside his house to prevent Tokes being taken away for questioning by the security police. On the following day the vigil turned into a major demonstration, when several thousand Romanians joined the Hungarian parishioners and began shouting 'We want bread'. These calls were then replaced by chants of 'Down with Ceauşescu' and the protesters marched into the town centre. They were dispersed by baton-wielding militiamen but no shots were fired, even though Ceauşescu had given orders that the security police and the army should fire on the demonstrators. The demonstrations continued on 17 December, but on that afternoon the army did open fire on the crowd. The number of casualties was initially put at several thousand, but subsequent investigations put the figure at less than 200. On Elena Ceauşescu's orders, 40 of the dead were transported by lorry to Bucharest and cremated to make identification impossible.

On 20 December Ceauşescu returned from a brief visit to Iran and made the first of three fatal errors. In a televised address to the nation he completely misjudged the mood of the people by displaying no hint of compassion for the victims of Timişoara and by dismissing the demon-strations as the work of 'fascists' and 'hooligan elements', inspired by Hungarian irredentism.

His second mistake was to convene a public meeting of support on the next morning in Bucharest, when the public was incensed by his lack of humanity. To his amazement, his speech was interrupted by cries of 'We are not hooligans' and the live television and radio coverage was cut for several minutes. When he resumed his speech, Ceauşescu attempted to placate the crowd by announcing salary and pension increases, but this stratagem only angered them further. At the end of his speech large groups of young people remained in the city centre and, encouraged by the warm, unseasonal weather, lingered into the evening. It was at this point that they were fired upon by the army and security police, and many of them were shot dead.

On the following morning of 22 December Ceauşescu committed his third error. He summoned yet another public meeting of support and attempted to address it. Stones were thrown at the balcony of the Central Committee building and Ceauşescu fled from the rooftop in a helicopter accompanied by his wife and two of his closest allies, Manea Manescu and Emil Bobu, and two bodyguards. Ceauşescu ordered the helicopter pilot to land at Snagov, some 30 kilometres to the north of Bucharest, where he had a country villa, and it was from here that he and his wife collected a suitcase of clothing. Manea and Bobu remained behind as the helicopter took off again with the Ceauşescus and their bodyguards in the direction of Piteşti, but shortage of fuel, and the danger of being spotted by radar, prompted the pilot to put down on a main road just outside Titu, some 35 kilometres to the south of Tîrgovişte. Here they parted company with their bodyguard and hijacked a car driven by a doctor, who took them to the outskirts of Tîrgovişte. They then commandeered a second car and tried to reach the local party headquarters, but were recognized. The driver took them to an agricultural centre, where they were locked in a room until the local police arrived. The couple were eventually taken to the Tîrgovişte military garrison, where they were tried and executed on Christmas Day 1989.

The Front for National Salvation

In the wake of Ceauşescu's flight from the roof of the Central Committee building on 22 December the Council of the Front for National Salvation was set up to run the country. Comprising 145 members, it represented an alliance of reform-minded Communists and prominent dissidents which initially enjoyed widespread support for its declared aim of steering the country towards free elections. On 26 December Ion Iliescu was declared president, and Dumitru Mazilu vice-president, of the National Salvation Front (NSF) and a government appointed with Petre Roman as prime minister. All were members of the Communist Party. An eleven-man Executive Bureau of the NSF was set up to act as a 'Cabinet', but in effect all major decisions, including the one to execute Nicolae and Elena Ceauşescu, were taken by a small group centred around Iliescu, Mazilu and Silviu Brucan, a leading Party critic of Ceauşescu and the *eminence grise* of the Front. It was this concentration of power in the hands of an inner circle of Communists and the secrecy of its decision-making processes that created a climate of suspicion about its intentions.

The turning point in the public's acquiescence in the NSF came with its decision on 23 January 1990 to stand as a political party, despite the pronouncement on 29 December of its ideologue, Silviu Brucan, that 'it is not necessary for us to become a political party'. On the following day the leading dissident, Doina Cornea, announced her resignation from the NSF Council, accusing it of being 'demagogic'. The Front's *volte-face* was also criticized by the three leading opposition groups, the National Peasant Party, the National Liberal Party and the Social Democratic Party, and prompted a large anti-Front demonstration in Bucharest on 28 January 1990. This was followed by a pro-Front demonstration by workers, many of whom were brought in by buses and brandished cudgels and chains. A number of them besieged the National Peasant Party leader, Corneliu Coposu, in his headquarters, and when he left he had to be taken away in an armoured car. The day after, on 31 January, Ana Blandiana, the dissident poet, announced her resignation from the Front's Council, opining that her membership was not compatible with her position as a writer who wanted to distance herself from the 'aggression, hatred and lack of tolerance produced by the struggle for power'.

This turbulence forced the NSF to open discussions with the opposition parties in order to enlarge the Council of the Front, which had been set up on 22 December 1989 on an *ad hoc* basis as an interim government. The new Council was set up on 1 February 1990 with the name of the Provisional Council for National Unity (PCNU), and its 241 members were to be drawn from representatives of the major parties and national minorities, together with figures 'active in the revolution', workers, intellectuals, and students. Nevertheless, the Front continued to dominate the new body, with 106 members, compared to the 105 representatives of the 35 registered parties (three from each) and the 27 members representing the nine national minority bodies. The membership of the PCNU was increased to 253 on 10 February to incorporate extra representatives from the Front and from two newly formed parties. The proliferation of new parties (on 19 April their number stood at 82) might be seen as a reaction to almost half a century of single-party rule, but many of them are regarded by the opposition as cover organizations for the Front and six of them indeed declared their support for it in late January. Such developments invite parallels with the tactics used by the Soviet Union to impose Communist rule in Romania at the end of World War II, when a National Democratic Bloc incorporating several Communist front bodies was used to bring a Communist regime to power.

On 19 March the PCNU passed a decree confirming 20 May as the date for parliamentary and presidential elections. In a statement the Council's chairman, Ion Iliescu, said that the electoral campaign, which would start the next day, would lead to the election of a bicameral parliament whose main task would be to draft a new constitution. According to the electoral law the parliament will operate as a constituent assembly with two chambers: an assembly of deputies with 387 seats and a senate with 119 seats.

Public distrust of the NSF's intentions and its anger at the Front's failure to grant equal air-time to the opposition parties led to the resignation of the president of Television and Radio, Aurel Dragoş Munteanu, on 9 February while a week later the Minister of Defence, General Nicolae Militaru, resigned following demonstrations outside the government's headquarters by young army and air force officers and civilians protesting at his association with the Ceauşescu regime. Reports of attacks in February on National Peasant Party officials and offices throughout the country heightened suspicion that the NSF was resorting to intimidation and violence in order to dampen opposition, and once again raised the spectre of the brutal authoritarian rule associated with the Communists.

Fears that the NSF's ultimate aim, if elected, is to engineer a return to single-party rule have been strengthened by its reliance on officials who served Ceauşescu and on senior *securitate* officers. Prime minister Petre Roman has countered that it is impossible to form an interim government without including figures who were members of the Communist Party and who have some administrative experience. Mistrust of the NSF is compounded, particularly in the eyes of the younger generation, by the prevalence of opportunism which so ravaged Romanian public and intellectual life during the Ceauşescu era, and which still threatens to turn the revolution sour. Dumitru Mazilu has been a victim of such a charge. A Communist turned dissident, Mazilu was appointed vice-president of the NSF Council on the morrow of the revolution, but when he appeared on the same platform with President Ion Iliescu to answer critics at an anti-Front demonstration on 12 January he was accused of attempting to manipulate the crowd to his own advantage. Three days later a number of letters appeared in one of the principal national dailies, claiming that Mazilu had some years earlier been Director of the State Security Training School. Despite his threat to sue the newspaper for libel, public suspicions were not allayed, and he resigned from the Front on 26 January, claiming that he was the victim of 'Stalinist' methods adopted by those who had access to *securitate* files.

In the degree of attention given to criticism of the NSF it is tempting to believe that it is completely lacking in public support, but this is not the case. The miners who came to Bucharest to show their support for the Front on 19 February 1990 did so, despite President Iliescu's plea to them to stay at home, and threatened to destroy the local railway station in the mining centre of Petroşani if trains were not provided for their transport to the capital. In the miners' view the Front's reformed Communist policies offer a better guarantee of their jobs than the market-orientated programmes of the other major parties. These parties have claimed that the miners are easy prey to manipulation by the Front for its own ends, but they have been far from docile in the past, and they staged the first major strike in protest at working conditions under the Ceauşescu regime in July 1977.

Ceauşescu's legacy

While the crisis of morality and the political problems of Romania might be alleviated by impartial and dignified conduct of the May elections, the solution of the economic problems left by the Ceauşescu regime will require drastic and painful measures. All the major political parties are agreed upon the need for decentralization, the transition to a market-based economy, and the dissolution of collective farms. Where there is a difference is over the speed at which these changes should take place, and the NSF, with its largely Communist composition, is in this respect the most cautious, for it derives most of its support from the industrial working class who stand to lose their jobs in any market-orientated rationalization of the economy, and who cannot fall back on a non-existent unemployment benefit.

The most comprehensive statement on the state of the Romanian economy was given by the prime minister, Petre Roman, on 4 January 1990. He told the National Salvation Front Council that the economy was in 'profound crisis'. Production targets had been imposed without any regard for the country's 'raw material and material resources'. Money was thrown away on 'lunatic investments . . . with no technical or economic justification'. Industry was using 'obsolete technologies', particularly the metallurgical and chemical industries, which had not been modernized since 1948. 'In the energy field we are working with pre-war technologies.' Due to the policy of rapid debt repayment, no new technology had been imported for 10 years, and for the same reason, health, education and transport services had all been starved of investment during the same period.

Roman announced at the same time that a number of Ceauşescu's prestige projects would be abandoned, including the construction of a canal linking Bucharest to the Danube, the Călăraşi iron and steel combine, and the second stage of the heavy-water plant at Turnu Severin. While the cancellation of these projects, and of the systematization programme announced on 26 January, will release funds for investment, they will not be sufficient for the modernization which Romanian industry so desperately requires. Industrial modernization can only be achieved with foreign collaboration, but the Front's declarations in this regard are less than encouraging for prospective partners, for they will not allow majority Western equity participation in Romanian companies. Roman seems to fear that aid from the industrialized West will not only bring a transfer of capital and technology but also concomitant divisions of wealth, privilege and labour.

The most immediate problems for the economy arise from energy production. Over the last decade the power supply network was not developed sufficiently to meet the needs of the energy-intensive and wasteful metallurgical and chemical industries, and as a consequence, draconian restrictions and quotas were imposed on domestic consumers. These restrictions were annulled on 1 January, but the subsequent diversion of power supplies to the household has badly affected industrial production. Domestic consumption of electricity rose in January 1990 by 50% compared with the same month in the previous year, and now represented 12% of total electric power generation, according to the Minister for Electric Power. In February it was announced that street lighting, which had been cut by 80% between 1972 and 1989, would be restored. In Bucharest alone 40,000 lamps would be reinstated by 1992.

The impact of these measures upon industry has been considerable. In January 1990 the Minister for National Economy, Colonel-General Victor Stănculescu, reported that factories were suffering from shortages of natural gas, electricity, coal and other raw materials. It is clear from the minister's remarks that industrial output fell in the first two months of 1990, and these difficulties make the case for economic reform even more cogent. The interim government's commitment to improve household supplies will further reduce the amount of energy available to industry unless the deficit is made up by imports from the Soviet Union.

The miners' protests in support of President Iliescu suggest a favourable response from the industrialized working class to the Front government's measures to protect workers' interests. They have been told that they will not have their wages stopped for failure to meet unrealistic targets, as was the case during the Ceauşescu period. Where production was halted due to shortages of energy or raw materials, 75% of wages would still be paid.

It was upon the workers that the Front pinned its hopes for victory in the May elections. The Front was to emerge victorious only by maintaining its support from large numbers of workers, and we can expect only a very gradual transition from a centrally planned to a market economy, unlike the developments in Poland. There are advantages in this. A slow restructuring of industry will reduce the threat of massive and rapid unemployment which could create political instability. Furthermore, Romanians' economic expectations are less ambitious at the moment because of their experience of Communism. Having endured the insanity of the Ceauşescu regime, they are relieved to have survived, and even though we can hardly describe the situation at present as one of even relative normality, it is undeniably preferable to what preceded it. Romanians will be happy to make do with half a capitalist loaf after having been completely denied the Communist one. The disadvantages in applying a slow pace to industrial change are that there will continue to be shortages of consumer goods, and that this will give little incentive for the new private peasant farmers to invest in agricultural machinery and increase production for the market if they have nothing to spend their income on.

Chronic shortages of consumer goods were a feature of the latter years of the Ceauşescu era, and the Front has frozen the export of foodstuffs. But despite the arrival of emergency food aid, many areas do not have food supplies sufficient to satisfy local needs. The abolition of rationing, introduced in 1982, has aggravated the problem, for there has been panic buying of meat, sugar, edible oil, butter and eggs, and stocks of these products are low. Food supply in the long term will be eased by the creation of private holdings of plots on state and collective farms. Two decrees issued by the Front on 31 January 1990 permitted collective farms in mountainous regions to allocate land to farmers for private use with production being delivered to what were termed 'the state's specialized units'. In lowland regions collective farms would be allowed to allocate up to 5000 square metres of land for private use to collective farm members, and up to 2500 square metres to those who were not collective members but who wished to return to the countryside, provided that they cultivated the land and paid rent to the collective. State farms would also be able to allocate up to 5000 square metres of land to agricultural labourers. The produce of these private plots could be sold in the market and the plots themselves, together with the farmers' houses, sold and inherited.

Private enterprise, albeit on a very limited scale, has also been permitted by the Front in industry. Under a decree issued on 6 February small enterprises with a maximum of 20 employees may be set up, and individuals who are already employed in state industry may move to private enterprises. The products of these businesses may be exported through the state foreign trade concerns and 50% of the hard currency income may be retained by the business. The rest will be credited in lei converted at the official exchange rate. What the decree does not address is the problem of obtaining investment capital for these small businesses, and the Front's cautious attitude towards Western economic co-operation, coupled with the unstable political situation, make the prospects for investment gloomy. The need for Western involvement in modernizing Romanian industry was recognized by prime minister Roman himself in an economic report which he gave on 5 February. Lack of investment had created conditions in factories which were 'impossible' while machinery had not been maintained and had broken down. Imports of what he called 'key technologies' would be needed in order to raise living standards: 'For these technologies we must and have already started to turn openly to the West, Western Europe in particular.' Exactly how this technology would be acquired was not made clear, although his reference in this context to the provision 'of proper laws for joint societies, for co-operation' seemed to indicate a preference. Under pressure from the opposition parties the proposed decree for attracting foreign capital in Romania was modified in the interim Parliament in March to allow Western companies to own outright Romanian enterprises, but profits from such companies must be reinvested in the country.

The threat of nationalism

The problems of underinvestment, of modernizing a backward economy, of creating a civic society undivided by generation divisions and ethnic tensions – difficulties which Romania's politicians faced at the end of World War I – must be confronted again today. If they remain unsolved, as they did in the interwar period, we shall witness a period of political turmoil. In such conditions nationalism, which has been a feature of Romanian politics for over a century, is likely to flourish.

The greatest threat to stability in Romania is posed by ethnic differences, and failure to solve them will endanger all efforts to set the country on the path to democracy and to economic reform. Sadly, the spirit of partnership shown by the Hungarian and Romanian communities in Tranvsylvania in the anti-Ceauşescu demonstrations in Timişoara which set off the revolution in December rapidly evaporated as the Hungarians used their newly gained freedom to present demands for more cultural autonomy. These included a restoration of secondary and university education in their native tongue and greater provision for the publication of Hungarian-language books and newspapers. Initially, the provisional government promised to meet these demands. A ministry for ethnic minorities was to be set up and a Hungarian, Attila Palffy, was appointed Deputy Minister of Education. However, measures to revive former Hungarian-language schools in Transylvania were resisted by local Romanians, especially those who had been settled by the Ceauşescu regime to provide manpower for the newly developed industries of the province. Palffy was dismissed, the provisional government abandoned plans for an ethnic minorities ministry, and the proposed educational reforms were postponed on the grounds of lack of money.

A hardening of the Romanian attitude was prompted by the creation in February 1990 of an ultra-nationalist Romanian cultural association in

Transylvania called Vatra Românească (Romanian hearth), which has attracted a considerable membership among professional people and workers by exploiting Romanian fears that the Hungarian agitation is a sinister stratagem to revive territorial claims to Transylvania, and by encouraging anti-Hungarian sentiment. Hungarian frustration at this change of direction by the provisional government found expression in a sit-in, organized by Hungarian students at the Institute of Medicine in the Transylvanian town of Tirgu Mureş in March, who demanded the restoration of teaching in Hungarian, as indeed had been the case in the pre-Ceauşescu era. The Ministry of Education countered that medical graduates must have a fluent knowledge of Romanian in order to practise throughout the country.

The problem is not just one of language. Behind it lies a mutual mistrust felt by the Hungarian and Romanian governments, which is the legacy of Transylvania's position as part of the ancestral homeland of both peoples, and, more basically, a differing conception of respect for minority rights. Until 1918 the province formed part of Hungary, and following World War I was awarded to Romania on the basis of its considerable Romanian majority. The Romanian government fears that granting separate education in Hungarian will encourage the 2 million Transylvanian Hungarians to then press for greater political autonomy and for a closer association with Hungary. The Hungarians feel that they can only reverse the process of forced assimilation and integration carried out by Ceauşescu by first protecting and then asserting their national identity, and in the event of opposition, calling upon Hungary to aid them in these endeavours.

The question of minority rights strikes at the heart of a democratic society. The principle of equal rights for all citizens is fundamental for any democratic society, and the guarantee of these rights has been given by all the political parties created since the revolution. However, Romanians of all social classes still show sympathy with the Romanian nationalist propaganda generated by the Ceauşescu regime, which was based on two premises. The first was the primacy of group rights over individual ones, and the second, that a people's group rights were to be accorded upon the basis of their historical antiquity in Romania. In support of the second premise, the theory of Romanian historical antecedence over Hungarians in Transylvania was consistently adduced to the exclusion of all other views on the subject. Linked to this idea was the slogan 'Romanians must be masters in their own home', which was interpreted by the regime to mean that since the Romanians were in their own home, they must therefore be masters in it. For the Romanians the idea of 'mastership', or supremacy, was confirmed by the measures taken under Ceauşescu to place minority institutions, such as schools, institutes of higher education, and theatres, under the aegis of Romanian ones, whose governing bodies were almost exclusively made up of Romanians. For most Romanians this system seemed perfectly normal, 'For after all', the argument went 'we live in Romania'.

This mentality is still exhibited by supporters of the nationalist association Vatra Românească, who see the relationship between the Romanians and Hungarians in terms of subordination of the minority to the majority. Hungarians want this relationship to become one of co-ordination, one of tolerance and not dominance. In their view, loyalty to the Romanian state, to have any meaning, must be one that is freely given and not extracted from them, and to give their loyalty they too must be allowed to feel at home in the ancestral homeland which they share with the Romanians. Hungarian demands for greater cultural autonomy have encountered powerful resistance from many Romanians in Transylvania, who see them as an attack on their own interests, which can be defined as both national and economic. It is precisely to defend these interests that Vatra Românească was established, drawing its support from members of the Romanian professional classes, who see the Hungarian demands as a threat to the position of supremacy which Romanian culture has been accorded in public life in Transylvania, and from the Romanian industrial working class, many of whom were brought from other parts of Romania during the last two decades as industry expanded in Transylvania and who fear the loss of their jobs. The latter have been encouraged by the leaders of Vatra Românească to believe that the restoration of Hungarian cultural autonomy will lead to greater Hungarian control of the local economy and that positive discrimination in favour of the Hungarians will leave many Romanians jobless. The association's manipulation of Romanian fears has contributed in a major way to the ethnic unrest in Transylvania.

In essence, Vatra Românească seeks to maintain the Romanian position of supremacy in Transylvania, and appeals to all those who still share Ceauşescu's aim of creating a uniform, homogeneous state. It is obvious that such an aim is alien to a democratic society, and the association's propaganda campaign of what can only be termed incitement to ethnic hatred threatens, in practical terms, to effectively undermine the process of democratization in Romania as a whole. It is in the interests of both Romanians and Hungarians to create a democratic society in which these ethnic tensions disappear, and yet the ethnic divide continues to be reinforced by the composition and character of the political parties which have emerged since the revolution. The largest of these, the Front for National Salvation, the National Peasant Party and the National Liberal Party, have drawn very little support from among the Hungarian community, which has identified itself almost exclusively with the Hungarian Democratic Union. Very little dialogue has taken place between this Hungarian party and the other political groupings, with the result that its pleas in the provisional parliament to discuss minority demands have fallen upon deaf ears. The failure of the Bucharest government to address the issue prompted a series of peaceful demonstrations by Hungarians in

Tirgu Mureş, but tension increased after celebrations on 15 March 1990 of Hungary's national day, when buildings in Transylvania were draped with Hungarian flags and thousands of Hungarians from Hungary joined their co-nationals in the ceremonies. On 19 March Romanians in Tirgu Mureş marched in peaceful protest at what they regarded as the connivance of local Hungarian officials in staging ceremonies which were considered provocative, but in the evening a crowd of several hundred Romanians stormed the local headquarters of the Hungarian Democratic Union party. After sacking the building, they beat party officials as they tried to leave, including the prominent Hungarian Transylvanian writer, Andras Suto, who was blinded in one eye. At the same time, the local headquarters of the predominantly Romanian National Liberal Party were attacked by a mob armed with staves and axes. On the following day, as some 5000 Hungarians staged a peaceful demonstration against the violence of the previous evening, they were charged by an estimated mob of 2000 Romanians armed with scythes and clubs. The attack left six people dead and more than 300 injured. It was only after the bloodshed that the army intervened with tanks to separate the rival groups.

Apart from the ethnic dimension to these clashes and the harm which they have done to community relations, there is the separate issue of the violence which was used on both sides. Violence has not been restricted to Transylvania, but has characterized political manifestations in other parts of the country, notably the attack on the National Peasant Party headquarters in Bucharest on 30 January 1990. The failure of the interim government to intervene on these occasions suggests, at best, weakness, and, at worst, collusion. How was it possible, for example, in Tirgu Mureş for several thousand Romanians armed with sticks and bars to be brought to the city in buses and lorries with the apparent acquiescence of the authorities, when private car drivers were prevented from reaching the town centre by the police? Organized violence was a feature of inter-war Romanian political life, and just as it eroded the flimsy edifice of democracy in Romania then, so it is in danger of repeating the process today.

The threat of instability in Romania will also give greater impetus to calls for a return to constitutional monarchy. By standing above politics, the monarch can offer hope of reconciliation. In the person of King Michael the monarchy is represented by a courageous figure who overthrew the pro-German dictatorship of Marshal Antonescu in August 1944 and who, uniquely among East European royalty, attempted to save his country from Soviet domination. The exiled King Michael was due to make a private visit to his native country on 12 April 1990 in order to celebrate Easter and to see his grandparents' tombs, but at the last minute the provisional government clumsily withdrew the entry visa which they had granted him several weeks earlier on the grounds that his visit was politically motivated.

The landslide victory awarded to President Iliescu (85% of the vote) and the National Salvation Front (67%) in the May presidential and parliamentary elections led the opposition to claim that there had been wholesale fraud. While most foreign observers were unable to find evidence of a total theft of the election by the Front, some of them were concerned at irregularities in the voting process, particularly in village areas, where the opposition parties, either as a result of intimidation or of poor organization, were not represented at the polling stations. Among the malpractices reported were voting by persons not on the electoral list and failure to stamp identity cards as a safeguard against voting more than once. The scale of these malpractices in some districts led observers with the Helsinki Watch to call for the annulment of the result.

In assessing the fairness of the elections one must consider both the timing and the nature of the electoral campaign which preceded them. It is perhaps unrealistic to expect the same democratic standards from a country which had only just emerged from the worst dictatorship Europe has known since World War II. Having said that, the electoral process was flawed from the moment in January when the Front, behind the mask of the provisional government, declared itself player as well as umpire in the elections. By inheriting the propaganda machinery of the former Communist regime, including two mass-circulation newspapers, they gave themselves a great advantage in presenting their case. By contrast, the major opposition parties had to start from scratch in building up their party and media apparatus. Although the contestants were granted equal airtime on the television, the inevitable identification of interim government and Front ensured that the latter always remained in the forefront of viewers' consciousness. The difficulties which the National Liberal and National Peasant Parties, with their respective presidential candidates, encountered in making themselves known to the voters, particularly in provincial areas, arose from a combination of party mismanagement and intimidation. Claims that intimidation was stage-managed by the Front were difficult to substantiate. It was probably spontaneous, resulting from an inability on the part of many Front supporters to accept the opposition as adversaries rather than enemies. However, it is not without significance that there were virtually no reported incidents of intimidation and physical assault directed against Front candidates.

However, violence and dirty tricks alone could not explain the Front's victory. Essentially, the vested interests of several sectional groups converged to provide the Front's overwhelming support. The large Communist bureaucracy and the *securitate* regarded their future as safer with the Front, the peasants were content with the land which they have been given, and the industrialized working class considered their jobs more secure with the Front's platform of gradual economic reform. President Iliescu was widely seen as the St George who slew the Ceauşescu dragon and the populist measures which he introduced immediately after the revolution were sufficient to earn him a decisive victory.

Nevertheless, the continued occupation of Bucharest's University Square by students demanding that politicians who had served as Communist Party activists or security officers should be disbarred from government showed that Iliescu and the NSF leadership had failed to convince them of their democratic credentials. Iliescu ordered the police to clear the square and, at dawn on 13 June 1990, they moved in. Groups of people gathered that same afternoon and later set fire to several cars and a police van. They then attacked the police headquarters, the offices of Romanian Television and the Foreign Ministry, where Iliescu and the government were based. Evidence was later produced that instructions had been given to the police to set fire to their own headquarters.

The failure of the police to disperse the rioters prompted Iliescu that evening to appeal to miners from the Jiu valley to defend the government which, he claimed, was facing a 'fascist putsch'. Special trains were laid on and some 7000 miners arrived in Bucharest at dawn on 14 June armed with wooden staves and iron bars. Under the direction of figures suspected of belonging to the *securitate* they terrorized the population of the capital, attacking the headquarters of the major opposition parties, and the University, where they beat students. On 15 June President Iliescu summoned the miners to a 'victory' rally, where he thanked them.

Iliescu's action was condemned by most Western governments and his inauguration was boycotted by the US ambassador. The EC postponed signature of a trade agreement with Romania and the European Parliament made its approval of the agreement conditional upon the NSF government satisfying criteria guaranteeing political and human rights. Dismayed by the ineffectiveness of the parliamentary opposition, extra-parliamentary groups such as trade unions and student unions joined in September to form the Civic Alliance.

On 18 October the government announced what it called 'emergency measures' to deal with the 'disastrous' state of the economy. The currency was immediately devalued by 60% and from 1 November price controls on all goods and services, except for bread, meat, heating and electricity, were removed, causing increases of between 100% and 120%. On 15 November some 200,000 people joined a peaceful demonstration organized by the Civic Alliance in Bucharest, where there were calls for the postponement of price rises.

As a result of widespread public protests and strikes against these increases, the government decided to postpone the second stage of price 'liberalization' – the removal of subsidies from the essential items not included in the first round of price increases, from 1 January to 1 April 1991. On this date the price of these exempted items, such as bread, milk, butter, cheese and sugar, more than doubled. At the same time, the official rate of the leu was further devalued by 58% to 60 lei to the US dollar. On 14

February 1991 a land reform allowing private citizens to reclaim a maximum of 10 hectares (24 acres) of land nationalized by the state was passed by both chambers of the Romanian parliament.

The adoption of these measures tempered international concern that the government was not doing enough to eradicate the totalitarian practices of the past. Furthermore, Romania's strong support of the United Nations position during the Gulf crisis, given despite the fact that the UN trade embargo deprived the country of securing repayment of Iraqi debts totalling almost $3 billion, while not relevant to the process of economic liberalization won Romania goodwill. This was reflected in the decision of the European Community Council of Ministers to extend the PHARE (Aid for Restructuring of Economies) programme to Romania in mid-January 1991; on 39 January the Group of 24 OECD countries agreed to give assistance while recognizing the need to monitor closely the implementation of political and economic reform. Two days later Romania was granted guest status by the Council of Europe, being the last East European country, with the exception of Albania, to be admitted. On 9 May it was announced that the British Know-How Fund, set up in June 1989 to assist the countries of Eastern Europe to move towards democracy and a free market economy, had also been extended to Romania.

However, distrust of Romania persisted in several quarters. Prime Minister Petre Roman's request to be included in the Visegrad summit of Czechoslovak, Hungarian and Polish leaders was turned down by President Havel on 15 February on the grounds that the process of rapid integration into Western Europe pursued by the three countries represented might be jeopardized by close association with Romania. At the same time, the US administration made it clear that it was not yet prepared to grant the country Most Favored Nation status.

A view that Romania was looking eastwards rather than westwards seemed to be confirmed by President Iliescu's signing of a treaty of friendship and co-operation with the Soviet Union on 5 April 1991 during a visit to Moscow, thus making Romania the first country in Eastern Europe to conclude such a treaty with its former overlord since the collapse of Communism in the region. Although not a treaty of alliance, one of its clauses stipulates that neither country will join any alliance directed against the other. Based on the provisions of the Helsinki Final Act and the Paris Charter for a New Europe, the treaty reaffirms the inviolability of borders and attracted criticism from the Romanian opposition that it validated the Soviet occupation of the former Romanian territory of Bessarabia, which is largely coterminous with the former Soviet Socialist Republic of Moldavia, now the self-styled Republic of Moldavia.

Domestically, for an increasing number of Romanians democracy has come to be identified with chaos, rocketing prices, rising crime and increasing unemployment. Voices are beginning to recall with nostalgia the 'order' of the past. Reform runs the risk of being compromised and with it the reformist voices of the economists in the NSF government. Whether the latter will prevail over the conservative elements within the NSF and surrounding the President depends to a large degree on how far the populace is prepared to accept further hardship.

In the longer term the chances for democracy depend on a change in the relationship between the people and government. Both sides have something to learn. The populace must accept that the exercise of freedom in society requires democratically approved constraints while the government must accept that those constraints be much less rigid than those of the Communist past. Furthermore, Romanians in public office must themselves change their attitudes towards power. Far too many politicians are interested not in increasing access to power for Romanian citizens but in securing power for their own personal ends. Public realization of this has added to the mistrust of authority felt by Romanians. That mistrust is the legacy of the Communist past when the truth was distorted by the regime. Cynicism and scepticism, attitudes developed by Romanians to combat oppression, are hallmarks of public opinion today and will only diminish if people and government alike recognize the need for a new political morality and make a conscious effort to introduce one. Consequently, there is growing support, especially among the intellectual elite, for the return of King Michael and constitutional monarchy as the sole means of instituting the moral regeneration which the country needs if it is not to remain on the periphery of the democratic family of nations.

8 YUGOSLAVIA

The Yugoslav situation can be defined in three sentences: (1) a society without a state; (2) an economy without a market; (3) a people without freedom and democracy. It is further characterized by high unemployment, acute social misery and galloping inflation. Has a programme been established, in real and exact terms, to get out of this apocalyptic situation?

Such was the opening question of a well-publicized interview with the head of one of the eight regional leagues of Yugoslav Communists in November 1989. In another set of interviews with leading economists two months later, a professor from Titograd University said 'We have the last Bolshevik-type party in Europe'. When interrupted with 'You have forgotten Albania', he retorted: 'Don't mention Albania, please. Must we always compare ourselves with the worst?' At the time of the first interview the pun was that Yugoslavia was in *RAJ* ('heaven' in Serbo-Croat, as well as being the initials for Romania–Albania–Yugoslavia). At the time of the second, it had become *AJ* ('Ouch!').

Such was the bleak view from within, but in the West who remembers the days when Yugoslavia's special brand of socialism elicited admiration and envy; when the claims of its Communist rulers about how they came to power, reunified the country and solved its problems were accepted at face value? Who remembers, now that the land of the South Slavs is the sick man of the Balkans and in danger of 'Balkanization'? (This ugly word is often used by people who know little about the Balkans, and who prefer not to have to pronounce Timişoara or look for Kurdzhali.)

The People's Liberation Struggle

On the eve of the German invasion in 1941 the Communist Party of Yugoslavia, ancestor of the later League of Communists (SKJ), was a Stalinist and revolutionary organization which Tito had rejuvenated since the Comintern had appointed him to take it over. With the war and liberation, it had acquired a good base of its own, and it stood out among the Communist parties that had taken power in east-central Europe as the one that had gone furthest on the way to copying the Soviet model before Stalin excommunicated it in 1948.

Finding itself rejected by its mentor, it was forced to look to its own base, and to adapt to a situation that would reflect the constraints of

YUGOSLAVIA

Official name	The Socialist Federal Republic of Yugoslavia
Area	255,804 sq. km (98,766 sq. miles)
Population	23,657,000 (1989) (annual growth rate 0.7%)
Capital	Belgrade (Beograd)
Languages	73% Serbo-Croat, 7.8% Slovene, 6% Macedonian, 7.7% Albanian
Religions	40% Eastern Orthodox, 30% Roman Catholic, 12% Muslim
Currency	dinar

geography and mentality, while drawing from its Stalinism the strength to hold out against Stalin, before extracting from its Marxism–Leninism the ability to indulge in ambitious experiments. Without relinquishing its totalitarian origins and aspirations, Tito's regime acquired a specificity which it owed partly to historical circumstances. Titoism was to be characterized by the People's Liberation Struggle as its source and inspiration, by workers' self-management and by non-alignment as principles of its domestic and foreign policies, respectively.

The People's Liberation Struggle was actually more of a civil war for the control of post-war Yugoslavia. As such, it did little to heal war wounds and to rally patriotic feelings in a country where memories are long. To support the claim that its monopoly of power was a defence against the threat of renewed strife between its domestic enemies, the Party had magnified and mythologized the partisan struggle. The recent interest in that period is a symptom of the dissatisfaction created by this policy.

A brilliant idea in terms of ideology and publicity, self-management could, arguably, have been a useful model for an economy of industrial take-off at the time when it was conceived, if it had really been applied. Exploited as an all-purpose slogan, it was claimed as a substitute for political democracy but it turned into an economic disaster. As for non-alignment, it was but the latest in a series of 'grey-zone' situations for the Yugoslav lands. For a while, it was of marginal international importance, but for the leadership it was a way of satisfying its foreign-policy ambitions.

Serbs and Croats

Serbs and Croats make up the core of the Yugoslav population. They are intermingled, speak the same language, have the most ancient collective self-awareness, and feel different. Together they form an absolute majority of about 60%. Religion remains the symbol of the differences. Serbs, nominally Eastern Orthodox, are the most numerous, followed by Croats, nominally Roman Catholic. On the eve of the collapse of Austria–Hungary these two groups, along with their Catholic Slovene cousins to the north, had already fully developed such attributes as a modern language, a literature, a national ideology, political parties and an aspiration to greater unity. In the movement towards unification, differences were underrated, while all the emphasis was placed on common origins and affinities.

The diversity of historical experiences can be reduced to two major trends which met in 1918: Serbia's, unitary and centralist, and Croatia's, born of the institutional and ethnic complexity of Austria–Hungary. For the Serbs, their local Orthodox Church, the only surviving institution of the medieval kingdom, had continued the development of a conscious entity during the centuries of Turkish rule. In the nineteenth century the growing embryo of a principality, and later kingdom, of Serbia provided the framework within which nationalism and politics could blossom, and contemplate the liberation and integration of kindred populations. This tradition assimilated the emancipation from Austrian and Hungarian overlordship to the wars of liberation against the Turks, and viewed the Yugoslav state as the final stage in the long process of liberation and unification.

The experience of the Croats was that of the continued separate existence of the 'Crown of Croatia'. It fell to the nobility, and later to the bourgeoisie, to continue to give shape to a wider national feeling during the centuries when that crown belonged to foreign dynasties, and the struggle for its rights kept it as a legal framework in which nationalism and politics were able to develop under the Habsburgs. By 1918, Croatia's political class yearned for a Yugoslavia where an extended Serbia would have been balanced by a consolidated Croatia. The Serbian tradition, modelled on the French post-revolutionary ideal, led to Serbian (then Yugoslav) integration of a nation defined by the state. The Croatian, on the model of Hungary, perceived Yugoslavia as an improved dualistic system which would have strengthened Croatia's historic rights.

The outcome of the constitutional confrontation was influenced by several factors which lent support to the unitarist trend, not least the romantic view of the one Yugoslav nation-to-be with its triple Serb–Croat–Slovene name. The Serbian conception prevailed. The 1921 Constitution set up a centralized parliamentary government under the Serbian royal house. Serbs were satisfied with the framework of the new state of Yugoslavia, which they viewed as the natural extension of their father-land. Divided into regions and parties, far from seeing themselves as a domineering element, they thought themselves to be the ultimate rampart of a unified country for which they had given up their own identity.

The disappointed Croats immediately began to demand a revision of the Constitution. Not numerous enough to change it by regular parliamentary procedure, they increasingly coalesced into one large ethnic party, which went back and forth between opposition and government, while a fringe, the fascist Ustašas, would turn to violence feeding on more general frustration. The tragedy of pre-war Yugoslavia was that parliament was closed down in 1929 by King Alexander. The Crown tried to foster 'Yugoslavism' from above, but in so doing it merely alienated the Croats, while it irritated many Serbs, and others too. Serbian and Croatian opposition coalesced in the 1930s, but it was with the Crown that the latter eventually struck a bargain which gave Croatia a special status. This divided the opposition and caused bitterness on both sides. The Axis then invaded and destroyed Yugoslavia. All possible ethnic tensions were inflamed by the Nazis. A greater and nominally independent (but satellite) Croatia was set up under the Ustašas, who tried to get rid of the Serbs in their state by massacres, expulsions and conversions. The country was to come back to life, however, albeit in another form, in the wake of the collapse of Hitler's New Order.

Postwar Yugoslavia

Yugoslavia was restored after the war as a multinational state of related nations, united under the Communist Party. The new federal division made additions to the three original components of Serbs, Croats and Slovenes whom the monarchy had failed to blend into a single Yugoslav people. The Macedonians to the south were acknowledged as a distinct nation, and the Yugoslav part of Macedonia was set up as a separate republic. The same status was granted to Montenegro, whose inhabitants were encouraged to identify with the territory's history rather than with the wider concept of Serbdom, and to Bosnia-Herzegovina, kept undivided because of its ethnic and religious compound of Orthodox Christians (Serbs), Catholic Christians (Croats) and Muslims (Serbo-Croat-speaking Slavs). This produced the six constituent republics of the Communist federation.

Furthermore, two autonomous regions were carved out of Serbia – Vojvodina to the north and Kosovo to the south, because of their mixed ethnic composition, according to the Soviet model. They had been the cradle of Serbdom, at the beginning of its medieval and of its modern development, respectively. But Serbia had to be cut down to a size not too large in comparison with Croatia. What many felt to be Serbia's dominant position had to be diminished, and satisfaction given to the differences that existed in these regions.

As internationalists, the Yugoslav Communists had not had a consistent record in national matters. They had started as unitarists, had dutifully turned disintegrationist to follow the Comintern line, before they were to convert to federalism. The Party had inserted itself into the resistance of Serbs during the war – mainly among Serbs outside Serbia – but it had also used the notion of Serbian hegemony to win support among other nationalities. It looked to the peripheral groups to weaken those at the core, Serbs and Croats, whom it wanted to equalize and neutralize. At first, federalism was no more than a form, for it was subordinated to a new political unitarism, that of the Party, and to a new ideology of integration, that of Communism. It did, however, immediately give birth to regional political elites, who were to prosper with the decentralization that expanded after the break with Moscow in 1948.

Federalism – and nationalism

By the late 1960s federalism was not only well established but was even turning to confederalism. The distribution of social goods had been one of the means initially used by the Party to acquire support. The creation of a new elite and Soviet-style industrialization had led to large-scale social mobility. After the chaos of the war years, people were more ready to accept rule from the centre, especially if backed by the lure of rapid economic progress. In the 1960s, however, these possibilities were no longer what they had been, and the Party gave up its control of certain areas of social life. Ideology became less significant, and the primary object of the political elite turned to enjoying the privileges of power rather than trying to change society. This was achieved by a combination of tactical concessions, selected repression, tolerance of particular interest representation within limits, and Western aid.

Having assumed more and more responsibilities, local Party leaderships took on the representation of territorial interests as a way of legitimizing their roles. Not able to satisfy the new post-revolutionary generations with more political or even economic freedom, the regime ignored the expression of nationalist feelings. To the extent that such a freedom weakened the more conservative wing of the Party, the decentralizing reformers encouraged it. No sooner had social and economic developments led to a pluralist reaction against ideological and political uniformity than the Party was faced with the same multiform nationalism it had hoped to eliminate. Meanwhile, it had prevented any attempt at Yugoslav integration by means other than those of official ideology. Driven by disappointment in the present, concern for the future and nostalgia for the past, feelings of nationalism flowed out again into old moulds.

Without the possibility of discussing openly the all-important problems the country had to face, national identity, because of its highly emotional character, was the question that tended to pervade all others. The craving for more freedom of expression was all too often reduced to a need to call oneself by the name of one's nationality. Faith in a supranational Communist ideology having failed, people fell back upon the collectivity to which they felt they belonged. Economic, social and even political grievances were increasingly seen as national grievances – in a state that had a minorities problem and no integrative national feeling. In the 1960s, it turned out that Yugoslavia's national question was much more serious than in the 1930s.

Before the war, the problem had been primarily seen in political and constitutional terms; 30 years later, it had become economic, social and cultural as well. More nationalities had been recognized, assisted in inverse proportion to their numerical importance and historic seniority, so as to divide the population into smaller categories and speed up their integration. Yugoslavia, which had been set up again as a federation of nations, was turned into a confederation of territories with the 1974 Constitution. That was the fourth of the Titoist regime's fundamental laws, the longest, most verbose and most confusing, bringing together what had become the twin evils of the SKJ – nationalism and *langue de bois*.

In principle and in rhetoric, it was made to appear as the final outcome of the country's socialist progress – a charter of the working class. In reality, it institutionalized the nationalism it could no longer oppose, by giving the parts – the federated units – greater rights than the whole – the federation. The autonomous regions, which had become autonomous provinces with increased prerogatives in the 1960s, were equated with the republics in all but name, while the domain of the federal government was reduced to defence, foreign affairs, certain limited prerogatives of economic and financial policy, and the overall maintenance of the constitutional system. Even in those areas, however, policies could only be adopted and implemented through the 'consensus' or unanimous consent of the federated units.

The trend towards identifying republics with ethnic groups thereafter increased the malaise of the Serbs, who were further hurt by developments in Kosovo. In what was theoretically still a part of the Republic of Serbia, Albanian demographic pressure was constantly reducing the Serbian proportion of the population, while local Albanian SK cadres were busy turning the province into an Albanian unit within Yugoslavia. In the 1960s Serbs had begun to ponder on the consequences of their dispersion. By 1981 there were 4.9 million of them in what had come to be called 'Inner Serbia' – Serbia without the provinces – as opposed to 3.3 million in other territories, with another 600,000 Montenegrin cousins, not to say brothers.

The territorial division of the country, which had been acceptable as an administrative structure, was no longer so as the framework for mini-nation-states in a 'Balkanized' Yugoslavia. Serbian public opinion resented that it had got nothing out of its leadership's identification with the federal leadership. Serbian national frustration began to resemble an opposition to the regime, culture and religion picking up what Party cadres had not dared handle.

Meanwhile in Croatia, the defenders of that republic's identity had been recruited from the local SK, making the Zagreb government fly in the face of the federal authorities in Belgrade, which were, once again, openly identified with Serbian influence. This heresy was brought to an end in 1971, along with other heresies elsewhere, notably that of the liberals in Serbia's SK, and in Croatia it led to a more orthodox, but weaker and unpopular, leadership. In exchange for losing a government that had become both populist and popular, Croatia would be appeased by the 1974 Constitution, which gave the new set in Zagreb a chance to legitimize itself.

In the more outlying regions, the then relatively level-headed nationalism of Slovenia and the still young nationalism of Macedonia simply carried on with the task of turning their territories into nation-republics. Whereas Slovenian particularism believed that a looser Yugoslav community would give greater scope for economic development to its republic on the borders with the Western world, Macedonian particularism felt the need for a strong South Slav federation in order to survive in the heart of the Balkans, unacknowledged outside Yugoslavia, caught between Albanian and Bulgarian aspirations.

Tito's legacy

Revolutionary turned conservative, Tito had harmonized all the contradictions of the Stalinist system he had had to adapt to the isolation of his country's geography and mentality. He had eventually come to solve all the problems by ignoring or condemning them, by his hold over the Party cadres, by the cult of his personality which equalled that of the greatest dictators of our century, and by the propaganda which was one of the regime's greatest successes. He had become monarch, originally anointed by Stalin but inheriting the traditions of the sultans in Stambul and the emperors in Vienna, along with the authoritarianism of Serbia's Obrenović and Karadjordjević rulers.

Tito had more palaces and villas, hunting lodges and islands, yachts and custom-built cars, uniforms and suits, medals and titles than any of his royal predecessors (who actually had very few of these) or of his Communist counterparts. While still alive, he had installed not one heir, apparent or presumptive, but a set of *diadochi*, mediocre apparatchiks selected to take the place of the up-and-coming elite of the 1960s that had been purged of its more popular and able leaders. His advanced years were accompanied by increasing court intrigues, and when he died in 1980, the system was paralysed. Without him as supreme symbol and moderator, the Constitution could no longer function. Trapped between nonsensical rhetoric and rival nationalist power factions, it ground to a halt once it had put its anointed monarch to rest.

At a popular level, the legitimacy of the SKJ was founded on three facts: it had ended the civil war, and brought the various ethnic groups out of the blind alleys into which the Axis had pushed them; it had then stood up to Stalin; finally, it had introduced the Yugoslavs to the joys of consumerism, and put the country on the map. By the time Yugoslavia remembered that it was 70 years old, at the end of 1988, all that had evaporated. The country was but one instance of the tension between regime and society in Communist Europe. The difference between Yugoslavia and the others was that Yugoslavia had started it all. For 40 years, the ruling Party had looked for ways of legitimizing itself independently of the Soviet Union, and of making the economy more efficient while maintaining its monopoly of power.

To acquire that monopoly and to preserve it had been at the fore of the Yugoslav Communist leaders' preoccupations. This had been the case in the initial period, when Tito was anticipating and fomenting revolution outside Yugoslavia's borders, while still fearing the possible victory of anti-Communist forces within. It had been true of the middle period, when Tito approached the nationalities issue as a balancing act, if not actually with a divide-and-rule policy, which accentuated the difference between nationalities and regions. It was so of the final period, when he delegated power to his trusties in the republics who then went on to draw on nationalistic feelings and international credit to build up their separate bases.

Shaken by the loss of faith, the SKJ bureaucracy clung tenaciously to those bases. Its fragmented nationalism, in search of a new make-up with which to restore its tarnished image, managed to break the enormous potential of opposition, but at the cost of promoting the primacy of national identities, of threatening the state with disintegration, and its component nationalities with the loss of feeling for their common interests.

After Tito

After Tito's death, a growing section of public opinion aspired to more pluralism, more legality, more rationality, more reality. Its educated elite clamoured for it in the years 1985–7, particularly in Slovenia and in Serbia. Throughout these years, several hundred intellectuals were standing up to be counted. An all-Yugoslav opposition platform, however inchoate, was emerging, and the mood was spreading to the more educated rank and file of the Party, aiming at introducing into government and society some basic rules of generally accepted civilized behaviour. An atmosphere of *glasnost* produced a public debate in which everything was discussed with frankness and at length, while action based on these debates remained small, slow and disorganized.

By 1987 the failure to grapple with the economic crisis had removed the last shreds of credibility from the people in charge. There was widespread popular agreement with the intellectuals that the political system was responsible, and that radical change must come, to include the political leadership put together by Tito in his last decade. A workers' revolt, caused by the sharp fall in their standard of living, spread to all sectors and all republics from its source in Croatia's heavy industry. It was the prelude to the year 1988, which saw the resignation of the Mikulić government, which had been thought tougher than its predecessors, coming after six months of criticism, and mass demonstrations that swept away Party leaderships and governments in Vojvodina and Montenegro. Whole groups of high officials, selected by the tried and tested processes of the *nomenklatura*, suddenly found themselves at the mercy of the working class, in whose name they had been ruling for so long.

These events were linked to the explosion of Serbian nationalism, which brought to the leadership of that republic the first Yugoslav politician since Tito to have made an impact, even if a negative one, on the West – Slobodan Milošević, head of the Party hierarchy and genuinely popular hero. Mass demonstrations called for the sacking of corrupt officials, exploiters of the workers, and traitors to Serbian interests. They were the result of discontent pent up since the 1960s, especially since 1974. The constitutional arrangements of these years appeared as a feudalization of Party power at the expense of Serbian interests, with the approval of Serbia's leadership. At the same time, the prominent position of Serbs in the country's political elite, at federal and regional level, left only Slovenia north and Macedonia south without relatively strong Serb Communist influence, and made them resented in most other regions. The Serbs felt that their historical past and consciousness had been sacrificed for the sake of a common Communist Yugoslav cause.

The Kosovo situation had burst the abscess. Set up originally as an autonomous region within Serbia, adjoining Albania, to ease the latter's hoped-for entry into the federation, Kosovo had been moving towards the status of Yugoslavia's Albanian component. This had been institutionalized in all but name in 1974. The demographic thrust of Albanian Muslims, together with the affirmation of their ethnic consciousness by the regional government, had dramatically accelerated the reduction in the proportion of Serbs living there. Pressures and intimidations of all sorts had turned Serbian emigration into an exodus, without the government of Serbia being able to do anything about it.

While being a relative majority in Yugoslavia, Serbs saw themselves as having just one vote in eight, as being out of favour and without protection. It was becoming clear to them that the original division, which historians are discovering to have been established with some arbitrariness and opportunism, had been made to find an immediate and practical answer, not only to the question of ethnic minorities but also to that of the Serbs' relative majority.

Milošević has made use of these feelings of humiliation, frustration and fear among Serbs, and of their resentment at the lack of sympathy in other regions for their predicament. He did what other regional Communist leaders had done in the 1960s and 1970s, but he did it with added advantages – a more numerous and extended basis, and rampant de-Titoization. His was the latest and most successful attempt to try to save the power of the Party by jumping on the bandwagon of nationalism.

Stumbling into a grey and uncertain dawn from the long anaesthetized sleep of ideological rule and the surreal dream of Titoist charlatanry, people huddled together in groups that recognized each other by language, religion and common memories of the past. In their resistance to a radical restructuring of society imposed from the top, they had usually taken the side of what had been erased from the history books, of the names and stones that had been removed from their cities, and blamed their misfortunes on others. All thought of themselves as being unequal, exploited and oppressed.

Once particularism had been taken over by the regional bureaucracies, communities tended to blame one another, and one another's history, one another's foreign overlords, religious or ideological centres abroad. Poets and novelists moved to the forefront of a vacant political scene with their moral exhortations and literary visions, while bankrupt Communist apparatchiks were left to mismanage economic wars between their republics.

Eight different models of Yugoslav Communism thus appeared in the 1980s. In the 1960s and 1970s, Slovenia had developed an increasingly humanized version that provided space for various interests to interact, that gauged the public mood before acting, and acted more openly, thus obtaining much-improved economic results. This opening out was, however, done in very special circumstances, with an ethnically homogeneous population already endowed with a more prosperous environment.

In the 1980s, however, Slovenia's privileged position was translated into the highest rate of decline in real income, thus inciting the local leadership to oppose, often stridently, all attempts aimed at giving the centre the power to implement an all-Yugoslav economic policy. A smugly chauvinistic rhetoric certainly did not contribute to allaying Serbian sensitivity or the anti-reformist vested interests of most Communist caucuses.

In Croatia, a weak, unpopular and dogmatic leadership had, since 1974, been trying to acquire a doubtful legitimacy by adopting an all-too-often negative attitude to what came from Belgrade. Placed between Serbia and Slovenia, it increasingly tended to side with the latter against the former. The leaders who fell from power in Montenegro and Vojvodina did not do so because they were more incompetent than most of their opposite numbers elsewhere, or as a result of ethnic clashes, but because they were defending their positions without the backing of strong particularist feelings. Of the new governments there, one can only say that they had younger faces and cleaner hands, and that they stood by Serbia.

The return to that republic of certain prerogatives in matters of defence, the maintenance of order, international relations and taxation, that had previously been devolved to the autonomous provinces, although it did not affect their basic autonomy, especially in cultural affairs, nevertheless posed a long-term problem in Kosovo, whose non-Slav population felt more and more alienated.

Macedonia kept quiet, concealing its own expanding Albanian minority. It is in need of Yugoslav solidarity to be able to stand economically and ethnically. Its neighbours outside Yugoslavia do not recognize the existence of a Macedonian nation, and all the richer republics – Serbia included – are unhappy about continuing to subsidize its economy. As for Bosnia-Herzegovina, that republic was barely emerging from a long reign of corruption, racketeering and arbitrary authoritarianism.

Yugoslav Communism had made compromises with forces hitherto perceived as hostile (such as the market, religion or nationalism) in order to remain somehow in power. A complex situation had arisen, all too often simplified by Western onlookers disappointed by the failure of a regime in which so many hopes, illusions and funds had been invested. Facile clichés presented it as a North–South or West–East opposition, consolidated into NW–SE to make it even simpler, with Slovenia (replacing Croatia for a while) – Catholic, Austrian-like, central-European, liberal, mercantile, industrious and pluripartite – threatened by a Serbia that is

Orthodox, Turkish-influenced, Balkan, authoritarian, peasant, militaristic, hegemonistic and neo-Stalinist. Yugoslavia's need for change was interpreted as an ethnic conflict, because it seemed to take the form of a confrontation between the Communist leadership of Slovenia and that of Serbia, whereas the ethnic conflict was the consequence, and not the cause, of the deadlock.

The 'agreed economy'

The leadership was still unified enough in 1985 to decide in principle to try to overcome existing constitutional obstacles to the further development of the market economy, and to extend federal powers over economic policy. It took time to obtain the necessary consensus on a scheme, which was limited to proposals for better guarantees to private small enterprises, a unified tax system, and rationalized planning as a way towards an integrated Yugoslav market. Finally submitted in 1987, it had been overtaken by events.

Serbia, which had so much wanted to change the Constitution of 1974, appeared in the late 1980s to wish to defend it against Slovenia, which wanted to loosen the links even more. The amendments of 1989 to Serbia's own constitution changed little, and it is difficult to see why they gave rise to such euphoria in Serbia and to so virulent an anti-Serbian reaction in Slovenia. Slovenia, which insisted on the sanctity of the 1974 settlement in the face of Serbia's onslaught, amended its own constitution to give itself the right to secede from Yugoslavia altogether.

In fact the Constitution of 1974 barely survived, as it was being amended piecemeal within the republics but could not be altered at federal level. The sole rationale for attitudes struck by various leaderships was their wish to hold on to the appearances and privileges of political power, but the only practical solution would have been to move towards a totally new settlement through a transitional period when different parties with varying programmes would have organized themselves into fully competitive politics.

In substance, this had been advocated for two decades or so by the Democratic Alternative forum of expatriates linked to the London- and Paris-based journal *Naša Reč*. Unfortunately, it had become difficult for most non-Serbs to regard any proposal of Serbian provenance as progressive if it implied the slightest interest for those Serbs living outside Serbia, or a minimum of real authority for the federal government. Likewise, it had become hard for Serbs to recognize that they could hold ideals or aims in common with people they suspected of camouflaging integrationist intentions towards Serbs living in their midst, even separatist thoughts, and certainly egoistical tendencies, under a Christian–Catholic–social-democratic discourse.

The last stage of the 'Yugoslav road to socialism' as it took shape in the 1970s was the 'agreed economy', where political pressures were applied to ensure that market forces, such as had been released, produced the right decisions. These reflected local Party officials' perceptions of local interests, often at the expense of other local or all-Yugoslav interests. The pursuit of regional aims under political patronage led to each ruling hierarchy investing within the boundaries of its territory, whatever the cost, to retain control over its capital, thus aggravating regional differences.

The aim of the Yugoslav Communists had been to change society according to a given model, whatever its capacities, and because their essentially political project cost more than it produced, the deficit was at first made up by revolutionary zeal, which dampened consumer expectations in the immediate post-war period. The continued exploitation of natural resources and pressure on the peasants to produce cheap food were another phase, before the export of unemployment and the injection of foreign credits took over until the 1980s. Meanwhile, consumer appetites had been whetted as bureaucratic structures grew with foreign debts, feeding the system with make-believe money in the absence of real money.

Yugoslav economists have long been saying that the system had always been inefficient. Some are now claiming that it has never produced a profit. As inflation passed from a trot to a gallop, more institutions issued bills of exchange, thereby increasing the number of those who benefited from inflation. All economic reforms since the 1960s had always been more cosmetic than real – compromise solutions adopted by a hesitant and divided government, half-heartedly applied, forgotten and then taken up again. All anti-inflationary measures failed, as they did not attack the roots of the problem, and the huge bureaucratic structure was not keen to confront it.

After almost 20 years of operating under this convoluted system the Yugoslav economy was in a desperate state. As banks were made to inject more money into bankrupt enterprises, economic management was, more often than not, reduced to trying to pay salaries at the end of the month. 1989 ended up with an inflation rate officially said to be 1225%, but estimated by Western observers to be somewhere between 2000 and 3000% (it had been a mere 50% at the end of 1984). Living with inflation had become a part of the national culture.

Under pressure from foreign creditors, however, the present federal executive chaired by prime minister Ante Marković had, in 1989, managed to pass laws on the free circulation of goods, capital and labour, on foreign-exchange markets, and on foreign ownership rights, thereby reviving some decisions already taken in 1985 and not acted upon. On paper at least, that legislation was on a par with the best that was being obtained elsewhere in east-central Europe. Some progress had also been achieved in external accounts, the balance of payments being in surplus again by over $2 billion, hard currency reserves going up to $6.5 billion, and the foreign debt being reduced to $17 billion (from over $21 billion in 1981).

On that basis, the government – which Marković had tried to put together on the competence of at least some of its members rather than as a result of regional patronage – at last managed to cobble together an apparently more rigorous package aimed, perhaps too ambitiously, at bringing inflation down to 13% in a year. As from 1 January 1990 the dinar was declared fully convertible, pegged to the West German mark, and devalued by being made to shed four zeros. Salary rises were severely curtailed but prices allowed to find their own level, except in the case of energy and infrastructural costs.

Economists in Yugoslavia argued that inflation was more political than economic, but an end to the political monopoly of the feuding components of the SKJ did not in itself produce a miraculous solution to the crisis of the country's economy, or to that of its national unity. An open debate between the legitimate and accountable representatives of different communities, interests and opinions would have been but a necessary condition. With the demise of Communist ideology, and fostered by the very disintegration of the ruling Party, nationalism has become the dominant ideology. To the extent that politics had for too long been appropriated by one ideology, resistance to it had turned to other dimensions – to the past and to religion, to feelings of wounded patriotism and to preoccupations with the survival of numerically small nations. As such, history, religion and the nation have moved in a basically anti-Western direction, and politics have become apolitical. A culture of resistance can, however, transform itself into one of democratic opposition, as has been seen sometimes in east-central Europe. After all, most Yugoslavs, along with most east-central Europeans, are imaginary Westerners and aspire to Western 'civilizational' (a favourite Yugoslav neologism) values.

Moves towards a multi-party system

More and more calls were then made to repeal the legislation on verbal offences, on the slandering of the state and the official posthumous cult of Tito, but even more so for the introduction of a multi-party system as the only way to tackle the crisis. These calls came from various quarters, mostly, but not exclusively, from intellectuals who rarely saw beyond the borders of their own republic. Public opinion around them was almost unanimous in thinking that the present system was at a dead end, and no more than 10% expressed any confidence in the SKJ. At the same time, people were still afraid of the cost of reforms, especially in the poorer regions and sectors, even though they had already been going through a difficult decade for no good reason and with no clear prospect of change.

It was in Slovenia, in January 1989, that east-central Europe's first independent political party since the Communist take-overs was launched. A multitude of 'alternative' groups emerged, and, for a while, helped the local Party leadership to increase its regionalistic stance, but eventually they pressed it into accepting the principle of allowing others to compete with it in the April 1990 elections. 1989 ended with a new electoral law for Slovenia that legalized political parties. In Croatia, a dozen or so similar groups, although kept under closer surveillance, were able to obtain enough public support to force the SK of that republic to follow that of Slovenia in accepting the principle of competition at the next elections. The Zagreb-based Yugoslav United Democratic Initiative which, however small, does have branches in other republics, was watched with particular dislike.

In Serbia, in the midst of the euphoria surrounding the secentenary of the Battle of Kosovo (1389) and the restoration of some control over the provinces, the dissident voices of intellectuals were no longer heard, but they were soon raised again very strongly in favour of an end to the power monopoly of the SKJ. Of the independent political groups that appeared, one stood out. A Democratic Party, Belgrade-based but devoid of an ethnic or regional attribute, set itself up as a political party of individual representation, in opposition to, and in competition with, the SKJ. Its manifesto called for a new constitution, to be drawn up through an agreement between the legitimate representatives of all communities, based on the equality of regions and citizens, on parliamentary government and on free enterprise tempered with social justice.

An affiliated group existed in Montenegro, and sympathizers appeared in all republics. Three parties were being organized in Macedonia. Even the nationalist Albanian students of Kosovo, whose militants belonged to underground Marxist–Leninist groups in the early 1980s, demonstrated in favour of multiple parties in the wake of the failed Fourteenth Congress, as the situation in the province deteriorated yet again, while a Democratic Alliance of Kosovo was set up to demand a constructive and reasoned dialogue between communities. Most of these groups held meetings and issued manifestos without hindrance.

Under such pressure, but also facing counter-pressure from conservatives, veteran partisans' organizations and generals, Party forums tried to show how democratic they were by accepting some degree of pluralism. Once again, the lead was taken by Slovenia, where public pressure was strongest. The declared concessions of the various leaderships were ambiguous. Political parties would have to be socialist, or should not be ethnic, or should conform to current legislation, or would be considered after the next elections. At best, initiatives were taken to turn the Socialist Alliance into a separate party, which would field candidates alongside those of the SK, and benefit from state support. The aim everywhere was to ensure the success of the SK in the forthcoming elections, and to delay the development of independent parties. Serbia had already held elections in 1989, in the wake of its nationalistic euphoria, according to the existing system, without independent candidates. The Party there had gained a respite, and could even afford to ban an ultra-nationalist alternative organization. In Slovenia, the Party still had to go to the polls and face competition.

The Fourteenth Congress

As far back as February 1989 it had been decided to call a Party congress to sort things out. By the time the Fourteenth Congress of the SKJ did meet in Belgrade, on 20 January 1990, the possibility of pluralism had been conceded in Moscow, and even in Ulan Bator. The Communist Party had been banned in Romania, and opinion polls had revealed that 80% of Yugoslavs thought their own SKJ incapable of pulling the country out of the crisis. The Congress had been summoned in an extraordinary capacity to launch a 'new democratic model of socialism', with tight financial constraints and no fraternal delegations. What remained of a federal leadership had just come round to accepting a draft declaration which pronounced in favour of the freedom of political association 'within the limits of the socialist democratic society and of the federal model', and in favour of the efforts being made by the government to integrate the Yugoslav market.

The Congress started off badly with a long wrangle over procedure, then accepted the draft document by an overwhelming majority, and eventually went to pieces over the rejection of amendments put by the delegates of Slovenia, to turn the League into an even looser 'League of leagues', with new forms to reflect its 'socialist' rather than 'Communist' nature. The tide which had initially gone in favour of the Slovene Communists' 'liberalizing' tendencies then turned against their 'disintegration-ist' demands. Insults were exchanged, the delegates from Slovenia marched out, and the Congress was adjourned on 23 January *sine die*. On that day, *Borba*, the one-time mouthpiece of the SKJ, at that time still appearing under the slogan 'Proletarians of all countries unite', on behalf of the Socialist Alliance, had a banner headline: 'The SKJ no longer exists.'

Historians of the Balkans know that the new Soviet concept of *perestroika* is but a literal translation of the old Ottoman *tanzimat*. Far from reforming itself into yet another 'democratic socialist project', the SKJ was disintegrating, and the false problem of how to restructure its regime was giving way to the real one of how to dismantle it. Its hesitating, contradictory and obfuscating policies manipulated the powerlessness of its apparatus. The abrupt interruption of the Fourteenth Congress had made it obvious that clarity, with all its risks, was the only way to give Yugoslavia a chance to avoid a breakdown.

In a Communist polity paralysed by the deadlock of eight antagonistic regional Party elites, hard-line warnings against the dangers of party pluralism in a polyethnic country carried little weight, even, and perhaps especially, among those who thought that it would be better to channel expressions of particularism in independent regional, ethnic and religious parties, rather than let (or encourage) it to spill out into the streets. The crisis of the Yugoslav federation was not a classical confrontation between a federal centre and federated components. The visible signs of disintegration were only the consequences of the malfunctioning of the whole system. Decentralization made little sense in economic terms as local bureaucrats took over the role of meddling decision-makers and unopposed rulers previously played by the central leadership. Redistribution of power, changes of personnel rather than of policies, watering down of Party rule, and recourse to crowd support were no substitute for political democracy, without which real economic reforms could hardly be made to take off.

Yugoslavia did have a point or two in common with Albania, which is why both countries, in spite of all the obvious differences, were the last of the Communist states of east-central Europe to confront the political monopoly of the ruling Party. Both regimes had had a smooth succession after the natural death of a long-ruling charismatic leader, both claimed that they were more truly socialist than the members of what used to be called the 'Eastern bloc', and, since they were outside it, they were less prone to the 'domino effect'. 'We would have found it easier to get rid of the Communist legacy if it had been clearly imposed from the outside . . . Today maybe we would come out of this mess sooner if we were to join the Warsaw Pact,' a student remarked in January 1990 (Srdjan Trifković, 'When the center no longer holds', *US News and World Report*, 8 January 1990).

The Communist Party of Yugoslavia had acquired its own credentials by emerging victorious in a bloody four-year civil war, with help from both the USSR and the Western Allies. The length of Tito's reign and the cult of his personality identified him with the Party leadership, its cadres, the state and the nation. Because of its independence from Moscow after 1948, the Titoist regime was first saved, then supported, increasingly subsidized, and constantly flattered by the West into thinking that it was a model to be followed by the other Communist-ruled countries of Europe. Although the West was by far its best patron, it was not the only one, for the Soviet Union also sustained it against the West through the Non-Aligned Movement. Trading on the confrontation between blocs and superpowers, it was fêted by all.

If Western aid was meant to help produce a Communist system that could become economically viable and politically acceptable, it did no more than enable Titoism to live beyond its aims and eventually to stagnate. Intent as they were on salvaging what they could from the initial project by half-hearted concessions, Yugoslavia's Communist leaders had admittedly been resourceful in holding out.

Eventually the regime did both liberalize and decentralize. It diffused power within the SKJ, and it tolerated more and more personal freedom, but with little structural change. It institutionalized local interests in an elaborate system of checks and balances that achieved a decade or so of internal stability, at a cost which not only worsened economic problems but weakened the means available to the leadership. In Tito's lifetime the system still appeared to work, as it was propped up by the ageing leader's personal authority and by heavy external borrowing. The simultaneous disappearance of both props was coincidental. When the Cold War was consigned to the archives, and left to historians, Tito's heirs realized that no-one was interested any longer in subsidizing their experiment, and the Titoist lobby in the West vanished almost overnight, leaving behind it a whiff of nostalgia, particularly in Britain.

The first and the last

The Communist regime that had been the first to set itself up outside the Soviet Union after World War II seemed, for all these reasons, to be almost the last to disappear. Having come to power on the basis of its identification with the working class, it ended up by hiding behind the primacy of national identity. Far from resolving Yugoslavia's national question, it has given nationalism the chance to return to the fore with a vengeance. It has interrupted political traditions that were still in their youth, while freezing atavistic attitudes. Because of its bureaucratic, anti-cultural and anti-intellectual stance it made it more difficult for people to distance themselves from instinctive reactions, and impaired their understanding not only of socialism but of democracy as well. On the one hand, it formally replaced the concept of political citizenship by a system of indirect delegations. On the other, it achieved the fusion of ethnic-religious communities in the Ottoman tradition with historic-territorial rights in the Habsburg tradition. All this appeared to have blocked the possibility of a democratic evolution within the existing constitution.

By 1990 the Socialist Federal Republic of Yugoslavia was a hybrid. In fact a confederation, it had not become that through the coming together of pre-existing states but through a process of degeneration. Indeed, it is so loose a confederation that it has either to break up completely or be turned back into a real federation as a third Yugoslavia, set up on deeper foundations than its monarchical and Communist predecessors. Today's stresses are, paradoxically, the result of common influences, moulds and mentalities, which gave birth to a Yugoslav idea and a Yugoslav movement even before these led to the formation of a Yugoslav state in 1918.

Initially unification went against the grain of 'Balkanization'. Yugoslavia had to prove itself before the West acknowledged its existence, and it had to stand up against the attempts of both Comintern and Axis to 're-Balkanize' it, before the country proved itself yet again under Communist leadership. The idea of survival helps to illuminate the way in which Yugoslavia seems to have spent 70 years lurching from crisis to crisis. Milorad Ekmečič, the author of *The Creation of Yugoslavia, 1790–1918*, says that the crisis of Yugoslavia has been going on for 200 years – a long historical process whose outcome is being decided now.

Both in 1918, when the united Kingdom of the Serbs, Croats and Slovenes (later Kingdom of Yugoslavia) was proclaimed, and in 1945, when it was formally reorganized as the Federal People's Republic of

Yugoslavia (later Socialist Federal Republic of Yugoslavia), there was no real alternative to a Yugoslav solution, but the question was never directly put to the population. The self-determination of Serbs, Croats, Slovenes and others living there was somehow exercised through a relative parliamentary majority, or the force of arms and circumstances, or unsatisfactory bargains with the rulers. Although there has generally been interest in the common enterprise, no party to these outcomes has ever had full confidence in either its partners or the community as a whole, and each has always tried to safeguard its own position through a centralistic state structure, or a special status, or a confederal arrangement. The state itself has been identified with its rulers. Rarely has there been real compromise between Yugoslavia's component groups, ethnic or political, preceded by a real debate. Rarely have any means of promoting integration been allowed, let alone encouraged, other than those of the official ideology of the time. Yet Yugoslavia's communities have not hitherto been at each other's throats except when shamelessly exploited by invading powers in European wars, and there are precedents of active co-operation between the political parties of the various nationalities, especially in trying to restore parliamentary government to set the common state on a new course.

The regional multi-party elections of 1990

Multi-party elections, according to different systems, took place in all the republics during 1990. Slovenia and Croatia came first, in April and May. Demos, a right-of-centre coalition, obtained power in Slovenia with 55% of the votes. In Croatia, 41% went to the very right-ring Croatian Democratic Alliance, led by the ex-Communist General Tudjman. The electoral system turned this into a parliamentary majority of more than two thirds. Frightened by Milošević's apparent bid for power through the SKJ, Slovenia's and Croatia's Communist leaders had gone straight for above-board multi-party elections, in the belief that they would be returned as 'Parties of Democratic Renewal', only to be beaten by new, *ad hoc*, right-wing nationalist movements.

Milošević heeded the lesson that there was no reward to be reaped from sharing out power. He turned the local SK into the Socialist Party of Serbia, became tough on Kosovo, and pushed a new Constitution through the tame Serbian parliament. This granted the provinces little more than cultural autonomy and gave him sweeping presidential powers. The ruling party lost its last shreds of legitimacy in the eyes of the Albanian minority, now approaching 2 million, and Milošević's popularity faded in inner Serbia, as he had failed to provide any solutions – as opposed to gestures – to his republic's problems. Yet his nationalist Communism still fed on the anti-Communist nationalism of Croatia's new President Tudjman.

The remaining republican elections then took place in November and

December. Proportional representation in Bosnia-Herzegovina returned three parties that reflected the ethnic composition of that republic, at the expense of the restyled SK apparatus: 37% to the (Muslim) Party of Democratic Action, 30% to the Serbian Democratic Party, and 19% to the Croatian Democratic Alliance. Three rounds of voting still left Macedonia with a hung parliament: 37 seats to the Democratic Party for Macedonian Unity, a nationalist movement; 31 to the renamed SK; 25 to the Albanians' Party of Democratic Prosperity; and 18 to the Alliance of Reformist Forces, Marković's federal government party.

Last came the sister republics of Montenegro and Serbia. Only in the former, Yugoslavia's smallest, did the revamped SK win a convincing 66% majority of its tiny electorate. In Serbia more than elsewhere, the ruling party was reluctant to share campaign facilities. Spreading fears of civil war and warnings that the army would stand by its constitutional duty to defend the established order were meant at least as much for Serbia's voters as for Slovenia's and Croatia's new leaders. Albanians in Serbia, in contrast to those in Macedonia, boycotted the poll. The ruling party thus eventually mustered almost four-fifths of members of parliament representing, however, no more than 43% of the electorate in the first round of voting. Milošević personally still had enough popularity to be returned to the presidency by a decisive 65%. Voting warily for the devil it knew, the electorate made his declining hold over Serbia as legitimate as that of nationalists, separatists and renamed Communists elsewhere.

The 1990 elections were preceded by developments in the two northern republics. Marković's federal government had had some success with its first package of reforms, which brought the 1990 inflation down to 120%, but the next phase – to include privatization as well as tax and bank reforms – encountered obstacles. Production had fallen along with living standards. The right-wing governments of Slovenia and Croatia, no less than the Communist government of Serbia, have been obstructing the implementation of Marković's plans – along with his not very successful attempts since May 1990 at launching his own pan-Yugoslav government party to back his reformist endeavour.

The governments of Slovenia and Croatia were worried about losing control over public ownership and fiscal policies. Their nationalism had thrived on declining economies, but they, too, were losing popularity as they had also delivered nothing beyond slogans and symbols. Afraid of being isolated between 'Europe' and 'Yugoslavia', they needed to reinforce their positions and improve their bargaining assets. Hence the decision by the Demos government to hold a plebiscite on whether Slovenia should become an 'independent state'. It waged a campaign full of pressures and rumours (which went beyond the sombre intentions of the Yugoslav People's Army, to Italian troop concentrations and US naval movements), but was nevertheless anxious to stress that its aims were not necessarily secessionist. Be that as it may, while Serbia was voting in a second round of parliamentary elections on 23 December, 94% of Slovenia's electors wrote 'yes' on their plebiscite papers. What is more, the parliament of Croatia approved a new Constitution which, like Serbia's, has a form that could suit a 'sovereign' Croatia either in Yugoslavia or out of it, and an impressive presidential prerogative.

Can Yugoslavia survive?

Yugoslavia is in transition from a disintegrating Communist regime to a post-Communist policy, but it is uncertain how long the present republican leaderships will remain in power, whether Yugoslavia will survive as a political community of related South Slav nations, and whether it will open out to genuine multi-party democracy or turn to nationalist authoritarian populism. For the time being, most of it is still in the grip of a party-state mentality, even where it has changed more than the name of the ruling group, even when it looks back to a romantic nationalism reminiscent of the late nineteenth century or to a leadership cult similar to that of the 1930s. Nationalism could be the first stage in the regeneration of political consciousness in a society long made insensible by authoritarian rule, but, as the last refuge of Communism, it could also be an escape from past responsibility and present reality.

Yugoslavia is a microcosm of the problems that beset the post-Communist states of Eastern Europe. Its generally incompetent nationalist regional politicians (ex-, anti- and revamped Communist) all retain a one-party mentality, with little respect for oppositions and minorities. The leaderships of the three most important republics in particular – Serbia, Croatia and Slovenia – have been losing popularity since the elections, and they are trying to regain it by competing in a dangerous game of bluff, blackmail and contradictions, appearing to go to the brink of the unthinkable, and then returning to the negotiating table. At each stage of this game, more media hysteria, more vandalism and a few more victims have made it more difficult for them to control the extremists that have been encouraged, to appease the fear and the distrust that have been aroused and to envisage compromises.

A common Yugoslavia is the only way for all Serbs and Croats to live within a common state. It would find it less difficult to cope with economic problems than a set of smaller states, and better economic prospects would contribute to easing the present political, social and ethnic tensions. If, however, the accumulated distrust is such that divorce is seen as the only way out, compromise will still be called for to avoid chaos, widespread suffering, and the slipping out of Europe. Outright dissolution, no less than a continued union of one kind or another, calls for compromise.

So far, however, the republican leaderships have shown little inclination to seek this. They have indulged in aggrieved nationalistic rhetoric, and have insisted on the inviolable territorial integrity and political unity of their own respective republics, but supported autonomist tendencies, and even encouraged irredentism, elsewhere. The leaders have sought assistance both in Yugoslavia and abroad. Legitimized through elections that were free and as fair as could be hoped for, they have not allowed the federal government to acquire a similar legitimacy through all-Yugoslav elections. The federal parliament has been marginalized, and the federal government has held on by dint of Marković's unflappable optimism, with the moral support provided by the international community and through the increasingly grudging endurance of the republics.

The only other federal institution worth mentioning is the Yugoslav People's Army, and this is a force of the past. Its constitutional role is to safeguard the country's territorial integrity and constitutional order, but it would be difficult for it to do so except as the arm of a legitimate acknowledged and united authority, that of its nominal supreme commander, the collective federal presidency. The top brass is divided. Some have supported the initiative of retired political generals for a revived SKJ. Others have tried (and failed) to have the presidency proclaim a state of emergency. Others still have been ready to accept the modest role of peace-keeper between local paramilitary forces and extremist militants so as to help the federal government hold the ring while the regional leaders negotiate.

Right from the beginning of 1991, Prime Minister Marković has worked to get the republican presidents to accept a minimum of federal authority to tide the country over its transition to some new order, and to work out an agreement of sorts. Early in March, the federal presidency practically gave them a mandate to do that, and they eagerly accepted it, anxious as they were to push out the federal government. They went on a tour of the republics, holding a series of roadshow 'summits' in Tito's former residences (re-opened for the occasion), and divided into three groups of two. Croatia and Slovenia argued for a loose union of sovereign states, or a 'dissociation' (a valid divorce accepted by all parties and by the international community), easier for Slovenia to achieve than for Croatia. Serbia and Montenegro stuck to a meaningful federation which allowed all Serbs to live in one country. Macedonia and Bosnia-Herzegovina, not endowed with similar ethnic strength, hovered between the two. The six leaders came up with two plans – for a reformed federation and for a confederal union – to be put to the electorates of all the republics in simultaneous referenda to be held before the end of May.

No sooner had they appeared to agree, than they disagreed. Some were accused of selling out. Slovenes argued that they had already voted. Croatia announced it would vote before the others. Not to be outdone, the self-proclaimed Serbian Autonomous Region of Krajina within Croatia organized a referendum of its own, in advance of that of the whole of Croatia, and voted almost unanimously to remain part of a Yugoslav federation, or to join Serbia. A week later, on 19 May, 94% of votes cast in Croatia went in favour of an independent state, which could unite with others in an alliance of states. With 'sovereignties' being proclaimed all over the place, a worker from Bosnia told the press he, his wife and his two children had voted unanimously to set up their own sovereign family unit, dissociated from the Republic of Bosnia and Herzegovina and from the Socialist Federal Republic of Yugoslavia, because they did not want to go along with the 'parastatal collective madness' of the political class.

On 15 May the representative of Croatia should have taken over as chairman of the collective presidency, but since Croats, Slovenes and Albanians in the federal parliament had refused to ratify the new representatives of Montenegro and of Serbia's provinces in the presidency, Serbia and its allies refused to ratify the new Croatian chairman. Both sides were intent on wrecking what remains of the old constitutional set-up insofar as they could not use it to advance their own plans. The Slovenian and Croatian unilateral declarations of independence on 25 June, rejected by the federal authorities, the army's failed intervention in Slovenia, and repeated interventions by the European Community eventually ensured that the legitimate representative of Croatia should take his turn to head a state his republic wants to leave, and the Yugoslav 'summits' have tentatively resumed amid more fighting.

The world is losing patience with Yugoslavia, now that this country no longer has much geostrategic importance and that the Powers have greater problems. The West has told the Yugoslavs that the Europe they are anxious to join is being built on different principles to those of nation states, historic rights and ethnic sovereignties. At the same time, some Yugoslavs have been trying to tell the West that it bears some responsibility for the chaos the country has sunk into, by lulling it into a false sense of its own importance when a bloated Titoist regime was helped to the point of surviving into post-Titoism.

Foreign governments and international organizations have made it clear that neither a violent maintenance nor a violent break-up of the country is acceptable, and that they would prefer to see a united and democratic Yugoslavia. Serious calls are being made from within Yugoslavia for outside mediation. With the leverage of aspirations to be accepted by Europe and of the need for Western capital, such a mediation is not impossible. It would probably lead in the first instance to an agreed dissolution of the federation as a damage-limitation measure. Something could later be rebuilt once all had come to their senses and realized that the Yugoslav republics cannot follow the example of Norway and Sweden in 1905, let alone that of Uri, Schwyz and Unterwald in 1291. The various parts might then want to come together again, after new and more sober political elites, backed by more rational public opinions, had emerged from post-Communist democracy.

Part 2
The
Soviet
Union

9 AN OVERVIEW

Historical background

The Soviet Union now appears an anachronism. Yet in the 1970s it was still commonly suggested that its social and economic system represented a successful model of modernization that other states might follow. It is now clear that despite the transfer of a large proportion of its workforce from subsistence agriculture to an urban, industrial environment and a rise in educational standards, the Soviet experiment has been a dead-end. It has isolated the country from a dynamic world economy and the spread of market consumerism. Despite a rise in living standards it has failed to establish a form of legitimacy to rival that enjoyed by representative democracies. Military superpower status masked the failures of the system. In the early 1980s one perceptive (if cynical) Western observer remarked that the Soviet Union resembled 'the Upper Volta with missiles'.

Whether the Tsarist regime was succeeding in breaking the cycle of Russian history in which a passive society was periodically modernized by the state, often in a bloody fashion, is a matter of historical controversy, but the seizure of power by the Bolshevik Party in October 1917 re-affirmed it. A totally new ruling elite was to be established to carry out a 'modernizing' project. Bolshevik rule was imposed after a bitter civil war in which, at first, it faced only the old Tsarist elite but later also a wave of popular protest, culminating in a revolt of sailors and workers in Petrograd and the Kronstadt naval base and peasant risings in early 1921. Many Russians finally accepted the Bolsheviks as the only force able to provide the country with a strong government. In non-Russian areas the re-establishment of rule from Moscow even in the guise of the Union of Soviet Socialist Republics, supposedly created by voluntary treaty in 1924, was less welcome.

The Bolsheviks seized power with the intention of implementing a Marxist social and economic revolution. Until Lenin's death in 1924 the utopian aspect of the Party's programme was tempered by a degree of pragmatism. Thus, faced with popular discontent in early 1921 he persuaded the Party to accept the New Economic Policy (NEP). The NEP, which forced industrial enterprises to prove their financial viability, allowed the private sector to dominate internal trade and encouraged peasant agriculture, was a retreat from earlier attempts to create a Communist society by force and fanning class war.

Stalin's emergence as the pre-eminent Bolshevik leader at the end of the 1920s saw a return to policies of mass coercion in the shape of the collectivization of agriculture and Communist enthusiasm in a five-year plan to carry out a rapid industrialization programme. By the mid-1930s a massive industrial base had been built which was to give the Red Army victory in World War II and the country superpower status after 1945.

The 'centrally planned economy' was a myth that masked a system based on coercion and improvization. The belief that every aspect of the economy of a vast country like the Soviet Union could be run from Moscow led to the proliferation of a stifling bureaucracy of ministries, the creation of twentieth-century 'Potemkin villages' as managers made exaggerated reports of broken production records to satisfy the centre and the squandering of the country's natural resources. Considerable increases in the production of steel, coal and electricity were achieved by savagely cutting the living standards of peasants and workers to the point of famine. Agriculture, industries serving the needs of the consumer and the service sector were permanently neglected. Soviet women suffered particularly badly from the backwardness of these sectors. Women were drawn into the urban workforce but continued to perform the bulk of the domestic duties – what came to be known as 'the double burden'. This position was reinforced by Soviet propaganda, which, after stressing sexual equality in the early days of the Revolution, later created a cult of motherhood, with the attendant reward of 'hero-mother' status for those who produce large families.

Appalling living conditions were only one side of the Stalinist nightmare. Against the background of social upheaval, extravagant visions of a Communist utopia and Stalin's pathological suspiciousness, many Soviet citizens were physically eliminated. Millions of peasants who resisted being herded into the new collective farms were labelled *kulaks* (rich peasants) and deported. Between 1936 and 1938 former political opponents of the regime and ordinary citizens were joined in the labour camps by millions of loyal Party and government officials arrested on trumped-up charges. Those who avoided execution found that camp conditions were often no better than a death sentence. During the Civil War the pre-revolutionary elite had been largely chased from their jobs into death or exile. The post-revolutionary elite of politicians such as Trotsky, Bukharin and Zinoviev, cultural figures such as the theatre producer Meyerhold and the poet Mandelshtam and, most absurdly of all on the eve of World War II, the cream of the Red Army such as Marshals Tukhachevskii and Blyukher were liquidated.

Stalin died in 1953, and the new leadership was determined to avoid the fate of its predecessors. After Khrushchev's 'secret speech' to the Twentieth Party Congress in 1956 the labour camps were opened and the inmates, many of whom had been re-sentenced on the expiry of their term, were released. The relatives of those who had not survived could apply for their rehabilitation. Greater intellectual freedom was permitted. Solzhenitsyn's *One Day in the Life of Ivan Denisovich*, which vividly described camp

UNION OF SOVIET SOCIALIST REPUBLICS (USSR)

Official name	The Union of Soviet Socialist Republics
Area	72,400,000 sq. km (8,646,400 sq. miles)
Population	286,717,000 (1989) (annual growth rate 0.9%)
Capital	Moscow (Moskva)
Languages	Russian, many regional languages
Religion	Russian Orthodox with Catholic, Jewish, Muslim minorities
Currency	rouble

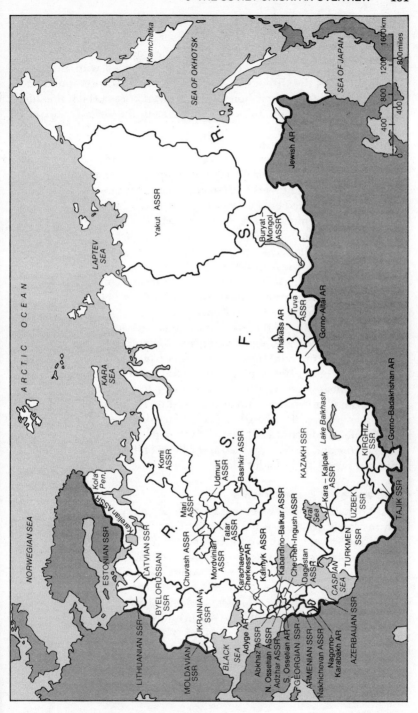

life, was published. However, disturbed by his unpredictable behaviour, his so-called 'hare-brained schemes', Khrushchev was deposed by his fellow Party leaders in 1964. Liberalization had not been indiscriminate even under Khrushchev. The cultural 'thaw' coincided with an intense campaign against the Orthodox Church, which had escaped annihilation by helping to rally the population during the war. But as Leonid Brezhnev gradually emerged as the pre-eminent leader in the 1960s, criticism of Stalin halted.

After the death of Stalin the apparatus of state repression continued to be employed against anyone who questioned the regime, but terror was no longer applied on a mass scale. The co-operation of the mass of the population was sought by the promise of rising living standards. Economic growth stagnated by the 1970s and Soviet GNP was later overtaken by that of Japan, a much smaller country, and West Germany was not far behind. This not only threatened rising living standards, it also jeopardized the country's status as a military superpower. By the early 1980s the economic slow-down was reflected in growing social problems, such as an epidemic of alcoholism, a deeply alienated youth, and corruption. The SDI (America's 'Star Wars' programme) presented the Soviet Union with new, insurmountable technological challenges.

The social stability of the Brezhnev period saw an increasingly well-educated population gaining in confidence. By and large, the new intelligentsia rejected the values of the Party and frequently turned to the West for inspiration or to national or religious traditions. However, the skills of the intelligentsia were vital if the Party was to maintain rising living standards and the country's superpower status. The problem of overcoming the scepticism of this alienated class and persuading it to collaborate in achieving the leadership's policies, even though the goal of Communism was put more and more feebly, lay at the heart of the dilemma of political legitimacy posed by destalinization.

Gorbachev's *perestroika*

When Mikhail Gorbachev became General Secretary of the Communist Party in March 1985 he was not alone in underestimating the malaise that afflicted the Soviet Union. For the best part of his first two years as leader Gorbachev believed that the system could be made to work better by a mixture of greater discipline and technocratic reform. The slogan then was *uskorenie* (speeding up), not *perestroika* (reconstruction). Many people have forgotten that Gorbachev was best-known at first for his anti-alcohol campaign. More substantially, he set up now half-forgotten bodies to improve the quality of goods produced (*Gospriyomka*) and agricultural production (*Gosagroprom*) by the traditional method of central directive.

Then towards the end of 1986 his reforms began to change character, and *perestroika* began. In one respect this was a response to reverses in foreign policy. Soviet diplomacy had failed to break European support for the SDI programme and the explosion of the nuclear reactor at Chernobyl in April 1986, and the subsequent delay in informing its international neighbours, undermined the international reputation of the Soviet Union. The return of Andrei Sakharov from exile in December 1986 was as much a gesture to world opinion as domestic. At home, technocratic reform had failed to make an impact against the resistance of the bureaucrats. Firmer discipline was not enough to make the system work. There had to be a much greater degree of commitment to reform by those who were supposed to implement it.

Over the next three years there was a turnover in government and Party personnel greater than at any time since Stalin. To remove the people whom he saw as the opponents of his reform, without resorting to Stalinist methods, Gorbachev had to break down the fear that was the legacy of the Terror. Under the slogan of *glasnost*, Stalin and his policies were subjected to fierce criticism, and as a sign of good faith many books and films which had been banned under Brezhnev were published. Almost all political prisoners were released and religious freedoms were greatly extended.

This stage of *perestroika* reached its apogee with the elections to the Congress of People's Deputies in the spring of 1989. Although single-candidate elections persisted in many places and almost everywhere else special commissions weeded out unacceptable people, Soviet citizens used the choices they now enjoyed to throw out local bureaucrats. In the Baltic states candidates with the endorsement of the nationalist popular fronts were triumphant, and in Moscow Boris Yeltsin, who had been forced out of the Politburo at the end of 1987 for criticizing the slow pace of reform, was elected by an overwhelming majority. The unprecedented outspokenness of the Congress debates attracted avid television audiences.

Political liberalization was at its peak in the early part of 1990. In the summer of 1989 striking miners had not only demanded better conditions but also that the Party give up its legalized monopoly of power. The revolutions in all the Soviet Eastern European satellites in the autumn undermined attempts at reform within the existing political parameters. At a plenum of the Communist Party Central Committee in January 1990 Gorbachev appeared to concede the right of republics to secede from the Union and accept the principle of a multi-party system. However, doubts about his good faith were raised as early as March, when the Congress of People's Deputies confirmed him as President with new wide executive powers. Gorbachev claimed he needed these new powers to push through radical reform. However, in the summer he failed to back the radical economic reform programme drawn up by Stanislav Shatalin, an economics professor. This envisaged a transition to the market economy in '500 days' by means of a massive programme of privatization and devolution of real powers to the republics. As the economy steadily deteriorated and the political impasse in the republics dragged on, the KGB head,

Vladimir Kryuchkov, and 'conservative' elements in the *apparat*, re-presented by the Union (*Soyuz*) group in the Supreme Soviet, made strident calls for a reassertion of authority. At the December session of the Congress of People's Deputies the foreign minister, Eduard Shevard-nadze, resigned, alleging that the country was drifting towards dic-tatorship. The advance of the 'conservatives' was also signalled by the appointment of Gennadii Yanaev as vice-president. In May 1991 an agreement with Yeltsin, which led to the coal-miners' returning to work, signalled a return to the centre ground by Gorbachev. A programme of economic reform, the so-called 'anti-crisis programme', advanced by the new prime minister, Valentin Pavlov, in the same month, kept alive the hope of some forward movement.

Gorbachev is a representative of the generation that has grown up since the death of Stalin, a generation that rejects both mass terror and Com-munist utopianism. It is greatly to his credit that he has pursued this very necessary corrective, but the Soviet regime was established by force, and the social and economic transformation of the 1930s was also achieved by force. This fact puts strict limits on the possibility of reform. As political controls have been relaxed, aspirations have risen to the surface which challenge the political, economic and social basis of the Soviet regime.

The economy

There is broad agreement on the nature of the problems that afflict the Soviet economy and the necessary remedy. The first attempts to decentralize decision-making and increase incentives were made in the 1950s and were repeated in the 1960s. Little progress was made, and now leading Soviet economists agree on the need to replace centrally laid-down plans with market mechanisms. In practice, it has proved difficult to introduce elements of a market into a system where, as a result of the setting of arbitrary prices, all goods for which there might be a demand are in short supply.

Shortages of basic foodstuffs are endemic, and time spent in queues acts as a serious brake on labour productivity. Raising agricultural produc-tion is a priority on the reform agenda. Most hopes have been pinned on the idea of leasing plots of land or livestock herds from the collective farms to small groups of peasants, usually families. After making deliveries to the state the lessees are free to dispose of their surplus on the market. Although highly successful individual cases have been given wide pub-licity in the media, leasing arrangements have not yet been taken up on a wide scale. To increase incentives, in the summer of 1989, farmers were promised bonuses in hard currency in return for improvements in output. At the beginning of March 1990 state ownership of land was abolished but the new law fell short of introducing full private ownership and a market.

The leasing of land is often justified by reference to the NEP, but 60 years have passed since the demise of the peasant agriculture that was at its base. The contemporary Soviet agricultural workforce tends to be elderly and younger workers no longer feel any real interest in the land. There have been institutional obstacles to agricultural reform as well. Peasant scepticism is not allayed by the relatively short term of most leasing agreements. Local bureaucrats, fearing the loss of their authority, hinder leasing by insisting on high deliveries to the state or, for example, refusing to supply fertilizers or animal feeds. Even if agricultural production could be increased, it would not solve the problems in the food distribution system. At present, a third of grain is lost through inadequate transport and storage. This was graphically demonstrated in 1990 when, despite a bumper harvest, queues outside shops grew longer.

Reform of industry has not been much more successful. A new law on enterprises, again drawing on the NEP model, which came into force in January 1988, transferred the bulk of industrial concerns to self-financing (*khozraschet*). In theory, this meant that they would no longer have to deliver their production to the state according to centrally laid-down plans, and instead managers would be forced to seek out the most profitable buyer. This measure should also have removed the massive state subsidies to unviable factories and given greater scope for the introduction of incentives. In practice, state production targets were replaced by priority orders from the centre.

There have been other more radical initiatives which have conflicted with Communist taboos on private property. First, some enterprises, particularly in the light industrial sector, have been leased to their managers and workers. Second, and best known, a policy of encouraging co-operative enterprises has been begun. In theory, co-operatives are not allowed to employ hired labour, and people are only supposed to work in co-operatives in their spare time. In practice, local authorities display considerable discretion either to further restrict co-operatives or sometimes to turn a blind eye to breaches of regulations. Where co-operatives operate, they are, to all intents and purposes, small private firms. In 1990 there were 260,000 active co-operatives, employing 6.2 million people producing 70 billion roubles of goods and services. A small number of co-operatives are in light industry but the great majority are involved in retail and wholesale trade, supplying goods and services to the ordinary consumer and sometimes to other co-operatives or even state organizations.

Great emphasis has been put on the need for the Soviet Union to re-enter the world economy. At present, foreign trade is a small part of the GNP. In the West the most important Soviet trade partner is Germany. Britain comes low down on the list and runs a regular deficit with the Soviet Union. Despite the number of Lada cars on Britain's roads, the bulk of Soviet exports are raw materials, oil, gas and timber, and most of its imports, apart from grain, consist of machinery. Until recently these were mostly made up of industrial goods but the emphasis has switched to consumer goods; most economists agree on the need to increase such imports to provide incentives for the workforce. The Soviet Union usually runs a foreign trade deficit, but the foreign debt rose from an estimated $40 billion in 1988 to $48 billion in 1989, and this will probably limit future growth. By the middle of 1990 many Western firms began to complain that payments from Soviet partners were being delayed. To earn hard currency quickly, the Soviet Union stepped up its sale of gold.

There is also a strong desire on the part of the Soviets to import foreign capital, management skills and technology. Most significantly, in the spring of 1989 the possibility of establishing 'Special Economic Zones' on the Chinese model was mooted. So far only Leningrad has taken concrete steps in this direction. The most widespread initiative in this area has been the encouragement of joint ventures. A substantial number of agreements, 1300 at the beginning of 1990, have been negotiated with foreign companies but only 200 are up and working. Only 5% of the ventures are in engineering and even fewer have been established in agriculture. Meanwhile, fully one third of them are in 'trade', tourism and light industry, and another third are categorized as consultancy or research development. The Soviet authorities regard this as speculative, and are responding by imposing restrictions.

Not only have the policies of the Soviet government failed to create a secure basis for the development of a market economy, they have led to a formidable crisis. During 1990 overall labour productivity fell by 3%. In the first quarter of 1991 national income went down by 10%. The warnings of serious food shortages made in the autumn of 1990, which had failed to materialize in the winter, were now given firmer statistical foundation. Figures were showing that there had been a reduction in the area prepared for sowing in the spring and agricultural production had fallen by 13% in the first quarter of 1991.

It is common in the Soviet Union to hear these problems attributed to deliberate sabotage by bureaucrats. A failure to satisfy rising expectations may also be important. While these factors cannot be ruled out in all cases, economic difficulties are much more a consequence of the half-hearted nature of reform. The service sector is still in a terrible state. Partly this is a problem of physical infrastructure (for example, the railways lack necessary rolling stock), but restrictions on co-operatives prevent them developing into a flexible consumer-orientated distribution system. As a result, tons of foodstuffs rot in railway marshalling yards and consumer goods purchased with precious hard currency lie in foreign warehouses because of a shortage of containers.

The introduction of small oases of private enterprise into the desert of a state economy where everything is in short supply inevitably creates a threat of inflation, and without real incentives production will not increase. Reforms that are generally agreed to be necessary, and which would allow private ownership of the means of production, permit citizens to employ hired labour and introduce a pricing system based on the market and a convertible currency, face serious ideological and social obstacles. Neither is the latest package of economic measures proposed under Gorbachev the 'anti-crisis programme', put forward by prime minister Pavlov in April 1991, a serious plan to establish a market economy. Instead, it attempts to prevent further disintegration by setting up various new controls.

Events are showing that some of the features of a market economy are developing, often despite government policy. In particular, the decentralization of decision-making to enterprises means that more and more economic activity in the Soviet Union is made up of bargains struck directly between enterprises rather than as a result of orders issued from the centre, according to the Plan. Auctions of hard currency and commodities have been established in some places to facilitate this activity. The privatization of retail outlets has begun in some cities, such as Moscow and Leningrad, where power is in the hands of non-Communist reformers, However, all the signs point to the fact that the Soviet economy is sliding into crisis without any real progress in economic reform having been made.

The decentralization of decision making before any of the institutions that support a market economy have been established is causing widespread dislocation of economic activity. The handful of enterprises boasting modern production are disappearing, so that the much-publicized conversion of the generally efficient military sector to civilian production is failing to produce significant results. The decentralization of decision making, in the absence of real incentives for managers to maximize production and in conditions of scarcity, has led to a situation where enterprises, regions and republics hoard their stocks. Most frightening of all are the prospects for inflation. The effective deregulation of wages is leading to rapid increases. More seriously, the budget deficit appears to be out of control. It was planned to amount to 26.7 billion roubles for the whole of 1991 but it was revealed in April that in the first three months it had already reached 31.1 billion roubles. The consequences could be disastrous.

The nationalities

Nothing has illustrated the fundamental nature of the difficulties facing the Soviet Union more than the re-emergence of the nationalities question. In every part of the country national groups are calling for a relaxation of control from Moscow, and sometimes for complete secession from the union. Nationalist unrest has considerably hampered Gorbachev's reform programme. At the most basic level, strikes and conflict in Azerbaijan and Armenia cost cost over 280 million roubles in lost production in 1989. The centralized economic system in the Soviet Union means that the consequences of such interruption are magnified. For example, most cigarette paper is produced in Armenia, and strikes in that republic caused shortages throughout the country. More seriously, in the long term, nationalist unrest is an issue on which opponents of reform can capitalize by stirring up a Russian backlash and strengthening demands for force to be used to ensure the territorial integrity of the country.

The rise of nationalist feeling in Russia, Ukraine, Byelorussia, Moldavia and the Baltic states are covered later in this book and will only be touched on in passing here. Nationalist tensions in the Transcaucasus have been in the world's headlines in a particularly tragic fashion. This region has great economic potential. It is strategically situated at a cross-roads between Europe, Asia and the Middle East. Its jumble of ethnic groups and ancient Christian and Islamic cultures are not just a source of conflict, they are also a symbol of its richness. The strategic importance of the Transcaucasus has made it a perennial target for outside conquerors. The Russian Empire did not really establish its power here until the middle of the last century. None of the three main Transcaucasian nationalities, the Georgians, Armenians and Azerbaijanis, are Slav, and all briefly established independent republics in the aftermath of the Revolution.

Nationalist feeling in Georgia is intense and support for total independence is strong. In its own referendum, held on 31 March 1991, 89% of the population of the republic supported the idea that independence should be re-established. At the end of 1988 the nationalist movement took on a mass character as tens of thousands of Georgians demonstrated in the streets of the capital, Tbilisi. The early mood of celebration turned sour after a peaceful demonstration was brutally broken up by special Soviet troops on 9 April 1989, killing at least twenty people. Ominously, this seems to have represented an attempt by anti-reform leaders in Moscow to rehearse a Tiananmen-style solution to the country's problems. The local Party leadership was also implicated and replaced. The inability of the Communist leadership to work with the national movement, as happened in the Baltic republics, combined with the 9 April killings led to a radicalization and polarization in Georgian politics. Unfortunately, the leadership of the Georgian nationalist movement has not always deserved the confidence it undoubtedly enjoys. Insensitivity on their part has inflamed anti-Georgian feeling among the Abkhazian and Ossetian minorities. Multi-party elections in October 1990 gave victory to a nationalist coalition led by the veteran dissident, Zviad Gamsakhurdia. A bloody conflict soon broke out in the Autonomous Region of South Ossetia and, at the beginning of April, Moscow sent in its forces. In response, on 9 April 1991, the Georgian Parliament declared independence.

If Georgia were to become truly independent it would face many problems as a small country, with a population of under 6 million, whose economy has been closely tied in with that of the Soviet Union as a whole. Conceivably, it might also come under pressure from Turkey as well as facing serious internal ethnic problems. As elsewhere in the Soviet Union, central planning has had a deleterious effect on the local agriculture. But the country is proverbially fertile, and Georgian wine and, with some effort, tea and citrus fruit could be valuable exports. The tourist industry has considerable potential and the Caucasus mountains contain valuable minerals. Georgian entrepreneurial skills are well known, although under the planned economy they have mostly frequently found an outlet in the black economy, which does not suit them immediately for modern business. However, reflecting its key position in Transcaucasia, there has already been a certain amount of foreign investment in Georgia and co-operative enterprises are well-developed.

Conflict between the republics of Azerbaijan and Armenia began in early 1988. Armenians took advantage of *glasnost* to restate a long-standing demand that the Armenian enclave of Nagorno-Karabakh in Azerbaijan be joined to their republic. A mass movement quickly grew up around this issue led by a Karabakh Committee, whose prestige rapidly overtook that of the local Party. Gorbachev refused to countenance any change in republican boundaries and took advantage of the disastrous Armenian earthquake in December 1988 to arrest most of the Karabakh Committee. Meanwhile, inter-ethnic conflict was rapidly growing worse, beginning with the murder of 31 Armenians in the Azerbaijani city of Sumgait in February 1988. A flow of refugees began, which eventually created a population of 300,000 displaced persons in the two republics and a permanent cause of instability. Furthermore, the Azerbaijants are able to impose an economic blockade on Armenia and have frequently done so.

In Azerbaijan the Soviet military were still maintaining a state of emergency after bloodily reimposing order in the capital Baku in January, when elections were held in September. The Communists, led by Ayaz Mutalibov, won on a programme that stressed the need to assert republican sovereignty. Mutalibov's decision to participate in negotiations on a new union treaty was rewarded by military support for Azerbaijan in its conflict with Armenia. In April Soviet helicopters co-operated with Azerbaijani forces in evicting Armenians from villages near Nagornyi-Karabakh.

Azerbaijan is the largest of the Transcaucasian republics in terms of territory and population. By the end of the 1980s there were nearly 7 million Azerbaijanis, the great majority of whom live in their native republic. Azerbaijani national identity is shaped and reinforced by the Muslim religion and ethnic proximity to the Turkic peoples of Central Asia and Turkey. Their national movement, which is dominated by the Popular Front, has shown great self-confidence. The Popular Front arose to articulate the Azerbaijani opposition to the Armenian claim on Nagornyi-Karabakh and the discontent of local workers, but quickly made independence its main goal. Azerbaijani self-confidence also stems from the mineral wealth of its republic. Although reserves have greatly diminished, Azerbaijan is still an important oil producer and, like Georgia, it enjoys a fertile soil and a good climate.

The Armenian national movement has been much more ambivalent in its attitude to Moscow. The massacres of about a million Armenians by the Turks at the beginning of the century have left a permanent scar on the national psyche. Armenians are skilled traders, and through their diaspora they have unrivalled international contacts. But Soviet Armenia is not agriculturally rich, and pressure from its neighbours means that the land is heavily populated. The earthquake of December 1988 dealt the country's economy a cruel blow from which it has still not recovered. An independent Armenia would be a small (its population is around 4 million), crowded, landlocked Christian territory surrounded by traditionally hostile Muslim Turks and Azerbaijanis. Nevertheless, the failure of Moscow to support Armenia in its campaign for Nagornyi-Karabakh has greatly strengthened pro-independence feeling. After elections in June 1990 a new government was formed, led by a former leader of the Karabakh Committee, Levon Ter-Petrossian. The new government refused to participate in the negotiations for a new union treaty.

The extent and nature of nationalist feeling in the five Central Asian republics, Uzbekistan, Kazakhstan, Kirgizstan, Tadzhikistan (Tajik) and Turkmenistan, is difficult to gauge. This not just because the local Party leaderships are hostile to *glasnost* but also because the population has determinedly maintained its culture, language and Muslim religion by carefully presenting a picture of outward conformity to Soviet norms. In the past five years organizations with the aim of promoting the local language and culture and supporting democratization, such as the Uzbek Popular Front (Birlik), have appeared. In practice, clan and ethnic identities (and possibly Muslim brotherhoods) have been more important in mobilizing the populace. Violent conflict has broken out on a number of occasions. In Alma Ata, the capital of Kazakhstan, in December 1986 mass demonstrations turned violent after the local Kazakh Party's first secretary was replaced by a Russian. In July 1989 the Uzbek population in the Fergana valley attacked Meskhetian Turks who had been transported there from Georgia by Stalin. In February 1990 in Dushanbe, the capital of Tadzhikistan, there were violent demonstrations by the local population who have close ethnic relatives in Afghanistan. In June 1990 over 200 people were killed in the Osh region of Kirgizia.

Agriculturally, these are potentially rich territories, but the local environment is in a terrible state. The economy of Central Asia has been geared to produce raw materials particularly cotton, for factories which are mostly situated elsewhere in the Soviet Union. The profligate application of chemical fertilizers and pesticides and the diversion of local rivers has created an ecological disaster in the Aral Sea, which has shrunk to a toxic puddle. These are already sizeable republics. Uzbekistan has the largest population of nearly 15 million, and the high local birth rate means that they will become even more important. The combination of a rapidly rising population with a ruined economy creating unemployment and land hunger and a strong identification with Islam has created a potentially explosive mixture in Central Asia. The Communist leader of Kazakhstan, Nursultan Nazarbayev, is trying to create a new appeal for his rule around technocratic reform and a strong defence of republican sovereignty while the Communist leader of Uzbekistan, Islam Karimov, is seeking to appeal more directly to Muslim sentiment.

This upsurge in nationalist feeling is the single largest problem facing the peoples of the Soviet Union. Gorbachev, with his Russian background and training in Marxism–Leninism, is not well equipped to deal with it. On a visit to Lithuania in January 1990 he asked a protester holding up a banner calling for independence who had told him to do so, apparently unable to believe that anyone would do this voluntarily. In his handling of the conflict between Armenia and Azerbaijan he has consistently underestimated the strength of local feeling, and has taken decisive action too late and in such a way that only exacerbates the situation.

In the spring of 1991 a possible future shape for the Soviet Union started to emerge. A referendum on the future of the union held in the RSFSR, the Ukraine, Byelorussia, Azerbaijan and the five Central Asian republics on 17 March 1991 showed strong support both for a continuation of the union in a looser form and for greater sovereignty for the republics. On 23 April the leaders of the nine republics that had participated in the referendum and Gorbachev signed an agreement, the so-called '9 plus 1 agreement', stating their commitment to the principle of a new union treaty. For his part, Gorbachev conceded that it should be a union of 'sovereign states'. The six republics which had refused to participate in the union referendum and had announced their intention of not signing any union treaty had their right of secession from the Soviet Union recognized, but they were told that they would not be able to enjoy any of the economic benefits available to those republics which remained within the union.

The dilemmas of reform

Between 1985 and 1990 the main dilemma of reform in the Soviet Union concerned the contradictions implicit in the attempts of an authoritarian regime to implement change without weakening its own legitimacy. In the Soviet case these did not merely stem from the relaxation of coercion but also from the weak hold of its Marxist–Leninist ideology. With the entry of the people of the Soviet Union onto the political stage, new dilemmas arise. In the past, radical Soviet reformers have sought merely to mobilize popular support for their programmes, but now the population is being asked to decide between different alternatives. Are Soviet citizens, who have never really experienced pluralist democracy and a market economy, capable of responding to the new challenges? What happens if reforms which are generally recognized to be necessary conflict with the interests of important social groups?

The introduction of the market economy in the Soviet Union will mean that many of its citizens will experience a drop in living standards. For some, this will entail merely a relative decrease as social inequalities increase, but for many, those on fixed incomes and workers in loss-making enterprises who face redundancy, the decline will be absolute. Despite occasional campaigns against 'petty bourgeois levelling', the official ideology in the Soviet Union has reinforced popular egalitarianism. This is now backfiring in the shape of popular resentment against Party privileges. Fear of widespread unrest consequent upon the introduction of policies which will raise prices, increase inequalities and create unemployment (Poland in the early 1980s is an example of what might happen) has been a considerable brake on reform.

The nationalities question poses seemingly intractable problems. Nationalist movements have been given great impetus by the adverse economic situation, but they have their own momentum. Pro-independence sentiment in the Baltic republics and Georgia would have been strong, whatever the economic outlook. Political liberalization has simply raised expectations rather than satisfying them. More seriously, the rise of nationalist feeling in one republic is met with suspicion both by Russians and minorities in the republic, who are often Russian as well. Inter-ethnic conflict has caused the loss of many lives over the past few years, and left the country with over half a million refugees. Complaints of discrimination by Russian minorities in the Baltic republics or Moldavia could provoke an authoritarian backlash.

Gorbachev's acceptance of the principle of a multi-party system is severely qualified. He may have abandoned the Party's 'leading role' but, in its place, asserted its position as a 'vanguard party'. Gorbachev has realized that the Communist Party is the bond that holds together the Soviet Union and has stressed the need for unity. Despite this, the Communist Party continues to fall apart. In the Baltic republics and Georgia the local parties have already seceded from the All-Union organization, and by the 28th Party Congress in July all its popularly elected leaders, Nikolai Travkin, Boris Yeltsin, Gavrill Popov and Anatolii Sobchak, had resigned. A significant group of reformers in the Democratic Platform also left the Party.

Furthermore, all over the Soviet Union political organizations are emerging to articulate the aspirations of the population. Sometimes they are tempted to play on the raw nerves of wounded national pride and the desire for scapegoats, but they have also displayed remarkable political skill. This is particularly so for the Baltic popular fronts, which have outmanoeuvred Moscow with a steady stream of small symbolic victories and the occasional tactical retreat. In Russia itself various groupings have sprung up covering the political spectrum, from monarchists to anarchists, reflecting an exceptionally rich political tradition. So far, despite their headline-grabbing demonstrations and an undoubted increase in the number of attacks on Jews, Russian chauvinist organizations like *Pamyat* have failed to attract a mass following. In the elections to the Congress of People's Deputies in March 1989 anti-reform and Russian nationalist candidates, even where they were not associated with the Party apparatus, did badly, and then did not do any better in the republican and other elections in March 1990. An often painful learning process is going on over the whole of the Soviet Union, and there is good reason to think that the great majority of its citizens do not want to return to international isolation and rule by coercion in the name of a failed ideology.

Prognoses

The future of the Soviet Union can appear very uncertain. This sense of uncertainty in a society which has always been assured that it is travelling towards the creation of the perfect human community (Communism) explains the apocalyptic prognoses that one sometimes hears in the Soviet Union. All the same, pessimism is widespread. An opinion survey carried out at the beginning of 1989 showed that 37% of Muscovites considered that their lives had improved over the past three years and 24% thought that their lives had got worse. When asked the same question at the beginning of 1990 only 24% considered that their lives had got better over the past four years while 33% said that their lives had got worse. It is often pointed out that political reform (*glasnost*) has gone ahead much faster than reform of the economy (*perestroika*) and there must be a real danger that economic failure will undermine popular support for political liberalization.

Over the past five years Gorbachev has shown himself to be a consummate politician. He has a knack of just keeping ahead of his critics by brilliantly timed concessions or purges. The failure of *perestroika* to improve the living conditions of ordinary Soviet citizens has critically undermined Gorbachev's personal popularity and hence his room to manoeuvre. The contrast between his popularity abroad and his unpopularity at home has become obvious. His persistent failure to secure a personal popular mandate means that he has to rely increasingly on the 'conservative' *apparat*. 'Conservatives' in the Union group, the KGB and the military have not been slow in pressing home their advantage, as the December 1990 session of the Congress of People's Deputies showed. There was a glimmer of new hope in the spring of 1991 with Gorbachev's move back to the centre of the political spectrum. The 'anti-crisis programme' and the '9 plus 1 agreement', despite all their faults, were the fruits of this. Together with thorough-going democratization they could provide the basis on which governments are established with a mandate to carry through change. Unfortunately, this progress looks like being overtaken by economic collapse.

An attempt to suppress the popular national and democratic movements in the near future, with or without Gorbachev, is a real possibility. However, such a move would be short-lived. The 'conservatives' do not have any coherent alternative to political and economic liberalization; all they propose is that it should go more slowly. Most importantly, the movement for radical change has attained such a scale that it has affected the main pillars of the Soviet state. The decline of the Communist Party has already been demonstrated and the willingness of conscript soldiers and many junior officers to confront the population is also open to question. There are even signs of division within the KGB. If the experience of the past five years has shown one thing it is the inseparability of political and economic reform. New forms of government will emerge which will reflect better the aspirations of the people. For good or ill, the Soviet Union has begun a process which will completely transform the lives of all its citizens.

Postscript: the August coup

This book goes to press against the background of the extraordinary events following the collapse of the hardline coup against Gorbachev in late August 1991. That the conservative reaction against Gorbachev might lead to an attempt to overthrow him was predictable; that its failure would unleash a tidal wave of reform was very much less so.

Wither the Soviet Union now? The decline of the Communist Party seems assured. The breakaway Republics likewise seem certain to be granted independence, though their economic relationship with the centre has yet to be established. Boris Yeltsin's star will surely soar as Gorbachev's wanes. Nonetheless, those who counsel caution and who fear the destructive effects of the economic and social chaos facing the Soviet Union – if indeed the Soviet Union can any longer be said to exist – should be heeded. The legacy of more than 70 years of Communist rule may yet prove bitter.

10 RUSSIA

The Russian Soviet Federated Socialist Republic (RSFSR) is the largest of the fifteen Union republics that make up the Soviet Union. Its population in January 1989 stood at 147.4 million. For such a large territory it is remarkably ethnically homogeneous. The RSFSR stretches from Vladivostok on the Pacific Ocean in the east (nearly 10,000 kilometres and eleven time zones) to the border of Byelorussia in the west. Even further to the west is the Baltic enclave of Kaliningrad, which is cut off from the rest of the RSFSR by Lithuania. This territory was originally part of German East Prussia, annexed to the Soviet Union after World War II, and is now settled by Russians. Then, the RSFSR extends from Murmansk on the Arctic Ocean in the north (2,800 kilometres) to Pyatigorsk in the Caucasus mountains in the south.

The republic's eponymous ethnic group makes up the overwhelming majority of its population (82.6% in 1979). There are many minority peoples, sometimes grouped in their own autonomous republics or national areas. The largest of these minorities are the 6 million Tartars, who have an autonomous republic on the Volga with Kazan as its capital. Nearby are the closely related 1.5 million Bashkirs. Apart from the other small Volga peoples such as the Mordvinians and the Chuvashes, there is also a patchwork of autonomous republics in the north Caucasus; Dagestan, North Ossetia, Chechen-Ingushia and others. There are two other minorities who do not have a national area: the Jews and Germans. (The Jewish national area of Birobijan in the far east was an artificial creation, and few Jews actually live there.)

The European Russian heartland was not well endowed by nature. The rigours of the Russian climate are proverbial. It is continental in pattern with harsh winters (Moscow's average winter temperature is $-8°C$) and relatively warm summers (July temperatures of $20°C$ are typical). The growing season is short and, for the most part, the soils are poor except for the fertile black earth region in south-central Russia and the steppe that extends eastwards. Despite the unpropitious environment in some parts of north European Russia, dairying is successfully practised. For most of central Russia mixed farming is the norm, with potatoes and hardy grains the typical crops. Further south, however, are rich grain belts with sugar beet and maize also grown on a wide scale.

European Russia lacks natural resources. There are no major coal fields

RUSSIA

Official name	Russian Soviet Federal Socialist Republic (RSFSR)
Area	17,078,005 sq. km (6,592,100 sq. miles)
Population	147,386,000 (1989)
Capital	Moscow (Moskva)
Languages	Russian, many minority languages
Religion	Russian Orthodox
Currency	rouble

or oil deposits and few minerals except in the Urals mountains, where there is copper, iron, nickel, zinc, aluminium and magnesium. The climate compounds with distance to make communications difficult. So although Russia does have extensive timber reserves, they have proved difficult to exploit. Russia is also constricted by a lack of ice-free outlets to the sea, thus hampering foreign trade. Murmansk, although it is in the far north, is navigable throughout the year, but its distance from the main population centres limits its importance. Leningrad, which is further south and the centre of a major industrial region, is closed for three months of the year. In contrast, Siberia is rich in minerals. It has extremely large oil deposits in west Siberia around the city of Tyumen, and coal reserves for several thousand years in the Kuzbass and east Siberia, at the present rate of extraction. There are extensive deposits of all kinds of ferrous and non-ferrous metals, including gold, aluminium, molybdenum, manganese and iron. There are also large diamond workings. West Siberia has considerable reserves of natural gas and east Siberia a large surplus of hydro-electric power.

Russia's economic strength has stemmed from its agriculture and the creativeness and hard work of its people. It is a potentially rich country, but realizing that potential requires an immense input of human effort, and for most of its history it is the peasants who have made the country productive. In the pre-revolutionary period the productivity of Russian agriculture was low compared with West European countries, but the gradual penetration of the market into the countryside began to transform subsistence agriculture. In the south large estates were producing grain for export and the Siberian dairy herds did the same with butter. One of Tsarist Russia's last prime ministers, Pyotr Stolypin, introduced measures to encourage the development of individual peasant farms out of the old semi-feudal structures based on the peasant commune, the *mir*. Fast industrial growth was also achieved.

The introduction of the market into the countryside and the inequalities that went with it caused social tensions. During the Revolution the peasants seized the large estates and divided them up. Individual peasant farmers were forced back into the *mir*, which was a major setback in the development of Russian agriculture. In 1917 the Bolsheviks had been able to secure the passive support of the peasants by calling for the division of the landlords' land, but gradually alienated them during the Civil War, until they rose in rebellion. The Bolsheviks abandoned their policy of grain requisitioning and their plans to introduce collective farms, and in early 1921 introduced the New Economic Policy (NEP). Under the NEP the problem of grain production was approached by offering peasants incentives, and recovery from the famine of 1921–2 was remarkably quick. The peasants showed that they were able to respond to these incentives, despite the restrictions placed on them by both the *mir* and the Soviet state. Under NEP, grain deliveries to the cities were dependent on the market, and if prices were not good enough the peasants would not and frequently did not sell. At the end of the 1920s, under pressure to get grain into the cities to support the industrialization programme, requisitioning was re-introduced and systemized under the collective farms. In its collectivization campaign the Communist Party tried to exploit the resentment that the more successful peasants, the *kulaks*, aroused.

Russia's lack of natural resources and poor communications has encouraged the state to play an important role in the development of the country's economy. Both under Peter the Great at the beginning of the eighteenth century, when industry was built up with serf labour, and the much more grandiose project of Stalin in the 1930s the state was used to pull the country up by its bootstraps. It is the negative consequences of this last 'revolution from above' which are now being tackled by Soviet economic reformers.

From the beginning of the 1930s a rapid process of industrialization was carried out in Russia, as elsewhere in the Soviet Union, and, as elsewhere, it transformed the traditional life-style and economy of the bulk of the population. In less than ten years Russia's traditional peasant agriculture was replaced by collective farms. This was a disaster. Many peasants regarded collectivization as a return to serfdom, with the forced labour for noble serf-owners (*barshchina*) being replaced with forced labour for the state. Production of most agricultural commodities fell, but the number of peasants needed to produce them fell faster. Although there was thus an apparent rise in productivity, Russian agriculture was now permanently depressed. This was partly due to the centre's persistent neglect, compounded by its failure to take account of local conditions and also because of the lack of incentives given to individual peasants. Some Russian intellectuals now argue that collectivization permanently destroyed the peasants' interest in the soil, but this is belied by the success of their private plots, which make a contribution to Russian food production out of all proportion to the size of their area.

Russia's rapid urbanization and the development of heavy industry gave the impression of modernization. The population of old-established cities grew rapidly and new ones were built from scratch. From being an overwhelmingly peasant country in 1928, by 1941 Russia was becoming a nation of city dwellers. During the 1930s the output figures for iron, electricity, coal and machinery shot up, and by 1941 a massive industrial potential had been created which was the basis of the Soviet war effort. The structural bias towards heavy industry was established in the early five-year plans, and Russia's economic geography was transformed by the establishment of large new metallurgical combines at Magnitogorsk in the Urals and Kuznetsk in west Siberia.

Soviet economic development has been particularly profligate with the country's two most precious assets, its natural resources and its people. Cheap natural materials have been made to substitute for capital and technology and waste has been compounded by the lack of proper controls on costs. As a result, it now takes three times as much energy to produce a tonne of copper in the Soviet Union as in Germany. Industrialization was wasteful in people not only because of the physical destruction of millions as *kulaks* and in famine. Low productivity is structural to the Soviet economic system. Western social scientists have described a sort of 'social contract', whereby the regime bought political quiescence with gradually rising living standards to be enjoyed roughly by all citizens, no matter what contribution they made to society. Wage differentials were small, job security almost total and pressure to increase productivity minimal. Russian workers called this the system of 'we pretend to work and they pretend to pay us'. The Soviet system has created a highly educated but greatly under-utilized workforce. Typically, across the Soviet Union today there are thousands of research institutes where highly educated graduates 'pretend to work'.

What is Russia?

Formally at least, it would be no exaggeration to say that 70 years of Soviet rule reduced Russia to the status of an administrative concept. Indeed, for many foreigners Russia is synonymous with the Soviet Union. In recent years, however, the fundamental questions that are being asked about the future of the Soviet Union are encouraging Russians to think about their own national identity. Russia's history, in many ways, separates it from the other nations that make up the Soviet Union and from those of Eastern Europe. In the past, both Russians and foreigners have tried to define Russia in terms of either its European or its Asiatic heritage. In practice, Russian culture has been European for over two centuries, although the Russian state and its relationship to society makes this a nation *sui generis*.

Modern Russian history began in the fifteenth and sixteenth centuries, with the campaigns of Ivan III and Ivan IV, the Terrible, to free Russians from Mongol and Tartar rule. To stave off its enemies in the east and later in the west (at first, Poland and Sweden, and later, France, Britain, Austria and Germany), the need for a powerful state to mobilize all available resources developed. However, the Russian autocracy was not merely a strong state: it was a very personal form of absolutism in which there were no intermediate institutions, such as an independent church, an aristocracy (as opposed to a service nobility) and rule of law. There were attempts to replace the 'bootstrap-pulling' convulsions to catch up with rivals who were always ahead and create a self-sustaining process of development by releasing the creative forces in society. Catherine II, the Great, tried to raise the prestige of the nobility, for example. In 1861 Alexander II abolished serfdom, and subsequently set up a judiciary and a representative form of local government, the *zemstva*. After the 1905 Revolution Nicholas II granted a limited representative assembly, the *Duma*. However, the

Bolshevik determination to industrialize the country through state planning represented a resumption of the state tradition.

The Communists have exploited aspects of Russia's political culture to
maintain their rule, in particular peasant egalitarianism, and this is one
reason for the ambivalence with which Russians have sometimes regarded
the Soviet regime. However, Communist rule has destroyed a great deal
more than it borrowed from Russia's traditions, and not just those of the
Europeanized elite. Collectivization did not entail just the destruction of an
economy, it also meant the elimination of a way of life. The *mir*, for
example, restricted individual freedom in some respects but it did provide
a basic form of mutual aid and even collective decision-making. The highly
developed village handicrafts industry (*kustar*), which provided the bulk of
the peasants' consumer goods and work tools, was destroyed during
industrialization. The *artel* was a peasant-based form of co-operative work
that had great social and economic potential, and it persists in various
forms to this day, both sanctioned by the state (*brigady*) and unofficially
(*shabashniki*).

The Soviet Union is, at least, the territorial heir to the Russian Empire,
and for many in the non-Russian republics they merge into one. While
many Russians feel a sense of patriotism about the Soviet Union, it is
usually not without reservations. Professor Geoffrey Hosking, the 1988
Reith Lecturer, put it very well:

> One nation in the Soviet confraternity is in a very singular position,
> and that is the Russians. They are to all appearances the imperial
> nation, the 'elder brother', in Stalin's words. They have no worries
> about their territory, or language, or alien immigration: in fact other
> nations feel threatened by *them*. Yet, curiously enough, in some
> respects the Russians feel like a national minority discriminated
> against in their own country. They know that the non-Russians are
> often more prosperous. And they can see that since 1917 their
> church has been undermined, their rural way of life mortally
> enfeebled, their finest writers, artists and thinkers banned, driven
> into the underground and emigration.

This discontent manifested itself in a search for roots among Russians
that began long before *perestroika*. The best recent Russian prose writers,
such as Valentin Rasputin and Viktor Astafev, eulogized the disappearing
village way of life. Among many Russians there was a growing interest in
and respect for religion. The Soviet regime reduced the Russian Orthodox
Church to a state of complete subservience, and it was in no position to
play a role similar to that of the Roman Catholic Church in Communist
Poland. Nonetheless, in recent years Russians have increasingly turned to
the Church both to express their rejection of Communist ideology and to
affirm their national identity. Gorbachev attempted to capitalize on this

when the marking of the millennium of the Russian Orthodox Church in 1988 was made the occasion for unprecedented offical celebrations.

At a time when politics could not be openly articulated, Russian national feeling also was expressed in opposition to the Siberian rivers project, whereby water from the north-flowing Siberian rivers would be diverted to irrigate the arid lands of Central Asia, with potentially serious ecological consequences, and occasional complaints that, alone of the Union republics, the RSFSR did not have its own capital (Moscow was better known as the capital of the Soviet Union) and did not have its own Academy of Sciences or even Party organization. When *glasnost* revealed the extent of national feelings in the non-Russian republics, Russians were forced to examine even further their own national identity.

As the tightly centralized Soviet state gives way to a much looser federation or even breaks up entirely, Russia will be forced to review its relationship with its Slav neighbours and the many minorities within the RSFSR. In September 1990 Aleksandr Solzhenitsyn, who still lives in the USA after being exiled from the Soviet Union in 1974, published a programme for the future development of Russia in Soviet newspapers. He advocated that Russia should separate itself from the three Baltic republics, Moldavia, the three Transcaucasian republics and the five Central Asian republics. On the other hand, the long political and cultural ties between the three Slav republics, Russia, Byelorussia and the Ukraine meant that they should remain united along with a large part of Kazakhstan, populated by Russians.

Solzhenitsyn is a key figure in contemporary Russian political thought, and the fact that his proposals attracted wide interest shows that for many Russians the Empire is no longer regarded as worth holding on to. However, despite the historical ties alluded to by Solzhenitsyn, many Ukrainians and Byelorussians look to the West rather than Russia. Furthermore, since the incorporation of Siberia into the Empire in the sixteenth century Russia has been geographically an Asian as well as a European power. The great majority of Siberia's population is ethnically Russian, the native peoples such as the Yakuts and the Buryat Mongols have their own autonomous areas, and it will remain closely tied to European Russia, but regionalist tendencies are bound to grow. Russians will also have to decide on their attitude to other minorities, Tartars, Jews and Germans. In particular, the increasing assertiveness of the 16 autonomous republics in the RSFSR poses serious problems. Most of them have declared sovereignty and several, including Tartaristan, Bashkirstan, North Ossetia and Chechen-Ingushia, refused to participate in the referendum about the establishment of an executive president in the RSFSR. Indeed Tartarstan deleted the paragraph in its constitution which said it was part of the RSFSR.

The rise of nationalism in the Soviet Union has made the way that Russians regard the Soviet Union, either as a genuine expression of their own statehood or as a system alien to their traditions, one of the crucial factors affecting the outcome of the present period of rapid change in the Soviet Union.

The prospects for economic reform

At various times the Communist regime has attempted to mobilize popular Russian hostility to social inequality. The campaign against the *kulaks* is a prime example, and has reinforced negative attitudes towards private enterprise. The problems encountered by the present reforms which call for greater incentives and a larger role for the market indicate that such attitudes are indeed commonly held by Russians. Mostly impressionistic evidence suggests that they are less common among the Baltic and Transcaucasian peoples. If *perestroika* is to avoid the fate of NEP it will be important to investigate the real extent of such attitudes. Opinion polling in the Soviet Union is not very sophisticated, but some polls have given interesting results.

During the present reforms the question of reducing the massive Soviet budget deficit, which stood at 36 billion roubles at the beginning of 1989, by closing unprofitable state enterprises has frequently been raised, but the government has always failed to take action in the face of the spectre of mass unemployment. Another way of reducing the deficit would be to cut subsidies on basic foodstuffs and utilities, such as electricity and rents, and to introduce market prices. At the end of May 1990 a decision by the Presidential Council to double the prices for staple goods such as meat, fish and milk and triple that for bread led to panic buying in major Russian cities, forcing the measure to be suspended. Food supply in Russian cities continued to deteriorate, and at the beginning of December the new popularly elected city councils in Moscow and Leningrad introduced rationing schemes.

The co-operatives have been a particular butt for popular hostility to private enterprise. A poll carried out in Moscow, one of the most liberal parts of Russia, at the beginning of 1989 found that 23% of men and 8% of women thought that people who worked in co-operatives 'were businesslike people full of initiative' and that they merited respect and support. Almost half of the men and about a third of the women had reservations about the co-operative movement and about a quarter of the men and 38% of the women thought that people who worked in co-operatives were 'swindlers and businessmen who make a lot of money at the expense of honest working people'. At the end of September 1989 an attempt by a group of deputies in the Supreme Soviet to ban all commercial co-operatives as opposed to production co-operatives was narrowly defeated, but in the middle of October the Soviet bowed to popular pressure and gave local authorities the right to set 'maximum price levels' on 'essential public goods' for sale in co-operatives. Such popular hostility and the activity of protection rackets run by organized crime, the so-called 'mafia', make the position of Soviet co-operatives unenviable.

There are more optimistic signs for reformers, though. A poll conducted in Moscow at the end of 1989 found that 57% of those asked agreed that the private ownership of the means of production should be allowed. Positive responses were much more common among the young. Many people seem to be prepared to give the co-operatives a chance. When asked whether the development of co-operatives would help to ease shortages, 39.4% of those questioned agreed, 37.9% disagreed and 22.7% did not know. A particularly bad sign for the co-operative movement was the demand of many of the strikers in the summer of 1989 for their closure, but by the end of the year a degree of understanding between the two sides seems to have been established when the co-operative union agreed to provide financial and material help to the strike committees.

In general, the old 'social contract' has broken down, and there does seem to be widespread acceptance of the need for greater incentives or, as it is put sometimes more hesitantly, payment by results. Many Russians feel that the present economic system does not give them the opportunity to realize their potential. The Russian government, formed as a result of the March 1990 elections, has consistently pursued more radical economic reform than the All-Union government. The failure of Gorbachev to come up with a radical reform programme prompted the Russian government to commission the economist Stanislav Shatalin to draw up an alternative. When the All-Union Supreme Soviet rejected his proposals for massive privatization and economic decentralization within '500 days' at the end of October the Russian Supreme Soviet agreed to it in any case. Meanwhile, Russia had been signing bilateral trade agreements with the other republics, which was an implicit challenge to the Union. At the beginning of December the Russian Supreme Soviet voted to allow, with some restrictions, full private ownership of land.

Political choices

Perestroika is presenting the Soviet citizen, for the first time, with political choices. This is so no less for Russia than elsewhere in the Soviet Union. As Marxist–Leninist ideology dissolves and the Communist Party fractures, groupings within the apparat are seeking new bases of support among the many informal organizations that are springing up. On the face of it, the Communist Party in Russia, untainted by deference to a foreign power, might expect to receive considerable support. At the end of June 1990 a Russian Communist Party was formally established but it was dominated by 'conservative' elements, some connected with the OFT (see below), symbolized by its leader, Ivan Polozkov, and as long as Russians continue to support further radical reform its appeal will be limited. By the middle of 1990 the Russian political spectrum looked something like this.

On the extreme nationalist right are organizations like *Pamyat* (Memory). *Pamyat*'s roots go back to officially sponsored organizations set up in the 1960s and 1970s to channel popular demands for action to preserve

Russia's national monuments, especially its devastated churches. When the organization, as such, surfaced in 1986 its ideology had clearly been formed under the influence of anti-semitic *samizdat* literature, such as that hoary old fake *The Protocols of the Elders of Zion*, which had been circulating in the 1970s. Gauging the support *Pamyat* really enjoys is very difficult, not least because the organization (if it was ever a single organization) has split into up to a dozen little *Pamyats*, the largest led by Dmitrii Vassiliev. *Pamyat* does not enjoy mass support, but it does have determined groups of activists in many Russian cities. More seriously, certain figures in the cultural intelligentsia give it their tacit support, and there is some evidence that elements in the KGB and the militia are sympathetic or even use it for their own ends.

The United Front of Workers (OFT) also has Russian nationalist tendencies, especially through its links with the Interfronts in the Baltic republics, but the OFT is more properly a child of 'conservative' elements in the apparat. In the search for a new base, some Communist politicians, most notably the Leningrad First Secretary, Boris Gidaspov, are trying to make capital out of the concerns of workers that the introduction of market mechanisms will lead to a fall in their living standards. The OFT undoubtedly has a resonance with popular anxieties, and has organized branches in different parts of the country. However, it has not been able to overcome workers' suspicions of the Communist Party and attract a mass following. Gidaspov's refusal to stand as a candidate in the elections to the RSFSR Supreme Soviet speaks volumes in this respect.

There are other radical political groupings which do not take part in electoral politics. Perhaps the most prominent is the Democratic Union (DS). With strong dissident roots a political party in opposition to totalitarianism was formed in Moscow in August 1988. Since then, they have been active in street demonstrations, with a radical programme for dismantling Soviet power. The DS is a small grouping. It has about 1000 members over the Soviet Union and does not have mass support – its attempts to link up with striking miners were rebuffed. On the other hand, it is well organized, with a strictly defined form of membership, in contrast to other informal organizations, and it produces a large number of publications. Anarchists have also made themselves visible but also (not surprisingly) do not participate in elections.

The strongest political force at present is represented by a coalition of radical Communists with liberal Russian nationalists, social democrats, Christian democrats and non-party radicals, particularly in the Russian popular fronts, which came together in January 1990 to form an electoral bloc, Democratic Russia, for the RSFSR Supreme Soviet elections in March. Democratic Russia draws its inspiration from the moral authority of the late Andrei Sakharov, includes members of the Inter-Regional Group of deputies, whose most well-known member is Boris Yeltsin, and has the grassroots support of some of the most active informal political associations. The elections marked an historic turning-point in Russian history. Approximately 35% of the deputies elected to the Russian Supreme Soviet were supporters of Democratic Russia. Although Gorbachev threw his personal authority against him, Yeltsin's authority was such that he was elected president of the republic. In Moscow and Leningrad the radicals' victory was total. In the capital the radical economist, Gavrill Popov, was elected leader of the council and in Leningrad the equivalent position was taken by Anatolii Sobchak, who had made his name as a leading radical member of the All-Union Supreme Soviet.

On 12 June the new RSFSR Supreme Soviet declared republican sovereignty, that is, the supremacy of its laws over All-Union laws and that all the resources of the republic come under its jurisdiction. Inevitably, the Russian Supreme Soviet quickly came into conflict with the All-Union government. Conflict over the Shatalin plan was only one aspect of this. At the practical level, in August, the Russian government moved to block an agreement between the All-Union government and De Beers over diamond sales. At the end of 1990 the All-Union government was unable to present a budget because the Russian government was determined to drastically reduce its contributions. At the same time, the failure of Yeltsin to come to an agreement with Gorbachev cast doubts over reform in Russia. By the beginning of 1991 there were signs that the Russian government was in danger of losing its way. In mid-October 1990 Grigorii Yavlinskii, a co-author of the Shatalin plan and a deputy prime minister, resigned from the Russian government in frustration, as did Boris Fedorov, the Russian Finance Minister, in December. Similarly, some radicals criticized the introduction of rationing in Moscow and Leningrad as a step back from market reform. However, the election, by a large majority, of Boris Yeltsin as executive president in popular elections at the beginning of June 1991 holds out the prospect of a new impetus being given to reform.

Many observers argue that Russia is, at last, experiencing the emergence of a 'civil society'. By this they mean that institutions and a political culture are being created which will allow forces in society to advance their aspirations, even against the state, in a coherent way. While great progress has been made in terms of political education, however, it is not clear that such institutions have really established themselves, and the Russian political scene continues to be dominated by a process of fragmentation. The contours of the new Russia are still obscure.

Conclusions

Russia is now going through a very painful transition process, a transition that has been made more difficult by 70 years of Communist rule. There is a risk of a backlash against political and economic liberalization: the treatment of minorities such as the Jews and Tartars will be a touchstone for this. In the nineteenth century intellectuals divided into those who saw

Russia as having its own particular path of development (the Slavophiles) and those who saw its future in representative democracy and in the development of a Western-style economy (the Westernizers). The isolation that Slavophilism implied and that the Bolsheviks imposed are not an option for Russia at the end of the twentieth century. The overwhelming majority of Russians appreciate the opening of links with the outside world. Polls have shown consistently that the most popular way of improving incentives is increasing the imports of foreign consumer goods.

The Slavophile/Westernizer controversy hinged not only on the relationship of Russia to the rest of the world but also on attitudes to private property. The sort of hostility to private property that the Slavophiles showed is not as strong a force now as it was at the beginning of the century. This is so first, for good or ill, because of the disappearance of the peasantry and second, because of the discrediting of Marxist–Leninist ideology. The experience of 70 years of authoritarian rule has also raised popular consciousness of the need for civil rights to be guaranteed. Despite these Westernizing tendencies, the political system of a sovereign Russia would probably differ in many ways from those prevailing in West Europe. Popular ecological concerns, which border on anti-industrialism, and decentralizing tendencies will be prominent. The main question facing Russians now (and the rise of nationalism in the Soviet republics has been shown in other chapters in this book) is the attitude they take towards the empire. If they refuse to accept demands for greater autonomy they will be forced to return to authoritarian styles of government. The indications at present are that as long as the process of liberalization is not discredited, Russians will become reconciled to this.

11 THE BALTIC STATES

Since 1940, when the independent Baltic states of Estonia, Latvia and Lithuania were annexed by the USSR and disappeared from the political map of the world, they have often been considered as a single entity. In fact they comprise three nations with different linguistic and historical backgrounds. For that reason, each is here given a separate analysis. Yet there are similarities in their recent historical developments. All three provinces of Tsarist Russia gained independence as a result of the simultaneous collapse of the Russian and German empires before the end of World War I. Lithuania declared its independence on 16 February, Estonia on 24 February and Latvia on 18 November 1918. Soviet Russia renounced all former rights of sovereignty 'voluntarily and for ever' in the 1920 peace treaties signed with Estonia on 2 February in Tartu, with Lithuania on 12 July in Moscow and with Latvia on 11 August in Riga. The Baltic states entered the League of Nations during the period 1921–2.

The states lost their independence as a consequence of the Molotov–Ribbentrop Pact (MRP) signed on 23 August 1939 between Germany and the USSR. Its secret 'additional protocol' assigned Estonia and Latvia to the Soviet 'sphere of interest' and Lithuania to Germany. A further secret protocol on 28 September also transferred Lithuania to the USSR. The Baltic states were forced to conclude Pacts of Mutual Defence and Assistance with the USSR in September and October, after which Soviet troops entered their territories. Although the treaties guaranteed independence, the total occupation of the Baltic states was completed between 15 and 18 June 1940, at the time when Germany invaded France. The incorporation took place behind a facade of legitimacy. Workers' demonstrations occurred on 21 June and the Communist parties became the only legal parties. Elections on 14–15 July were in clear violation of the electoral laws of the three states. Before the elections, non-Communist leaders and activists were arrested. Voting was according to a single Soviet-assigned candidates' list. The new assemblies requested entry into the Soviet Union and their requests were accepted on 3 August (Lithuania) and on 6 August 1940 (Estonia and Latvia). Most Western countries to this day do not recognize *de jure* the annexation of the Baltic states by the USSR.

During the first year of Soviet rule, Estonia lost around 60,000 people (4% of its pre-war population), Latvia 35,000 and Lithuania 34,000 (1.5–2% each) through deportations, mobilizations and massacres. The deportations of June 1941, coming on the eve of the German–Soviet war, served as a shock to the people, which explains their passive welcome of the German armies. They hoped that the Germans would restore their independence, but German actions did nothing to encourage such feelings. Before the return of the Soviets in the autumn of 1944 there was large-scale emigration of the Baltic peoples to the West (6% of the Estonian, 8% of the Latvian and 3% of the Lithuanian populations). Nearly half of these had benefited from higher education. Guerrilla resistance continued until 1952. At their most numerous, the guerrillas constituted up to 1% of the total population.

Collectivization of agriculture was accompanied by mass deportations of farmers to Siberia. In the month of March 1949 the Baltic nations lost about 3% of their populations.

Large numbers of Russian workers were brought into the republics to man new heavy industrial plants. Whereas in 1939 there were 8% non-Estonians, 23% non-Latvians and 20% non-Lithuanians living in the republics, by 1989 the figures had risen to 39%, 48% and 20% respectively. Large-scale industrialization has considerably damaged the local environment, and the ecological crisis has come to symbolize the colonial system under which the countries have no control over their natural resources or environmental protection. Ninety per cent of their industries are directly under all-union control through Moscow ministries.

The deterioration of the standard of living, the destruction of the environment, the demographic situation, and the suppression of national cultures have contributed to the disillusionment of the Baltic peoples with the occupying power. The tradition of dissent, the existence of strong, locally educated elites capable of articulating the needs of their people and mobilizing them into movements, the memory of their independent democratic statehood are all factors motivating them for a change.

In the Baltic context, Gorbachev's policy of *perestroika* has become a movement for restoration of independence. Moscow reformers failed to understand that, by promoting social initiatives and creativity from below, they strengthened the national identity of the Baltic peoples. The policy of *glasnost* has endangered the Communist Party's prestige and has burdened it with responsibility for the past repressive policies. Being a symbol of occupation, the Party has no chance of survival. When Soviet reformers criticize the central bureaucracy, in the Baltic context this means Moscow's colonial rule over the republics. When Moscow radicals attack Stalinist policies, the Baltic peoples include Stalinist foreign policies, as a result of which they were occupied. When Moscow promotes democratic elections, Estonians, Latvians and Lithuanians vote for their political independence.

Estonia

The Estonians are a Finno-Ugric people, related to the Finns and, more distantly, to the Hungarians. They were subjugated by German and

Danish invaders in the thirteenth century and later ruled by Sweden from 1561 to 1721, after which the Estonian lands became part of Tsarist Russia. Economic development between the wars was similar to that of Finland. The gradual deterioration of Soviet Estonia's living standards when compared to those of Finland (and the ability to see this on Finnish television) has always reminded Estonians of what might have been an alternative path of development had they not been occupied in 1940.

The tradition of dissent has ranged from small symbolic acts (such as laying flowers at places connected with independence or hoisting the prohibited national flag in public places) to large student demonstrations (1980) and to the existence of small dissident groups (the Association of Concerned Estonians, the Estonian Democratic Movement). In 1980 40 prominent intellectuals signed an open letter to *Pravda* objecting to the Russification of the republic. By 1983 nearly all open dissidents were arrested and protests became even more muted.

When Mikhail Gorbachev came to power in 1985 and launched his campaign against ageing Brezhnevite officials to secure his position, nothing changed in Estonia. The conservative leadership of the Communist Party of Estonia (CPE) remained intact and it launched a campaign against Estonian nationalism. Under these circumstances people became even more frustrated, expecting relaxation but seeing the opposite. This was the background of the anti-phosphorite campaign.

The environmental protests of 1985–7 started after the decision of the Soviet Ministry of Fertilizer Production to increase open-pit phosphorite mining in the already highly polluted region of north-east Estonia. The most polluting industries of Estonia are subordinate to all-union ministries. Although Estonia was first in the USSR to pass a Nature Protection Act (1957), this legislation does not apply to Moscow-controlled industries (90% of Estonian industries). Estonian youth organized small protest demonstrations in April–May 1987 and public discussions took place in the media. As a result of public pressure, the planned mining of phosphorite was postponed. The success increased the confidence of the people and prepared the ground for further protest actions.

The anniversary of the Molotov–Ribbentrop Pact was for the first time commemorated at Tallinn's Hirvepark on 23 August 1987 with 2000 participants. The demonstration's organizers (ex-prisoners and dissidents) knew that they were supported by the instincts of most Estonians. After the meeting, the Estonian Group for Publication of the Molotov–Ribbentrop Pact (MRP-AEG) was formed.

The Economic Self-Management proposal (IME in Estonian) was published on 26 September 1987. Closet reformers within the establishment were afraid to lose the initiative to the openly pro-independence dissident movement. It was also a logical solution to the ongoing anti-phosphorite campaign. IME proposed that the republic should be granted jurisdiction over its economy, the establishment of a convertible currency and

ESTONIA

Official name	Republic of Estonia
Area	45,100 sq. km (17,413 sq. miles)
Population	1,583,000 (1990)
Capital	Tallinn
Languages	Estonian, Russian
Religion	Lutheran
Currency	rouble

complete autonomy in trade relations with other countries. Throughout 1987 the proposal was criticized by the Communist Party leadership, but it gained growing public support.

Freedom of the press reached Estonia by 1988, when formerly prohibited subjects (Russification and destruction of the environment) were widely discussed. Since then it has played a major role in mobilizing people for change.

The Estonian Heritage Society (EHS) was formed on 12 December 1987, becoming the first grassroots organization. Its membership grew from 3000 to 10,000 during 1988. The EHS collected personal testimonies from victims of the occupation years, restored monuments destroyed by the Soviets, and organized collections of money for the restoration of the Estonian People's Museum.

A demonstration on 2 February 1988 to commemorate the Estonian–Soviet Peace Treaty of 1920 in Tartu was attacked by the police (the last such case). It brought about a sharp disagreement about tactics between MRP-AEG, standing for confrontational measures, and reformers within the establishment, who, fearing a backlash, were more moderate.

The Independence Day demonstration in Tallinn on 24 February 1988 was organized by the MRP-AEG with 10,000 people participating.

The Popular Front (PF) was unofficially established on 13 April, the Estonian Green Movement (EGM) on 23 May. The national flag colours of blue, black and white were first displayed at a meeting of the EHS in Tartu on 14–17 April 1988.

Spring was the beginning of the 'Singing Revolution' of 1988, which continued into September, when tens of thousands of Estonians waved flags and sang. The summer of 1988 was important because people lost their fear and became active participants in the movements. This frightened the non-Estonian population of the republic, and on 12 July the Intermovement was formed (formally constituted on 6 March 1989).

After the publication of the secret protocol of the MRP in a party daily newspaper, the MRP-AEG had achieved its short-term goal and re-emerged on 20 August as the Estonian National Independence Party (ENIP), the first opposition party to the CPE. On 2 October 1988 the Popular Front (PF) was formally constituted when it held its first Congress. It included both Communist and non-Communist Party members and was formed as an umbrella organization to support *perestroika* in Estonia. Its programme called for political changes, including a 'transformation of the USSR from a federal state into a confederation of states' with juridical guarantees and the establishment of a political mechanism for leaving the union. The Communist Party of Estonia had lost its leading role in practical terms, but it tried to rehabilitate itself. The new CPE First Secretary, Vaino Väljas, told the republican party organization in September that there was little to distinguish the new-look party from the Popular Front. Demands for future sovereign rights were met by the formal granting of symbolically important demands: the restoration of the tri-colour and of local rather than Moscow time, the adoption of Estonian as the state language (January 1989), and the celebration of Christmas as a public holiday.

When the Estonian Supreme Soviet adopted the Declaration of Sovereignty on 16 November, giving the republic the right to veto all-union laws, Vaino Väljas declared that the decision was consistent with the policy of the CPE to encourage local autonomy. Although the Presidium of the USSR Supreme Soviet declared the Estonian sovereignty legislation unconstitutional, the Estonian Supreme Soviet affirmed its decision on 7 December 1988. As a result of all these measures, the CPE was split along national lines.

At dawn on 24 February 1989 when the Estonian tricolour was hoisted in Tallinn by the leaders of the Communist Party and the Popular Front, the Estonian National Independence Party (ENIP), the Estonian Heritage Society (EHS) and the Estonian Christian Union called on the Estonian people to form local committees to register citizens of the interwar Estonian Republic, their descendants and post-1940 immigrants as applicants for Estonian citizenship. After registration a congress of Estonian citizens would be called to discuss the future of Estonia.

Further political confrontation developed over elections to the USSR Congress of People's Deputies in March 1989. This was between the ENIP and EHS on the one hand, who stood for the re-establishment of the Republic of Estonia and considered sending Estonian delegates 'to the parliament of a neighbouring state' absurd, and the Popular Front, who supported the elections. About 95% of Estonians and 75% of non-Estonians voted. The supporters of the PF won 27 out of the 36 seats and Interfront won five.

By August the Communist Party of Estonia had come to support the Popular Front's demand for a treaty of confederation between Estonia and the Soviet Union but delivered several attacks on the Citizens' Committees, equating them with the conservative Russian Interfront. Their primary fear was that the Citizens' Committees would create an alternative state power structure.

From 11 to 16 August 1989 Interfront organized strikes and lock-outs, with 30,000 non-Estonian workers protesting against the new electoral law. The week was the high point of inter-ethnic tension in Estonia.

By September, some 300,000 people had registered as citizens. Faced with this competition, the Popular Front in October set an independent Estonian Republic as its final goal. This programme coincided with that of the Citizens' Committees (even in calling for the convocation of the Estonian Congress), in all but one crucial point. The PF requested a referendum on independence and on a new Constitution. The ECC denied the need for a referendum because under international law, the Republic still exists *de jure*, a position supported by the Western nations' policy of non-recognition.

The end of 1989 and the beginning of 1990 was a time for forming new political parties, blocs and organizations, on the one hand, and on the other, for the already existing movements to further define and consolidate their strategies. During 1989 the role of the Communist Party diminished very sharply. A poll in December showed that no more than 2% of Estonians and 19% of non-Estonians supported the CPE.

By 24 February, the first day of the elections to the Congress of Estonia, 700,000 citizens and applicants had been registered. It was not until 28 January that the Popular Front announced its formal backing to the Congress. By delaying its endorsement the PF could no longer claim to be the leading force among the popular movements. In consequence, the leaders of the PF began to form parties, mainly of a social-democratic type.

The Congress of Estonia was convened on 11 March 1990. It was not organized along ethnic lines but was based on citizenship of the Republic of Estonia. Of the non-Estonian population, 5% had petitioned for citizenship and were represented by 43 non-voting delegates. The Congress created a further structure, a 71-member Council of Estonia (including ten members from the exile communities), who elected from among themselves an 11-member Executive Committee, with Tunne Kelam as chairman. The Congress claimed it was prepared 'to accept parliamentary responsibility should the need arise'. The Supreme Soviet of Estonia, as an organ of the occupation authorities, was to maintain public order and the normal functioning of everyday life, while the Congress was to exercise sole authority over the questions of Estonia's status and its international relations. The majority view at the Congress and in Estonia at large was that there need not be a proclamation of independence, since this was done in 1918.

After multi-party elections on 18 March the Prime Minister, Edgar Savisaar, formed a new government, which at its first session declared that Estonia was now in a transition period towards full independence.

The Estonian Supreme Soviet also passed a law on 8 May on state symbols, restoring the name of the pre-war Estonian state – 'the Republic of Estonia' – and abandoning the state emblem, anthem and flag of the Estonian SSR.

On 26 May about 200 local and Supreme Soviet Russian deputies set up the Inter-Regional Soviet of People's Deputies and Workers of the ESSR in Kohtla-Järve to preserve Soviet rule in north-east Estonia, but there was increasing confusion among Moscow-loyalists as demands for sovereignty began mounting in the Russian Federation itself. According to a poll conducted in the spring, about one-third of the Russian-speaking population supported Estonian independence.

In the course of 1990 a full spectrum of political parties emerged, totalling around ten. Although they represent left-wing, right-wing and centrist policies, real differences will appear only when the common goal of establishing real independence has been achieved. A pattern of uniting similar movements under a single party is also emerging. For example, on 9 September four small social democratic parties were united under the leadership of Marju Lauristin in the Estonian Social Democratic party. As a consequence, the role of the Popular Front has decreased. The same can be said of the Estonian Congress. Although in opposition to the policies of the Savisaar government (and politically very important for that reason), no alternative programme for socio-economic development by its executive Estonian Council has been proposed.

Following the passage of legislation on border controls, a customs border was set up in November 1990. Tension started mounting in December, when the USSR People's Deputies Congress in Moscow was informed that Estonia, Latvia and Lithuania would refrain from signing the Union Treaty. At the end of December the Tallinn City Council set up a committee for liaison with the Tallinn garrison, which resulted in a declaration by the military that the garrison would not participate in political developments. In January the Estonian leadership had a series of talks in Moscow which succeeded in securing Soviet Defence Minister Yazov's undertaking that no additional troops would be sent into the republic. On 10 January food prices were raised and a sales tax introduced by the Estonian Supreme Council. This increased the discontent among the non-Estonian population. The Estonian Communist Party (which favours the Communist Party of the Soviet Union) called for a strike demanding the dissolution of the Estonian Supreme Council and the lowering of prices (these strikes lasted until the end of January). Under these tense circumstances treaties on political and economic co-operation were signed between Estonia and the Russian Federation in Moscow on 12 January. The next morning, Boris Yeltsin arrived in Tallinn and, together with the three Baltic leaders, sent an address to the United Nations Secretary General protesting against the previous night's bloodshed in Vilnius. Estonia was the only one of the Baltic countries where military confrontation did not take place.

It is almost certain that the positive result among the non-Estonian population in the referendum organized on 3 March 1991 was a result of the failure of the military coup: 82% of the population took part in the referendum and 78% voted for Estonian independence.

Estonia has been the most successful of the three nations in establishing small enterprises. There are 227 joint ventures, including Finnish (123), Swedish (33), German (15), USA (10) and British (8) businesses, compared to 162 in Latvia and 43 in Lithuania.

Latvia

The Latvians are members of the Baltic group of Indo-European peoples. The territory was invaded in the twelfth century by the Germans and later by the Poles and Swedes, and in 1795 it became a part of the Russian Empire. In the interwar years Latvia already had a high percentage of ethnic minorities (24.5% in 1935). Under the Soviet occupation the

LATVIA

Official name	Republic of Latvia
Area	64,500 sq. km (24,590 sq. miles)
Population	2,687,000 (1990)
Capital	Riga
Languages	Latvian, Russian
Religion	Lutheran
Currency	rouble

Latvians' share has decreased to 51.8% (1989), which gives the nationalist issue a special urgency.

Latvia fared worse than Lithuania and Estonia during the 1960s and 1970s because of the Latvian purge of 1959–61 by Khrushchev, who accused the Latvian leadership of pursuing a policy of Latvianization. Some 2000 party and government officials were expelled, and were replaced by Russians and the *latovichi* (Soviet-born people with nominal Latvian lineage who came to Latvia after 1945). Since then, Latvians have been in the minority in the Communist Party of Latvia. The worst policies of Russification were carried out by two *latovichi*, Arvids Pelše and Augusts Voss, who favoured extensive immigration. During the postwar period over 700,000 immigrants have settled in Latvia. The political purge of 1959 also changed the cultural atmosphere of the republic. As late as 1967, an ex-Stalinist critic considered the stagnation in Latvian literature to be worse than under Stalin. Even folklore groups were prohibited. But Latvians, like Estonians and Lithuanians, learned to channel their national feelings into their culture. The young poets, Ojars Vacietis, Imants Ziedonis, Maris Caklais and Janis Peters, were popular in the 1960s because their poems were the only means of telling the truth about the past and the present. The revival of folklore groups at the end of the 1970s also became part of the Latvian struggle for self-esteem. They told the people that the continuity of the generations had been kept alive through folk songs and folk wisdom and that this link could not be broken.

During the 1980s groups of young people started restoring derelict churches and architectural monuments. All this activity helped to raise the Latvian national consciousness which the authorities had tried to suppress. These groups later joined the Environmental Protection Club (EPC) in the spring of 1986.

In July 1986 five people in Liepaja founded Helsinki 86 to monitor Soviet compliance with the 1975 Helsinki accords. These were people who had consciously remained outside the establishment, and although their work was manual, their background was often intellectual. Their *samizdat* bulletin *Tevija* (Fatherland) informed people about the activities of the KGB and human rights campaigns at a time when the republican press kept silent on such issues. They were also the first to organize mass demonstrations on 14 June and 23 August. Both were disrupted by the police. The group had no desire to become a mass-membership organization, but they tested the ground for the coming mass movements.

In October 1986 a campaign was launched to stop construction work of the Daugavpils Hydro-Electric Station on the Daugava River. An important role in the upsurge in public protest was played by an article by Dainis Ivans and Arturs Snips in the newspaper, *Literatura un Maksla*. On 6 November it was announced that the Soviet government had discontinued the project. For the first time in 50 years, Latvian public opinion had gained a victory.

In 1988 the leadership was taken over by the Latvian intelligentsia and other reformers within the establishment. A demonstration held in Bralu Kapi cemetery on 25 March to commemorate the deportation of 43,000 Latvians in 1949 was organized by the Creative Unions, and was the first peaceful demonstration without police interference in the postwar period.

On 27 April the EPC organized a demonstration against the planned construction of the Riga Metro. They argued that this would lower the water table, affect the fragile foundations of old historical buildings and bring in thousands of immigrant workers. The EPC made it possible to hold an alternative point of view, and was especially popular among young people, who saw environmentalism as an expression of spiritual values.

The Latvian Writers' Union convened a plenum for representatives from all the Unions of creative workers on 1 June, which was a turning-point in the events of 1988. The speeches showed a degree of political expression and openness not hitherto seen at an official gathering in Soviet Latvia. The plenum adopted a resolution demanding the recognition of Latvia as a sovereign national state within a Soviet Federation with diplomatic representation. This helped to form an alliance between seventeen leading intellectuals, human rights activists from Helsinki 86, and clergy, who formed an organizing committee with the aim of founding a Popular Front (PF). But in order not to be too confrontational, the human rights activists were excluded from the committee, and the PF became more closely affiliated with the Latvian intelligentsia. Like the Estonian Popular Front, the Latvian PF became an umbrella movement accommodating a variety of political outlooks.

In June 1988 the National Independence Movement of Latvia (NIML) was established under the leadership of Eduards Berklavs among others (purged in 1959). The existence of NIML and its openly pro-independence programme was instrumental in forcing the PF to adopt a similar stance later. In many cases, the NIML has taken credit for parts of the PF programme. The main point of difference between the NIML and PF is in tactics. While the PF seeks to achieve independence through 'step-by-step' parliamentarian means (working with the present Soviet Latvian government), the NIML views the existing Latvian government as illegal and has taken a more confrontational approach.

In July in the procession of a folklore festival, 'Baltica', folklorists were among the first to bring out the Latvian national flag. They had proved themselves to be, in a real sense, the flag-bearers of Latvia's heritage.

The founding congress of the PF took place on 8 October. One-third of the 1000 delegates were Communists. A Governing Council with 100 representatives was elected and after the congress this body elected a 13-member board, with Dainis Ivans as president. From the start, the PF has promoted pluralism and has included representatives from the NIML, the Environmental Protection Club, Helsinki 86 and the Lutheran Movement for Rebirth and Renewal. In October the PF began publishing a weekly newspaper, *Atmoda* (Awakening), which has become the most widely read weekly in Latvia. At its inception, the PF adopted a programme calling for Latvia's sovereignty within the USSR.

As a reaction to the congress, the Latvian International Working People's Front (or Interfront) was formed mainly by Russian speakers. Claiming the support of 48% of Russian speakers, it held its founding congress on 7 January 1989. Latvians view Interfront as a group of neo-Stalinists.

The significance of 1988 was that it saw the eclipse of the previous atmosphere of fear and hopelessness by a new enthusiasm and optimism. The following year was one of large-scale demonstrations and the foundation of new political organizations.

On 18 and 19 February 1989 the NIML held its first congress in Ogre. Many NIML members were also members of the PF. The Presidium of the Latvian Supreme Soviet declared the programme, statutes and resolutions of the NIML to be in conflict with the Latvian SSR Constitution, and the Communist Party of Latvia publicly denounced the NIML as unconstitutional. Following government threats to ban the organization, the NIML organized an extraordinary congress on 28 May. The congress, however, further consolidated its demands for total economic and political independence.

On 26 March about 70% of the population voted in the National Congress of the USSR elections. Candidates endorsed by the PF won 26 out of 34 Latvian seats. The Communist Party of Latvia's First Secretary, Janis Vagris, won barely 51% of votes in his district, largely due to the 'offshore' vote of the Baltic merchant marine fleet, which was conveyed by telegram from ships at sea at the last minute.

A political opposition party, the Latvian National Rebirth Party, was formed in Riga on 2 April.

A delegation of 24 PF leaders went on a one-month tour of Canada and the USA to legalize, within Latvia, the western Latvian emigré organizations such as the American Latvian Association. A symposium with over 100 West Latvian social and business leaders took place in Gananoque, Canada.

On 10 April a co-ordinating body for the registration of all citizens of the Latvian Republic and their descendants, the Latvian Citizenship Committee (LCC), was formed, sponsored by four informal organizations – the NIML, Helsinki 86, EPC and the Riga Chapter of Helsinki 86. The goal of the LCC was to convene a Congress of Latvian Citizens which would serve as the legal representative of the citizens of the Republic of Latvia. The PF expressed support for the concept of the Citizens' Committees, but the support of the Executive Board was lukewarm, although the local chapters were actively involved in the registration process. Registration started in June.

Inspired by the National Independence Movement congress, the Executive Board of the Popular Front proposed a referendum on 'total political and economic independence' for Latvia on 31 May. It was declared that 'the goal of the PF is to achieve national Latvian independence'. This appeal marked a major departure from the previously stated goal of a 'sovereign' Latvia within the framework of a federation of Soviet states.

In July a new party, the Christian Democratic Party, was formed by a pastor, Oskars Bogdanovs. The leadership of the Latvian Lutheran Church disassociated itself from the new party. The oldest Latvian political party, the Latvian Social Democratic Workers Party (LSDWP), resumed its activities under the leadership of Valdis Steins but subsequently split into two parties.

The proclamation of sovereignty and economic independence on 28 July 1989 was not as bold as the similar declarations adopted by the Estonian and Lithuanian Supreme Soviets. The Latvian legislature chose to follow in the footsteps of its neighbours rather than initiating something new, a course of action that illustrates the inherent cautiousness of the Latvian leadership.

On 7–8 October the Second Congress of the Popular Front adopted a programme with an open call for total political and economic independence, outside the USSR. It also supported a free market and a multi-party system.

Candidates supported by the Popular Front won some 70% of the seats at the election to the local councils in December. This was a major victory, which demonstrated that non-Latvians take less interest in political changes.

A multi-party system was introduced in Latvia on 11 January 1990. After that, a number of new parties were established (the Latvian Green Party, the Latvian Social Democratic Party, the Liberal Party, the Democratic Party, etc.).

Elections to the Latvian SSR Supreme Soviet on 18 March were real multi-party elections. The nationalist parties and movements won over two-thirds of the total of 201 seats.

The Latvian Citizenship Committee was formed on the example of a similar movement in Estonia in April 1989. The First Congress of Latvia took place on 1–2 May 1990 and elected the Committee of Latvia with Aigars Jirgens as chairman. Throughout 1991 the role of the Congress has diminished.

The newly elected Supreme Soviet held its first session on 3–4 May and elected Anatolijs Gorbunovs as President and Ivars Godmanis as the Prime Minister. On 4 May the Supreme Soviet renamed the country the 'Republic of Latvia' and annulled the annexation of Latvia by the USSR.

Because of the large non-Latvian population the Latvian leadership has had to move very cautiously. As Latvians fare worst demographically, the threat to use force to 'protect the Soviet military and their families' is loudest in Latvia. In December 1990 numerous bomb blasts in Riga took place, with no group claiming responsibility. In January the special units of the Soviet Interior Ministry, the 'Black Berets', occupied the Communist Party Central Committee Publishing House. The Latvian Strike Committee, the Interfront and the newly founded Public Salvation Committee demanded that the democratically elected Latvian government resign, that price rises be rescinded and that presidential rule be introduced. Their goal was to provoke public dissatisfaction, to threaten Latvian institutions with the help of special militia units (OMON) and to paralyse Latvian economic life through mass strikes. On 13 January the Central Committee of the Latvian branch of the Communist Party of the Soviet Union asked the Public Salvation Committee to assume absolute state power in Latvia until new elections to the Supreme Council could be held. On the same day Gorbunovs and Yeltsin signed the Latvian–Russian Federation co-operation treaty in Tallinn. On the night of 20 January the 'Black Berets' occupied the building of the Ministry of Interior. In the heavy gunfire five people were killed and 10 wounded. On 28 January the Public Salvation Committee rescinded its decision to assume power. Without the support of the non-Latvian population the conservative forces suffered a humiliating defeat. As a result, 88% of the population participated in the referendum on 3 March and 74% of them supported the independent Republic of Latvia.

In May, an agreement was reached between Latvia and exile organizations in the West. The co-ordinator of the Latvian Foreign Service in the West is the Latvian Embassy in Washington.

The Latvian government has been the most successful of the three in establishing trust among the local non-Latvian population. This is especially significant in view of the fact that every tenth inhabitant of Latvia is a member of the Soviet military.

Lithuania

The Lithuanians are members of the Baltic branch of the Indo-European peoples. Unlike Estonia and Latvia, Lithuania can look back on a period when it was itself 'a great power'. United dynastically and later constitutionally with Poland, Polish–Lithuanian Union was the greatest force in Eastern Europe, extending from the Baltic to the Black Sea, in the fifteenth and sixteenth centuries. The Lithuanian territories fell under Russian rule in 1795, and the policy of Russification also included suppression of the Roman Catholic Church. As a result, the close identification of Catholicism with nationalism has persisted to the present day.

The establishment of independence was more complicated than in Latvia and Estonia because of the dispute with Poland over Lithuania's historic capital, Vilnius. Lithuania was unable to prevent Poland from occupying Vilnius in 1920 and was forced to nominate a temporary capital

LITHUANIA

Official name	Republic of Lithuania
Area	65,200 sq. km (25,165 sq. miles)
Population	3,723,000 (1990)
Capital	Vilnius
Languages	Lithuanian, Russian, Polish
Religion	Roman Catholic, Lutheran minority
Currency	rouble

in Kaunas. The 1939 Molotov–Ribbentrop Pact assigned Lithuania to the German sphere of interest, but after September 1939, when the USSR invaded East Poland and occupied Vilnius, Hitler was obliged to consign Lithuania to the Soviet sphere. After the Mutual Assistance Pact with the USSR on 10 October 1939, Soviet troops were stationed in Lithuania. In November Vilnius became the Lithuanian capital. Unlike Latvia and Estonia, Lithuania was a predominantly agrarian country.

Armed guerrilla resistance was maintained into the 1950s and a total of about 100,000 Lithuanians are estimated to have been involved.

After the war, religious dissent was the strongest manifestation of organized opposition to the Soviet regime. The main *samizdat* publication, *The Chronicle of the Lithuanian Catholic Church*, dates back to 1972. In 1978 (after the election of Pope John Paul II) five priests formed a Catholic Committee for the Defence of Believers' Rights, which became the unofficial spokesman for the Catholic Church in the USSR. In the 1970s and 1980s Lithuania produced more *samizdat* per capita than any other area of the USSR.

Mikhail Gorbachev's first campaign in the USSR was against alcoholism. This only followed that of the Lithuanian bishops, who had proclaimed 1980 to be 'The Year of Temperance'. The Lithuanian Supreme Soviet passed a similar decree, but that remained the only issue in which the Communist Party of Lithuania followed Gorbachev with any enthusiasm.

The anxiety about Chernobyl in April 1986 was higher in Lithuania than elsewhere in the USSR because people discovered the full scale of the disaster through Polish radio and television. The evasive official Soviet press reports were in sharp contrast to precautions taken in Poland, and left Lithuanians uneasy. Less than 80 miles from Vilnius at Ignalina, the first reactor of the world's largest nuclear power station was already operating with a Chernobyl-type reactor and the second was to go on-line in 1986. Some Lithuanians were aware of reports by Swedish experts in August of cases of increased radiation levels from Ignalina. The absence of any information about Ignalina in the local press until April 1988 prepared the ground for environmental protests, which led to demands for economic autonomy and to the formation of a movement for the support of *perestroika*.

At the beginning of 1987 several leading dissidents were released from prison. This helped to restore dissident groups, including the Lithuanian Freedom League (chairman: Antanas Terleckas). Since its foundation, the group had advocated full independence, and had been the first to test the credibility of democratization by organizing public demonstrations on 23 August 1987 and on 16 February and 22 May 1988 (the anniversary of the 1948 deportations). The League helped to raise national consciousness and, by uncompromisingly promoting independence, radicalized other movements.

The Lithuanian Restructuring Movement (commonly referred to as *Sajudis* or the Movement) was founded on 3 June 1988 by Party and non-Party intellectuals. Since *Sajudis* had been formed against the wishes of the Communist Party, its creation heralded a split within the Party itself. During the summer *Sajudis* increased its support among the people by organizing mass demonstrations.

Of special importance was a demonstration by the Freedom League on 28 September, when a violent confrontation between police and demonstrators took place. *Sajudis* formed an alliance with the Freedom League by protesting against the violent action.

The policies of the Communist Party of Lithuania were criticized not only by *Sajudis* but also by the Communist Party of the Soviet Union. When a Politburo member, Aleksander Yakovlev, came to Lithuania in August 1988 he had pressed the Communist Party of Lithuania to be more active in directing change, to harness the 'national factor' as a force for reform, and not to lose its leading role (which it had already lost). It was announced that further construction of the Ignalina nuclear power station would cease. Communist Party members could remain in *Sajudis*; and *Sajudis* would be allowed television coverage. After the Party order to suppress the September demonstration, Moscow decided to remove the inflexible leadership by promoting Algirdas Brazauskas as the Party's First Secretary a few days before the *Sajudis* congress.

The constituent congress of *Sajudis* on 22–23 October was a middle-class gathering, dominated by intellectuals. The congress elected a 220-member Assembly (*Seimas*) and a 35-member Council. *Sajudis* acted as an informal movement, but, by public consent, it had deprived the Communist Party of Lithuania of its leading role.

The popularity of the Party increased with the introduction of Lithuanian as a state language. The co-operation of the Communists with *Sajudis* lasted until 18 November (two days after the Estonian Supreme Soviet had declared the sovereignty of Estonian law), when Algirdas Brazauskas managed to persuade the Lithuanian Supreme Soviet not to follow the Estonian example. That was the day when the Communist Party of Lithuania won in Parliament but lost in the country, and *Sajudis* lost in Parliament but won in the country. From its first defeat, *Sajudis* emerged as a much stronger body by electing Professor Vytautas Landsbergis as its chairman of the council, and clarifying the criteria of membership. Despite the fact that the Communists had made further concessions (the release of political prisoners and the designation of Christmas and Independence Day as public holidays), by the time of the spring elections to the USSR Congress of People's Deputies in 1989, the Party had already lost control of the media, youth, higher education and part of its own membership.

Sajudis had other challengers in the Freedom League, the Democratic Party and the Helsinki Group, all three of which boycotted the elections. Nevertheless, 82.5% of those eligible to vote took part in the March elections to the USSR Congress of People's Deputies. *Sajudis* won 36 of the 42 Lithuanian seats in the Congress. Algirdas Brazauskas and his second secretary, Vladimiras Beriozovas, were elected because *Sajudis* did not contest their candidacies. A number of other top-level party officials were defeated.

On 18 May 1989 (exactly 6 months after the first rejection of sovereignty) the Lithuanian Supreme Soviet issued a declaration on state sovereignty and a law on economic sovereignty, asserting that all Lithuania's natural resources and all its territory, transportation, energy and communications enterprises were the property of the republic, and assuming its own right to veto legislation and legal acts by the USSR state government. It also established Lithuanian citizenship and control over immigration. The Communist Party of Lithuania had to accede to the demands of the voters and was forced to recognize that the movement for *perestroika* had become a national liberation movement against Soviet occupation and Communism. It was at this time that the Party, in order not to be completely defeated, took the decision to become an independent Lithuanian Communist Party.

In such a political climate Lithuanian political leaders took steps to establish closer links with Lithuanian exile communities in the West. Their meeting took place on the island of Gotland, Sweden, in August.

Since autumn 1989, Lithuania has acted in direct confrontation with Moscow. In September the Lithuanian Supreme Soviet passed laws on referendums and amended Article 50 of the Constitution to give greater rights to believers.

On 6 December 1989 the Lithuanian Supreme Soviet decided to abolish the Communist Party's monopoly and establish the first multi-party system in the USSR. The Lithuanian Communist Party won much political capital by declaring its independence from Moscow on 20 December. The Party also benefited from the leadership of Lithuania's most popular politician, Algirdas Brazauskas. The independent Communist Party of Lithuania had a membership of 70,000. The continuing Communist Party of Lithuania, loyal to the CPSU, draws its support mainly from Russian-speaking Communists. The Lithuanian Christian Democratic Party, re-established in January 1990, could become an influential force. It was the largest party in pre-war Lithuania and has the backing of the Catholic Church.

The first test of the new multi-party system took place on 24 February, when *Sajudis* won 88 seats in the 141-seat Lithuanian Supreme Soviet. The newly elected Supreme Council proclaimed Lithuanian independence on 11 March 1990. Vytautas Landsbergis was elected as president, and Mrs Kazimiera Prunskiene became prime minister. The strategy of the Lithuanian government was to establish a legal basis for negotiations with Moscow founded on the presumption that Lithuania is already an independent state. Had this been acceptable to Moscow, they would have been prepared to be extremely flexible on the question of ownership of sections of the economy. In the event, the Supreme Soviet of the USSR declared Lithuania's declaration of independence invalid, and Moscow's immediate response was to rule out negotiations. Shortly afterwards, Gorbachev declared himself in favour of a dialogue. On 16 April the central government imposed economic sanctions on the rebellious republic. By the middle of June, Lithuania had exhausted its reserves of energy. Despite lobbying by the Baltic communities in the West on behalf of their compatriots, Lithuania failed to become a major factor in the summit meeting of President Bush and President Gorbachev at the beginning of June, being eclipsed as a priority by the settlement of the German question. The declaration of independence on 11 March 1990 was an open challenge to Gorbachev's leadership and demonstrated effectively how weak both sides were. The Moscow-imposed blockade was not efficient (soldiers themselves sold petrol to the locals) and helped to increase President Landsbergis' government's popularity both at home and abroad. To break the blockade treaties with other republics were concluded. On 29 June the Lithuanian parliament voted to place a moratorium on its declaration of independence when negotiations with Moscow began. Although the Kremlin started talks with Lithuania in August, a week before signing the 'four plus two' German Unification Treaty, the Soviet side unilaterally broke off the talks.

Although the economic blockade was ineffective, the tension between the Kremlin and Lithuania remained very high. At the beginning of January 1991 the Lithuanian government decided to raise retail prices on foodstuffs. The decision was followed by protest meetings with the participation of the Russian- and Polish-speaking populations. *Sajudis* organized a counter-rally in support of the government in front of the Parliament building (Supreme Council). In the increasing tension Kazimiera Prunskiene and her cabinet resigned and the decision to raise the price of foodstuffs was suspended. Gediminas Vagnorius became the new Prime Minister. Soviet troops seized the Press House, the Publishing House and the Department of Defence. President Landsbergis appealed to the people to stand vigil in front of the Parliament building. On the night of 13 January Soviet troops seized the Lithuanian radio and television buildings and the television tower. Thirteen civilians were killed and over 500 wounded. On 14 January the Vilnius strike committee addressed the Supreme Soviet of the USSR demanding its support for the National Salvation Committee and the establishment of presidential rule. On 23 January Mikhail Gorbachev said at a meeting with three Lithuanian cultural representatives that the National Salvation Committee was an unconstitutional body and should be punished. The events of January strengthened popular support for the Landsbergis government as the results of the 9 February referendum demonstrated amply. 84% of the population took part in the referendum and 90% voted for an independent

Republic of Lithuania. After the events of 13 January there has been a considerable increase of support from Western countries.

Conclusion

From the time of Gorbachev's accession to power in March 1985 the political aspirations of most of the people of the Baltic republics have evolved along with (and in certain cases determined) the general flow of *perestroika*. While the initial goal in 1986 was for greater cultural sovereignty, by 1987 it had come to include economic and, by late 1988, political sovereignty. The consensus by late 1989 and early 1990 was a clear desire for fully fledged independence.

During the period 1987–9 it was possible to discern an interplay between three basic political forces. The first was represented by restorationist movements, the aim of which, from the very beginning, has been the restoration of the independent republics. The most significant are the National Independence Party of Estonia, the National Independence Movement of Latvia and the Lithuanian Freedom League. Their members are former political prisoners, human rights activists and people who have not co-operated with the political establishment. Their uncompromising confrontational tactics appealed to young people. This force radicalized the centrists, who formed the second force. Centrists comprise movements working within the existing political structures (the Supreme Soviet, the Communist Party, Unions of Writers, Architects, Journalists, etc.) who preferred to work for change step by step. The intellectuals, technocrats and rank and file Communist Party members took up this position. Both the Estonian and Latvian Popular Fronts and the Lithuanian *Sajudis* were numbered within this force. All of them had stood for the sovereignty of the Baltic republics within the Soviet confederation, but because of pressure from the restorationists they later came to support political independence. The third force, anti-reformist or conservative, includes Russian-speaking Party officials, the military, bureaucrats and immigrant workers who do not wish to lose their privileged status. Almost none of them speak the local languages and all feel isolated from the present political movements. This force is represented by the Estonian Intermovement, Latvian Interfront and the Lithuanian *Yedinstvo*.

The co-operation of Lithuanians, Latvians and Estonians has been another key to their success. All the larger movements, both centrists and restorationists, have been organizing meetings to work out future tactics. The restorationists have tried to involve Ukrainians, Armenians, Georgians, Moldavians and others.

Of great importance in co-ordinating the work of the Popular Fronts and *Sajudis* has been the Baltic Council, founded at a 'Baltic Assembly' in May 1989 in Tallinn, which worked out a united programme for reform.

A Baltic parliamentary group formed by 90 of the deputies of the three republics in 1989 pressed for the creation of a commission of the USSR

Supreme Soviet to investigate the Molotov–Ribbentrop Pact and for the acceptance of Moscow of Baltic economic self-management. Before the fiftieth anniversary of the signing of the MRP on 23 August, 14 members of the USSR Supreme Soviet commission (but not its chairman, Aleksander Yakovlev, who maintained that the Pact had no connection with the incorporation of the Baltic states) concluded that the pact had infringed the rights of third countries, including the Baltic states. They recommended that the USSR Supreme Soviet should declare these protocols invalid. The Congress of People's Deputies adopted a watered-down version of the report on 24 December 1989.

The three popular fronts organized a 400-mile human chain on 23 August 1989, with nearly 2 million people commemorating the 50th anniversary of the MRP. It was the largest anti-Soviet demonstration ever held.

Another Baltic joint action was to press the USSR Supreme Soviet to adopt a law on Baltic economic self-management. Although the law was adopted on 27 November 1989 and was to go into force on 1 January 1990, the Moscow ministries refused to hand over key areas of the economy to the Baltic authorities. By the end of 1990 it had become increasingly clear that economic independence was impossible without political sovereignty.

Although in January 1990 Gorbachev had offered a new looser federation with great autonomy, and a mechanism by which a republic could secede, the Baltic deputies did not believe that such decrees were practicable.

The economic blockade imposed by Moscow on Lithuania brought the three Baltic republics closer together. Although Moscow was trying to use a policy of 'divide and conquer' by offering Estonia and Latvia a special status, the Baltic unity was sealed with the renewal of a 1934 Treaty on Unity and Co-operation by the presidents of Estonia, Latvia and Lithuania on 12 May in Tallinn.

After the Russian blockade the Prime Minister Kazimiera Prunskiene visited Western and North American leaders and politicians. The blockade confronted the international community once again with the status of the Baltic countries. Although the Estonian Foreign Minister, Lennart Meri, together with his Latvian and Lithuanian counterparts, Janis Jurkans and Algirdas Saudargas, did not gain the requested 'observer status' at the Paris European Security and Co-operation Conference (CSCE) in November, the Nordic countries, Britain, Poland, Czechoslovakia and the Vatican supported their request, signalling their view that the Baltic states constitute a special case in view of the illegality of the occupation. The Baltic states want to join the Nordic nuclear-free zone.

The three Baltic states have entered a difficult period of transition: they are not yet independent states in control of their borders. At the same time, all three refused to participate in an all-Union referendum on 17 March

1991. The Baltic argument runs as follows. Stalin forced the Baltic States into the Soviet Union through a military occupation which is still continuing; Estonia, Latvia and Lithuania are not talking about secession from a Union they have never willingly joined but about restoring their independence. In order to prove that the restoration of independence is supported by the majority of the populations, independent referenda were organized in Lithuania, Estonia and Latvia before 17 March. The Baltic States did not sign the Union Treaty on 23 April; instead they sought – and continue to seek – real negotiations with the USSR. Consultations between Soviet delegations and each Baltic state started in 1991, as it became clear to the Kremlin that the Baltic question would not go away and could be solved either by peaceful means or by the use of force. The Balts claim that the latter threatens the whole democratization process of the USSR. Were the democratically elected Baltic governments overthrown, the whole process of *perestroika* would come to a halt. The balance of power in Moscow depends largely on developments in the Baltic area. Neither the conservatives nor the democrats are free any longer to do as they choose because events in Estonia, Latvia and Lithuania are setting the pattern for the whole of the Soviet Union. It is becoming clear that by restoring their independence the Baltic States may help to create a new power structure in which the centre loses absolute control and the constituent republics gain greater sovereignty. Should the democratically elected Baltic governments be suppressed, a new Soviet dictatorship would follow.

12 BYELORUSSIA

Byelorussia is one of the fifteen constituent republics of the Soviet Union. As a founder member of the United Nations, it has full representation, alongside the USSR and Ukraine, both on that body and its dependent agencies.

The composition of the country's population reflects the complex and turbulent history of an area which for centuries had consisted of large landed estates – and therefore a mainly peasant population – and small, predominantly Jewish, towns. A breakdown into urban (65.5%) and rural (34.5%) population reveals the increasing rate of urbanization. The corresponding figures for the previous census of 1979 were 55% and 44.9%, respectively, and 7.9 million of the population declare themselves to be Byelorussians, of whom 80.2% regard Byelorussian as their first language, as against 83.5% in 1979. There are 1,342,000 Russians, of whom only 24.5% claim a fluent command of Byelorussian, a decrease from 29.4% in 1979. Some connection is discernible between the increase in numbers of Russians and the growth of the urban population. The number of people who regard themselves as Poles has increased (418,000 as compared with 403,000 in 1979), whereas the Jews continue to decline (112,000, down from 135,000 in 1979), largely as a result of emigration to Israel.

History

The earliest medieval Byelorussian state can be said to have developed around the city of Polotsk on the river Dvina. From the thirteenth century onwards Byelorussian lands were incorporated into the growing Grand Duchy of Lithuania. Despite its name, the Grand Duchy was a predominantly Slavonic state throughout its history, with a form of Byelorussian serving as its official language until 1696. As a result of union with Poland in 1569, the nobility became increasingly Polish in language and religion, switching from Orthodoxy to Roman Catholicism, and leaving the peasantry with no kind of leadership. The partitions of Poland at the end of the eighteenth century brought the Byelorussians into the Russian Empire. The growth of a new Byelorussian national consciousness can be traced to about the middle of the nineteenth century, largely as a result of the interest taken by ethnographers and folklorists in the inhabitants of the poorest and most backward part of European Russia. The first attempts

BYELORUSSIA

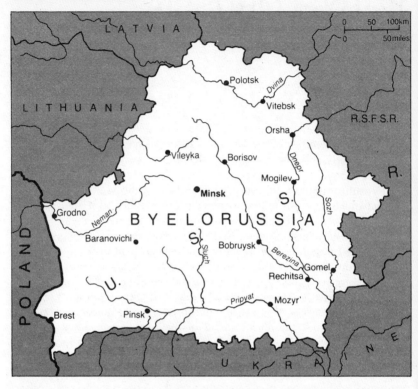

Official name	Byelorussian Soviet Socialist Republic
Area	208,000 sq. km (80,290 sq. miles)
Population	10,200,000 (1989)
Capital	Minsk
Languages	Byelorussian, Russian
Religion	Roman Catholic, Russian Orthodox, with Baptist and Muslim minorities
Currency	rouble

were made to revive the language as a means of written communication, although they soon fell foul of the Tsarist censorship.

The national revival really commenced at the beginning of this century, and here, as elsewhere in east and central Europe, writers and intellectuals were in the vanguard. In 1914 the country once again became a battleground. The front line divided the country, and as a result national activities were split between Vilnia (Wilno, Vilnius) under German occupation and St Petersburg. The Bolshevik October Revolution of 1917 and the ensuing chaos gave what national leadership there was a chance to try to establish some form of autonomy or even an independent state. A Byelorussian National Republic was declared on 25 March 1918, but without armed forces of its own or international recognition it was doomed to fall prey to marauding Polish bands and German troops. Undoubtedly as the result of nationalist pressure, a Byelorussian Soviet Republic was declared in January 1919. The ensuing war between Soviet Russia and Poland led once again to the division of Byelorussia.

The Byelorussian Soviet Republic in the 1920s, based on little more than the province of Minsk, gave every appearance of developing into a truly national state. The language was encouraged, a national educated elite was in the process of formation. All this changed under Stalin. Writers and intellectuals were exiled; many of them were killed or died in Siberian labour camps. We now know, as a result of the discovery of the mass graves at Kurapaty near Minsk and elsewhere, that extermination was taking place on a grand scale in Byelorussia itself in the late 1930s. Language laws were promulgated to ensure that Byelorussian became more like Russian.

Life for Byelorussians under Polish rule was better, because they were at least spared the worst excesses of persecution. The Polish civil and religious authorities, however, did not tolerate too much cultural independence on the part of their Byelorussian minority, some 6% of the total population.

The Nazi–Soviet pact of 1939 is often viewed as paving the way for the division of Poland. It is equally valid to say that it led to the reunification of Byelorussia. The western frontier came to correspond more or less to the Polish-Soviet demarcation line that had been proposed by the British Foreign Minister, Lord Curzon, in 1920. The pact did not, of course, save Byelorussia from war and suffering during the German occupation in 1941–4. The present western frontier of Byelorussia was established by agreement with what was then the Polish People's Republic.

Politics

The political life of Byelorussia has inevitably been dominated by the Communist Party of the Soviet Union and the subservient line that its leaders, with the notable exception of P. M. Masherov, have followed in their dealings with Moscow. The new First Secretary, elected at the

31st Congress of the Byelorussian Communist Party (BCP) held in late November 1990, is A. A. Malofeev. The demise of Article 6 of the constitutions of both the USSR and Byelorussia guaranteeing a leading role for the Party in society has not yet brought about many changes. It continues to wield great authority by virtue of its wealth and limitless access to the media. Not surprisingly, both the Party and the government are viewed in many quarters as reactionary. A public opinion poll conducted in April-May 1990 revealed that, on a 5-point scale, the Party has a rating of 2.02 and its Central Committee 1.89.

They are being judged on past performance. A deliberate policy of Russification was being pursued in the 1960s and 1970s. Fewer books in Byelorussian were produced, the print runs of Byelorussian newspapers were cut, the country's history was subjected to gross distortions, many writers were either completely banned or had selected works excised from their total output and the language was taught in an ever-decreasing number of schools. By the middle of the 1980s the situation had become so dire that there was not a single school in the capital city teaching its children in Byelorussian.

As with the national revival earlier in the century, writers and intellectuals were the first to sound the alarm. Boldness inspired by *glasnost* has led to the publication of more and more previously banned works. A new and fresh look is being taken at Byelorussia's history with the aim of demonstrating that they are not simply Russians with a different name. A Byelorussian Language Association has been set up to foster the use of language in all spheres.

The Byelorussian Popular Front was compelled to hold its inaugural meeting in 1988 in Vilnius, in accommodation provided by its Lithuanian counterpart, *Sajudis*, because of the hostility of the authorities. Only in June 1991 was it given official permission to exist. It has gained considerable publicity as the result of demonstrations in memory of the victims of Stalin's terror in Byelorussia and its counter-demonstration on Revolution Day (7 November) 1990. Other political parties have also been founded, some specifically Byelorussian, others as branches of Russian or All-Union organizations. For example, the 'Democratic Platform' within the BCP has joined with other groups to form a United Democratic Party. They are all small and exert no tangible influence as yet on the political life of the republic.

Depoliticization of the workplace is one of the main platforms of an as yet small Workers' Union which comprises representatives of strike committees from enterprises throughout Byelorussia and is linked to the miners' committees in the Donbass area. Picketing in front of the Minsk City Council building when the Council was due to discuss depoliticization led to arrests on charges of 'disobedience to the authorities'. Similar demands for the depoliticization of factories led to major strikes in Minsk on 4 April 1991. A strike committee under the leadership of Sergei Antonchik, a deputy of the Supreme Soviet, still functions. Byelorussian intellectuals have, in general, failed to support the strike movement so far.

The increased desire to separate Party from State has given rise to developments in the world of journalism throughout the Soviet Union. Newspapers that once belonged to both Party and Soviet organizations may now choose their allegiance. It is significant that this has happened less in Byelorussia than elsewhere in the USSR, but the Minsk evening newspaper has become the subject of an ownership dispute. Probably the nearest to regular opposition newspapers in the republic are the former Byelorussian Young Communist League paper *Znamia iunosti* (Banner of Youth), now styling itself a 'Byelorussian social and political newspaper' without the previously ubiquitous slogan urging workers of the world to unite, and the weekly *Litaratura i mastatstva* (Literature and art). The advent of the market economy has caused a number of difficulties. The supply of paper does not match demand; many Byelorussian-language newspapers and journals will require a subsidy if they are to survive.

Multi-candidate (but not multi-party) elections for the 360 seats in the Supreme Soviet were held on 4 March 1990. Without official registration, the Popular Front was unable to field its own candidates. The 'national ticket' was therefore frequently represented by candidates from organizations like the Byelorussian Language Association or the Byelorussian Ecological Union. Nevertheless, the Front now has a fraction in the Supreme Soviet (27 members) and has taken the initiative in forming a Deputies' club with a statute accepted by some 100 deputies. It is now an opposition group with the ability to stop business by staging walk-outs when the agenda of items for discussion excludes any of its proposals. The leader of the club is Z. Pazniak, chairman of the Popular Front. The Chairman of the Supreme Soviet is N. I. Dementei, a Party *apparatchik*. One of his deputies, S. S. Shushkevich, professor of nuclear physics in Minsk University, had considerable support among 'progressive' sections of opinion, but has, to some extent, forfeited it by aligning himself with the *status quo*.

Given that the overwhelming majority of deputies are representatives of the Party old-guard and the *nomenklatura* (some 84%, in fact), it is perhaps surprising that a far-reaching law declaring sovereignty was passed on 27 July 1990. If it were to be acted upon, Byelorussia would be independent of Moscow in its conduct of political, economic, judicial and military affairs.

Rumours alleged that Dementei had been instructed by Gorbachev to declare sovereignty, so that the new USSR – when the draft treaty has been accepted – could be claimed as a voluntary union of sovereign states. The item had not been on the agenda, and only 230 deputies were present for the discussion. (One of the absentees was the then Party First Secretary, E. E. Sokolov.) Two sub-commissions of the Supreme Soviet, one 'conservative' and the other 'progressive', are now working on draft texts of a new constitution to reflect sovereignty. As an alternative to a renewed USSR, the Popular Front has proposed the formation of a union of Baltic States, Byelorussia and Ukraine. A meeting to discuss this proposal was held in Minsk in November 1990.

The government has, to some extent, adopted the Front's policies on sovereignty and language. The law declaring Byelorussian the official language of the republic came into force on 1 September. It is evident that Russian will continue to occupy a major place in the life of the state. A period of three years has been granted for Byelorussian to become the language of the media, but on matters of education, ten years are deemed necessary for the transfer from Russian.

There are nationally minded ministers who seem determined to take a more independent line in presenting Byelorussian affairs, both within the USSR and abroad. Contact with Byelorussian émigré communities is being actively sought. Direct agreements have been made with other Union republics (Russia, Latvia, Azerbaijan). Foreign Minister P. Kravchenko used his recent visit to the United Nations to highlight the scale of the Chernobyl disaster and stress the urgent need for international aid.

Precisely because it exposed serious flaws in the government of the country and the relations between Minsk and Moscow, the Chernobyl disaster poses a real political as well as economic problem, in that the clean-up operation has become a test of the trust that the people can place in the authorities.

The affected area of Byelorussia, with a population of 2,200,000 people, amounts to 70% of the total area of the USSR polluted by radioactive fallout from Chernobyl. About 20% of Byelorussia's agricultural land and almost 15% of its forests are unusable. The explosion occurred in April 1986; the Byelorussian government produced its first figures on radiation levels in July 1988 and made its first appeal for international assistance in February 1990. It is estimated that if the present rate of support from central sources (500 million roubles annually) is maintained, it will take 100 years to resettle everyone now living in areas with radiation levels of more than 1 curie/km^2. An appeal was recently sent to Gorbachev protesting that the situation in Byelorussia resulting from Chernobyl was placed no higher than item 33 on the agenda of the current session of the USSR Supreme Soviet, adding that 400 million hard-currency roubles will be needed in the period 1991–5 for the purchase of the necessary special foodstuffs, medicines and equipment.

On 3 November 1990 an incident occurred in the industrial town of Novopolotsk which has all the makings of yet another ecological disaster. A quantity of a highly toxic substance leaked into the River Dvina. Preliminary estimates for the clean-up already amount to 30 million roubles. A newspaper report appeared on 24 November revealing both incompetence and a desire to suppress the facts. The town is already heavily polluted, with a higher-than-average incidence of sickness among children, and yet there are plans to build more chemical plants there.

Severe industrial pollution, of which Chernobyl is only a part, is already the cause of major strains on an inadequate health service. That service will be stretched even further if the AIDS projections are realized; it is estimated that by the year 2000 there could be 84,000–112,000 sufferers in Minsk alone unless preventative action is taken now.

Inevitably, the solution of Byelorussia's pressing political problems requires a sound economic base. A glance at the business of the session of the Supreme Soviet that began on 21 May 1991 shows just how much ground has to be covered even to create the right conditions for successful economic growth. Legislation to be discussed includes forms of ownership, taxation and banking. An additional difficulty will be caused by the inevitable rise in unemployment; estimates vary from 60,000 to 170,000 by the end of 1991. One in three people in Byelorussia are already on or below the poverty line, with the minimum monthly wage calculated as between 114 and 125 roubles. The housing shortage has been exacerbated by the arrival of officers in the armed forces after their withdrawal from Eastern Europe. The BCP, in its draft programme for the 31st Congress, sees itself as defending the working man in the new conditions of the market economy, as well as still playing the leading political role in society.

Religion

The attitude of the authorities and the Warsaw-administered Catholic Church was, and essentially still is, that if you are a Roman Catholic in Byelorussia you must be Polish. However, it is estimated that there are 2 million Catholics in the country. With only 418,000 declared Poles, who are all the others? Pleas for the Church to take more account of Byelorussian national aspirations have so far fallen on deaf ears. There are 65 parishes in the country. A new seminary is to be opened in Grodno.

The Orthodox Church (370 parishes and 383 priests), once a bulwark of 'Russianness', is beginning to discover that Byelorussia is in fact different. Its status has been raised to that of an exarchate, in line with the Church in Ukraine. A seminary has been opened in Zhirovitsy, where there is already a monastery. The Church has commissioned a translation of the Bible into modern Byelorussian. Sunday schools have opened and are already forced to turn children away for want of space.

The Eastern-Rite Catholic (Uniate) Church, now so important in the Ukraine, was abolished in Byelorussia in 1839. A group of predominantly young lay nationally minded Byelorussians is seeking to re-establish it. Appeals for support have been made to the Pope. This development is regarded as sufficiently important to warrant hostile attacks in the Party press. A more numerous (but not specifically Byelorussian) Christian denomination is the Baptist Church, with 195 chapels attached to the All-Union council and 26 autonomous chapels.

A Jewish Sunday school opened recently in Minsk (where there are some 40,000 Jews). An informal group (*Atikva*) exists to promote Jewish culture. Also primarily cultural is the Tatar group *Al-Kitab*. The Hare Krishna sect has attracted some adherents.

The increase in poverty and unemployment will lead to an increased need for charitable activities. At present, the most obviously active group seems to be the Byelorussian section of the Russian Christian Democratic Union, with plans to open a Christian cultural centre and dining room equipped by a Finnish Christian organization. Mention should also be made of a Social Defence Fund set up by Communists (but not by the Party).

Economy

1 January 1990 marked the changeover to self-management and self-financing, a move timed to coincide with the final year of the current five-year plan and to lead into full regional cost-accounting in January 1991. Byelorussia and the Baltic republics had been chosen to spearhead this development because they were regarded as the economically most advanced areas of the USSR. However, these plans have now been superseded by the rapidly deteriorating economic situation of the USSR as a whole. Early in 1990 it had still been possible for official statistics to show a budget surplus. On 1 November 1990, when the market economy was officially introduced into Byelorussia, a spokesman for the Council of Ministers forecast a budget *deficit* for the current year of 5000 million roubles. The dawning of the market era was accompanied by the opening of 35 customs posts on Byelorussia's borders with other Union republics to prevent the export of prescribed foodstuffs and other items, including hard currency and precious metals.

The economic plan adopted for Byelorussia reserves the right of the republic to issue its own currency, to be used, if necessary, alongside the rouble. Prices of 90 major consumer items will be frozen until the end of 1991, by when 70% of prices will have been freed from control. State orders will be placed for essential goods to ensure adequate supply. Price-freezing means high subsidies; the meat and milk subsidy costs 4000 million roubles a year, the new fixed purchase price for grain will cost 1890 million.

Virtually without natural resources except its land, forests and water-courses, Byelorussia has had to rely on agriculture and manufacturing industries for its wealth. Over half of the country's industrial base comprises heavy engineering (trucks and tractors), the chemical (oil and oil-based products) and hi-tech (computers and electronic components) industries, i.e. precisely those areas which are normally controlled from Moscow. The economic plan allows for the privatization of 50% of all enterprises by the end of 1991. Proposals for the future of the All-Union enterprises include making them joint-stock companies, with Moscow holding 51% of the stock. The development of co-operatives has been handicapped by the hostility of the authorities, in the form of high tax levels and the absence of anti-monopoly legislation, and the public, who suspect profiteering. A stock exchange began to operate in Minsk on 23 May 1991 with 12 founder-members, places for 200 brokers and an initial capital of 20 million roubles.

There are some 30 joint ventures (JVs) registered in Byelorussia, with many more agencies of JVs based in Moscow. Byelorussian operations are hampered by the impossibility of opening an account in the local branch of the USSR Foreign Trade Bank and the inability to participate in hard-currency auctions. The taxes levied on Byelorussian-based JVs end up in Moscow; it has been estimated that the Byelorussian budget lost US$3 million in the past year in this way. These JVs operate mainly in the hi-tech area, especially computer systems and programming, with the Byelorussian side providing intellectual expertise. The firms Dialog (official Microsoft representative in the USSR), Interkvadro (contract with IBM) and Belkom (for hardware production; a JV with an Indian firm) seem particularly prominent.

Agriculture does not present a very promising picture. The current All-Union policy of allowing farmers to lease and work private holdings on a family basis has met with poor response in Byelorussia. By 1 July 1990 there had been only 21 takers. The rural population is evidently unconvinced that the policy changes are irreversible. No real legal or economic guarantees have been provided. There are as yet no land banks, no land registers, and there is always the danger that, if land is privatized, the owners of land in what was eastern Poland before 1939 will return to claim their property.

Conclusion

The prospects for peaceful change are not good. The strongest political force in Byelorussia, the Communist Party, hankers after a constitutionally guaranteed leading role and the command economy. No real political dialogue has taken place between the Party and the Popular Front, unless the superficial adoption by the Party of much of the Front's programme on sovereignty and cultural issues can be regarded as 'dialogue'.

It has become clear that Byelorussia cannot rely on increased aid from Moscow in solving the problems caused by central control of much of its economy and by Chernobyl. Any assertion of economic sovereignty must be accompanied by moves to make the country attractive to foreign investment, and to ensure that the money yielded by such investments remains in Byelorussia. More international recognition of Byelorussian sovereignty might help: the new united Germany appears willing to maintain the consulate of the former GDR in Minsk.

Byelorussia, long regarded as the quietest and most amenable of the republics, is slowly moving towards increased independence. At present, the driving forces seem to be the workers, certain sections of the government and the Supreme Soviet. Some kind of conflict with the entrenched Party seems almost inevitable.

13 UKRAINE

The Ukrainian Soviet Socialist Republic was established by the Bolsheviks after the 1917 Revolution and Civil War. It had a population of approximately 30 million people on a territory of 443,000 square kilometres, encompassing present-day Central and Eastern Ukraine. Western Ukraine came under control of the newly established states of Poland, Czechoslovakia and Romania. In December 1922 the Ukrainian SSR formally joined the USSR on the basis of the Treaty of Union. It was further enlarged during World War II with the annexation by the Soviet Army of Galicia and Volyn from Poland in 1939, northern Bukovyna and sections of Bessarabia from Romania in 1940, and Transcarpathia from Czechoslovakia in 1945. With the transfer of Crimea in 1954 from the Russian SFSR to the Ukrainian SSR, the republic further grew to its present size of 603,700 square kilometres.

When Czarism collapsed in 1917, political control of the Ukrainian provinces of the Russian Empire was contested by the Provisional Government based in Petrograd, the Central Rada based in Kiev and the workers' parties (mainly Mensheviks and Bolsheviks) based in the urban soviets. The Rada emerged the strongest contender in October 1917. It took power with the overwhelming support of peasants on the land and in the army, and with a growing base among workers, especially in the northern provinces. In November the Rada declared the formation of the Ukrainian People's Republic.

Although the Bolsheviks entered the 1917 Revolution largely convinced that new nation states were an anachronism, their branches in Ukraine supported the Rada against the Provisional Government in October and then sought a place in the leadership of the Ukrainian People's Republic. Having failed to find agreement on their proportional representation, the Bolsheviks withdrew and established a competing Ukrainian People's Republic in December 1917, with headquarters in Kharkiv and based mainly on the urban soviets of the Donbas region in south-eastern Ukraine. The Kharkiv-based UPR became the Russian Bolsheviks' fig leaf for their military intervention against the Kiev-based UPR in January 1918, which led the latter to declare independence from Soviet Russia on 22 January 1918 and to seek military support from the Austro-German armies.

After three years of civil war, foreign interventions by Axis, Entente,

UKRAINE

Official name	Ukrainian Soviet Socialist Republic
Area	603,700 sq. km (233,030 sq. miles)
Population	51,704,000 (1989)
Capital	Kiev
Languages	Ukrainian, Russian
Religion	Orthodox and Greek Catholic, with Roman Catholic, Protestant, Jewish and Muslim minorities
Currency	rouble

White and Red armies, and no less than 14 separate governments, the Bolsheviks finally took power in Ukraine with the military and economic backing of Soviet Russia. They consolidated power here during the 1920s by conceding the New Economic Policy to the peasantry, which gave them a chance to prosper as individual producers, and by admitting left-wing sections of the patriotic intelligentsia to the Communist Party, to government office, the educational system, mass media and the trade unions. Through such institutions the Ukrainian intelligentsia set out in the 1920s to make Ukrainian the language of civic life, education and economic activity, and to strengthen the republic's rights *vis-à-vis* Moscow.

The first post-revolutionary decade is considered a golden era of national rebirth. The second decade leading up to World War II saw a brutal collectivization of agriculture, the death of approximately 7 million peasants in the genocidal famine of 1932–3, the extermination by Stalin's secret police of an entire generation of Ukraine's political, cultural, scientific and religious leaders, and the crash industrialization programme with which Stalin prepared his country for war.

World War II, which brought about the unification of practically all Ukrainian territories into the Ukrainian SSR, also cost the republic 6 million lives, or 30% of the USSR's total human losses, and the destruction of much housing, industry and communications, amounting to 47% of the USSR's material losses. These were compounded by the outbreak of famine in Ukraine in 1946–7, the continuing campaign by Soviet units in Western Ukraine against the guerrilla Ukrainian Insurgent Army and the mass deportations to Siberia and the Far East of this region's villagers on suspicion of nationalism and disloyalty to the Soviet regime. 'When the casualties of the civil war, collectivization, the purges and the Second World War are combined, more than half the male and a quarter of the female population perished' (Bohdan Krawchenko, *Social Change and National Consciousness in Twentieth-century Ukraine*, London: Macmillan, 1985, p. 171).

The *status quo* in Ukraine was challenged in the latter half of the 1950s and 1960s (the period of de-Stalinization throughout the USSR) by the opposition or dissident movement. Unlike its counterpart in Russia, the Ukrainian opposition movement was supported actively by workers, both in membership of its various organizations and participation in meetings, petitions, etc., particularly in its early years. This movement had as its primary objectives the restitution of civil rights and national self-determination for the republic. It gained support within the Communist Party of Ukraine and a number of key republican state institutions, in response to which the central Communist leadership under Leonid Brezhnev ordered the movement to be crushed. A wave of arrests of prominent oppositionists swept the republic in January 1972 and many were subsequently incarcerated to long terms in labour camps, psychiatric prison hospitals and internal exile. The Communist Party of Ukraine was purged of its patriotically inclined members and its First Secretary, Petro Shelest, was removed from office.

Volodymyr Shcherbytsky, Brezhnev's faithful ally, replaced Shelest in 1973. He ruled the republic until 1989, when he retired from office and died soon afterwards, in February 1990. By the end of his term in office Shcherbytsky had discredited himself publicly by his iron rule, subservience to Moscow and his cover-up of the immediate and long-term effects of the 1986 Chernobyl disaster. His failure to cope with the July 1989 miners' strike in Donbas or the emergence of the Popular Movement of Ukraine for Restructuring (Rukh) made him appear out of step with the times and a liability for the Party. In September 1989, after careful preparation in Moscow by the CPSU Politburo, a plenum of the CPU Central Committee in Kiev elected Volodymyr Ivashko as the Party's new republican First Secretary. At 57 years of age and a Party member since 1960, Ivashko was described by Mikhail Gorbachev as 'intelligent, cultured and simply very accessible' (Moscow Radio, 28 September 1989). His task was to steer the republic through an impending storm of political change, which was already blowing in adjacent Eastern Europe, and to keep the Party in office.

The political terrain

Four key political forces were evident in Ukraine in 1990 – the Communist Party, Rukh, a fledgling workers' movement and a student movement. Also, several new political parties were founded in anticipation of a multi-party electoral system. The signal for such a system was given in February 1990 by the CPSU's declaration that it would give up its monopoly of power. The Ukrainian republican elections in March came too soon for a genuine multi-party contest here, but their outcome showed clearly that the CPU was destined to share power or to become a minor party in opposition.

The Communist Party of Ukraine claimed 3.3 million members at the beginning of 1989, one-sixth of the CPSU's total. However, it was losing both members and authority within society at large, because its leadership under Shcherbytsky was associated with the Brezhnev era. It was failing to improve the economic situation or to make any concessions to popular demands for change in linguistic and cultural policy, nuclear energy and environmental protection or political reform.

Through its control of electoral commissions, the Party prevented the nomination of all but a few Rukh candidates to stand in the first all-Union elections in March and April 1989 to the Congress of People's Deputies. The electorate responded with a boycott of many single-candidate constituency elections, thus defeating unpopular nominees of the CPU apparatus. On the other hand, reform-minded Communists in other constituencies who had publicly declared support for Rukh's programme were elected to the Congress.

Ivashko's first months in office saw the Party leadership steering several progressive pieces of legislation through the Ukrainian Supreme Soviet (parliament): on improving the status of the Ukrainian language in the republic; making its electoral law more democratic; and declaring the need to close the Chernobyl nuclear power station for good. Such measures were intended to improve the CPU's image, and to convince the population that Ivashko's elevation signalled a major turn to responsible and accountable government in the republic. But they did not arrest the flow of resignations from the Party. More alarming still, a wave of mass protest against oblast Party leaders on charges of corruption and patronage swept the republic in the first three months of 1990, forcing their resignation in five of the 25 oblasts. Ivashko acknowledged in March 1990 that it was no longer easy to attract professionals and people of standing in the community to the Party, and spoke of his previous career as a college lecturer as 'the better years of my life' (interview in Kiev with Marko Bojcun for HTV Wales, 1 March 1990).

Rukh has its origins in 1988 when attempts were made in various cities to launch popular-front organizations on the model of those in the Baltic states. The most active participants in such attempts were former political prisoners just released from labour camps and exile, radical students and members of the Ukrainian Writers' Union. Many of the last were also members of the Communist Party. However, all these attempts were crushed by the authorities until November 1988, when an initiative committee composed of prominent Kievan writers and other intellectuals was formed in Kiev. The committee wrote Rukh's draft programme, which was published in February 1989 in *Literaturna Ukraina*, the writers' union newspaper. Local Rukh branches sprang up in all 25 oblasts, the strongest centres being Kiev, Lviv and the towns of Central and Western Ukraine.

Despite intense pressure applied by the CPU leadership against its own members in Rukh, as well as a continuous campaign of slander and abuse against the organization in the state-controlled media, Rukh prepared and convened its first national congress in Kiev on 8–10 September 1989. Of the 1,158 delegates in attendance representing 280,000 Rukh members, almost a quarter were CPU members. Engineers, teachers, industrial and cultural workers were well represented. Ukrainians made up a majority of those in attendance, followed by Russians and Jews. Among the informal groups whose members were active also in Rukh, the Ukrainian Helsinki Union was the best organized and most prominent.

The founding congress adopted a new programme that deleted all previous acknowledgements of the 'leading role' of the Communist Party and declared 'humanism, democracy, openness, pluralism, social justice and internationalism' as its guiding principles. It elected Ivan Drach, a well-known writer, as its head and Mykhailo Horyn of the Ukrainian Helsinki Union as chairman of its ten-member Secretariat. It declared its intention to issue a national newspaper, establish permanent head-quarters in Kiev and run its candidates in future election campaigns.

The retirement of Shcherbytsky and his replacement by Ivashko soon after Rukh's first national congress was interpreted by many political observers as the Party's attempt to stem defections from its ranks to Rukh. Some in the CPU leadership like Leonid Krawchuk, Ideological Secretary in the Politburo and its emissary to the Rukh Congress, saw that a clear split in the CPU's ranks might result from the rapidly changing political conjuncture, and entertained the idea of a 'Hungarian evolution': a split between the old conservative wing and the younger reform Communists, but with the latter seeking to draw the more moderate and federalist wing of Rukh into a new formation with them.

As noted above, the CPU leadership also launched a number of legislative initiatives to improve its image. Finally, it skilfully dragged out negotiations with Rukh over the latter's access to printing facilities for a national newspaper and its legal registration. Both questions were critical to Rukh's participation in the March elections. In the end, Rukh was not registered until mid-February 1990, after nominations of election candi-dates were closed, and so its candidates were forced to seek nomination by other, registered organizations or on the basis of place of residence or occupation (as permitted in the new electoral law). Rukh managed to produce the first issue of *Narodna hazeta* (People's Newspaper) at the end of February, too late to have a significant impact on the first round of elections on 4 March. Yet it was still in the ascendant in the first months of 1990, with a membership surpassing half a million and an ability to organize, for example, a 300-mile human chain across the republic on 21 January to mark the anniversary of Ukrainian independence in 1918.

The third important political force to consider in Ukraine is the inde-pendent workers' movement, centred in 1989 and 1990 around Donbas mining communities. This movement was triggered by the July 1989 miners' strike, which spread from the Russian SFSR into Ukraine and encompassed all of Donbas and the Galician-Volynian coalfield. As in other parts of the Soviet Union, Ukrainian miners first established strike committees to lead them, negotiate with the government and maintain order in the towns. The strike committees evolved into workers' control committees in August, after negotiations were concluded, which were charged with monitoring implementation of the agreement. The control committees united into a regional organization in August and set out in September to found the Donbas Union of Workers, an independent union encompassing workers in all industries.

The workers' movement first emerged in Donbas for several reasons. Ukrainian miners have a long tradition of struggle, even in the most difficult years. The Association of Free Trade Unions, established in 1978 by Vladimir Klebanov and suppressed mainly by psychiatric abuse of its leading members, was based here. Problems of housing, food supply and working conditions became worse in the 1970s and 1980s as the central government shifted capital investment away from Donbas into Western Siberian open-cut mining. The accident rate soared. In 1987, in the midst of a spate of fatalities in the pits, the Ukrainian republic's coal ministry was abolished and control of the industry was recentralized in Moscow even more. By 1989 the situation here was clearly coming to a breaking point: in the first three months there were eleven strikes. A lull followed, and the twelfth strike on 17 July brought Donbas into the country-wide miners' strike.

The strikers did not limit themselves to economic demands, although these were clearly of paramount immediate importance. The miners wanted a form of enterprise autonomy and regional cost accounting that gave their own organizations control of capital investments, the wage fund, management appointments, domestic wholesale trade and a part in international trade of their coal as well. They demanded the removal of unpopular trade union, government and police officials; the Chervonohrad miners in Western Ukraine demanded Shcherbytsky's removal. Most important of all, strike committees in Ukraine, as in other parts of the Soviet Union, were the first to raise the demand for abolition of Article 6 of the Soviet Constitution that guaranteed political power to the Communist Party.

Further evidence of a rapid politicization of miners included: participation of their strike leaders (as observers) in the September Rukh congress; readiness to mount a general strike if the original CPU draft of the new republic election law was not withdrawn (the original draft reserved a number of uncontested seats for CPU-sponsored organizations); fielding candidates in the March elections; and the mounting of strikes and demonstrations in Donetsk oblast on the eve of the elections to force the oblast CPU leadership to resign.

The miners' strike and its aftermath had a lasting impact upon other groups of Ukrainian wage-earners. First, it demonstrated to them how the strike weapon could be applied effectively, without creating pretexts for a violent reaction from the authorities. This led to the formation of strike committees in numerous towns and cities that accepted the strike as a weapon of last resort in the pursuit of all manner of popular demands. Second, the miners impressed upon other workers the value of independent organization, which took form later in the Donbas Union of Workers, the Horlivka Workers' Union and Yednist (Unity), formed in February 1990 in Kharkov by workers' committees from 16 towns and cities across the republic. In October, the Association of Independent Unions of Miners (a USSR-wide organization) was founded at a delegated congress in Donetsk.

The republican elections

All 450 seats in the Ukrainian Supreme Soviet, as well as those of municipal and oblast governments, were contested in the March 1990 elections. An average of six to seven candidates vied for each seat in the Supreme Soviet. Because Rukh was unable to field candidates in its own name, it entered into a Democratic Bloc with other registered and informal organizations that shared its programme, and had its candidates nominated by such registered organizations as the Taras Shevchenko Ukrainian Language Society, by work collectives or resident voters' meetings. In a number of constituencies protests were levelled against the Party-controlled electoral commissions for refusing to register Democratic Bloc, Green World (Zeleniy Svit – an ecological organization) and other candidates. Demonstrations against the commissions broke out in February in Vynnytsia, Kiev, Ternopil, Chernivtsi and Poltava.

The election campaign period was marred also by persistent rumours of impending pogroms against Jews and attacks by civilians on Soviet troops stationed in the republic. At rallies and in public appeals to soldiers and civilians, Rukh denounced these rumours as an attempt by conservatives in the Party leadership, KGB and military command to intimidate voters and strengthen their own nominees' chances in the elections.

In the end, 129 Democratic Bloc candidates and 72 independents supported by the Bloc stood in the elections. They were well represented in the western oblasts of Lviv, Ternopil and Ivano-Frankivsk, moderately so in the central oblasts, and poorly in the south and east, particularly Odessa, Crimea and Poltava, where they fielded no candidates at all. The Communist Party fielded its candidates in all 450 constituencies, but it was by no means clear that all those elected would remain loyal to the CPU leadership and not defect to the Democratic Bloc. A number of strike committees also managed to field candidates, mainly in the coal, steel and machine-building centres of south-eastern Ukraine. Many of them were supported by the Democratic Bloc.

In the first round of the elections 120 out of the 450 seats were filled by 71 Communist Party candidates, 36 Democratic Bloc candidates and 13 independents supported by the Bloc. In Western Ukraine, the Bloc did particularly well, taking a large majority of the available seats. In the remaining 330 constituencies, where no candidate had received 50% of the vote in the first round, and which had to go through to a second round runoff between the two leading contenders, the Democratic Bloc remained in the running in 103 constituencies. It secured another 72 seats in the second round, giving it a total of 108 deputies in the Ukrainian Supreme Soviet. Supported by independent deputies, the Democratic Bloc commanded up to 170 votes, against 280 behind the CPU leadership.

While Rukh functioned well in this period as an umbrella organization of various democratic and patriotic political tendencies, the imminence of a multi-party system encouraged such tendencies to prepare for life as fully fledged parties. Thus in the first months of 1990 plans were put in motion to establish the following: a Ukrainian Democratic Party by reform Communists in Rukh; a Ukrainian Social Democratic Party by local groups in six cities; a Ukrainian Republican Party by the Ukrainian Helsinki Union; a Ukrainian National Party by a breakaway group from UHU; a Ukrainian Peasant Democratic Party by an initiative committee based in Lviv; and a Green Party by the Green World association.

Volodymyr Ivashko was elected chairman of the Ukrainian Supreme Soviet, and in June resigned as CPU First Secretary in the face of Democratic Bloc criticism that his occupation of these two posts was unconstitutional. Second Secretary Stanislaw Hurenko replaced Ivashko in the CPU leadership. In July, however, when Ivashko was elected CPSU deputy secretary to Mikhail Gorbachev, he also relinquished the chairmanship of the Ukrainian Supreme Soviet. It was filled subsequently by the election of Leonid Kravchuk, who had long waited in the wings for a chance to prove himself a statesman of the new era.

Kravchuk's elevation coincided with a surge forward by the opposition, flushed by their success in the recent elections and buoyed by widespread public encouragement. It culminated in the adoption by the Supreme Soviet on 16 July of the Declaration of State Sovereignty of Ukraine by an overwhelming majority. Setting forth the parliament's desire to become truly supreme within the republic and to make Ukraine an independent, neutral and non-nuclear subject of international relations, the Declaration effectively laid down the political agenda for the months that followed. The government under Prime Minister Vitali Masol were obliged to start implementing the Declaration.

A massive student strike broke out across Ukraine at the beginning of October, when the Supreme Soviet returned from summer recess. It was aimed at forcing the Communist majority to press ahead more energetically with the Declaration's stated tasks. After two weeks of demonstrations and hunger strikes in the capital, Prime Minister Masol resigned and the Supreme Soviet agreed to the following other student demands: not to negotiate a new Union Treaty with Moscow until Ukraine has a new constitution entrenching its sovereignty; to bring home all citizens of Ukraine serving outside its borders in the Soviet Army by the end of the year; to establish a commission to nationalize CPSU/CPU property; and to hold a republic-wide referendum of confidence in the existing government.

Vitold Fokin, CPU member, parliamentary deputy and head of the Ukrainian State Committee of the Economy, was elected Prime Minister by the Supreme Soviet on 14 November. His first decisive move was to introduce a coupon system to protect the Ukrainian trade network from collapse under pressure of inflation, the black market and purchases by citizens of other Soviet republics and states (amounting to 8 billion roubles in 1990). Second, he secured bilateral economic agreements with other

Soviet republics that completely bypassed Moscow. The first of these were with the Russian Federation, Kazakhstan, Turkmenistan, Latvia, Lithuania and Georgia.

The issues

The major issues that shaped the election contest and will continue to dominate the political terrain in the future are: democratization, the economic crisis, the environment, and the complex and long-term question of national sovereignty.

In view of the Communist Party's declared readiness to relinquish its monopoly on power, the issue of democratization is now a question of *how* to end this monopoly and make the transition to a genuine multi-party system. The Communist Party is naturally concerned to retain some role in future governments and not be completely marginalized in the process. Rukh, on the other hand, faces the task of maintaining unity of all the groups under its wing in order to enforce this transition to a multi-party democracy, while at the same time allowing these groups to prepare themselves as competing political parties. A thoroughgoing process of democratization must also address the delicate issue of the KGB, the Soviet Army and other means of coercion available to the state authority. Without their subordination to a democratically elected government, the process will be incomplete.

Although its economic weight has declined since World War II in relation to the country as a whole, Ukraine remains a crucial economic region of the Soviet Union. Today it produces one-quarter of the USSR's food and one-fifth of its industrial goods. Donbas provides a quarter of the Soviet Union's annual coal output, while the republic's five nuclear power stations account for 40% of the USSR's nuclear generating capacity. Producer goods, which make up 70% of the republic's GNP, include rolled steel, diesel locomotives, coal mining and agricultural machinery.

The republic's economy is characterized by its intense use of fuels, raw materials and labour, both in the agricultural and industrial branches; by its relatively worn-out, technologically backward and ecologically harmful capital assets; and by grave disproportions between its base industries, manufacturing, social infrastructural and consumer goods sectors. Soviet Ukrainian economists estimate their economy is in a worse state than those of Russia, Byelorussia and the Baltic republics. Four years of *perestroika* have left it with a less desirable output structure than before (the consumer goods sector shrinking below 30% of GNP), in eleventh place in the average republican wages table, and below the Soviet average in provision of social services, trade turnover in consumer goods, per capita housing space and educational levels (*Radianskiy ekonomist*, 9 October 1989, pp. 2–3; and *Ekonomika Radianskoyi Ukrainy*, No. 4, 1989, p. 60).

The republic's leaders have been able to do very little until now to combat shortages, disproportions in output and other problems because economic decision making (investment allocations, wholesale and retail prices, tariffs, etc.) has been determined in Moscow and implemented by union ministries. The Ukrainian republic controls only 5% of the gross national product created on its territory. Enterprises run by union ministries control the rest, and these enterprises deposit into the republic's budget a mere 3.5% of their income as payment for labour and infrastructural costs (*Robitnycha hazeta*, 18 April 1989).

The terms on which Ukraine trades are disadvantageous to its own interests. Payments for its annual exports to other parts of the Soviet Union are 1 billion roubles less than the costs calculated to produce those exports. Its electricity exports to Central and Eastern Europe are sold at 1 kopek per kilowatt hour (*Izvestiya*, 9 September 1989). Although comprehensive analyses of the republic's trade are not yet available, the general feeling both in Rukh and the Communist Party is that Ukraine suffers a net outflow of wealth and has practically no say in the matter. Not surprisingly, insistent calls are now made to reclaim control of economic strategy, domestic production and trade from the central government and its agencies.

Five objectives, first articulated by Rukh but co-opted in large part by the Communist Party leadership, have been articulated: republican economic independence exercised by the Ukrainian Supreme Soviet and its Council of Ministers, with veto power over any centrally initiated project; customs duty, banks, and other fiscal instruments under republican control; a new Treaty of Union laying down the division of powers between the union and republican government, with a radical increase in the powers of the latter; independent access to the world market; and the promotion of a mixed economy with personal, co-operative and state ownership enjoying equality before the law.

Serious differences do exist, however, between Rukh and the Communist Party in their interpretation of these objectives and the procedures needed to realize them. Fundamentally, the differences are as follows. The Party is seeking a new economic arrangement in a renewed Soviet federation, guaranteed and arbitrated by a powerful executive presidency, whereas Rukh seeks recognition of full republican economic independence first, to be followed by negotiations with Moscow and other republics about trade and co-operation. It is, nevertheless, important to stress that, as in the Baltic republics, Ukraine's entire political spectrum now wants a radical increase of its power over the economy.

Closely related to the economy, but an important issue in its own right, is the environment. The republic is facing a serious water shortage. Pollution has destroyed many sources of potable water. Irrigation systems covering more than 5 million hectares, various industrial processes and nuclear power stations all impose a heavy burden on available supplies.

Attempts to increase agricultural yields by irrigation and the intensive use of phosphate fertilizers have, over the years, exhausted and then poisoned Ukraine's once fertile black-earth zone, and contributed in turn to the further pollution of water. Industrial pollutants in the air, water and soil, particularly in the south-east, have pushed up the incidence of disease, genetic defects and infant mortality. A qualitatively new dimension was added by the 1986 Chernobyl disaster, which seriously contaminated 3.7 million hectares of land with its fall-out and damaged the health of still unknown numbers of people.

A growing awareness of the ecological situation, particularly after the Chernobyl disaster, has led to a widespread movement in defence of the environment, of which Green World is the main republic-wide organization. This movement has managed to block all further construction of nuclear power stations in Ukraine, including the abandonment of those close to completion. It will most likely force the complete closure and dismantling of the Chernobyl station, which has operated practically without interruption since the disaster there. The republic's leading scientists and economists are preparing a new energy strategy in the context of a decisive shift in economic strategy overall away from energy- and resource-intensive technologies and processes.

The question of national sovereignty in a renewed federation or outright independence is the overriding long-term political issue. Both Soviet and Western observers accept that without Ukraine the Soviet Union cannot be a superpower. It is conceivable that Moscow will let the Baltic republics go, but to lose even control of Ukraine would greatly accelerate the already-evident fragmentation of the Union and embolden all the non-Russian peoples seeking greater national self-determination.

What, then, will determine the outcome of this issue in the long term? The evidence so far suggests that a worsening Soviet economy will generate more urgent demands for political separation, an internal economic reorganization in the direction of self-sufficiency and proportionality within a single national/republican market, and the renegotiation of trade terms with other states. Similarly, the deepening political instability across the Soviet Union will strengthen separatist sentiment in Ukraine and weaken the central government's ability to combat it. Young men, for example, do not wish to serve in the Soviet Army if that means they will be sent to the Baltic republics, Transcaucasia or Soviet Central Asia to put down nationalist movements there. On the contrary, the mass demonstrations across Ukraine in late March and April in support for Lithuania's bid for independence showed that growing numbers of people support such movements elsewhere and the peaceful resolution of their demands.

These are negative features of the all-Union situation that are promoting the idea of Ukraine's separation. The positive feature is, above all, the re-awakening of national pride and dignity among the Ukrainians, which brings with it a confidence that their republic can stand alone if it wishes to and should determine its relations with other republics as equals with them. But the republic will stand alone only if the majority of its population becomes convinced that independence is needed to bring greater freedom, better living standards and greater security than they presently enjoy under Soviet rule.

There was a fairly strong desire within Rukh at the beginning of 1989 to renegotiate the terms of the Treaty of Union. Only after that option had been tried and had proved unsatisfactory was independence going to be considered as a serious alternative. The CPSU leadership and central government in Moscow responded to such a desire (here, as in other republics) by drafting new proposals on the national question, on economic independence, mechanisms for negotiated disengagement from the Union, and finally at the end of 1990 a new Treaty of Union. However, their actual content showed that the central government was not interested in real concessions to the republics. The April 1989 Tbilisi massacre, the military intervention in Azerbaijan and Armenia, the response to Lithuania's bid for independence, and Gorbachev's threats in December 1990 to preserve the Union by any means necessary, reinforced such a view. At its second congress in October 1990, Rukh redefined itself as a movement, no longer for restructuring but for Ukrainian independence. By the end of the year, the polarization between the central government in Moscow and Ukraine's pro-independence forces had become acute, with the republican Communist Party stretched out painfully between them.

The main weakness of previous bids for Ukraine's independence – in 1917 and during World War II – lay in the historic division between Western Ukrainian nationalism and the Eastern Ukrainian proletariat. The former saw national unification and independence as a panacea, without considering fully the political and social-egalitarian aspirations of workers in such a movement for a new state. The latter, a multinational working class with a sizeable Russian component in the most industrialized part of Ukraine, was radical in social and political demands, but not quite sure whether its region should belong to Ukraine or to Russia. The conservative wing of the Communist Party of Ukraine is very much aware of this historic division, and has worked hard to re-create it, without much success, in the present situation. Of course, the size, location and composition of the working class has changed a great deal since World War II. By 1970 it accounted for more than a half of the total population; it was more evenly spread across the republic and three quarters of its members were Ukrainian. The important question, however, is what political outlook the just emerging workers' movement will take on the issue of national self-determination, and whether its leaders will look to Moscow or to Kiev as their political centre. This still largely unknown factor will have immense relevance for the future course of events in Ukraine.

14 MOLDAVIA

The Moldavian Soviet Socialist Republic is an artificial republic created by the Soviet Union in 1940 from the region between the rivers Dniester and Prut, formerly known as Bessarabia, which had, and still has, a predominantly Romanian population. According to the 1979 census, the major peoples of the republic are Moldavians (Romanians) who number 2.5 millions and represent 64% of the population, Ukrainians 560,000 (14%), and Russians 500,000 (13%). Except for a period under Russian rule between 1812 and 1918, Bessarabia formed the eastern half of the Romanian principality of Moldavia and its population shared a common ancestry, language and, for the most part, history with the Romanian people. In March 1918 a national assembly of Bessarabian Romanians voted for the union of the province with Romania. The new Soviet government refused to recognize the union and, in order to formalize its opposition to Romania's annexation of the province and to offer a nucleus for a 'liberated' Bessarabia, created in 1924 the Autonomous Moldavian Republic (AMR) in the partly Romanian inhabited area of south-western Ukraine on the east bank of the Dniester. The Soviet interest in Bessarabia was conceded by Germany in a secret protocol to the Nazi–Soviet Pact of August 1939.

On 26 June 1940 the Romanian government received a Soviet ultimatum demanding the cession of Bessarabia and Northern Bukovina and, bereft of international support, decided to accede. From the union of most of Bessarabia with the western part of the AMR (the areas around Tiraspol, Dubossary and Rebnitsa) the Moldavian Soviet Socialist Republic was created on 2 August 1940. The greater, eastern, part of the AMR was returned to the Ukrainian Soviet Socialist Republic, thus revealing that its creation in 1924 was merely a political stratagem to give credibility to the Soviet claim to Bessarabia. By restoring most of the AMR's territory to the Ukrainian SSR the Soviet government admitted the fiction of 'Moldavian' in the autonomous republic's official name.

Immediately after the annexation of Bessarabia the Soviet authorities nationalized the land and private enterprises were taken over by the state. The process of sovietization was facilitated by the transfer of 13,000 specialists from Russia, the Ukraine and Byelorussia. Romanians were deported from the new republic to Central Asia in order to work in factories and collective farms as replacements for those drafted into the

MOLDAVIA

Official name	The Republic of Moldavia
Area	33,700 sq. km (13,010 sq. miles)
Population	4,341,000 (1989)
Capital	Kishinev (Chişinău)
Languages	Moldavian (Romanian), Russian
Religion	Orthodox
Currency	rouble

army. Estimates of the total number of Romanians resettled in this way vary from 100,000 to half a million. The deportations were interrupted by the German attack of 22 June 1941 on the Soviet Union in which Romania, under General Ion Antonescu, participated in order to recover Bessarabia and Northern Bukovina. These lost provinces were regained by 27 July.

The reconquest of Bessarabia was accomplished by the Red Army on 20 August 1944, when the Soviet generals Malinovsky and Tolbukhin successfully launched a massive assault of almost one million troops and 1,500 tanks against the combined German and Romanian forces straddling the Prut. Most of Bessarabia was reincorporated into the Moldavian SSR in its August 1940 frontiers, the former southern Bessarabian districts of Ismail and Cetatea Albă being assimilated into the Ukrainian SSR. These territorial realignments were formalized in the Soviet–Romanian Armistice Convention of September 1944 and confirmed by the Peace Treaty of 1947 with Romania.

The fierce rearguard action fought by the German and Romanian armies in Bessarabia caused the virtual destruction of the towns in the province. The capital Chişinău (Kishinev) was reduced to ruins and the damage to roads, railways and bridges posed considerable supply problems for the Soviet authorities. The difficulties faced by the recreated Moldavian SSR, the economy of which was based almost entirely upon agriculture, were exacerbated by the severe droughts of 1946 and 1947, which created a widespread famine. Several thousand party activists were brought from the Ukraine and Russia to supervise the establishment of the republic's organizational infrastructure, thus diluting the Romanian element in the population, which was further weakened by mass deportations to the republics of Central Asia in the 1950s. Most of the Romanian schools were given over to teaching in Russian, for which teachers were imported from the other Soviet republics, while the ubiquity of Russian and Ukrainian activists in the republic's official apparatus provided the Soviet authorities with a justification for the priority given to the use of Russian in the official life of the republic. At the same time, the influx of Russians and Ukrainians acted as a check against potential nationalist agitation among the Romanians, who were now officially christened Moldavians.

Soviet difficulty in winning over the native Moldavians to the party was exemplified by the choice of First Secretaries of the Moldavian Communist Party (MCP), none of whom were of Romanian origin. The best-known was Leonid Brezhnev, who held the position between 1950 and 1952. Throughout the republic's postwar history the percentage of Moldavians who have been members of the MCP has been the lowest among any indigenous nationality in a Soviet republic.

Urbanization and migration

The process of russification in the Moldavian SSR was accelerated by enforced socio-economic changes, the most important of which were urbanization and migration. The urban growth rate in the republic since 1944 has been among the most rapid in the Soviet Union. Indeed, comparison of the 1959 and 1979 censuses showed that it was the highest of any republic during that period. When considering this development it should be borne in mind that before World War II, Moldavia (i.e. Bessarabia) was a predominantly agricultural province largely starved of Romanian investment. Its towns were mainly peopled by Russians, Ukrainians and Jews. The demographic changes registered between 1959 and 1979 reflect not only a period of intense urban development but also a shift in the balance between urban and rural populations. The rural population fell from 77.7% of the total in 1959 to 61% in 1979, while the urban population increased from 22.3% in 1959 to 39% in 1979.

A concomitant of Moldavia's urbanization was migration, both within the republic from rural to urban areas and from outside it. Of the migrants who came from outside Moldavia between 1968 and 1970 (the only years for which these figures are available), 46% came from the Russian Republic and 36% from the Ukraine. Between 1959 and 1979 the numbers of Russians in Moldavia increased considerably from 290,000 to over 500,000. This influx not only consolidated the use of Russian as the republic's official language but, more significantly for the position of the Moldavian language, led to an increase in the adoption of Russian as the native language among the other peoples of the republic. As language is considered by Moldavians to be the badge of national identity, their fears about assimilation by the Russians grew as more of their number became bilingual in Moldavian and Russian.

Economic and language reform

These trends, coupled with the fact that the number of Moldavian-language newspapers published in the republic had been surpassed in 1975 by Russian-language ones, and that the Moldavian percentage share of the number of books published had been declining steadily since 1960, were highlighted by *glasnost*, which brought to the surface previously repressed dissatisfaction among the Moldavian intelligentsia of the republic about the status of their language and provision for schooling in Moldavian. The authorities in the republic responded to such complaints by issuing a decree in May 1987 which increased provision for teaching Moldavian in schools and expanded air-time given to radio broadcasts in Moldavian. This concession could not remedy the fact, revealed at a Moldavian Communist Party meeting in September 1987, that in the republic's medical and agricultural institutes not a single subject was taught in Moldavian, and that in the town of Tiraspol, which included 25,000 Moldavians in its population, there was not one Moldavian school.

It was further disclosed at this same meeting that the 600,000 Ukrainians in the republic did not have a single school or newspaper.

The encouragement of *glasnost* prompted further demands from Moldavian intellectuals, which were encapsulated in the call on 1 September 1988 from the editors of *Literatura şi arta*, the principal Moldavian literary review, that immigration from the other republics be stopped immediately, that the Moldavian language become an official language, that textbooks containing the true history of Moldavia be written, and that the Latin alphabet be restored.

At the same time, the model of the Baltic states provided an example and precedent to the Moldavians as to how far they could press their demands. It was not without significance that *Glasul* (The Voice), the first newspaper to appear in Moldavian in the Latin alphabet since 1944, was printed in Latvia in March 1989 in 60,000 copies, which were sold out on the day of distribution in Chişinău on 13 March. Three months later a number of Moldavian journals renounced the Cyrillic for the Latin alphabet.

Pressure for economic and language reform continued to be exerted by a number of newly created groups, the most notable of which were the Moldavian Democratic Movement in Support of Perestroika and the Alexei Mateevici Cultural Club. Semyon Grossu, the Communist Party leader, not only refused to consider reform but also attempted to persuade the non-Moldavians in the republic to oppose the Moldavian demands. Denied access to the media and the possibility of legal registration, the unofficial Moldavian groups decided in May 1989 to join together to found the Popular Front of Moldavia. The Front set itself two objectives: to act as an umbrella organization for its constituent groups in any dialogue with the republican or Soviet authorities and to create links with other unofficial movements elsewhere in the Soviet Union, and second, to co-ordinate public actions in pursuit of common aims.

Two public demonstrations organized by the Popular Front in the following month demonstrated its rapidly growing influence and an embitterment of Moldavian opinion. On 25 June 1989 the Front held a mass rally in Chişinău to mourn the Soviet annexation of the territory of the republic on 26 June 1940. According to the organizers, about 70,000 people attended, making it the largest unofficial rally in the history of the republic. In contrast, the authorities' attempts to celebrate the anniversary of the entry on 28 June 1940 of Soviet troops into Bessarabia was foiled by a mass counterdemonstration in the capital. Profiting from the momentum gathered by these protests, the Front mobilized support for language demands in a series of demonstrations in Chişinău, which culminated in a rally attended by half a million people in the capital on 27 August, two days before the Moldavian Supreme Soviet was due to consider draft laws making Moldavian the official language of the republic. Opposition to the laws came from Russian-speakers in the republic, 100,000 of whom went on strike on 29 August 1989, demanding that Russian also be proclaimed a state language and the language of inter-ethnic communication. In Moldavia's second largest city, Tiraspol, which has a Russian-speaking majority, 30,000 protesters called for the withdrawal of two Moldavian books recently printed in the Latin alphabet from local bookshops. Faced with these conflicting pressures, the Moldavian Supreme Soviet approved on 1 September legislation which made Moldavian the state language of the republic, which reinstituted the use of the Latin alphabet, proscribed by Stalin following the annexation of Bessarabia, and which designated both Moldavian and Russian as languages of inter-ethnic communication.

Party leader Semyon Grossu's opposition to language reform and *perestroika* finally led to his sacking on 16 November. His dismissal was caused by disturbances which marred the 7 November Revolution Day celebrations in the capital Chişinău, and a riot three days later during which the headquarters of the Interior Ministry was set on fire. Grossu was replaced by Pyotr Luchinsky, aged 49, a man said to be more in tune with the ideas of Mikhail Gorbachev. Luchinsky, a native of Moldavia and, unlike his predecessor, a fluent speaker of Romanian, had previously served as Second Secretary in the Central Asian republic of Tajikistan. He immediately made a gesture of goodwill by organizing the withdrawal of 2,000 Soviet Interior Ministry troops who had been rushed to the republic to restore order after the riot. The Moldavian Popular Front responded by promising to avoid a confrontation in order to give the new leader a breathing space.

Reunion with Romania?

The Romanian revolution and the Lithuanian Communist Party's decision to break with Moscow led to calls from the Moldavian Popular Front for reunion with Romania. In this respect there is a different and (for the Soviet Union) more dangerous element to Moldavian nationalism. The Baltic states do not have a large sister sovereign state adjacent to them whereas Moldavia does. While independence is the limit to the demands of the Baltic states, Moldavian aspirations can go one step further. By reincorporation into Romania, Moldavia's loss to the Soviet Union will represent a neighbouring sovereign state's gain.

At a mass rally in Chişinău on 30 December there were calls from representatives of the Moldavian Popular Front for the republic to follow Lithuania's example and to establish an independent Communist Party, and for union with Romania. But at a later rally on the same day, Party Secretary Luchinsky was pressed by Russians in the republic to take strong action against Moldavian nationalists and opponents of Communist rule. The Russians and Ukrainians in Moldavia are extremely concerned that they will now lose their privileged positions in the republic, since the decision to make Moldavian a state language would relegate them to the status of second-class citizens, and that independence and union with

Romania would leave them exposed to the same kind of linguistic assimilation which formerly threatened Soviet Moldavians. To defend their interests, they have formed themselves into an association called the Yedinstvo, which is virtually a mirror-image of the Moldavian Popular Front.

Elections

Elections for a new Moldavian parliament were held on 25 February 1990. Although the Communist Party was the only party that was officially recognized, the most significant political forces in the elections were the Moldavian Popular Front and the Yedinstvo. Of the 370 deputies elected to the parliament, 85% were Communists, 70% were Moldavians, with 112 deputies receiving the backing of the Moldavian Popular Front, 15% were Russians, and about 10% Ukrainians. The question of sovereignty was foremost on the parliamentary agenda. Significant signs of the recognition of historical and political identity between Moldavia and Romania appeared in rapid succession. The first was the adoption on 27 April of the Romanian flag as the flag of Moldavia by the Moldavian parliament. On 5 June the parliament decided to rename the Republic 'The Soviet Socialist Republic of Moldova', thus adopting the name for the area in use in Romania. Following the example of other Soviet Republics the Moldavian parliament made a declaration of Moldavian sovereignty on 23 June, giving primacy to the constitution and laws of the Republic over those of the Soviet Union and making Soviet laws and presidential decrees subject to the Moldavian parliament's approval. (In December 1990 the parliament dropped the words 'Soviet Socialist' from the republic's name).

This declaration of national self-determination by the Moldavians acted as an invitation to secession to the republic's minorities. On 5 June deputies from the predominantly Russian area of the republic east of the river Dniester demanded the right to form their own autonomous republic, which they named the 'Transdniestrian Moldavian Soviet Socialist Republic' and proclaimed the town of Tiraspol its capital. At a meeting on 19 August in the southern town of Komrat deputies representing the 150,000 Gagauz population, Turkified Bulgarians who retained their Orthodox faith and settled in the area in the nineteenth century, called for the secession of Gagauz-inhabited territory from Moldavia and appealed to President Gorbachev and the USSR Supreme Soviet to back their demand. Gorbachev gave his support to the Moldavian government in ruling the minority Russian and Gagauz actions illegal, and when Gagauz representatives defiantly held elections on 25 October for a 'parliament' of the 'Gagauz Republic', thousands of Moldavians were bussed to the area in an attempt to halt them, and Soviet Interior Troops were called in.

While a compromise solution was reached over the Gagauz demands, the leaders of the breakaway 'Transdniestrian Republic' remained determined to press ahead with elections for their own parliament. On 22

December President Gorbachev issued an ultimatum to the Moldavian government, giving it ten days to adopt the following measures: to ensure that the laws of the USSR were valid in the republic; to review the language law of August 1989 in order to protect the interests of all inhabitants; to consider null and void the declarations of independence of the Gagauz republic and the Moldavian Dniester Soviet Socialist Republic and the elections held in them; and to revoke the resolution of parliament of 2 November setting up Moldavia's republican guard. The Moldavian parliament, unwilling to challenge Gorbachev's authority and risk direct rule, resolved on 28 December to accept the ultimatum and on 2 January 1991 President Snegur vowed to implement the resolution.

Evidence of the Soviet military leadership's hostility to any attempt by Moldavia to leave the Soviet Union came on 15 January in a radio broadcast from Tiraspol, the capital of the self-proclaimed Dniester republic, when Colonel-General Ivan Morozov, commander of the Odessa Military District, which includes Moldavia, said that his troops would not allow Moldavia to become independent because 'too much blood had been shed to obtain the territory in 1940'. Despite this pressure, the Moldavian parliament voted on 19 February, largely on ethnic lines, to boycott the all-Union referendum on the grounds that the Soviet parliament's decision to hold the referendum 'sought to dictate to the peoples of the USSR, including the Moldavian people, what to do, how to live, and what fate to accept'. The same session voted to reject the Union treaty in favour of Moldavia's own proposal for a confederation of sovereign states.

In the light of this refusal to organize the referendum the Soviet military authorities and all-Union organizations, with the backing of city and district councils in mixed population areas still controlled by the Communist Party, set up 50 polling stations, which opened on 14 March, three days before the date fixed for the vote. The voting continued for four days, but was boycotted by 95% of the Moldavian population. In the two breakaway Gagauz and Dniester republics the turnout was high among the non-Moldavians. Even according to the official returns (considered inflated by the Moldavians) only 28% of those registered voted. Major irregularities in the voting were reported, and the presidium of the Moldavian parliament declared the returns unreliable. On 20 March a constitutional committee met for the first time to draft a new Moldavian constitution 'based on the principles of liberty and independence'.

Between 11 and 16 February Moldavian President Mircea Snegur paid an official visit to Romania, the first by any leader from the republic since the Soviet annexation of Moldavia. It marked the end of a ban on ties between Romania and the Moldavian republic imposed by the Soviet Union. Snegur made an address, broadcast nationwide, to both chambers of the Romanian parliament in which he recognized a shared Moldavian–Romanian national identity and made a claim to the former Moldavian areas of southern and northern Bessarabia and northern Bukovina that were transferred to the Ukraine following their annexation by the Soviet Union in 1940. He called for closer economic ties with Romania and agreed to the establishment of a Moldavian consulate in Iaşi in northern Romania and a Romanian consulate in Chişinău.

These steps were welcomed by the Moldavian Popular Front, the Moldavian republic's largest political grouping, but the Front was strongly critical of Romanian President Iliescu's conclusion on 5 April of a treaty of Friendship and Co-operation with the Soviet Union, declaring on 21 April that the treaty 'contradicted the natural process of European reconstruction, which also involves the Baltic States, Georgia and Armenia as independent states'. In a clear reference to Moldavia's situation the declaration continued: 'The Soviet–Romanian treaty denies the right of captive peoples in the Soviet Empire to national and state independence.' The treaty did not mention the Moldavians, but it did encourage links between Romania and the Soviet republics. The Romanian leadership has shown that it is anxious to avoid any actions that might cause irritation in Moscow. Even Moldavian supporters of full independence from the Soviet Union have accepted for the moment the concept of the existence of 'two Romanian states'. Cultural integration between Moldavia and Romania is the path chosen by both states. From the Moldavian viewpoint it does not present an obstacle to Moldavian independence, and from that of Romania it does not assume a political union that would place the country in danger of conflict with the Soviet Union.

Appendix 1   EASTERN EUROPE AFTER THE FIRST WORLD WAR

The peace treaties of 1919, following the end of World War I, created as many problems as they tried to solve. Some were solved by plebiscites under League of Nations auspices. Others were the result of unilateral action (Teschen, Fiume, Vilnius, see below). Some national groups achieved independence or autonomy, only to lose it by force to those whose temporary weakness had made their emergence possible (particularly true of the Byelorussian, Ukrainian and Caucasian republics). Nevertheless, the most significant achievement of the peace treaties was the creation of a belt of central European states from the buffer zones of the pre-war German, Austro-Hungarian and Russian empires. Their true independence proved short-lived; within two decades the expansion of Nazi Germany and the Soviet Union had erased their autonomy, if not their actual independence.

Areas of dispute
Aland Is: disputed between Sweden and Finland. Granted to Finland (1921) and neutralized
Memel: Allied occupation 1920–23, annexed by Lithuania 1923, autonomous 1924
Vilnius: annexed by Poland 1920, plebiscite for Poland 1922
Marienwerder and Allenstein: Plebiscite to join E. Prussia (Germany) 1920
Polish Corridor: Continuing German demands for access to E. Prussia
Poznan: disputed between Germany and Poland. Reverted to Poland 1918
Upper Silesia: divided between Germany and Poland by plebiscite 1921
Teschen: partitioned between Czechoslovakia and Poland 1920
Sopron: granted to Austria in 1918, reverted to Hungary after plebiscite 1921
Fiume: disputed between Italy and Yugoslavia. Free state established 1920. Italian Fascist *coup* 1922. Partitioned 1924
Macedonia: Greek–Bulgarian conflict 1925
Western Thrace: ceded to Greece from Bulgaria 1919
Adrianople: occupied by Greece 1920–22
Corfu: Disputed between Italy and Greece 1923–24

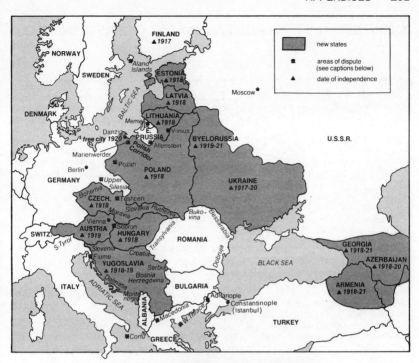

Appendix 2   NATIONS AND LANGUAGES OF EASTERN EUROPE

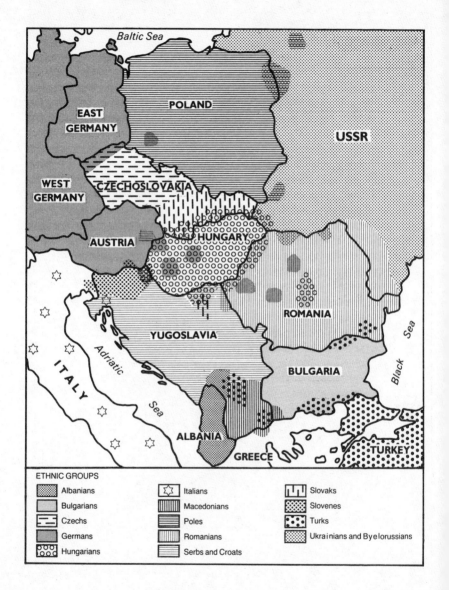

ETHNIC GROUPS

Albanians	Italians	Slovaks
Bulgarians	Macedonians	Slovenes
Czechs	Poles	Turks
Germans	Romanians	Ukrainians and Byelorussians
Hungarians	Serbs and Croats	

Appendix 3   NATIONALITIES IN THE USSR

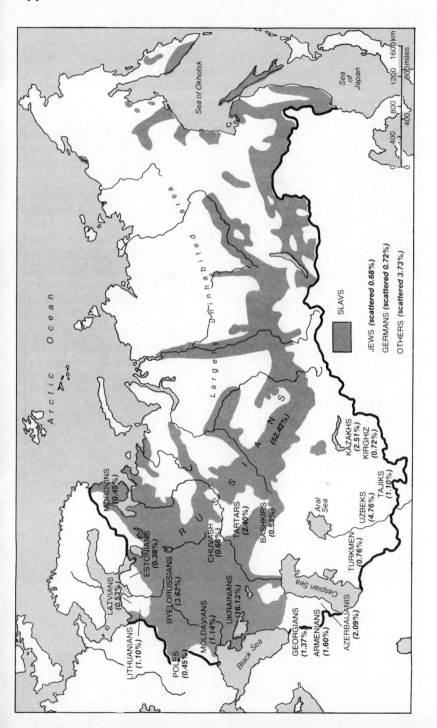

Appendix 4   EUROPEAN ECONOMIC AND DEFENSIVE BLOCS

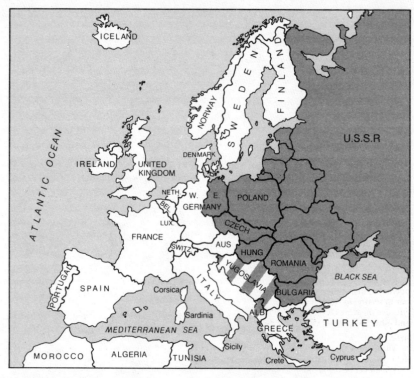

ECONOMIC BLOCS, WITH DATES OF MEMBERSHIP
★ European Community (EC)
▲ Benelux Customs Union, 1947
▼ Council for Mutual Economic Assistance (CMEA/COMECON)
● European Free Trade Association (EFTA)

MILITARY PARTITION, WITH DATES OF MEMBERSHIP
■ North Atlantic Treaty Organization (NATO)
○ Brussels Pact, 1948
□ Warsaw Pact Organization

The Twelve		FDR (W. GERMANY)	★ 1957 ■ 1955	ITALY	★ 1957 ■ 1949	PORTUGAL	★ 1986 ■ 1949
BELGIUM	★ 1957 ▲ ■ 1949 ○	FRANCE	★ 1957 ■ 1949 ○	LUXEMBOURG	★ 1957 ▲ ■ 1949 ○	SPAIN	★ 1986 ■ 1982
		GREECE	★ 1981 ■ 1952			UNITED KINGDOM	★ 1973 ● 1960–72 ■ 1949 ○
DENMARK	★ 1973 ▲ 1960–72 ■ 1949	IRISH REPUBLIC	★ 1973 ● 1970–72	THE NETHERLANDS	★ 1957 ▲ ■ 1949 ○		

AUSTRIA	● 1961	TURKEY	★ applied for EC membership 1987 ■ 1952	ALBANIA	▼ 1949–61 □ 1955–68	ROMANIA	▼ 1949 □ 1955
FINLAND	● (ass. member 1961–85)			BULGARIA	▼ 1949 □ 1955	USSR	▼ 1949 □ 1955
ICELAND	● 1970 ■ 1949			CZECHO-SLOVAKIA	▼ 1949 □ 1955	YUGO-SLAVIA	▼ limited involvement from 1964
NORWAY	● 1960 ■ 1949			GDR (E. GERMANY)	▼ 1950 □ 1955		
SWEDEN	● 1960			HUNGARY	▼ 1949 □ 1955		
SWITZER-LAND	● 1960			POLAND	▼ 1949 □ 1955		

Appendix 5   THE WARSAW PACT, 1955
(*SIGNATORY STATES:* ALBANIA, BULGARIA, CZECHOSLOVAKIA, GDR, HUNGARY, POLAND, ROMANIA, USSR)

Key statements include the following:

The Contracting Parties,

Reaffirming their desire to create a system of collective security in Europe based on the participation of all European States, irrespective of their social and political structure, whereby the said States may be enabled to combine their efforts in the interests of ensuring peace in Europe;

Taking into consideration, at the same time, the situation that has come about in Europe as a result of the ratification of the Paris Agreements, which provide for the constitution of a new military group in the form of a 'West European Union', with the participation of a remilitarized West Germany and its inclusion in the North Atlantic bloc, thereby increasing the danger of a new war and creating a threat to the national security of peace-loving States:

Being convinced that in these circumstances the peace-loving States of Europe must take the necessary steps to safeguard their security and to promote the maintenance of peace in Europe;

Being guided by the purposes and principles of the Charter of the United Nations;

In the interests of the further strengthening and development of friendship, co-operation and mutual assistance in accordance with the principles of respect for the independence and sovereignty of States and of non-intervention in their domestic affairs;

Article 1

The Contracting Parties undertake, in accordance with the Charter of the United Nations, to refrain in their international relations from the threat or use of force and to settle their international disputes by peaceful means in such a manner that international peace and security are not endangered.

Article 2

The Contracting Parties declare that they are prepared to participate, in a spirit of sincere co-operation, in all international action for ensuring international peace and security and shall endeavour to secure, in agreement with other States desiring to co-operate in this matter, the adoption of effective measures for the general reduction of armaments and the prohibition of atomic, hydrogen and other weapons of mass destruction.

Article 3

The Contracting Parties shall consult together on all important international questions involving their common interests, with a view to strengthening international peace and security.

Whenever any one of the Contracting Parties considers that a threat of armed attack on one or more of the States Parties to the Treaty has arisen, they shall consult together immediately with a view to providing for their joint defence and maintaining peace and security.

Article 4

In the event of an armed attack in Europe on one or more of the States Parties to the Treaty by any State or group of States, each State Party to the Treaty shall, in the exercise of the right of individual or collective self-defence, in accordance with Article 51 of the United Nations Charter, afford the State or States so attacked immediate assistance, individually and in agreement with the other States Parties to the Treaty, by all the means it considers necessary, including the use of armed force.

Article 5

The Contracting Parties have agreed to establish a United Command, to which certain elements of their armed forces shall be allocated by agreement between the Parties, and which shall act in accordance with jointly established principles. The Parties shall likewise take such other concerted action as may be necessary to reinforce their defensive strength, in order to defend the peaceful labour of their peoples, guarantee the inviolability of their frontiers and territories and afford protection against possible aggression.

Article 8

The Contracting Parties declare that they will act in a spirit of friendship and co-operation to promote the further development and strengthening of the economic and cultural ties among them, in accordance with the principles of respect for each other's independence and sovereignty and of non-intervention in each other's domestic affairs.

Article 9

The present Treaty shall be open for accession by other States, irrespective of their social and political structure, which express their readiness, by participating in the present Treaty, to help in combining the efforts of the peace-loving States to ensure the peace and security of the peoples.

Article 11

The present Treaty shall remain in force for twenty years. For Contracting Parties which do not, one year before the expiration of that term, give notice of termination of the Treaty to the Government of the Polish People's Republic, the Treaty shall remain in force for a further ten years.

In the event of the establishment of a system of collective security in Europe and the conclusion for that purpose of a General European Treaty concerning collective security, a goal which the Contracting Parties shall steadfastly strive to achieve, the present Treaty shall cease to have effect as from the date on which the General European Treaty comes into force.

Appendix 6   THE HELSINKI CONFERENCE, 1973–75

The Helsinki Conference or, to give it its full title, the Conference on Security and Co-operation in Europe (CSCE), was originally proposed by the Soviets. No general peace conference had ever taken place following World War II (although the Great Powers had met), and the Soviet Union saw such an assembly as a means to consolidate, or 'legitimize', the favourable strategic position it had attained in Europe as a result of the war. That is, it sought not only recognition for postwar boundaries (including the division of Germany) but also for the political order imposed in much of the region. Although Moscow had established Communist rule in its satellites and had stationed tens of thousands of troops there, it remained nervous about the prospects for 'socialist rule' given continuing evidence of popular discontent. The advent of *détente*, coming on the heels of Brandt's *Ostpolitik*, made the atmosphere favourable to such talks.

Preliminary negotiations began in 1972. Eventually on 3 July 1973 the representatives of 35 nations (all the European states – except Albania – with the USA and Canada) sat down for talks in the Finnish capital. Far from being a speedy 'summit' though, the talks dragged on and on. As Vojtech Mastny has written '. . . the conference that Brezhnev has hoped to finish quickly and climax in a glittering summit, with himself as the superstar, turned into a two-year diplomatic marathon instead'. The Final Helsinki Document was not signed until 1 August 1975.

While the Soviet Union wanted the Conference to concentrate on security matters, and was prepared for some general statements on economic and cultural co-operation, the West wanted a broader overall programme for the improvement of pan-European relations. Western nations felt that for real *détente* to be achieved, the rights of individuals would have to be secured. This meant:
i) a minimum consensus on the development of human rights.
ii) liberalization as regards exchanges of people and ideas.
The Soviet side was hostile to the thrust of Western moves. The Western emphasis upon the freedom of the individual in relation to the state contrasted with the notion that had developed in state socialist societies that such freedoms as the individual possessed were inextricably linked – and even conditional upon the individual's duties and obligations to state and community. According to the latter precepts, socialist régimes arrogated to themselves the right to prescribe the limits of acceptable behaviour of their citizens. Moreover they refused to countenance intervention in defence of their citizens' rights, branding it 'unwarranted interference' in the internal affairs of the given state.

Eventually, however, Soviet resistance to discussion on human rights was overcome by Western persistence. There was agreement to consider humanitarian and cultural questions on the conference agenda as a separate item. The Swiss delegation had proposed the idea of dividing the agenda into more manageable units – 'baskets'. So it was that the concerns of the conference became divided into three 'baskets'; the first dealing with security in Europe, the second dealing with economic matters, and the third dealing with human rights. The main link was between the first and third baskets. The Soviets were forced to recognize that the security and stability they so earnestly desired could not be guaranteed by weapons or inter-governmental treaties alone. It was dependent also upon their willingness to take the aspirations of individual citizens into account. Furthermore the Western nations made clear that they were not prepared to talk about peace and security without reference to human rights.

The Helsinki Final Act (or Helsinki Accord, as it is sometimes called) is not an international treaty. The participating states at the conference had made clear that they did not want one. The Act had limited legal significance, therefore, although the participant states declared their resolve to pay due regard to, and to implement, its provisions. But the Final Act did contain clauses with reminders of the legal obligations which participating states had assumed previously (for example, by ratifying the European Convention on Human Rights, or the UN Covenant on Political Rights). It therefore strengthened the principles underlying these earlier treaties. Moreover, the Soviet Union adopted the principles of the Final Act into its 1976 Constitution, thereby strengthening their universal validity regarding standards of international conduct.

Finally, it should be emphasized that the Final Act established a basis for continuing dialogue on the matters dealt with. It initiated a process for seeking information and exchanging views on the issues raised by the conference, as well as monitoring compliance. Subsequently, Helsinki 'follow-up' conferences (such as those at Belgrade (1977), Madrid (1979), Stockholm (1984–5) and Vienna (1986)) were held to review the working of the agreement.

Extracts from the Helsinki Accord
Questions Relating to Security in Europe (Basket 1)

The 'Declaration on Principles Guiding Relations between Participating States' bound the signatories to:

I Respect each other's sovereign equality and individuality, as well as all the rights inherent and encompassed by its sovereignty . . .

II Refrain from the threat or use of force . . .

III Regard as inviolable all one another's frontiers as well as the frontiers of all States in Europe . . .

IV Respect the territorial integrity of each of the participating States . . .

V Settle disputes among them by peaceful means in such a manner as not to endanger international peace and security and justice . . .

VI Refrain from any intervention, direct or indirect, individual or collective, in the internal or external affairs falling within the domestic jurisdiction of another participating State, regardless of their mutual relations . . .

VII Respect human rights and fundamental freedoms, including the freedom of thought, conscience, religion or belief, for all without distinction as to race, sex, language or religion . . .

VIII Respect the equal rights of peoples and their rights to self-determination, acting at all times in conformity with the purposes and principles of the Charter of the United Nations and with the relevant norms of international law, including those relating to the territorial integrity of States . . .

IX Develop their co-operation with one another and with all States in all fields in accordance with the purposes and principles of the Charter of the United Nations . . .

X Fulfil in good faith their obligations under international law, both those obligations arising from generally recognized principles and rules of international law, and those obligations arising from treaties or other agreements, in conformity with international law, to which they are parties . . .

This section dealing with the first 'basket' contained two further sections. The first set out matters 'related to giving effect to certain of the above principles'; the second was a 'Document on confidence-building measures and certain aspects of security and disarmament'. The latter carried provisions for the prior notification of military manoeuvres and exchange of observers in the event of manoeuvres being held.

Co-operation in the Field of Economics, of Science and Technology and of the Environment (Basket 2)

I Commercial exchanges

The participating States resolved to promote the expansion of trade and to ensure conditions favourable to such development by:

a) improving business contacts,

b) promoting the publication of economic and commercial information

c) encouraging organizations, enterprises and firms connected with foreign trade to develop further the knowledge and techniques required for effective marketing

II Industrial co-operation and projects of common interest

The participating States resolved to encourage industrial co-operation between their countries, and to encourage major projects of common interest (in the fields, for example of energy exchange, research for new energy sources, transportation).

III Provisions concerning trade and industrial co-operation

The participating States:

a) reaffirmed their interest to achieve the widest possible international harmonization of standards and technical regulations

b) recommend, where appropriate, to organizations, enterprises and firms in their countries to include arbitration clauses in commercial contracts and industrial co-operation contracts, or in special agreements

c) would consider favourably the conclusion, in appropriate cases of specific bilateral agreements concerning various problems of mutual interest in the fields of commercial exchanges and industrial co-operation (e.g. with a view to avoiding double taxation; to facilitating the transfer of profits).

IV Science and technology

The participating States expressed their awareness of the need to develop scientific and technological co-operation, and affirmed that such co-operation could be developed and implemented bilaterally and multilaterally at the governmental and non-governmental levels.

V Environment

The participating States agreed to the following aims:

a) to study those environmental problems which, by their nature, are of a multilateral, bilateral, regional or sub-regional dimension.

b) to increase the effectiveness of national and international measures for the protection of the environment.

c) to take the necessary measures to bring environmental policies closer together and, where appropriate, to harmonize them.

d) to encourage efforts by interested organizations, enterprises, and firms to develop, produce and improve equipment designed to monitor, protect, and enhance the environment.

VI Co-operation in other areas
  The participating States considered it desirable to encourage, promote and safeguard:
  a) the development of transport
  b) the promotion of tourism
  c) the economic and social aspects of migrant labour
  d) the training of personnel

Co-operation in Humanitarian and Other Fields (Basket 3)

I Human Contacts
  The participating States expressed their aim to facilitate freer movement and contacts, individually and collectively, whether privately or officially, among persons, institutions or organizations of the participating States and to contribute to the solution of the humanitarian problems that arise in that connection. They expressed their intention to facilitate movement arising from the following situations:
  a) contacts and Regular Meetings on the Basis of Family Ties
  b) reunification of Families
  c) marriage between Citizens of Different States
  d) travel for Personal or Professional Reasons
  e) improvement of Conditions for Tourism on an Individual or Collective Basis
  f) meetings among Young People
  g) sport
  h) expansion of Contacts
II Information
  The participating States express their intention in particular to improve:
  a) Circulation of, Access to, and Exchange of Information
  b) Co-operation in the Field of Information
  c) Working Conditions for Journalists
III Co-operation and Exchanges in the field of Culture
  The participating States set themselves the following objectives:
  a) to develop the mutual exchange of information with a view to a better knowledge of respective cultural achievements.
  b) to improve the facilities for the exchange and dissemination of cultural property.
  c) to promote access by all to respective cultural achievements.
  d) to develop contacts and co-operation among persons active in the field of culture.
  e) to seek new fields and forms of cultural co-operation.
IV Co-operation and Exchanges in the Field of Education
  The participating States sought to strengthen the links among educational and scientific establishments and to encourage their co-operation in sectors of common interest by:
  a) concluding co-operation agreements in education and science
  b) facilitating and intensifying exchanges between educational, scientific and cultural institutions
  c) increasing the exchange and dissemination of scientific documentation
  d) encouraging the study of foreign languages and civilizations as an important means of expanding communication among peoples, and for the strengthening of international co-operation.
  e) promoting the exchange of teaching methods at all levels of education as well as the use of teaching materials.

Sources: *Conference on Security and Co-operation in Europe. Final Act*. HMSO Cmnd.6198.
  V. Mastny, *Helsinki Human Rights and European Security. Analysis and Documentation*. Duke University Press. Durham, 1986.
  T. Buergethal (ed), *Human Rights, International Law and the Helsinki Accord*. Allanheld, Osman, New Jersey, 1977.

Appendix 7 POSTWAR SUMMIT MEETINGS

Since the last of the Great Power conferences took place at Potsdam following the end of World War II, the following meetings have taken place between US and Soviet leaders:

1955 (July) *Geneva*
Eisenhower and Khrushchev met, together with British and French leaders (Eden and Fauré). They gave instructions to their foreign ministers to draw up proposals on European security and Germany, disarmament and East–West contacts. Nothing came of it.

1959 (September) *Camp David, Washington*
Eisenhower and Khrushchev agreed to reopen negotiations on Berlin. No progress was made on disarmament or German reunification.

1960 (May) *Paris*
Eisenhower, Khrushchev, Macmillan and de Gaulle met. Khrushchev walked out after U2 spy plane piloted by Gary Powers was shot down over Soviet territory.

1961 (June) *Vienna*
Kennedy and Khrushchev met. No progress made.

1967 (June) *Glassboro, New Jersey*
Johnson and Kosygin met, but the Soviet offer to act as an intermediary in the Vietnam War was rejected.

1972 (May) *Moscow*
Nixon and Brezhnev signed ABM (anti-ballistic missile) and SALT-1 (strategic arms limitation) treaties.

1973 (June) *Washington*
Nixon and Brezhnev signed agreements on the prevention of nuclear war and the principles of a further SALT pact.

1973 (July) *Helsinki* – see Appendix 6

1974 (June–July) *Moscow*
Nixon and Brezhnev signed protocol strengthening ABM treaty and a treaty limiting underground nuclear tests. The latter remained unratified.

1974 (November) *Vladivostok*
Brezhnev and Ford reached outline agreement on SALT-2.

1975 (July–August) *Helsinki*
Brezhnev and Ford met twice; no progress made.

1979 (June) *Vienna*
Brezhnev and Carter signed SALT-2, but it was never ratified.

1985 (November) *Geneva*
Gorbachev and Reagan pledged to speed up arms talks.

1986 (October) *Rejkjavik*
Gorbachev and Reagan narrowed their differences on an INF treaty and agreed limits for a new strategic arms reduction (START) pact. The plan to abolish ballistic missiles fell through owing to the American determination to go ahead with the 'Star Wars' programme.

1987 (December) *Washington*
Gorbachev and Reagan signed INF treaty abolishing land-based medium-range missiles; progress was made on START.

1988 (May–June) *Moscow*
Gorbachev and Reagan exchanged instruments of ratification for the INF treaty, but failed to bring the START treaty within reach. They signed agreements on ballistic missile testing, nuclear test monitoring, space research and cultural exchanges.

1988 (December) *New York*
Reagan made promise to Gorbachev that existing US policies would continue under incoming President Bush, who also attended the meeting.

1989 (December) *Malta*
Bush and Gorbachev reached agreement on pursuing START talks in time for a further summit in the US in June. Some progress was made on chemical weapons. There was agreement that neither side should interfere with the liberal reforms in Eastern Europe. The US proposed moves to integrate the USSR into the Western economic system.

1990 (May–June) *Washington*
Bush and Gorbachev agreed to stop producing chemical weapons and halve existing stocks by the year 2000. They signed a START treaty providing for a 30% reduction in long-range nuclear missiles. There was provisional agreement on increasing trade links, but no consensus on the future strategic alignment of a united Germany.

1990 (September) *Helsinki*

Bush and Gorbachev jointly condemned Iraqi aggression against Kuwait and called upon Iraq to withdraw its forces from Kuwait in compliance with UN resolutions. They called for all countries to observe the sanctions against Iraq approved by the UN and stated their preparedness to consider 'additional steps' against Iraq if current steps failed.

1991 (July) *Moscow*

Bush and Gorbachev signed the START treaty, providing for a reduction in nuclear weapon stockpiles. They also issued invitations for a Middle East peace conference to be held in October.

Appendix 8 NATO SUMMIT (LONDON, 5–6 JULY 1990)
'NATO declares formal end to the Cold War'

Preamble (point 1 of the 23-point declaration)
'Europe has entered a new promising era. Central and Eastern Europe is liberating itself. The Soviet Union has embarked on the long journey towards a free society. The walls that once confined people and ideas are collapsing. Europeans are determining their own destiny. They are choosing freedom. They are choosing economic liberty. They are choosing peace. They are choosing a Europe whole and free. As a consequence this alliance must and will adapt.'

Main NATO decisions

1. *Peace declaration*
   The Warsaw Pact states are invited to sign a joint declaration with NATO committing them to non-aggression.

2. *Gorbachev invitation*
   President Gorbachev and other East European leaders are invited to address the North Atlantic Council.

3. *Conventional forces*
   CFE (Conventional Forces in Europe) negotiations to be intensified. When the treaty is signed, NATO will give a commitment on troop levels in united Germany and seek a new agreement on further cuts.

4. *Nuclear strategy*
   NATO to make nuclear arms 'weapons of last resort' – moving away from the 'flexible response' doctrine. NATO to withdraw all US nuclear shells from Europe if the USSR reciprocates.

5. *Stronger CSCE*
   New CSCE institutions are to include: a secretariat, a body to monitor elections, a conflict prevention centre and an Assembly of Europe.

(From *The Times*, 7 July 1990)

Appendix 9   CSCE PARIS SUMMIT (19 NOVEMBER 1990)

A joint declaration was issued by the member states of NATO and the Warsaw Pact. The signatories stated:

(a) That they no longer regarded themselves as adversaries and would seek friendly relations with each other.
(b) That, mindful of the obligations under the UN Charter and their commitment to the Helsinki Final Act, they would refrain from the use of force against the territorial integrity or the political independence of any state.
(c) That the security of each state was linked to the security of all participating in the Conference.
(d) That each state had the right to be a party to a treaty of alliance.
(e) That they approved the intensification of political and military contacts to promote understanding and confidence.
(f) That they were determined to agree to disarmament agreements and welcomed the new negotiations between the US and the USSR and the reduction of short-range nuclear forces.
(g) That they would work with other CSCE states to enable the body to make an even greater contribution to security and stability in Europe.

(Adapted from *The Independent*, 20 November 1990)

Appendix 10　THE TREATY ON THE FINAL SETTLEMENT WITH RESPECT TO GERMANY

The main points of the German unification treaty are as follows:

1. The united Germany shall comprise the territory of the Federal Republic of Germany, the German Democratic Republic and the whole of Berlin . . . The united Germany and the Republic of Poland shall confirm the existing border between them in a treaty that is binding under international law . . .
2. According to the constitution of the united Germany, acts tending to and undertaken with the intent to disturb peaceful relations between nations especially to prepare for aggressive war, are unconstitutional and a punishable offence . . .
3. The governments of the FRG and the GDR reaffirm their renunciation of the manufacture and possession of and control over nuclear, biological and chemical weapons. They declare that the united Germany, too, will abide by these commitments.

   The government of the FRG, acting in full agreement with the government of the GDR, made a statement on 30 August 1990 in Vienna undertaking to reduce the personnel strength of the armed forces of the united Germany to 370,000 (ground, air and naval) within three or four years. . . .
4. The governments of the FRG, the GDR and the USSR state that the united Germany will settle by treaty the conditions for and the duration of the presence of Soviet armed forces on the territory of the present GDR and of Berlin, as well as the conduct of these armed forces which will be completed by the end of 1994 . . .
5. Until the withdrawal of the Soviet armed forces from the territory of the present GDR and of Berlin is completed, only German territorial defence units which are not integrated into the Western alliance structures will be stationed in that territory.

   For as long as Soviet troops remain on German territory, the armed forces of France, Great Britain and the United States will, upon German request, remained stationed in Berlin.

   Once the withdrawal of Soviet armed forces from German territory is completed, German units integrated into the Western alliance structures may be stationed there, but without nuclear weapons carriers. . . . Foreign armed forces and nuclear weapons or their carriers will not be stationed in that part of Germany or deployed there.
6. The right of the united Germany to belong to alliance structures, with all the rights and reponsibilities arising therefrom, shall not be affected by the present treaty.
7. The four wartime Allies (France, Great Britain, the USA and the USSR) hereby terminate the rights and responsibilities relating to Berlin and to Germany as a whole.

Signed in Moscow on 12 September 1990 by France, Great Britain, the USA, the USSR, the German Federal Republic and the German Democratic Republic.

Appendix 11   THE PENTAGONALE INITIATIVE: POLICY DOCUMENT

1. Reasons for the establishment of the Pentagonale Initiative

The Pentagonale Initiative is a new form of co-operation for promoting joint efforts, taking into consideration the emergence of a new era in Europe. It is a follow-up to the former quadrilateral co-operation established in Budapest on 10 and 11 November 1989 between Italy, Austria, Yugoslavia and Hungary. It assumed the pentagonal form in Vienna on 20 May with the accession of Czechoslovakia.

The co-operation takes into account the following:

(a) The established tradition of co-operation between the five countries and their mutual bilateral co-operation;
(b) The major changes which have occurred in East–West relations;
(c) The revolutionary changes that took place recently in the Central and East European countries.

2. Objectives pursued by the Pentagonale Initiative

The Pentagonale Initiative is a contribution towards creating security and stability for the change-over from the old to the new order, particularly through:

(a) Establishing and strengthening mutually beneficial partnership structures based on the shared values of parliamentary democracy and human rights;
(b) Co-operating on specific matters between a number of Central and East European countries, taking advantage of the complementarity and contiguity;
(c) Beginning to work, within its geographically defined limits, on a solution to the problems of minorities within existing borders, while awaiting a broader codification of such matters within the framework of the Helsinki process and the Council of Europe;
(d) Contributing towards the consolidation of democratic institutions and economic recovery and development;
(e) Promoting general participation in the construction of a new Europe, a process that has been accelerated following the democratic changes and in particular the free elections held in some of the member states;
(f) Establishing ties with other existing regional groupings.

3. Characteristics of the group

The Pentagonale Initiative is a component of a much broader European architecture. In this context, the five participating countries recognize the essential role of the CSCE in setting up a lasting order of peace, security, justice and co-operation in Europe and they attach special importance to the activity of the European Community and other European organizations.

The Pentagonale Initiative therefore represents a level of co-operation which will be helpful in bringing those member countries not yet participating in – or candidates to – the EC, closer to the European Community. The Pentagonale Initiative is geographically circumscribed: it covers the east-central European area, which gives it compactness and a globality of common interests. Other neighbouring states, be it at government or regional level, could also be involved in specific initiatives, particularly those dealing with the environment. At the same time, encouragement must be given to the creation of other regional associations to the north and south-east, with which profitable co-operative relations can be established.

4. Identification of particular spheres of co-operation

The Pentagonale Initiative has no rigid institutional structures, and is designed to be flexible and pragmatic. The various projects can be carried out by all or by some of the participants.

The Pentagonale Initiative must make allowances for the extremely fast-moving events in Europe, and therefore needs continually to update its tools and objectives in order to keep pace with a general situation in a state of constant development.

The Pentagonale Initiative concentrates on the implementation of concrete, action-oriented projects of common interest to the five participating countries, especially in the fields of transport, environmental protection, energy issues, co-operation between small and medium-sized enterprises, scientific and technological co-operation, information and telecommunication as well as in education, culture and tourism.

The Pentagonale Initiative also foresees a regular exchange of views between the five member states on matters of a political nature and of common interest. Wherever possible, joint initiatives will be carried out within the latitude permitted by the international obligations of each member state in this respect.

Venice, August 1990

Appendix 12   CHARTER OF THE COUNCIL FOR MUTUAL ECONOMIC ASSISTANCE (COMECON), 1959
(*SIGNATORY STATES:* ALBANIA, BULGARIA, CZECHOSLOVAKIA, GDR, HUNGARY, POLAND, ROMANIA, USSR)

Purposes and principles

1. The purpose of the Council for Mutual Economic Assistance is to promote, by uniting and co-ordinating the efforts of the member countries of the Council, *the further deepening and perfecting of co-operation and the development of socialist economic integration,* the planned development of the national economies and the acceleration of the economic and technical progress of those countries, the raising of the level of industrialization of the countries with a less-developed industry, a continual growth in the productivity, *the gradual approximation and equalization of the levels of economic development,* together with a steady increase in the well-being of the peoples, of the member countries of the Council.

2. The Council for Mutual Economic Assistance is based on the principle of the sovereign equality of all the member countries of the Council.

Economic and scientific-technical co-operation between the member countries of the Council shall take place in accordance with the principles of *socialist internationalism, on the basis of* respect for *state sovereignty, independence and national interest, non-interference in the internal affairs of countries,* complete equality of rights, mutual advantage and friendly mutual aid.

Appendix 13 ECONOMIC STATISTICS

i) External Trade with OECD countries, 1988 (in $US million)

	Exports	Imports	Balance
Albania	n/a	n/a	
Bulgaria	780	2436	−1656
Czechoslovakia	3804	3588	−316
East Germany	2748	2976	−228
Hungary	3804	4008	−204
Poland	5652	4968	684
Romania	4056	1284	2772
Yugoslavia	7386	6483	−903
USSR	23652	24804	−1152

Sources: OECD data; Economist Intelligence Unit country reports, 1989/90.

ii) Estimated convertible currency debt (1988–89) (billion US$)

	1988		1989	
	Gross	Net*	Gross	Net*
Bulgaria	7.7	5.9	9.0	7.7
Czechoslovakia	5.2	3.5	5.1	3.1
East Germany	20.2	10.7	20.6	11.0
Hungary	19.6	18.2	20.6	19.5
Poland	39.2	35.6	39.9	36.5
Romania	3.1	2.3	1.4	−0.1
Eastern Europe	95.0	76.3	96.5	77.7
Soviet Union	41.7	26.5	48.3	34.1
E. Europe +				
Soviet Union	136.8	102.7	144.8	111.8

*The net figure represents gross debt minus assets held with Western banks – those reporting to the Bank of International Settlements. The data do not take into account indebtedness to countries outside the BIS area (e.g. developing market economies).

Source: Norman Scott, 'East–West Trade on the Threshold of the 1990s: Current State and Prospects' (Nato Economics Directorate, Brussels)

iii) United Kingdom Trade with Selected Countries, 1988*

	UK Exports	UK Imports	UK Balance
Bulgaria	161	45	116
Czechoslovakia	269	263	6
East Germany	202	272	−70
Hungary	234	175	59
Poland	313	532	−219
Romania	89	163	−74
USSR	1009	1178	−169

*(in millions of US$, annual totals)

Source: The Economist Intelligence Unit country reports, 1989

iv) Estimated annual* per capita income (in US$)

Albania	860
Bulgaria	3200
Czechoslovakia	6000
East Germany	5400
Hungary	1722
Poland	1900
Romania	2687
Yugoslavia	1850
USSR	4200
UK	7156

*for 1985

Source: *The World in Figures* (Economist Publications, London 1987)

v) Possession of luxury items (per '000 of the population)

	Telephones*	Radios	TVs	Cars
Albania	n/a	167	83	1.6
Bulgaria	200	221	189	115
Czechoslovakia	226	256	285	171
East Germany	212	663	754	199
Hungary	134	586	402	135
Poland	105	289	263	98
Romania	67	288	173	11
Yugoslavia	132	235	209	125
USSR	98	685	310	40
UK	523	1145	434	292

*1984/5. All other figures for 1987.

Sources: *UNESCO Statistical Yearbook*, 1989; *The World in Figures* (Economist Publications, 1987)

Appendix 14   POLLUTION IN EUROPE

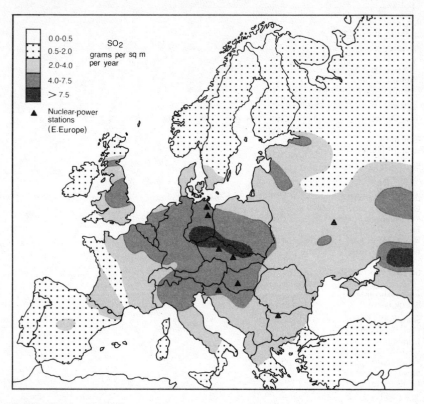

Sulphur dioxide emissions*

	1980 A.	1980 B.	1987
Albania	n/a	39	n/a
Bulgaria	517	508	570
Czechoslovakia	1550	1832	1450
East Germany	2500	2415	2500
Hungary	817	813	710
Poland	2050	1741	2270
Romania	100	757	100
Yugoslavia	588	837	588
USSR**	6400	8588	5100
UK	2335	2342	1840

Statistics listed in column A, and those underlined in the 1987 column, are provided by governments. Those under 'B' are independent estimates.
*Figures refer to thousands of tons.
**The European part only.

Source: *Environment*, vol. 30, no. 2 (March 1988)
Acid Rain, no. 8, September 1989.

Appendix 15   ELECTION RESULTS 1990 AND 1991

Albania
31 March and 8 April 1991

(Total seats: 250)

Albanian Workers' Party (Communists)	168 seats
Democratic Party	75 seats
Omonia (Ethnic Greek Party)	5 seats
Albanian War Veterans (pro-Communist)	1 seats

(98.9% of the electorate voted in the first round.)

Bulgaria
10 and 17 June 1990

Seats in the Grand National Assembly (Total: 400)
200 seats were be decided by direct election and 200 by proportional representation.

Bulgarian Socialist Party	211	(45.6% of the vote)
Union of Democratic Forces	144	(36.6%)
Movement for Rights and Freedoms	23	(5.8%)
Bulgarian Agrarian Party	16	(7.8%)
Fatherland Union	2	
Independent	2	
Social Democratic Party	1	

Czechoslovakia
8 June 1990

Seats in the Federal Assembly (Total: 300)

Civic Forum/Public Against Violence	164
Communist Party	40
Christian Democrats	35
Society for Moravia and Silesia	16
Slovak National Party	11
Co-Existence	10

The Czechoslovak electoral system is made simpler by the stipulation that parties must achieve 5% support in order to receive representation. However, percentage voting returns are calculated on the basis of elections to two chambers, and are also divided according to whether they are from the Czech lands or from Slovakia. Consequently, it is extremely difficult to give an overall figure for percentage support.

Eastern Germany
18 March 1990

Seats in the East German Volkskammer (Total: 400)

Alliance for Germany	193	(48% of the vote)
of which, Christian Democrats	164	(41%)
German Social Union	25	(6%)
Democratic Awakening	4	(1%)
Social Democrats (SPD)	87	(22%)
Party of Democratic Socialism (PDS) (former Communists)	65	(16%)
Free Democrats	21	(5%)
Alliance 90	12	(3%)
Democratic Peasants' Party	9	(2%)
Greens + Independent Women's League	8	(2%)
Others	5	(1%)

Hungary
25 March and 8 April 1990

Seats in the Hungarian parliament (Total: 386)

Democratic Forum	164 seats	(42.49% of the votes)
Alliance of Free Democrats	92	(23.83%)
Independent Smallholders	43	(11.4%)
Socialist Party	33	(8.55%)
Christian Democrats	21	(5.44%)
Alliance of Young Democrats	21	(5.44%)
Independents	6	(1.55%)
Agrarian Alliance	1	(0.26%)
Joint Party Candidates	4	(1.04%)

Romania
20 May 1990

Seats in the Romanian Chamber of Deputies (Total: 387)

National Salvation Front	263	(66.3% of the vote)
Hungarian Democratic Union	29	(7.2%)
National Liberal Party	29	(7.1%)
Christian Democratic National Peasants Party	12	(2.5%)
Ecological Movement	12	(2.45%)
Romanian Unity Alliance – AUR	9	(2.15%)
Agrarian Democratic Party	9	(1.59%)
Romanian Ecological Party	8	(1.38%)
Socialist Democratic Party	5	(1.11%)

A further 7 political parties gained less than 1% of the vote each and between them 9 seats in the Assembly.

Yugoslavia

All population figures taken from the 1981 Yugoslav census

Slovenia (pop. 1.9 million)
Results of elections to the Social and Political Chamber of the National Assembly (8 and 22 April 1990)

DEMOS (Democratic Opposition Alliance)	47 seats
Party of Democratic Renewal of Slovenia	14
(former League of Communists)	
Liberal Party (centre)	12
Socialist Alliance	5
Others	2
Total	80

(Milan Kučan elected president by direct suffrage. Kučan, representing the Democratic Renewal Party, received 52% of the votes in the second round of the election.)

Croatia (pop. 4.6 million*)
Results of elections to the Social and Political Chamber of the Croatian National Assembly (22 April and 6 May 1990)

Croatian Democratic Alliance (HDZ)	171 seats
Democratic Renewal	48
(former Communists)	
Centre Coalition + Independents	45
Serbian Democratic Party	5
Total	269

Macedonia (pop. 1.9 million)
Results of elections to the Macedonian National Assembly (two rounds held in three stages, 11 and 25 November and 9 December 1990)

Democratic Party for National Unity – VMRO		37 seats
Coalition of the Left		56
(includes: League of Communists	31	
Alliance of Reformist Forces	18	
Others	7)	
Party of Democratic Prosperity (Albanians)		25
Others		2
	Total	120

(President to be elected by Parliament)

Bosnia and Herzegovina (pop. 4.1 million)
Results of the elections to the Chamber of Citizens of the National Assembly (18 November and 2 December 1990)

Ethnic Parties		201 seats
Party of Democratic Action (Muslims)	86	
Serbian Democratic Party	70	
Croatian Democratic Party	45	
The 'Left'		35
League of Communists	23	
Alliance of Reformist Forces	12	
Total (4 seats still undetermined)		236

(Collective Presidency to be elected by parliament)

Serbia (pop. 9.3 million)
Results of elections to the Serbian National Assembly (9 and 23 December 1990)

Socialist Party of Serbia (former Communists)		194 seats
United Opposition		56
(includes: Movement for Serbian Renewal	19	
Democratic Alliance of Magyars of Vojvodina	8	
Independents	8	
Democratic Party	7	
Others	14)	
	Total	250

(Slobodan Milošević elected President by direct suffrage in the first round with 65.34% of the votes cast (42.72% of registered voters). Milošević was a candidate of the Socialist Party)

Montenegro (pop. 0.6 million)
Results of the elections to the Montenegrin National Assembly (9 December 1990)

League of Communists		83 seats
Alliance of Reformist Forces		17
Democratic Coalition (Moslems + Albanians)		13
National Party		12
	Total	125

(Momir Bulatović elected President in second round by direct suffrage, with 76% of the votes cast. Bulatović was the Communists' candidate)

Appendix 16   USEFUL ADDRESSES

Diplomatic and Consular*

Bulgarian Embassy,
188 Queen's Gate,
London SW7
071-584 9400

Czechoslovak Embassy,
25 Kensington Palace Gdns.,
London W8
071-229 1255

Hungarian Embassy,
35 Eaton Place,
London SW1
071-235 4048

Polish Embassy,
47 Portland Place,
London W1
071-580 4324

Polish Consulate,
2 Kenya Road,
Edinburgh EH3 5PE
031-552 0301

Romanian Embassy,
4 Palace Gdns.,
London W8
071-937 9666

Soviet Embassy,
10 Kensington Palace Gdns.,
London W8
071-727 6888

Soviet Consulate,
5 Kensington Palace Gdns.,
London W8
071-229 3215

Yugoslav Embassy,
5 Lexham Gardens,
London W8
071-370 6105

Banking and Trade

Anglo-Romanian Bank Ltd.,
42 Moorgate,
London EC2
071-588 4150

Anglo-Yugoslav Bank Ltd.,
11 St Mary at Hill,
London EC3
071-283 6111

Bank Handlowy w Warszawie
(Polish),
4 Coleman St.,
London EC2
071-606 7181

British–Soviet Chamber of
Commerce,
2 Lowndes St.,
London SW1
071-235 6477

Bulgarian Foreign Trade
Bank,
1 Gracechurch St.,
London EC3
071-626 1888

Department of Trade and
Industry,
Overseas Trade Division 3/5,
1–19 Victoria St.,
London SW1
071-215 5265 (USSR)
071-215 5152 (Czechoslovakia,
E. Germany, Romania,
Yugoslavia)
071-215 4735 (Albania,
Bulgaria, Hungary, Poland)

East European Department,
Confederation of British
Industry,
Centre Point,
New Oxford St.,
London WC1
071-379 7400

East European Trade Council,
25 Victoria St.,
London SW5
071-222 7622

Hungarian International
Bank,
95 Gresham St.,
London EC2
071-606 0237

London Chamber of
Commerce and industry,
69 Cannon St.,
London EC4
071-248 4444

Moscow Narodny Bank Ltd.,
81 King William St.,
London EC4
071-623 2066
071-623 2500

Yugoslav Economic
Chambers,
Trade Promotions Office,
143 Regent St.,
London W1
071-437 2870
071-734 2581

Yugoslav Trade Agencies
Ltd.,
58a West Heath Drive,
London NW11
081-458 1001

Zivnostenska Bank
(Czechoslovakia)
104–106 Leadenhall St.,
London EC3
071-623 3201

Further points:
  The embassies of the
respective country will have a
Commercial Counsellor who
should be contacted for more
information about trading.
  As moves are made to
open up the economies and
to encourage trade with the
West, more trade offices with
responsibility for particular
industries will be opening up.
Information on these can be
obtained from the
Department of Trade and
Industry.
  Most of the major banks,
including the big four clearers
(Barclays, Lloyds, Midland
and NatWest) have
departments dealing with
east and east-central Europe.

Travel and Tourism

Aeroflot Soviet Airlines,
70 Piccadilly,
London W1
071-493 7436

Balkan and Bulgarian
Airlines,
322 Regent St.,
London W1
071-637 7637

Balkan Holidays (Bulgaria,
Romania, Yugoslavia)
19 Conduit St.,
London W1
071-491 4499
071-493 8612

Bulgarian Tourist Office,
18 Princes St.,
London W1
071-499 6988

*Anglo–Albanian diplomatic relations were re-established in May 1991, but at the time of writing
there was no Albanian diplomatic mission in London.

Czechoslovak Airlines,
17 Old Bond St.,
London W1
071-499 6445
(reservations 071-499 6442)

Czechoslovak Travel Bureau
(CEDOK) Ltd.,
17 Old Bond St.,
London W1
071-629 6058

Danube Travel,
6 Conduit St.,
London W1
071-493 0263

Fregata, Polish Travel
Bureau,
100 Dean St.,
London W1
071-734 5101

Hungarian Airtours,
3 Heddon St.,
London W1
071-437 1622

Intourist Moscow Ltd.,
Soviet Tour Operator,
292 Regent St.,
London W1
071-631 1252/071-580 4974

Malev Hungarian Airlines,
10 Vigo St.,
London W1
071-439 0577

Polish Airlines (LOT),
313 Regent St.,
London W1
071-580 5037

Polorbis Travel,
82 Mortimer St.,
London W1
071-636 2217 (five other
numbers listed)

Romanian Tourist Office,
29 Thurloe Place,
London SW7
071-584 8090

Romania Airlines,
29 Thurloe Place,
London SW7
071-584 7955

Tazab, Polish Travel Agency,
273 Old Brompton Road,
London SW5
071-373 1186

Travellines,
154 Cromwell Road,
London SW7
071-370 6133

Yugoslav National Tourist
Office,
143 Regent Street,
London W1
071-734 5243/071-734
8714/071-439 0399

Yugoslav Airlines,
37 Maddox St.,
London W1
(Fare Quotations 071-409
1544)
(Flight reservations 071-493
9399)

Cultural and Educational

British–Bulgarian Friendship
Society,
69 Upper St.,
London N1
071-359 0507

British–Soviet Friendship
Society,
36 St John's Square,
London EC1
071-253 4161

British–Yugoslav Society,
121 Marsham St.,
London SW1
071-828 2762

Collett's International
Bookshop,
129 Charing Cross Road,
London WC2
071-734 0782

Czechoslovak News Agency,
59 Kensington Pl.,
London W8
071-727 7354

Polish Cultural Institute,
34 Portland Place,
London W1
071-636 6032

Polonez (Polish Book and Gift
Shop)
129 Shepherds Bush Centre,
Shepherds Bush Green,
London W12
071-749 3097

School of Slavonic and East
European Studies,
University of London,
Senate House,
Malet St.,
London WC1
071-637 4934/38

INDEX